Inspecting Jews

INSPECTING JEWS

American Jewish Detective Stories

LAURENCE ROTH

RUTGERS UNIVERSITY PRESS
New Brunswick, New Jersey, and London

Library of Congress Cataloging-in-Publication Data

Roth, Laurence, 1960–
  Inspecting Jews : American Jewish detective stories / Laurence Roth
     p. cm.
  Includes bibliographical references (p.) and index.
  ISBN 0-8135-3368-6 (alk. paper) — ISBN 0-8135-3369-4 (pbk. : alk. paper)
  1. Detective and mystery stories, American—History and criticism. 2. American fiction—Jewish authors—History and criticism. 3. Judaism and literature—United States. 4. Judaism in literature. 5. Jews in literature.

PS374.D4 R67 2004
813.0872098924 dc21

2003009380

British Cataloging-in-Publication information is available from the British Library.

I wish to thank the following publishers for permission to reprint material in the epigraphs:
  Excerpt from *Unheroic Conduct: The Rise of Heterosexuality and the Invention of the Jewish Man,* by Daniel Boyarin. Copyright © 1997 The Regents of the University of California.
  Excerpt from *A Lover's Discourse* by Roland Barthes. Copyright © 1977 by Editions du Seuil. English translation copyright © 1979 by Farrar, Straus & Giroux, Inc. Reprinted by permission of Hill and Wang, a division of Farrar, Straus, and Giroux, LLC.
  Excerpt from *The Angel of History,* by Carolyn Forché. Copyright © 1994 by Carolyn Forché. Reprinted by permission of HarperCollins Publishers, Inc.
  Excerpt from *By Words Alone: The Holocaust in Literature,* by Sidra DeKoven Ezrahi. Copyright © 1980. Reprinted by permission of the University of Chicago Press.
  Excerpt from *The Imaginary Jew,* by Alain Finkielkraut, trans. Kevin O'Neill and David Suchoff. Copyright © 1994 University of Nebraska Press; copyright © 1980 Editions du seuil. Reprinted by permission of the University of Nebraska Press.
  "Anyone," from *The Missing Jew: New and Selected Poems,* by Rodger Kamenetz. Copyright © 1992 Time Being Books. Reprinted by permission of Time Being Books.

Copyright © 2004 by Laurence Roth
All rights reserved

No part of this book may be reproduced or utilized in any form or by any means, electronic or mechanical, or by any information storage and retrieval system, without written permission from the publisher. Please contact Rutgers University Press, 100 Joyce Kilmer Avenue, Piscataway, NJ 08854-8099. The only exception to this prohibition is "fair use" as defined by U.S. copyright law.

The publication program of Rutgers University Press is supported by the Board of Governors of Rutgers, The State University of New Jersey.

Manufactured in the United States of America

למאריאשע אלישבע

For Mary

Contents

ACKNOWLEDGMENTS ... ix

INTRODUCTION: INSPECTING JEWS ... 1

Cases of Gender

1 TALMUDIC SISSY OR JEWISH DUPIN? ... 19
2 UNRAVELING "INTERMARRIAGE" ... 53
3 THE JEWISH WOMAN AS AMATEUR ... 76

Cases of Memory

4 TWICE-TOLD TALES OF ASHKENAZ AND SEPHARAD ... 111
5 HARD-BOILED HOLOCAUST ... 139

Cases of Alterity

6 UNDERCOVER GENTILES AND UNDERCOVER JEWS ... 173
7 AM I MY BROTHER'S DETECTIVE? ... 200

| 8 | THE FAITHFUL DEFENDED | 226 |

APPENDIX: AUDIENCE RECEPTION SURVEY 249
NOTES 253
BIBLIOGRAPHY 269
INDEX 279

Acknowledgments

The traumatic events and profound global changes that occurred while I researched and wrote this study often led me to question the willful self-involvement, and even the necessity, of my project. I am deeply indebted to the following people and organizations for their invaluable help, but most of all for their belief that this book matters.

My foremost thanks go to David N. Myers for his early and unflagging encouragement, as well as for his astute advice about the foundations of my argument, and to Norman Finkelstein, whose continual support and probing conversations suffuse this study. Thanks also to Adrienne Johnson Gosselin who included an earlier version of chapter 2 in *Multicultural Detective Fiction: Murder from the "Other" Side*.

Over the course of this project I was fortunate to work with a number of people who incited my thinking and helped me to formulate my ideas. Arnold Band's formidable intellectual presence and seminal article, "Popular Fiction and the Shaping of Jewish Identity," inspired me to start thinking about this subject after I finished my graduate studies at UCLA. Sidra DeKoven Ezrahi was a marvelous colleague during one semester, and her insights into Jewish literature were particularly helpful as I began drafting the book. Shari Jacobson, who tutored me on the art of audience reception surveys; Gabriel Finder; and David Imhoof all pushed and prodded my argument and my organizing concept of "kosher hybridity." I am especially lucky to have befriended Karen Bloom who guided my research into the Gothic for chapter 4, and who was always willing to listen and to critique. The indispensable Kathy Dalton, reference librarian *par excellence,* not only tracked down books and articles but also suggested a number of productive lines of investigation. My deepest appreciation goes to Susan Bowers who, as department chair, made it her job to fight for this project and for resources to enable it, and then at the end volunteered to proofread the entire manuscript.

I have also benefited immensely from the students in my continuing education course on American Jewish detective stories at the University of Judaism during the spring of 1997, and from those here at Susquehanna University who took "Multicultural Detective Fiction" during the spring of 1998 and "The Detective in Fiction and Film" during the spring of 2002. Their questions, insights, and papers all helped to deepen and sharpen my understanding of detective fiction.

A University Research Grant from Susquehanna University provided a reduced teaching load and much-needed time to research and write large sections of the study, and a National Endowment for the Humanities (NEH)/Gates Award from the School of Arts, Humanities, and Communications funded the audience reception survey. I am grateful to my colleagues on the committees that reviewed my applications, and to Laura DeAbruña and Warren Funk for clearing a great many administrative roads for me. Cheers to Ken Kopf and Eric Knepp who put the audience reception survey online, and to my research assistant, Adam Cole, who helped organize and maintain the data. Crystal VanHorn prepared the manuscript and provided many small kindnesses throughout the project that lightened my workload and speeded the study along. The prodigious talents of Mark Fertig brought the cover to life—thank you.

David Myers, Kristi Long, and Adi Hovav at Rutgers all were gracious and instructive guides to the publishing process, and I am in their debt for helping to make this book a reality. My gratitude as well to Paula Friedman, whose copyediting was astute and superb; it was a pleasure to work with her. And my thanks to the anonymous reader whose incisive suggestions improved the manuscript.

Finally, I am forever thankful to all of my extended family and to my friends across the country who patiently listened to me talk about this project for five years. In particular, my brother, Alan Roth, my father, Jack Roth, and my in-laws, Bob and Betty Bannon, never seemed to tire of my monomania, and they volunteered many useful suggestions and heartening words. They know better than anyone that this book was written *l'fi aniyut da'ati,* according to the paucity of my knowledge. This book is lovingly dedicated to my wife, Mary Bannon, who believed in it when I didn't, listened to it in the middle of the night, and read it with skill and care. She and Jonah Isaac *are* my American Jewish life—*La-yehudim hayeta orah ve-simcha, ve-sason vikar*... The Jews had light and gladness, joy and honor. So be it with us.

Inspecting Jews

INTRODUCTION
Inspecting Jews

The publication of Lawrence Raphael's *Mystery Midrash: An Anthology of Jewish Mystery and Detective Fiction* (1999) and *Criminal Kabbalah: An Intriguing Anthology of Jewish Mystery and Detective Fiction* (2001) acknowledged a remarkable phenomenon: more and more contemporary short stories, novels, and films feature American Jewish detectives. Harry Kemelman, James Yaffe, Rochelle Krich, David Rosenbaum, Marissa Piesman, Stuart Kaminsky, Faye Kellerman, Ira Levin, Janice Steinberg, Ronald Levitsky, and Richard Zimler are important representative writers in this genre, and their work, as well as the Devora Doresh and Bina Gold children's mystery series, and the films *A Stranger among Us* and *Homicide*, comprise the prooftexts for this book. At first glance the rise of what I call American Jewish detective stories seems easy to explain, and even easier to dismiss. Most obviously, they reflect the success of Jewish writers in America. Those writers are a creative presence now in both high and popular culture. Also, as Raphael argues, Jewish mystery and detective fiction appears yet another way in which Jewish writers "give us ourselves—contemporary American Jews."[1] Nevertheless, when less generous critics compare such fiction to American Jewish stories and novels by, say, Rebecca Goldstein, Melvin Bukiet, Tova Reich, Steve Stern, Allegra Goodman, and Nathan Englander, they judge it, and the entire phenomenon, to be faddish and/or shallow. One reviewer for *Pakn Tregr* characterized the phenomenon of Jewish women's crime novels as one that, like Jewish science fiction, "inevitably evokes parody"

(Woody Allen's "Match Wits with Inspector Ford" comes to mind), and asserted that there's "nothing deeply Jewish about the novels' form or content."[2] I offer this introduction theorizing American Jewish detective stories as a rejoinder to those who, like that reviewer, see nothing Jewish in these stories, and in order to illustrate how Jewish cultural studies, and my concept of "kosher hybridity," can help bring what is Jewish about them into focus. By doing so, I hope to expand our current conception of Jewish literature in America, an expansion that is a larger goal of this study.

American Jewish detective stories thrive in the busy and contested intersection of modern Jewish literature and American popular culture—which is to say, from a broader perspective, between narrative and popular culture—so let me first explain why I am drawn to a crossroads where literary conventions, mass media, and ideologies merge and collide. I believe that there are insights to be gleaned from American Jewish popular fiction that are different from, but neither inferior nor superior to, those that can be gleaned from American Jewish fiction that is perceived by readers and critics as "literary." Like most critics and theorists of popular literature and culture, I reject knee-jerk assertions that genre fiction is, by its very nature, inferior to other types of fiction. Nevertheless, the commercial and culturally propagated distinction between genre fiction and other types of fiction must be attended to and examined if we are to understand better the varieties of—and the sometimes antithetical relationships between—representation, expression, and instruction that describe "literature," Jewish or American, non-generic or popular. As Jon Thompson points out in his study of modernism and detective fiction, the detective formula's "intrinsic interest in society" (this fiction is, after all, about law and the breaking of laws) provides a tightly focused point of view on the confusions of living in a modern society: it means to provide a way in which the ambiguities of the modern social order can be resolved and made safe.[3] Hence, resolving the social conflicts that arise out of the interaction between Jewish and American sensibilities is a primary social function of American Jewish detective stories, whereas American Jewish "literary" fiction, especially the kind collected in anthologies of American Jewish literature, is often ambivalent, or even more perplexed than its readers, about that interaction. Muriel Rukeyser, who was keenly attuned to the traffic between narrative and popular culture, offered her contemporaries a still-useful observation about such a difference in social function, even though her point was to underscore a hierarchy of values within literature and art. As she put it, the amusement arts are about "the solving of emotion . . . that thus we distract ourselves from our conflict."[4]

I am, of course, implicated in my own study because, as I watch American Jews acted out in books and on screens, I too have conflicting feelings that beg for distraction. Like other American Jews I am entertained, but also anxious about the meaning of such pantomimes. Delmore Schwartz's short story "In Dreams Begin Responsibilities" (1938) captures some of the same feelings. Watching the silent film of his parent's courtship, the protagonist is both riveted and riven; he's shocked by the roles they play, yet all he can do to voice his fear about his and his family's fate is to shout at the screen, vexing the usher and the audience around him. In that story, as in one of his first publicity photos, Delmore Schwartz stares at his reflection, conflicted and self-absorbed. Reflecting on my particular intersection between writing and popular culture, I see a recognizably American Jewish perspective on identity in an American Jewish genre that is virtually ignored by scholars. Like Philip Roth's double in *Operation Shylock* (1993), the Philip Roth who midway through the novel declares himself a "Jewish private detective from Chicago,"[5] American Jewish detective stories are the absurd but provocative Jewish *Other* of Jewish literature.

I take that genre seriously. Taking it seriously means examining American Jewish detective stories not only as genre fiction, but also as reflective of contemporary acculturation in the American Jewish popular arts.[6] Over the last ten or twelve years, scholarship on the American Jewish popular arts has increased dramatically, and the new Jewish cultural studies, as this scholarship is sometimes called, is distinguished by its focus on issues of gender, sexuality, race, ethnicity, class, mass media representations, and material culture (foodways, folk art, ephemera, etc.).[7] In general, that scholarship—variously modified by recent ideas imported from gender studies, queer theory, Marxist theory, ethnic studies, postcolonial theory, psychoanalytic theory, etc.[8]—builds on two hypotheses: that all cultures process inchoate existence into organized fields of knowledge, and that culture, as a system of meanings and practices, is not only inherited (or opposed) but also adapted and transformed by the diverse individuals within a society.[9] Although literary critic Mark Bauerlein rightly points out that the definition of culture generally employed by cultural studies scholars is disputed by many anthropologists, and Arnold Eisen cautions against our privileging the individual and idiosyncratic over "the normative and communal components of culture,"[10] I find the above hypotheses both persuasive and challenging. They embody a pragmatic and skeptical attitude toward cultures and the way cultures function to make existence intelligible and meaningful. They foreground how fragmented, contentious, and contradictory cultures are, and so help illuminate the vexed nature of public discourse about who we are and the knowledges we possess. By looking at the American Jewish popular arts through the lens of currently fashionable, but also intriguing and productive, critical perspectives, scholars in Jewish cultural studies have provided a warrant for my description of American Jewish detective stories: taken as a whole, these stories are a complex public text about contemporary American Jewish culture, a public text that sustains a multiplicity of meanings and readings.[11]

My concept of kosher hybridity enables me to grapple with that multiplicity, whether called multiculturalism, the borderlands, or diversity.[12] I specifically use "hybrid" because it is a term that signifies multiplicity, in three ways important to American Jewish detective stories. First, I use it as a way of deploying a general concept indebted to postcolonial studies that denotes "the property of being informed by differing social and cultural positions," and as shorthand for one of Mikhail Bakhtin's three main devices for creating language-images in the novel (hybridization, dialogization of languages, and pure dialogues).[13] Second, I use it in the sense that Stephen J. Whitfield uses the term in *American Space, Jewish Time* to describe a distinctively American Jewish expression of cultural assimilation, a kind of cultural "straddling" that "constitutes an effort to bridge the chasm between the fashionable and the transcendent, the ephemeral and the exalted. It is a hybrid, composed both of some high cultural memories and pretensions and of the commercial necessities and ambitions of popular culture."[14] Third, I am acknowledging that kosher hybridity is another way of wording the poststructural phase of "the cult of synthesis," Jonathan Sarna's term for a central theme in American Jewish culture that, in its clearest expression between the 1830s and the 1970s, reflected "an ongoing effort on the part of American Jews to interweave their 'Judaism' with their 'Americanism' in an attempt to fashion for themselves some unified, 'synthetic' whole."[15]

Thus, reading American Jewish detective stories as "hybrid" is to acknowledge that they are a kind of identity-shaping project.[16] American Jewish detective stories fabricate an America and a portrait of Jews that are mutually compatible, and as a whole reflect contemporary middle-class life and concerns. The writers of these popular cultural texts, which are informed by contradiction and which thrive on intended and unintended ironies, formulate idioms for American Jewish identities that intentionally and unintentionally phrase social, ethnic, and religious syntheses in American Jewish life.[17] In general, these idioms reflect a troubled mixture of curiosity, unease, and an imperfectly remembered Torah. Indeed, the "kosher" of kosher hybridity references that imperfect memory, and Jewishness in general, within the context of such a mix. Kosher literally means "fit" or "proper," and I use it here as a conceptual improvisation on "fitness" as a religiously and culturally informed desire for separation and restriction—in other words, what is "fit" is that which is "set apart." In this sense, "kosher" is both a synecdoche and a floating signifier whose connotations and associations mobilize Jewish difference and help snap my organizing concept into sharp focus: Examined closely, the narrative strategies, topoi, and tropes of American Jewish detective stories, like all texts in the American Jewish popular arts, reveal a textual language with a hybrid logic resembling that of the oxymoron, jarring and sometimes absurd juxtapositions and fusions of contradictory ideas and terms from American space and Jewish time—kosher hybridity, the coalescence of the "set apart" with the "intermingled" ready for mass consumption by both Jews and non-Jews.

The term "coalescence" is here a purposeful reference to Sylvia Barack Fishman's description of the unconscious merger in the psyches of contemporary American Jews of American and Jewish value systems, a merger that today "permeates virtually all strata of American Jewish life, from Orthodox through Reform, from well-educated leaders through the Jewish masses."[18] Jonathan Sarna reads coalescence as a "transformed and internalized" version of his cult of synthesis,[19] yet coalescence better delimits my definition of kosher hybridity, for in defining her term Fishman makes an overt analogy between the social phenomenon she observes (a merging of values) and the way that people now access and negotiate, without really thinking about it, a multiplicity of texts on a single computer screen (a merging of texts).[20] Thinking of coalescence *as* a textual phenomenon is one way to understand kosher hybridity, but kosher hybridity raises a specific set of questions about the formation of identity and the function of unwitting collaboration in a popular cultural text (I will pose those questions shortly). Hence, kosher hybridity situates the general argument of my study, that American Jewish detective stories are representative and entertaining cases in the American Jewish popular arts of textual and cultural hybridity examined and made fit for mass consumption.

Of course, their textual language is also, in part, a product of the detective formula and its source materials. A variety of narratives provided those source materials, "medieval morality tales, the Romance, the gothic, the bildungsroman, the picaresque tale, domestic fiction, the adventure tale, and so on."[21] Film theorist Robert Ray even implicates photography and the nineteenth-century French *physiologies* (pseudo-scientific guides to urban "types") as sources, for like those two contemporaneously invented mass mediums, detective stories "offered to make the world, and particularly the urban scene, more legible," and reflected "the anxiety to interpret."[22] Given the variety of source materials, and the panoply of variants current within the genre (classic and locked-room mysteries; the cozy; pulp, and hard-boiled detective fiction; police procedurals; anti-detective stories; etc.), it is not surprising that a variety of critical perspectives have been employed to explicate and analyze texts in the genre. I find, however, that the critical perspectives Stephen Soitos and Adrienne Johnson Gosselin employ for their analyses of African American detective stories are especially helpful in making a way for a criticism that attends to the textual and cultural hybridity I have outlined.[23] Both Soitos and Gosselin close-read the detective formula in order to examine how African American writers hybridize and modify it with African American tropes, characters, and settings. They thereby show how distinctively African American material "infuses the detective text with African-American cultural expressions and value systems,"[24] how that material becomes source material for African American detective stories. In addition, Gosselin draws on the insights of three literary and cultural critics in order to posit that there is a pedagogical dimension to multicultural detective fiction: Stanley Ellin and Peter Freese, both of whom viewed detectives as cultural mediators who convey "inadvertent" lessons about life within a multicultural society, and Gloria Anzaldúa, whose concept of the borderlands serves a heuristic function for those who seek self-knowledge and knowledge of the Other.[25] The "inadvertent learning," as Gosselin terms it, that occurs in such fiction is that readers are engaged by stories that model how individuals and cultures bear witness to the disputations within pluralist societies, to how borders and bridges among individuals and among cultures are made.[26]

Given Soitos's and Gosselin's critical perspectives, these are the questions to pose about American Jewish detective stories: One, how are we to identify the distinctively Jewish source material for these stories, material that infuses the American Jewish detective text with Jewish cultural expressions and value systems? Two, what kind of pedagogical function, beyond the self-reflection Raphael notes, does kosher hybridity serve? James Yaffe's 1990 essay "Is This Any Job for a Nice Jewish Boy?" the first to address the subject of American and Anglo-Jewish detective stories critically and in its entirety, provides a starting point for addressing these questions. Yaffe, a writer of detective stories himself, identifies God in Genesis as the first detective and the first model for a Jewish detective. When Adam explains to God that he fled, when he heard God's voice, because he was naked, God's logical deduction of Adam's lie and his sin "sets the pattern for all those later, more elaborate deductions that have delighted readers since Poe invented the detective story."[27] Yaffe then draws parallels between "Judaism, as expressed in the Old Testament, and the underlying assumptions of detective fiction" based on his reading of Adam's crime and punishment.[28] Human justice, bringing out the truth, and the pleasure of "Talmudical" argument and analysis are Jewish cultural preoccupations and teachings that, according to Yaffe, make the genre ripe for Jewish intervention and appropriation. Using these cultural "traits" as his criteria, Yaffe divides Jewish detectives into three categories: the "officially religious," those whose "Jewishness is more closely involved with their personalities and the cases they solve," and "Jewish-in-name-only."[29]

Ultimately, Yaffe's categories are the most valuable part of his essay. Raphael, both in *Mystery Midrash* and in an earlier essay, revises the categories into more accurate sociocultural terms, calling them "affirming," "acculturated," and "assimilated."[30] Yaffe's formulation of Jewishness, however, is problematic. As his use of "Old Testament" indicates, his biblical source is a Judeo-Christian plexus, and he cites no specific source in the Talmud to illustrate what he means by "Talmudical" analysis. Given the recent theoretical arguments about culture, I am hesitant to claim Yaffe's Jewishness for American Jewish detective stories, although I cannot rule it out either. Even Stephen J. Whitfield is extraordinarily cautious when he tries to identify the *content* of Jewish culture in America, a culture "not merely synonymous with Judaism."[31] He suggests, with caveats and many examples, that it consists of emotionalism, logocentricity, and a predilection for urban settings.[32] Are either Yaffe's or Whitfield's formulations of Jewish culture useful for identifying the Jewish material that infuses texts featuring "affirming" and "acculturated" American Jewish detectives?

Consider the first Jewish detective in American detective fiction: Alvan Judah in Colonel Prentiss Ingraham's dime novel *The Jew Detective; or, The Beautiful Convict,* published July 1, 1891, by Beadle's Dime Library.[33] Ingraham's philo-Semitic and pro-intermarriage story resembles the novels of his contemporary, Henry Harland, who, writing as Sidney Luska, stereotyped Jews as models of ethical behavior and as "better educated individuals who were anxious to cast loose from their

Judaism and to amalgamate with their neighbors in order to help form the American people of the future."[34] Judah is a "noble specimen of manhood" who is reserved, whose physical strength is more important than his ratiocination in solving the mysteries of the story, and who at the end of the story retires to the country to marry the gentile heroine. Given how completely Judah has been forgotten by Jewish writers and critics, it is clear that the Jewishness of this story provides no tenable source material for American Jewish detective stories, but it does reflect an image of the Jew in late nineteenth-century American literature. Thus Whitfield's formulation of Jewish culture, as opposed to Yaffe's, is a good litmus test here: according to Whitfield's criteria, Alvan Judah is a Jew who is not Jewish.

If we compare Yaffe's and Whitfield's formulations of Jewish culture, however, we find that both see logocentrism as an important cultural trait, and so Yaffe rightfully points our attention to the Talmud. Consider, then, the first Jewish detective in *Jewish* literature: Rabbi Eleazar son of Rabbi Simeon (end of 2nd century C.E.), who, in a legend from tractate Bava Metzia 83b, teaches a thief catcher how to be a better detective. Keep in mind that the thieves the detective catches are Jewish, and that the king who employs the detective is Roman:

> R. Eleazar son of R. Simeon once met a detective who was a thief catcher. R. Eleazar asked, "How can you recognize them? Are they not like wild beasts that prowl at night and hide during the day? Perhaps you sometimes arrest the innocent and let the guilty go free?" The detective answered, "What shall I do? It is the king's command." R. Eleazar: "Come, I will teach you what to do. At nine o'clock in the morning, go into a tavern. Should you see a man dozing with a cup of wine in his hand, inquire about him. If he is a disciple of the wise, [you may assume that] he had risen very early in the morning to pursue his studies [and that is why he is dozing]; if he is a laborer, he too must have been up early to do his work. But if he is neither, he is a thief—arrest him." The report [of this conversation] was brought to the king's attention, and the decision was [as the proverb puts it]: "Let the reader of the message become the messenger." R. Eleazar son of R. Simeon was accordingly sent for and was appointed to catch thieves. At that, R. Joshua ben Korhah sent word to him: "O Vinegar son of wine! How long will you deliver up the people of our God for slaughter!" R. Eleazar sent back: "I weed out thorns from the vineyard." R. Joshua replied, "Let the Owner of the vineyard come and Himself weed out its thorns."[35]

Note that this passage is about resistance to a kind of colonialism, and so, in that light, note too that logocentrism, as well as human justice, bringing out the truth, and emotionalism are all implicated. Some readers may recognize this *aggadah* from Daniel Boyarin's *Unheroic Conduct,* to which I am indebted for providing the textual reasoning that authorizes my "Talmudic" interpretation here. But whereas Boyarin considers the implications in this passage for our understanding of gender in the Talmud and in Ashkenazi culture, I want to focus simply on the issue of political collaboration (I will take up Boyarin's insights on gender and collaboration in chapter 1, and on the Jewish body in chapter 6). The well-meaning Rabbi Eleazar brings his training in Jewish law and textual analysis to bear on discerning the innocent from the guilty. When he employs his hermeneutic gaze on humans, he and his apparently successful method are enlisted by the Roman state to serve its interests. This unleashes an emotional response from his colleague, Rabbi Joshua, upbraiding him for delivering up Jews to the Roman authorities. When Rabbi Eleazar protests that his weeding is for the best, Rabbi Joshua's response, "Let the Owner of the vineyard come and Himself weed out its thorns," implies that, first, human interpretation of the truth is fallible, and second, that the primary lesson to be learned here is about unwitting collaboration with a non-Jewish state power. Since God is the King of the King of Kings (*melech malchei ham'lachim*) the Jewish detective's fidelity is to Jews, Judaism, and Jewish tradition, and not to any power that may harm the faithful or the faith. A Jewish detective is above all a defender of the faith.

Now I am able to address the two questions I posed about American Jewish detective stories. Rabbi Eleazar helps us to identify distinctively Jewish source material for these stories by pointing our attention not to content per se but to a model: the Jewish detective who works in a non-Jewish political system. In other words, Rabbi Eleazar embodies an insight into the situation of those who, wittingly or unwittingly, are collaborators with the non-Jewish world. His legacy? That despite disagreements over the content of Jewish culture (and over how to interpret it), Jewish detectives in the non-Jewish world ought to defend Jews, Judaism, and Jewish tradition, whatever the class of Jew, thief or rabbi. *Ought to*—but, as Rabbi Eleazar shows, that is not guaranteed. In this sense, Rabbi Eleazar's legacy is that Jewish detectives defend the faith(s), defend the diversity of Jewish culture, though sometimes they must also interrogate their own defense to clarify who and what they are defending. Let me hasten to add that I am aware there is a vast difference between what "diversity of Jewish culture" may have meant in Talmudic times and what it means today. I am not arguing for a direct line of influence between Rabbi Eleazar and the detectives in contemporary American Jewish detective stories—it would be silly to claim, for example, that he might defend, or that the Talmud mandates defending, modern Jewish pluralism, or the ethical Jewishness and libertarianism of the Abe Lieberman mysteries.[36] I am arguing that he models, and is the model for, a particular kind of struggle for Jews living in non-Jewish political states and cultures, a struggle given expression in the Talmud as a lesson about fidelity to co-religionists oppressed by the Romans. What are our allegiances? Where do we draw the line between us and them? How do we build bridges between us and them? These are precisely the questions that animate "affirming" and "acculturated" American Jewish detective stories. Like Rabbi Eleazar's story, they exemplify how collaborations and borders between Jewish individuals and political states and cultures are made and remade, and this, finally, is the pedagogical function that kosher hybridity serves. It models for Jewish readers how to make—but often, too, how difficult it is to achieve—secure borders and acceptable bridges.

American Jewish detective stories thus provide a window onto contemporary versions of Rabbi Eleazar's situation, onto sites of struggle in the American Jewish popular arts over border-making and collaboration, over the meaning of fidelity to Jewish culture when that culture is variously defined by writers and artists and when such fidelity is coupled with a creative desire to improvise on cultural tradition.[37] These sites of struggle are evidence of what Geoffrey Hartman calls an "involuntary or insubordinate midrash," the involuntary or insubordinate retelling and refashioning of a Jewish tale or motif, in this case of Rabbi Eleazar's tale.[38] Midrash? Popular cultural midrash, yes, although I admit that "midrash" has become a voguish and slippery term. It translates as "probing" or "searching," and it technically refers to a rabbinical mode of literary exegesis and religious speculation—this is classical midrash, and the Talmud is its textual lodestar. But American Jews have unfastened the term from its traditional exegetical and theological referents, most notably in service of feminist re-visionings of Judaism and Jewish identity. In Hartman's usage (employed in service of a general description of Jewish literature), midrash, or "midrashic," describes the modern Jewish writer's relation to Jewish tradition, a relation the dynamics of which the poet and critic Norman Finkelstein dubs the "modern ritual of new creation."[39] According to Finkelstein, by "ritually troping on the past," which is to say by figuring and refiguring the meanings of Jewish memory and Jewish experience, Jewish writers "intend to create a space for themselves in whatever comes to be understood as the Jewish cultural tradition of the future."[40] This view of modern and postmodern Jewish writing provides a useful map of the terrain in which contemporary Jewish writers work, including the writers in this study. True, we might quibble over the degree of intentionality exhibited by writers who engage in modern midrash, and be justifiably concerned that a careless and reflexive use of the term simply reanimates an androcentric and elitist notion of how Jewish literature and culture is made. Nevertheless, in this map we find a geography of the contradictions and problems that face those who would recast the very meaning of midrash to authorize their place (to legitimate it, to write it) within Jewish cultural tradition; in this study I also overlay this map on the American Jewish popular arts.

In short, I agree with Hartman and Finkelstein that involuntary or insubordinate midrash remains one of the hallmarks of the modern Jewish imagination, and so the revisions of and improvisations on Rabbi Eleazar's "tradition" (however imperfectly understood or imaginatively rendered) are what make the American Jewish detective text distinctively Jewish, even as they raise fruitful questions about the very meaning of "distinctively Jewish." While there continues to be a great deal of contentiousness about how to define Jewish source material and Jewish writing—the title of Hana Wirth-Nesher's introductory essay, "Defining the Indefinable," in *What Is Jewish Literature?* gets right to the point—Rabbi Eleazar's situation and Yaffe's/Raphael's categories of "affirming" and "acculturated" detectives provide the criteria in this study for what detective stories will count as Jewish detective stories.

Taking American Jewish detective stories seriously leads us, therefore, to the recognition that the textual language and thematic concerns of those stories are a part of, and not separate from, the canon of Jewish literature and the process of modern Jewish self-definition and self-explanation. These stories bear traffic between American popular culture and Jewish literature, which is why I include two films and an informal audience reception survey in this study; the former illustrates how visual culture informs and has been informed by these stories and this process, and the latter helps to raise questions about the role of Jewish consumers in directing such traffic. Taken seriously, the detectives I investigate in this study reveal themselves as figures from an intersection: the American Jewish detective embodies the imperfect, popular balance between improvised Jewish reasoning and American mystification on which the American Jewish detective story turns, a balance the tensions and challenges of which open the detective formula to possibilities that can be exploited by various Jewish writers.[41]

The stories these writers tell reveal an imperfect, popular acculturation to, and interrogation of, the American diaspora, and they provide imperfect, popular defenses for defending the diversity of what it means to be Jewish in America.

Now for some organizational business. I have divided my study into three cases of kosher hybridity that manifest three generalized sites of struggle in American Jewish detective stories: cases of gender, cases of memory, and cases of alterity. I do not rigidly compartmentalize these issues here—I make references to gender, memory, and alterity throughout this study. The three cases simply make it possible for me to focus my argument in what I hope is both a coherent and an engaging fashion.

Cases of gender and kosher hybridity explore sites of struggle for control over the meaning of gendered American Jewish identities. Such cases are an appropriate starting point for this study since the question of who and what constitutes the beginning of American Jewish detective stories is really a question about whether to begin with Harry Kemelman's Rabbi David Small mysteries (published between 1964 and 1996) or James Yaffe's Mom mysteries (his initial series of short stories published between 1952 and 1968).

Alvan Judah produced a number of heirs in the twentieth century, all of whom I disqualified as contenders.[42] Those detectives and their stories say more about the image of the Jew in American literature than they do about the meaning of Jewishness in American Jewish literature and culture. Consequently, in looking for the beginning of American Jewish detective stories I looked for stories that embodied the criteria I have just reviewed, which, boiled down to a series of search parameters, came to this: a Jewish detective, created by a Jewish writer, whose character was developed over the course of a series in which issues of Jewish identity and Jewish experience were integral to the mysteries.

My decision? I argue in chapter 1 that, while Mom may be the first affirming or acculturated American Jewish detective to star in her own series, Rabbi Small is the first influential affirming Jewish detective. His rise illustrates that the rise of American Jewish detective stories is the result of a transitional period in the acculturation of Jews to postwar America, and his enduring legacy to the American Jewish detective story is his very struggle to exert authority over what it means to be American, Jewish, male, and middle class during and after the social and cultural changes of the 1960s and 1970s. In chapter 2, I examine how Faye Kellerman, in the Peter Decker and Rina Lazarus mysteries, revises Rabbi Small's misogynist teachings and Kemelman's model of American Jewish masculinity; in this chapter, I analyze how "intermarriage" functions as a description of Kellerman's reshaping of the detective formula and the detective figure, and as a coded reference and solution to the bane of American Jewish life during the 1990s. In chapter 3, I return to Yaffe's Mom to consider the ways Yaffe's stories illustrate midcentury images of American Jewish women, the infiltration of those images into American Jewish detective stories, and the ways Marissa Piesman's Nina Fischman mysteries "talk back" to Mom's gender masquerade.

Cases of memory and kosher hybridity explore sites of struggle over the meaning of the Jewish past and the American Jewish future. In "Cases of Memory," I continue my illustration of generic and cultural hybridity in American Jewish detective stories by analyzing the deployment of detectives into Jewish time as agents of American justice. In chapter 4, I consider the function and significance of "Jewish Gothic" in short stories by Janice Steinberg and Ronald Levitsky, in David Rosenbaum's *Zaddik* (1993), and in Richard Zimler's *The Last Kabbalist of Lisbon* (1998). The seduction and the terror of memory given voice in these works manifest a weird kosher hybridity that expresses anxiety and fear not about the future per se but about whether all the memory available to American Jews in the present is well-preparing them for the future. My argument in chapter 5 is that Ira Levin's *The Boys from Brazil* (1976), Zachary Klein's *No Saving Grace* (1993) and Rochelle Krich's *Angel of Death* (1994) and *Blood Money* (1999) exemplify how the social and cultural functions of narratives about American justice and Holocaust crimes correspond to the changing image of Holocaust victims in the American Jewish popular imagination, and to the changing image of their agent, the "Nazi hunter." In addition, the incorporation of conventions and character traits associated with the hard-boiled detective in the stories of all three writers underscores the influence not only of an American popular genre, but also of gender, in determining the meaning of heroism and in meeting the challenge of doing justice to Holocaust victims.

Cases of alterity explore sites of struggle over "spectatorship" and the meaning of Jewish difference to American Jews. By considering the problematics of viewer/reader positioning in American Jewish detective stories—the point of view that their readers are asked to collaborate with—I consider in more detail the complexities, and confusions, of the inadvertent learning attending the kosher hybridity of American Jewish detective stories. In this last section, I am most concerned with emphasizing that these confusions arise out of the contradiction of positioning Jewish identity as both different from, yet the same as,

American identity. Thinking in chapter 6 about the involuntary or insubordinate embodiment of Rabbi Eleazar in Sidney Lumet's *A Stranger among Us* (1992) and David Mamet's *Homicide* (1991), I consider the visibility of the Jewish body and its uses as a public symbol for borders and border crossings between Jews and non-Jews. Both these films visualize Alain Finkielkraut's observation about the desirability and the painfulness of Jewishness as an object of reflection. Chapter 7 takes up a question that chapter 6 raises about the inadvertent learning of kosher hybridity—is the positioning of an audience as spectators to border-making always a suspect activity?—through a reading of ethics in Stuart Kaminsky's Abe Lieberman mysteries. In those mysteries, Jewishness is reduced to ethical behavior, and so helps to distinguish between good guys and bad guys, good Americans and bad Americans. The result is a wobbly and confused fictional multiculturalism that betrays an anxiety about the role readers play in shaping the meaning of Jewish difference, and of Jewishness as a desirable object of reflection, in American Jewish detective stories. That leads me in my eighth and final chapter to a consideration of kosher hybridity and audience reception, and to my concluding thoughts on defending the faith(s), juvenile American Jewish detective stories, and the implications of this study for future work in the field.

Throughout this study I make it a point to describe, either in the narrative or in a footnote, the salient characteristics of, and the relevant critical commentary on, whatever variant of the detective genre I think is being hybridized in the story or stories at hand. However, there are two main formulas, the classical detective formula and the hard-boiled detective formula, that I refer to so often it seems best to define those formulas in brief here.[43] The classical detective formula refers to stories in which the detective possesses an idiosyncratic and markedly superior intelligence; classical detectives always work for or with the authorities, though often in a competitive relationship. The classical detective solves crimes primarily through a reasoned approach to understanding a crime's planning and execution, but especially to understanding a criminal's motive for committing a crime in the first place. The emphasis in the classical detective formula is on the puzzle aspects of the genre. The hard-boiled detective formula refers to stories in which the social background of the mystery appears to take precedence over the puzzle; in the hard-boiled formula the detective solves a crime primarily by unraveling a series of clues that lead, often by chance, to an investigation of the politically corrupt and morally ambiguous world in which the crime takes place and with which the detective is at odds.

The criminal or criminals responsible for a crime help to foreground the detective's idiosyncratic code of conduct as well as the reasons the detective must mete out the justice and punishment that the authorities cannot or will not dispense.

One final note before closing this introduction. I obviously do not survey every affirming and acculturated American Jewish detective story in this fast-moving and rapidly growing phenomenon. There are titles in this study that are already out of print. Still, there are sure to be readers who will object that I have omitted a favorite story or, in their opinion, a significant text. My aim here, however, is to provide a clear and cogent picture of American Jewish detective stories, and to do this I must focus on representative texts rather than on representing every text with a claim for inclusion. One of the exciting and frustrating outcomes of this study was my realization that the subject matter is deeper and larger than I at first thought, and that it easily exceeded the space and scope of one book. My hope is that others will see these omissions not as an attempt to create a canon but as an invitation to join the discussion.

CASES OF GENDER

TALMUDIC SISSY OR JEWISH DUPIN?

> I find in the nineteenth-century Austrian notion of the feminized Jewish male only one example of a Jewish ideal that goes back to the Babylonian Talmud. In this ideal I hope to locate a model for a gentle, nurturing masculinity (no matter how often it was, or was not, realized); a man who could be so comfortable with his little fleshy penis that he would not have to grow it into "The Phallus," a sort of velvet John.
> —Daniel Boyarin, *Unheroic Conduct*

Though his penis is never mentioned in the eleven books that comprise his eponymous detective series, Rabbi David Small is a popular cultural example of Boyarin's feminized Jewish male, which means that he both illustrates and contradicts the Jewish ideal for which Boyarin longs. Harry Kemelman's protagonist is not the first affirming or acculturated American Jewish detective to star in his own series. James Yaffe's "Mom" appeared in a series of short stories published in *Ellery Queen's Mystery Magazine* between 1952 and 1968. But those stories were not collected into one volume until 1997, and their impact on the American Jewish detective story pales in comparison to the Rabbi Small mysteries, which, because of their immediate recognition by the national press, and with over seven million copies in print at the height of their popularity, have become the introductory series for American Jewish detective stories, and so introduce this section on gender and kosher hybridity. (I will return to Yaffe's detective and her contribution to the gendering of American Jewish detectives in chapter 3.) Rabbi Small is the first influential affirming Jewish detective, an ultra-intellectual detective whose masculinity is flaccid compared to Roger Simon's dope-smoking, hard-boiled Moses Wine, Zachary Klein's cigarette-smoking, hard-boiled Matt Jacob, David Rosenbaum's mystic, hard-boiled Dov Taylor, and David Mamet's confused but hard-boiled Bobby Gold in the film *Homicide*. In comparison to these "tough" or "muscle" Jews, Rabbi Small's unprepossessing physique, gentleness, and absentmindedness, and his use of Talmudic logic and precedent rather than physical force or weaponry to solve murders or disputes, seems evidence enough that he is, indeed, a version of Boyarin's Talmudic sissy.[1]

Determining what kind of version is another matter. Outing a fictional American Jewish sissy like Rabbi Small means rummaging around "the Jew's closet," a term that cultural theorist Daniel Itzkovitz borrows from Eve Kosofsky Sedgwick as a spatial shorthand for repressed and repressive popular cultural fantasies about Jewish identity.[2] The "popularly constructed contents" of that closet, says Itzkovitz, reveal the "definitional slipperiness of Jewishness" in America, how definitions of Jewishness and Americanness are, in fact, "bound up" inside that closet.[3] Looking in, we see that the dangerous, even criminal, economic and sexual secrets that describe Jewish difference have different social and literary functions depending on how they help to delimit and control the meaning of heterosexual Americanness. Reading Itzkovitz, I was reminded of two Jewish characters from American literature: the scheming, newly moneyed Simon Rosedale in Edith Wharton's *The House of Mirth,* portrayed as a kind of economic and sexual predator who helps define the "spiritual fastidiousness" of the *haute bourgeois* Lawrence Selden; and the self-pitying, pathetic Robert Cohn in Ernest Hemingway's *The Sun Also Rises,* portrayed as a kind of economic and sexual masochist who helps define the wounded masculinity of Jake Barnes.[4]

But what if the Jewish suspect is also the American detective? For where an enthusiast of Boyarin's project might see in Rabbi Small a Jewish ideal, however imperfectly realized, mystery enthusiasts see a descendent of the first classical detective, C. August Dupin. After all, Edgar Allan Poe's effete, ultra-intellectual sleuth also employs knowledge rather than weaponry to survey and control his opponents.[5] Like Rabbi Eleazar, then, Rabbi Small also collaborates with a non-Jewish authority, with a precursor who polices his social and literary functions. In this chapter I will explore the collaborations that (en)gender Rabbi Small's character and which describe the kosher hybridity in Kemelman's series, thus shedding light on how the rabbi sheds light on the secrets in the Jew's closet. Tracing how the figures of the Talmudic sissy and of the detective as a middle-class agent of social control are embodied in Rabbi Small illustrates that Kemelman's model for the first affirming male American Jewish detective is different only in form, not in kind, from the later, hard-boiled American Jewish detectives and their definitions of masculinity. For it is Rabbi Small's very struggle to exert authority over what it means to be American, Jewish, male, and middle class, during and after the social and cultural changes of the sixties and seventies, that is his enduring legacy to the American Jewish detective story.

TEACHING AUTHORITY

Before close-reading Rabbi Small's collaborations, I should first explain Kemelman's own collaborations: why did he associate authority with didactics, and what in his background formed his educational model? Put simply, the answer to the first question is that teaching was Kemelman's calling and the rationale for all his fiction; however, consideration of the second question complicates this answer. Although Kemelman claimed to have studied "some Talmud" until college, it wasn't his Jewish education but rather his secular education at the Boston Latin School that really determined the trajectory and tenor of his educational life.[6] Boston Latin enabled him to attend Boston University where he studied English literature, and then Harvard, where he earned an M.A. in linguistics. He became a high school English teacher, taught evening classes at Northeastern University, worked as a civilian administrator for the U.S. Army during World War II, and then for the War Assets Administration until 1949. After the war he owned his own business and worked as a freelance writer until 1963, when he returned to academia as an assistant professor of English at Franklin Technical Institute. In 1964, when *Friday the Rabbi Slept Late* appeared, Kemelman, then fifty-five, was hired as an associate professor of English at Boston State College. It was the capstone appointment of his academic career and, together with his education, underscores the important role that teaching, along with the mid-century values of the American academy, played in his life and his fiction.

Little wonder, then, that Kemelman's early detective stories for *Ellery Queen's Mystery Magazine,* later collected in *The Nine Mile Walk* (1967), featured Nicky Welt, Snowden Professor of English Language and Literature at a New England university. The cerebral Welt, who appeared in eight stories written between 1947 and 1967, is an appropriate protagonist for the classical detective formula that Kemelman employed, and is also a standard-bearer for the kind of academic world that Kemelman admired: the liberal arts college whose mission, as Kemelman argues in his 1970 book, *Common Sense in Education,* is to instill a love of knowledge for its own sake into the hearts of undergraduates. Equally important, as he states in chapter 1, "The Problem," such a college must be a bulwark against the intrusion of politics—meaning the economic, cultural, racial, and gender politics of the sixties—into academic life. In Kemelman's view, that intrusion made liberal arts colleges little different from professional schools, turned professors into political partisans, and led middle-class students to "readily follow revolutionary leaders in courses that are not only normally repugnant to them, but that are contrary to their best interests."[7]

Welt, "with his white hair and lined, gnomelike face" (14), also gives voice to the competitiveness and elitism that Kemelman associates with his apolitical liberal arts college. Welt treats the narrator, his friend the county attorney, like a "schoolmaster hectoring a stupid pupil" (14), "like an immature schoolboy" (34), like a "not overbright sophomore" (111), and like "some luckless freshman asking for an extension on a term paper" (150). In response, the county attorney, himself a former faculty member in the School of Law, continually relishes the chance of "scoring" on Welt, of getting the better of him either in a deduction or an inference. Their competition is meant to be like that between a professor and his favorite student, but it is also indicative of the intellectual sniping necessary to survive in Kemelman's elitist, and entirely male, college where academic competition often has deadly results. Neither the competitiveness nor the elitism is cast in a negative or critical light—both are often the catalyst for a sly humor in the stories, where the punch line is witnessing Welt or another professor get the better of someone. When Kemelman says in the introduction to *The Nine Mile Walk* that "Nicky Welt was born in the classroom," it is a telling statement, not because it refers to the reading exercise at Northeastern University that provided the idea for the first Nicky Welt story, but because it makes clear the connection between Kemelman's idealization of the academy and his fiction.

The classroom, in fact, proved an apt model for the relationship between Kemelman and his readers, for Nicky Welt reflects Kemelman's long-stymied desire to be a professor of English. That desire went unfulfilled until 1963 for a number of reasons, one of which was his father's opposition to what he saw as a limited career. "My father was less than pleased when he learned of my intention to become a teacher," Kemelman recounts, in the preface to *Common Sense in Education*. "Then as now it was a poorly paid profession. But this was not his chief reason for disliking it. In part, it was because a teacher had to work for an institution, a school or a college, and this meant being obligated to a president or a dean or a principal for his livelihood. He would have much preferred that I go into business—and of course he meant in business for myself—because a businessman was his own master."[8] It is tempting to see here primarily a father–son conflict that played itself out in fiction, but Isaac Kemelman's preference that his son become an independent businessman also reflects a pragmatic concern for economic survival in early twentieth-century urban America; when Kemelman entered graduate school in the thirties, a tenured professorship in a New England college English department, much less an Ivy League English department, would not have seemed to Isaac Kemelman an easily attainable or sustainable career choice for a Jewish man.[9] Kemelman and his father were both actors in and witnesses to the drama of Jewish embourgoisement—not only to the adaptation by American Jews of middle-class values and behavior (which begat psychological conflict between generations), but also to their desire to enter the professions: medicine, the law, the academy.[10] Working outside the academy after the war, Kemelman imaginatively made his way into the academic game through Nicky Welt. Teaching was an integral part of Kemelman's life, even as he was making a living as a civil administrator and freelance writer, and the Nicky Welt stories provided him with a textual classroom, an entertaining simulacra of the academy where the writer/professor lectures to reader/students.

Psychologically, then, Kemelman redirected his professorial ambitions into fiction, fashioning a teacher who lectures not only to students but to working adults like the county attorney. Eventually, the author began sifting for a meaningful and more compelling lecture topic. "I got to the point where I could produce them with practically no effort whatsoever," Kemelman said of his *Ellery Queen* work. "But I was increasingly troubled by the fact that with this sort of writing, I wasn't saying anything of significance. And so I finally stopped, cold. Eventually I developed Rabbi Small, which is a vehicle that allows me to use a highly popular genre—detective fiction—to put across what I want to say."[11] Rabbi Small the teacher developed out of a social novel about Jews in the suburbs, *The Building of a Temple,* that was turned down by all the publishers to whom Kemelman sent it. But the social theme of that rejected novel, exploring the burgeoning American openness to Jews, and its effect on Jewish identity, was retained in *Friday the Rabbi Slept Late.* The idea for the novel came to Kemelman as he watched the sudden growth of his own Jewish community in Marblehead, Massachusetts, where he had moved in 1951, and the subsequent building of its new synagogue: "Very few of the people had any knowledge of Judaism, any knowledge of the religion. They were young lawyers, doctors, dentists, and they had almost no religious training. It was very interesting how the temple developed under the tutelage of one or two of the older people."[12] Kemelman's story, in which a newly built suburban temple becomes a literal and symbolic house of Jewish education, is critical of Jewish acculturation to the suburbs, yet it depends on those who live in those very suburbs for its audience, and thus for its commercial success.

This irony helps to date Rabbi Small's beginnings in literary history, and suggests why this Jewish teacher was in the right place at the right time. On the face of it, Rabbi Small seems a pure product of the "Jewish decade," as Louis Harap calls the 1950s, of a literature uneasy about postwar American success but still very much a part of it, a literature in which Jewish writers depicted their Jewish protagonists as uneasy insiders and ambivalent Jews.[13] By 1964, however, the middle-class acculturation of American Jews had been under way for a number of decades, even though as a literary theme it is primarily associated with Jewish writers of the late fifties and early sixties—for example, Saul Bellow, Bernard Malamud, Philip Roth—who entered the mainstream of American letters.[14] In fact, Robert Alter felt that the literary efflorescence accompanying that embourgoisement was nearly exhausted by 1965.[15] Looking back on that period, however, Philip Roth sees in the ambiguities and vicissitudes of American Jewish middle-class life the makings of a new kind of American Jewish "folk fiction," as Roth calls it in his preface to the thirtieth-anniversary edition of *Goodbye, Columbus*. Whether set in Short Hills or, as in *Friday the Rabbi Slept Late*, Barnard's Crossing (based on Marblehead), such folk fiction reveals "contradictory yearnings that can perplex the emotions of an ambitious embryo—the desire to repudiate and the desire to cling, a sense of allegiance and the need to rebel, the alluring dream of escaping into the challenging unknown and the counterdream of holding fast to the familiar."[16]

Alter's and Roth's conflicting observations make clear that the late fifties and early sixties were a transition period in American culture and in American Jewish life.[17] The significance of 1964 as the debut year of *Friday the Rabbi Slept Late* is that it places Rabbi Small's beginnings and his educational mission amid events and publications that illustrate the tenor of that period. For American Jews, events of those years precipitated a variety of reappraisals and widened the horizon of the possible in American Jewish literature and culture, enabling new improvisations. In 1964 the Freedom Summer; the murder of James Chaney, Andrew Goodman, and Michael Schwerner; the Civil Rights Act; and the Berkeley Free Speech Movement galvanized many young American Jews politically. For Jews in the period's social movements, the Black struggle for civil rights prompted questions about middle-class Jewish morality and identity. For some Jews, participation underscored their dissatisfaction with a tepid Judaism and a shallow ethnicity, but the burning of Jewish stores in Harlem that same year also revealed serious class and race antagonisms between Blacks and Jews. In 1964 the Second Vatican Council repudiated the notion of Jews as cursed or guilty of deicide, and Pope Paul VI visited Israel. In May, the Palestine Liberation Organization was founded in Jerusalem. In bookstores Saul Bellow's *Herzog*, the paperback reissue of Henry Roth's *Call It Sleep*, Karl Shapiro's *The Bourgeois Poet*, Bruce Jay Friedman's *A Mother's Kisses*, I. B. Singer's *Short Friday and Other Stories*, and Salo Baron's *The Russian Jew under Tsars and Soviets* were new in stock. *Fiddler on the Roof* and *Funny Girl* opened on Broadway.

Interestingly, although the works cited above are wildly divergent in content and style, all except one (Friedman's) look backward in time. Bellow's novel is a portrait of Moses Herzog, a historian taking stock of his "schooling in grief," who writes letters to the dead as he tries to stave off madness. He is a Jewish intellectual who is loved and rejected and who loves and rejects his own life as a Jewish intellectual at midcentury. *Call It Sleep* was a celebrated rediscovery, both of the novel and of the pain and strangeness of an immigrant childhood. Shapiro abandoned traditional rhyme and meter, for the first time in his career, to look back at the self-complacencies and self-deceits of the middle-class poet. "Lower the standard," he declares, his pun expressing a desire to bring down the long-reigning flag of modernist high art, and therefore to reinvigorate his own poetic voice. Singer's and Baron's works provide glimpses of a world destroyed less than twenty years before, and though neither book was a best seller, their availability in American bookstores was a stark reminder that the "destruction of European Jewry shattered the familiar contours of the Jewish world and transformed American Jews into the largest, wealthiest, most stable and secure Jewish community in the Diaspora."[18] The ambivalence with which most Jews responded to that transformation is exemplified by the two Jewish musicals of 1964. By looking back to vaudeville and musical theater, to Fanny Brice as self-made woman and Tevye as guardian of "tradition," American Jews, as Arnold Band notes, were invited to be spectators of an immigrant life and a supposedly authentic Judaism they no longer had to live, their middle-class lives validated by the success of these Broadway entertainments.[19]

Enter Harry Kemelman, an acculturated, older writer and teacher who looks to the future through the eyes of a traditional-minded young rabbi taking on his first job after ordination. Kemelman launches his mystery series at a time when attenuated American Jewish memories are being renewed and reinvented, both in service of building a new communal life in the gentile suburbs and in reaction to other social and cultural changes in America.[20] These combinations and contradictions reveal Kemelman as a bridge, a writer whose work connects two halves of the twentieth-century American Jewish experience. Kemelman has at his disposal his childhood memories of the value of Jewish learning and teaching (gleaned from his afternoon Hebrew school), his later memories of aspiring to, and eventually working in, an elitist, male-dominated, and educationally conservative midcentury American academy, and an optimism about embourgoisement all ready to be invested in the reinvented figure of a Jewish rabbi—an in-house professor and male authority figure for the temple Kemelman appropriated from his unpublished social novel. Kemelman's theme in the Rabbi Small mysteries remains the building of a new synagogue: he creates a work of fiction with which to teach middle-class American Jews about their religion and their ethnic difference, and to help them feel good about their Jewishness, however thin it may be. With Kemelman's memory as Rabbi Small's *smicha,* his rabbinic ordination, the author sends his newly formed protagonist into the suburbs, where he lives long enough in print to be a contemporary of both Moses Wine, whose cultural points of reference in *The Big Fix* (1973) are protests against the House UnAmerican Activities Committee (HUAC), the FSM, Students for a Democratic Society (SDS), Hell's Angels, and Ken Kesey's Merry Pranksters, and Matt Jacob, who nonchalantly observes in *No Saving Grace* (1993) that "the measure of my Jewishness had been tossed into a hospital's foreskin container a couple of minutes after my birth."[21]

Rabbi Small's beginnings are thus exemplary of the burgeoning collaborations shaping acculturation by 1964, evidenced by Kemelman's creative weaving of a useable past with his experience of contemporary social needs and political arrangements. Knowing this, we must be wary of the groundswell of critical approval that greeted Rabbi Small's arrival, of the articles that appeared during the sixties and seventies commending Rabbi Small as an authentic spokesman for Judaism and Jewishness, and of contemporary critics who see Kemelman and Rabbi Small as "demystifying" American Jews for a gentile public.[22] Rabbi Small is, in fact, a transition figure from a transition period. As a teacher, he is the heir to Nicky Welt's midcentury academic ultra-intellectualism and air of superiority. As a problem solver, he is an optimistic amateur from midcentury American Jewish life, not a revisionist of the sixties, though both in *Friday* and in the novels that follow he continually revises and remystifies in order to resolve.

AN AMERICAN JEWISH TALMUDIST

What does it mean to be an American Jewish Talmudist? Unlike the ambivalent Neal Klugman in *Goodbye, Columbus,* whose story ends in a reverie over his reflection and transparency in the glass front of Harvard's Lamont Library, David Small's story begins with the reveries of a committed Jew who refuses to disappear, even though he has already escaped into the unknown, the suburbs. This hook, of certitude entertaining contradictions, is evident in the opening scene of *Friday the Rabbi Slept Late,* when Kemelman's detective arrives in Barnard's Crossing, a fictional Boston suburb south of Lynn, Massachusetts:

> The rabbi, now prepared for morning service, strolled up and down the center aisle, not impatiently, but like a man who has arrived at the railroad station. Snatches of conversation reached him: talk about business, about family and children, about vacation plans, about the chances of the Red Sox. It was hardly the proper conversation of men waiting to pray, he thought, and then immediately rebuked himself. Was it not also a sin to be too devout? Was not man expected to enjoy the good things of this life? the pleasures of family? of work—and of resting from work? He was still very young, not quite thirty, and introspective, so that he could not help raising questions, and then questioning the questions. (2)

The tension between the profane and the sacred, between escape from Judaism (business, family, vacation, sports) and holding fast (the ritual of prayer), is made palpable here. Rabbi Small "is like a man who has arrived at the railroad station," a simile that provides a fitting image for a masculine Jewish character in transit at the end of the 1950s and the beginning of the 1960s. Kemelman, however, clearly allies Rabbi Small's contradictory yearnings with Judaism through a Jewish stereotype—Rabbi Small is the humorous image of the Jew who answers a question with a question, a positive Jewish self-image in this context, juxtaposed as it is with the image of men at a morning service, men who both embody and enact Judaism.

Kemelman's hook signals to readers how the tension resulting from the contradictory yearnings Roth describes in his preface to *Goodbye, Columbus* will be resolved in *Friday.* Whereas Roth tries to maintain the tension of contradictory yearnings in order to explore the ambivalences and ambiguities that attend the middle-class male romance of American Jewish acculturation, Kemelman sets his story in a town whose evocative name suggests that it is the "X" clearly marking an American Jewish crossroads, and he incorporates into Rabbi Small's character the role of "settling differences," as Rabbi Small reveals to two disputing congregants when he explains to them, in those first pages, the function of temples and rabbis: "The temple is not really a holy place. The original one was, of course, but a community synagogue like ours is just a building. It's for prayers and study, and I suppose it is holy in the sense that anywhere a group of men gathers to pray is holy. But settling differences is not traditionally the function of the temple, but of the rabbi" (3). Kemelman means to portray Rabbi Small as an *ohev shalom,* a lover of peace, but when Rabbi Small offers to resolve the congregants' dispute about damages to a car he settles more than their argument. He offers to resolve their differences through a *Din Torah,* a hearing based on Jewish law, and this illustrates how Rabbi Small also settles differences between the supposedly incompatible worlds of Judaism and modern suburban life.

How Rabbi Small accomplishes such a feat in this episode is illustrative. Although both parties are initially wary and even dismissive of getting justice at the *Din Torah,* Rabbi Small, applying the Talmudic distinction between a docile and a vicious ox, and the responsibilities of their respective owners, rules that responsibility for damages to the car rests with the owner and not the borrower. Before the owner can reject the ruling, Rabbi Small quickly explains that his Talmudic reasoning has also revealed that ultimate responsibility rests with the car's manufacturer who must make good under the warranty, so that ultimately the fault for the whole affair rests not with the Jewish parties but with the non-Jewish manufacturer. That is, the fault lies not with Jews but in their cars. Rabbi Small thus resolves differences by applying a neat Jewish solution to a typical middle-class problem, reasoning rather than hectoring, and thus supplying readers with a leading example of, and a clear judgment about, the kind of values real American Jewish men abide by.

Here, Rabbi Small does seem an embodiment of Boyarin's Talmudic sissy, especially for those who might read Boyarin's ideal as simply a gentle, spiritually nurturing Jewish male whose critique of the gentile world and gentile masculinity can be made to illustrate how "the incongruities of values" are resolved by Jewish apologetics.[23] Begin, for example, with the values of appearances. The murder in *Friday* is of a housekeeper who is found in Rabbi Small's car, throwing suspicion on the rabbi and embarrassing Jewish congregants who are in a headlong rush to emulate the middle-class dress, decorum, and business ethos of their non-Jewish neighbors. Given Rabbi Small's physical and sartorial appearance, however, few readers can share the congregants' doubts about the rabbi's innocence. As Jacob Wasserman, chairman of the temple's board of directors, notes:

> [T]he young rabbi's appearance was not imposing; he looked like a very ordinary young man. However, as they talked, he found himself beguiled by David Small's friendliness, by his common sense. Then there was something about his gestures and tone vaguely reminiscent of the bearded patriarch from whom he himself had learned the Talmud when a lad in the old country; the young man's voice had that gentle coaxing quality, a certain rhythm that stopped just short of developing into the chant that was traditional with Talmudists. (52–53)

Small's "ordinariness," and his unconcern and carelessness about his clothes (49, 55), is how Kemelman shifts attention away from Rabbi Small's body to focus attention on the attractiveness, and positive valuation, of his Talmudic "voice." On first meeting the rabbi, Wasserman observed that he "was thin and pale and wore eyeglasses, and although in excellent health he was obviously no athlete" (53), but Rabbi Small's ability to articulate tradition in the sensuous tones of Talmudic chant inevitably charms his listeners, as both Wasserman's observation and the episode of the damaged car illustrate. Even Rabbi Small's wife, Miriam, seems married more to his voice than to his body. She takes her cues for when to prepare his breakfast according to what he is chanting in the morning prayer (63), and she is seduced by his reasoning and convictions, certainly not by his physical charms, into serving at a temple where she feels they are not really wanted (66). Rabbi Small's effeminate body, gentleness, and studiousness reflect the desirable and even sexually attractive East European Jewish ideal of *Edelkayt*, nobility, which Boyarin claims has "origins that are very deeply rooted in traditional Jewish culture, going back at least in part to the Babylonian Talmud."[24]

Compare these qualities to the ones evident in the temple's board of directors, men whose valuation of outward appearances is often undercut by the comic effect of a less than perfect fit between costumes and actors. At a meeting of the all-male board of directors, in chapter 3, Kemelman clothes the chairman of the board, Jacob Wasserman, and the board members in the Sunday garb of the typical corporate boardroom:

"Wasserman was dressed in a lightweight business suit, but the others wore the conventional costume in Barnard's Crossing for a warm Sunday in June—slacks, sport shirts, and jackets or golf sweaters" (24). The emphasis of Kemelman's description of this meeting is on how much the white-collar board members want to ape a masculine gentile corporate culture. A number of board members seem concerned primarily with adhering to every last jot and tittle of Robert's Rules of Order, and when the rabbi's contract is brought up for discussion it is not his performance—his "voice," if you will—but the issue of a raise that prompts the following lampoon:

> "There's a motion on the floor."
> "Well, it's the same idea. All right, I'll make mine an amendment to the motion."
> "Any discussion on the amendment?" asked Wasserman.
> "Just a minute, Mr. Chairman," called Meyer Goldfarb. "That amendment is to my motion, so if I accept it then we don't have to have any discussion. I just change my motion, see."
> "All right, restate your motion then."
> "I move that the motion to extend the rabbi's contract—"
> "Just a minute Meyer, there was no such motion."
> "Jacob made the motion."
> "Jacob didn't make any motion, he just made a suggestion. Besides, he was in the chair—"
> Gentleman," said Wasserman, banging with his ruler, "what's the sense of all this motion, amendment, amendment to the amendment . . . ?" (27)

Rabbi Small's relatively recent arrival (he is, at this point, finishing his first year as the new rabbi) enables readers to see how the business of business has infiltrated the business of running a Jewish temple. Though the members are trying to operate the temple as if it were IBM, this lampoon makes it clear that such masculine corporate conduct is often comically incompatible with a "traditional" relationship between congregation and rabbi. When Wasserman notes that the temple has more members on its board of directors than has General Electric, Jewish readers understand the joke as one about acculturation, about the Jews of Barnard's Crossing being just like everyone else, only more so.

Rabbi Small wants those Jews simply to be themselves, (in other words, like him), but his valuation of a community based on tradition is consistently contrasted with the male congregants' valuation of secular "teams" and corporate hierarchies. Al Becker, congregant, board member, and co-owner of the Ford dealership that had to make good on the warranty of the defective car, virtually accuses Rabbi Small of not being a team member when he says, "I'll tell you what I've got against the rabbi. He's not the man for the job; that's what I've got against him. He's supposed to be our representative, yet would you hire him as a salesman for your company, Ben? Come on now, be truthful" (22). Equally damning for the vindictive Becker is that, when the rabbi introduces a baseball player at the Fathers and Sons breakfast, he "gives the kids a long spiel about how our heroes are scholars instead of athletes" (22). Becker himself is the leader of a kind of competitive team, the snobbish and cliquish crowd of upper middle-class congregants (6). As Becker reveals, competitiveness and fractiousness are key attributes of these teams. Abe Casson, a board member and chair of the county Republican committee, underscores this point when he explains the gentiles' perception of the congregation's behavior: "They don't understand that twenty minutes after a rabbi lands in town, there's a pro-rabbi and an anti-rabbi party. They can't understand how some members of the congregation can become anti-rabbi just because they don't like the kind of hats his wife wears" (116). Such infighting and "causeless hatred" (in Hebrew, *sinat chinam,* a grave sin in Judaism), a by-product, ironically, of American, middle-class acculturation, threatens the cohesiveness and spiritual life of the Jews of Barnard's Crossing. It is only when Rabbi Small manages to clear Al Becker's partner, Melvin Bronstein, who falls under suspicion in the novel, that Becker understands the value of Jews supporting each other as a community instead of competing against each other as in business and sports. It's no surprise, given the rabbi's solution of the damaged car issue, that, when Rabbi Small solves the housekeeper's murder, it turns out that the murderer is not a Jew but a policeman who, by denying he had seen the rabbi on the night of the murder, exemplifies how team thinking (gentiles as authorities versus Jews as scapegoats) can cause needless harm to others. In his appearance and through his values, Rabbi Small represents a Jewish male comfortable with being Jewish and who possesses a Jewish sense of community, a man without desire to ape non-Jewish costumes and attitudes that, at worst, can foster anti-Semitism.

Rabbi Small's explanation of Judaism in *Friday* as the rejection of a masculine gentile corporate culture is a kind of pop cultural midrash on *goyim naches,* a term that broadly describes non-Jewish activities and pursuits supposedly antithetical to a Jewish sensibility and temperament. For Daniel Boyarin, however, goyim naches is more specifically "the contemptuous Jewish term for those characteristics that in European culture have defined a man as manly: physical strength, martial activity, and aggressiveness, and contempt for and fear of the female body."[25] According to Boyarin, goyim naches is a result not of Jewish racism but of the difference in how Judaism and Christianity conceive the relationship between body and spirit. Traditional Jewish culture, argues Boyarin, does not split spirit from body, and so has little use for romance, romantic love, or a romantic ideology of masculinity.[26] A number of critics who have analyzed Rabbi Small's explanation of the differences between Judaism and Christianity have noted this dichotomy between spirit and body in Kemelman's series, and Kenneth Barker has rightly pointed out that "Rabbi Small's description of Christianity as a mystical religion and Judaism as an ethical religion is overly simplistic."[27] But such a simple description, and the absence of contempt in Kemelman's explanation of Catholic dogma or Christian belief (but not in his depiction of American Jewish women, as I will show in the last section), makes clear that it is not Christian faith itself that threatens Jews but rather faith in the masculine gentile corporate culture fostered by a Christian America. Rabbi Small's American Jewish midrash, ultimately in service of acculturation, means to make the conflicts between American Jews and American Christians intelligible and resolvable. Thus the point of Rabbi Small's midrash is that Judaism can still coexist with such a corporate culture in a way that enables Jews to have *naches* in a world of goyim naches.

The key to that coexistence is explained in *Saturday the Rabbi Went Hungry* (1966). Just before sundown on Yom Kippur eve, the Rabbi is told that the temple's public-address system is faulty, and the cantor, who treats the robing room like a backstage dressing room, and who sees his chanting of the *Kol Nidre* as his most important performance of the year, frantically asks Rabbi Small what he should do. Faced again with a fellow Jew who wishes to ape gentile culture, Rabbi Small applies a *pilpul*, a fine distinction, in which he points out that, since Yom Kippur falls on a Sabbath, the cantor should abjure using the microphone at all. Using the microphone is akin to turning electricity on and off, an act forbidden on the Sabbath, and "if the rule applies for the Sabbath for the Orthodox synagogue, then it should apply for us Conservatives on Yom Kippur, and on a third-degree Sabbath such as we're having this year, it ought to apply even to Reform congregations" (9). Without directly addressing either the cantor's desire to be seen as a performer like other gentile performers, or the cantor's performance of a theatrical gentile masculinity, the rabbi simply makes the one drawback to that performance an affirmation of Jewish difference. As Rabbi Small says, "I have converted into a blessing something that has to be tolerated anyway" (9).

Rabbi Small's act of adaptation is more than a commentary on Conservative Judaism in the sixties and its co-optation of Orthodox hegemony (the theme of one subplot in *Saturday*). Not only the lack of a microphone is converted into a benefit, in the episode above. The cantor's performance is converted as well, from a gentile to a Jewish one. Since the rabbi cannot stop or prohibit the cantor's behavior, which is portrayed in the same comical vein as the behavior of the temple board in *Friday*, that behavior is simply made "Jewish." That is, Rabbi Small's revision enabling a resolution to the conflict between Jewish culture and gentile culture sanctions coexistence between those cultures as long as that coexistence can be converted into a blessing, into a benefit for the Jews or their community. In the case of the cantor, Rabbi Small comments to his wife that his *pilpul* made the cantor "feel pious and devout instead of aggrieved" (9–10), thereby ensuring a moving *Kol Nidre* for both the cantor and the congregation.

Similarly, when Mortimer Schwartz, an architect and president of the temple, proposes to build an addition, his desire to increase the temple's physical size rather than improve the congregants' attendance provides Rabbi Small with an architectural illustration of his midrash. Schwartz feels slighted that a non-Jew designed the current temple. Although his design for the addition of a new chapel incorporates double cylinder columns that represent Torah scrolls, his real intention is to mimic the imposing physicality and the spiritual aggressiveness of European churches and cathedrals (56). By conceiving of the temple addition as a Jewish version of the church triumphant, where size equals importance, Schwartz sets in motion a conflict between the rabbi and those congregants whose designs on the temple are to transform it into a body similar in stature to Christian bodies. Ironically, the same congregants do an injustice to the short, fat, and balding body of the Jewish alcoholic whose death this particular mystery is about. Isaac Hirsch is irreligious, married to a non-Jew, and possibly a suicide, and his burial in the Jewish cemetery infuriates the wealthy and orthodox Moses Goralsky because, according to Jewish law, burying a suicide in a Jewish cemetery renders it unclean. Since Goralsky's wife is buried there, and since Goralsky also wishes to fund the new chapel as a memorial to her, Schwartz comes up with a plan to build a circular road in the cemetery that in effect "leaves Hirsch's grave outside—and in a corner" (97). Rabbi Small's moral outrage over this "criminal" plan, which privileges a kind of gentile body over a Jewish body, leads him to investigate the cause of Hirsch's death.

Once he solves Hirsch's murder, however, Rabbi Small focuses on the more troubling mystery in *Saturday,* how to settle the differences between all the competing bodies in this story. In the last chapter, he helps Goralsky, who feels beholden to his vow to fund the temple addition, to see that this vow is absolved because attaching the new chapel to the old temple violates the Biblical law of *shatnes* that prohibits Jews from mixing linen and wool together. Observing that the prohibition appears in both Leviticus and Deuteronomy, Rabbi Small explains that "we can interpret this to mean that the precept is intended to forbid various mixtures of two things of different kinds" (218). He then convinces Goralsky that his vow can be honored by building the new chapel in the cemetery, where it would be a more appropriate memorial to Goralsky's dead wife. Rabbi Small's revision, applying the law of *shatnes* to architecture, resolves the inevitability of dealing with some kind of "addition" to the Jewish architectural and corporate body by conjoining it to the cemetery rather than to the temple—to a Jewish space where both the spirit and the body rest in peace. Since it must be tolerated, Rabbi Small "kills" the initial project and converts the chapel into one of the dead, making it a blessing rather than a curse because in the cemetery it testifies to the Jewish community's inclusiveness and ethical largesse, as does the burial there of the irreligious Hirsch. Once both bodies have, in a sense, been buried by Rabbi Small in ostensibly Jewish ground(s), they are no longer a problem. They coexist quite nicely.

Thus, the pop cultural midrash of an American Jewish Talmudic sissy is an ethical commentary on the Jewish male's response not only to social conflict, but also, and especially, to the cultural conflict that goyim naches instigates in an American Jewish community. As Rabbi Small teaches, a Jewish man looks to the sources of these conflicts to settle the differences between Judaism and modern suburban life, and to convert into a blessing a masculine gentile corporate culture that must be tolerated anyway. Rabbi Small's critique of goyim naches in the suburbs depends upon his ability, modeled as the acme of Jewish male talent, to read and revise Jewish law so that the social differences between Jews as well as the cultural differences between Jews and non-Jews are settled. To be Jewish and male, then, means the responsibility, and the right, to transform and remystify tradition in its own defense, as well as in defense of the Jewish community's enjoyment of the benefits of an acculturated life in the suburbs. Ruth Wisse is right, therefore, when she points out that, as the embodiment of such a Jewish male protagonist, "Rabbi Small resists the inflation of obvious heroism," because to be Jewish and male means to be Small, to value an intellectual, redirecting, and apologetic heroism—a "feminine" heroism—rather than a phallic heroism.[28] Indeed, Kemelman emphasizes this in a rather blunt way in *Thursday the Rabbi Walked Out* (1978) by making a short but gun-toting gentile male character the murderer, while the short and apparently weak Rabbi Small heroically clears the short, nebbishy, but strong-willed adolescent boy accused of the crime. Wisse is right, too, though not at all in the way that she intends, when she lauds the rabbi for projecting "the steady disciplined intelligence of Jewish legal analysis" (47). There is nothing intellectually steady in Rabbi Small's revision of Jewish law—as he says in his ruling about *shatnes*, the logical test for deciding if an action is prohibited is "if it seems wrong to you" (218). Although such a test may seem logical to the rabbi's "A" students (to whom "you" is really Rabbi Small), its subjectivity and intellectual wooziness is problematic, to say the least. But Rabbi Small's intelligence is indeed disciplined, and the power exerting that discipline and collaborating in the production of his rulings on civil rights, Israel, the chavurah movement, neo-hasidism, and feminism is not conveyed by Jewish legal analysis but by the classical detective formula.

A FORMULA FOR COLLABORATION

An unremarked connection between Dupin and Rabbi Small is that both come into being during transition periods where the displacement of authority—social authority in the former, cultural authority in the latter—foregrounds the ambiguities of identity and of the social order.[29] In Dupin's case, Jon Thompson theorizes that Dupin's superciliousness and rationalism "ultimately derives from Poe's investment in the southern valorization of an aristocratic code."[30] The anti-democratic and alienated Poe renews and reinvents "reason" as a powerful, complete form of knowledge in order to indirectly survey and criticize a newly industrialized American society, powered by an empirical, "scientific" mode of knowledge, that threatens to displace the social authority of the South's "aristocracy of the mind" and agrarian ideal of American life.[31] Thompson's analysis is helpful in showing how Dupin's alienation from, and feelings of superiority to, a burgeoning industrialized society bequeaths to the classical detective formula a kind of asocial attitude: Dupin is the self-sufficient outsider critical of "authorities" who aid and abet a suspect social order. In ratiocinative detective fiction the "fascination with the power of knowledge is almost always associated with a lack of interest in the interaction between the individual and society."[32] The Rabbi Small mysteries are in no way as devoid of everyday detail and social character as the Dupin mysteries, but the rabbi's resistance, even antagonism, to the social changes transforming the relationship between individuals and society during the sixties and seventies is a reflection of Dupin's legacy to the formula that Rabbi Small inhabits. Moreover, keeping in mind the Nicky Welt stories and Kemelman's conservative idealization of an academy where the politics of social change are banned from campus, the rabbi's resistance also illuminates the usefulness to Kemelman of Rabbi Small's collaboration with the classical detective formula. If social and cultural change cannot be banned from Kemelman's "campus," the American Jewish community of Barnard's Crossing, it can certainly be surveyed and controlled by his Jewish Dupin.

In *Sunday the Rabbi Stayed Home* (1969), civil rights and social action are redefined and delimited by the rabbi as general concepts and as matters of individual conscience. Set, tellingly, in the days before Passover—the festival commemorating Jewish slavery and the Exodus from Egypt—the tale has Rabbi Small having to confront a group of congregants on the temple board who wish to change the function and meaning of the temple's social action program. Their self-serving goal is to abolish reserved seating on the High Holidays so that they can sit in the more prestigious pews closer to the Ark where the Torah scrolls are kept, but they sell their program to the congregation as the desire "to help make democracy work" (33). They pitch the idea that funds from the social action program ought to be contributed to causes like the Poverty March on Washington, legal aid for civil rights workers, and funding candidates for public office who support civil rights. Kemelman counterpoints such cynical "radicalism" with the behavior and intellectual hunger of the Jewish college students, home for Passover, who meet with Rabbi Small as part of a post-confirmation discussion group. The students are appalled at the board's hypocrisy, and are fascinated by Rabbi Small's informal lectures on Judaism that make such hypocrisy, and the intrusion of politics into the temple's organization, seem not just shallow but also a threat to Judaism. As one son tells his father, "Yeah, you can go and wreck an organization that's just a sideline with you, a hobby that makes you feel like a big shot. You don't even care about it enough to keep kosher or anything like that, but if someone whose life is involved in it tries to preserve it, then you got to rub him out" (77).

In fact, Kemelman uses the issue of civil rights to show that the Jewish historical knowledge Rabbi Small possesses obviates his having to be a part of the "trendy" social protest movements swirling around his congregants and students. As readers are shown at the beginning of the mystery, Black animus against Jews makes participation in these movements problematic for Jews, anyway. Rabbi Small, filling in for a week as the Hillel rabbi at "Mass State, Western Division, at Binkerton," is invited to have a cup of coffee with the Black poet-in-residence, Lucius Rathbone. Instead of the pleasant interreligious and intercultural gathering that the rabbi expected, he finds himself the target of Rathbone's anti-Semitic tirade, accused of economic profiteering in the inner city and of oppressing Blacks for four hundred years. Naturally, Rabbi Small knows the last four hundred years of Jewish history intimately, and he uses that knowledge as both a defense and a challenge: "Those four hundred years you speak of, Mr. Rathbone, my people lived in the ghettos of Europe—Poland, Russia, Germany—and there were no Negroes there. My Grandfather, who came to this country from a small town in Russia at the turn of the century, like the rest of my ancestors, had never even seen a Negro, much less enslaved and brutalized and robbed him of his manhood.... Can you say the same of your ancestors, Mr. Rathbone?" (47). The power of the Jewish historical knowledge that Rabbi Small wields here is twofold. First, it is a manly knowledge, understood as such by its comparison to, and overpowering of, an aggressive and belligerent African American historical knowledge; the prestige of manhood itself becomes symbolic of Jewish honor, decency, and strength. Second, this knowledge provides the logic for Rabbi Small's argument that a lack of social interaction with Blacks proves that Jews have never been and thus could never have been their oppressors or racists. As the rabbi's question makes clear, African Americans themselves cannot claim such a moral high ground. This logic is repeated later when a congregant mentions that he heard Rabbi Small give a talk in which the rabbi observed that "the modern civilized world was finally coming around to the positions that the synagogue had been preaching for a couple thousand years or more—social justice, civil rights, rights of women, importance of learning" (121). Kemelman, reflecting on how the civil rights movement also revealed the social tensions between Jews and Blacks, has Rabbi Small police Jewish involvement in that and other social protest movements by underscoring Black animus toward Jews, and by suggesting that for sympathetic Jews in suburbs like Barnard's Crossing the best course of social action is no action at all. Armed with a knowledge of Jewish history and its moral teachings, Jews need only wait for everyone else in America to catch up with Judaism.

Kemelman, however, does not mean to equate Jewish communal inaction with a complete indifference to the changes transforming American life, and he uses the arrest of Alan Jenkins, a young Black art student, as the catalyst for Rabbi Small's illustration of how Jewish historical knowledge supplements American social justice. *Sunday* is a mystery that links drug dealing with murder, a combination that plays on contemporary stereotypes of Blacks and makes Jenkins the immediate suspect. Discussing the possibility of Jenkins's guilt with Police Chief Lanigan, Rabbi Small intuits that Lanigan suspects Jenkins because of these stereotypes, and when Lanigan suggests that the rabbi ought to be glad that it's a stranger like Jenkins and not a Jew who is a suspect, Rabbi Small takes the opportunity to compare Jenkins's situation to that of the Jews during their bondage in Egypt. He tells Lanigan that Passover is not merely a holiday but a series of rituals whose purpose is to enable Jews to remember that "if a stranger sojourn with thee in your land, ye shall not do him wrong . . . he shall be as the homeborn among you; for ye were strangers in the land of Egypt" (169–170). In this one-on-one dialogue, Rabbi Small illustrates how an individual Jew who acts on his Jewish historical knowledge in the approved American time and place, and with the right American authority, can have a greater effect on a person's civil rights than could a mass protest. Rabbi Small may be wary about the displacement of authority, but he is still a good American—he supports the idea of American social justice, not social protest movements. In this way, Rabbi Small defends and supports Jenkins's civil rights without ever having to meet him, and so the crime of social indifference, of appearing un-American, is solved, for both the rabbi and the American Jewish reader. Rabbi Small's gendered lesson teaches that social change is best negotiated when a Jewish man acts in concert with Jewish historical knowledge and American law, when he accedes to a witting collaboration with the authorities.

Of course, the irony in this passage is that, to demystify Lanigan's stereotype of Blacks and of the stranger, Rabbi Small remystifies Jenkins into a literary trope from the Passover Haggadah, converting him into a kind of Jew that, conceptually, he knows quite well. This irony and revision are clues to Rabbi Small's unwitting collaboration. As Kemelman's Jewish Dupin, Rabbi Small disciplines American Jewish men to abjure "radicalism" and support for group rights, considered deviant, in favor of Jewish ethics (based on the rabbi's actions and his Jewish historical knowledge) and a secular faith in the American legal system's protection of individual rights, considered normal. Social action, as compared to individual action, is always suspect because, as the rabbi tells his wife Miriam, the baleful power of crowds is that they incite precisely the stereotypes Lanigan brings to light, and so also "religious war" (192). As a Jewish Dupin, then, Rabbi Small surveys a major social change of the sixties, the rise of interest in group rights and concerns sparked by sympathetic interest in civil rights for African Americans, and offers American Jewish men a self-policing method for safely negotiating that American social change without jeopardizing either themselves or their successful acculturation into middle-class American life.

In the mysteries that follow, Kemelman's Jewish Dupin repeats this pattern, disciplining American Jewish men to think "Jewishly" but act appropriately "American" in the face of social and cultural change. In *Monday the Rabbi Took Off* (1972), the change that must be negotiated is the galvanizing cultural effect of a post–Six Day War state of Israel on American Jewish identity. Taking a sabbatical in Israel, Rabbi Small explores and explains the attraction and "meaning" of Israel to American Jews—the communal nature of Israeli society (it's like a vast temple board!), the altruism, toughness and technological know-how of Israelis (such modern Jews!), and, above all, the normalization of Jewish identity in a modern Jewish nation-state (it's no big deal to be a Jew!). As literary critic Andrew Furman helps us to see, these "meanings" are related to images of Israelis, circulating in the American Jewish popular imagination between 1948 and the period just after the Six Day War, that replaced the image of "the nebbisheh (weak) Diaspora Jew, the victim of Hitler's Holocaust."[33] But whereas many similar novels, following the earlier example of Leon Uris's *Exodus,* attempted to "forge an appealing Israeli ethos that would bolster the image of the Jew in the Diaspora,"[34] Kemelman uses his Jewish Dupin to forge an appealing American ethos that bolsters the image of the Jew in Israel. In *Monday,* two "extremes" dominate Israeli society: the "fanatical" Orthodox who "try to impose their customs on the rest of us" (251), and "antireligious" secular Israelis, like the kibbutzniks the Smalls meet, for whom Israel is a place in which to escape the Diaspora burden of having to act out their Jewishness. This secular, yet "authentic," Jewish society is so attractive to the rabbi that he allows himself to skip synagogue on the Sabbath morning (90), and even doubts his choice of profession (120). In the course of solving the nearly insignificant murder mystery in this novel, Rabbi Small discovers that the modern observant Jew in Israel is, in fact, in danger of disappearing, either into the conservatism and pedantry of the Orthodox (91–92), or into the cosmopolitanism of secular Israeli society (252).

The answer? As in *Sunday*, Kemelman has Rabbi Small articulate a belief in the protection of individual rights and in the law as a pragmatic guide for negotiating social change, a belief that for Rabbi Small reflects a fundamental character of American society to which Jewish tradition is a supplement. As his Israeli hosts debate who is a "real" Israeli and the intolerance of Orthodox interpretations of the laws of religious conversion, Rabbi Small interjects: "And what law, anywhere, has ever affected everyone exactly the same? There are always exceptional cases which are unfair to the individual. But society tolerates them because a perfect law is impossible and life without law is unthinkable" (252). Law is what guarantees that the majority will have their individual rights protected. But given what readers have seen through Rabbi Small's eyes, it is clear that, in comparison to Israeli society, where there is no separation between religion and state, American society offers Jews a closer approximation to laws that are fair to the individual (because conversion is a private and not a state issue), and thus to the kind of moderation and pragmatism that the Israelis, for all their positive attributes, still need in order to sort out heated questions of social and cultural identity.

When he finally returns home and tells Police Chief Lanigan about his adventures, the rabbi mentions that despite his yarmulke an Israeli police inspector doubted his religious orthodoxy. Lanigan asks, "What kind of place is it where a cop would question a rabbi on his religious views?" (287–288). To the rabbi it's a special place, obviously, but to Lanigan, as to many of Kemelman's readers, a nation that does not separate religion and state is not a "normal" place. In America, Rabbi Small's identity as a Jew goes without question, primarily because his yarmulke is the gendered sign of Jewishness that no American would presume to doubt. In Israel, as the rabbi sadly notes, Jewishness is so healthy there is no need for another rabbi (273)—a yarmulke is just another kind of Jewish hat. A Jewish identity "whose work carries with it responsibility for others" (273) is really better served in the American Diaspora. Visiting Israel, therefore, is a fine and important way for American Jews to learn about and support Zionism, but Rabbi Small's experience teaches that Jewish men, even those in Israel, are in fact more Jewish when they act American, when they allow secular law to broker social arrangements.

This lesson is especially true when, in *Wednesday the Rabbi Got Wet* (1976), Kemelman's Jewish Dupin surveys the chavura movement and neo-Hasidism. Contemporary interest in mysticism and in alternative religious organizations, incited by the youth movement of the late sixties and early seventies, is Kemelman's real target in this novel. Indeed, the desire to change American Jewish men's religious observance so as to return to an authentic Jewish "spirituality" is seen to be the product of yet another trendy American social movement, and it provokes a strong reaction from Rabbi Small. He calls the chavurah movement a withdrawal from the world and "contrary to traditional Judaism" (31), and he lambasts neo-Hasidism: "They're terribly concerned about such things as having the mezuzah affixed to the doorframe exactly right and that it be handwritten by a scribe on real parchment. Otherwise, presumably, it won't work. And all of them are so self-righteous and so condescending to what they call 'establishment Judaism' as though for the last couple of thousand years we've just been going through the motions and haven't really understood what it's all about. It's the same attitude that led to the recent 'improvement' in our colleges" (32). As we have seen in his midrash, Rabbi Small understands "establishment Judaism" to be a code of ethical conduct—*his* conduct. Therefore, the focus on mysticism and religiosity in neo-Hasidism and the chavurah movement, and not on right conduct, is what makes them "errors" of Judaism (257), and even, in a sense, un-American.

It's no accident, then, that the way American Jewish men conduct themselves in accordance with both American and Jewish law is crucial to solving the murder mystery in *Wednesday,* where for the first time in the series the murderer turns out to be a congregant. The temple board's desire to purchase a Jewish men's retreat in New Hampshire with the proceeds from the sale of commercial real estate willed to the temple by Mr. Goralsky is stymied by a Jewish tenant's insistence that the lease he had been renegotiating with Goralsky, but which had not been signed, be honored. According to American law the temple board need not bother with the tenant, who owns a pharmacy, but, as Rabbi Small tells the board, according to Jewish law they must abide by Goralsky's intention to renew the lease. The rabbi's argument is that Jewish law is only obviated by secular law when there is a conflict between the two, but in cases such as the one before them, where there is no conflict because both laws "are interested in having the wishes of the testator carried out" (206), Jewish law is supplemental to secular law, is an added responsibility that Jews have to one another. If the temple board unquestioningly obeys American law, then so too, and with the same willingness, must they obey Jewish law, and thus Rabbi Small's logic reiterates again that Jewish men are more Jewish when they act American. The impasse with his board is finally broken when Rabbi Small discovers that the wealthy congregant who wanted to purchase Goralsky's property to build a shopping mall on it is the one who substituted a lethal prescription so as to ruin the pharmacy and clear the way for his mall. In their rush to embrace a trendy social movement that promised to put them in touch with their "inner" Jewishness, the temple board had lost touch with American conduct, and so they were unable to see that one of their own was acting outside the bounds of both American and Jewish law. Indeed, the fact that Jewish law was being ignored should have been a warning to them.

This temporary blindness to true American conduct is humorously underscored at the end of the novel when Rabbi Small learns that the last retreat the chavurah members organize is a bust, because the land they were going to purchase turns out to be a highly popular and very noisy summer vacation site. In terms of American conduct, in the sense here of normal American behavior, it is the wrong locale for religion; for Rabbi Small, that's what "establishment" temples are for.

In Kemelman's series, then, to be American and middle class means to have respect for the separation between religion and state, and belief in an American ethos that the best way to negotiate acceptable social change is through law, ideas that Kemelman links to Judaism in order to invest Jewish law with authority over changes in Jewish religious organization and culture. In short, Kemelman's Jewish Dupin uses law as a synecdoche for a normal American social order and as a stopgap for the displacement of social and cultural authority. Rabbi Small's fictionalization of American law thus bears out the observation made by literary theorist Joseph Riddel that Dupin's legacy in "The Purloined Letter" is his modeling of how authority is made in American literature: "It is necessary to maintain the fiction of authority if meanings are to be produced, if the game of signification is to be repeated, if a simulation of 'truth' is to be revealed or rendered. The game of detection, then, produces a representational model for the fictional production of presence, authority, power."[35] During a transition period in which what it meant to be American was under contention, Kemelman simplifies for his readers the meaning of "true" Americanness so that his fictional production of American authority is consonant with, and lends power to, Jewish tradition.

It also lends power and prestige to Jewish men, for just as Jewish historical knowledge is masculinized in the Rabbi Small mysteries, so is Rabbi Small's definition of "true" Americanness. All of the agents of American law are male, and Kemelman's focus in *Wednesday* on the egregious effects that failing to act American has on Jewish men underlines an important point: what is at stake in trying to define Jewish, American, and middle class is primarily at stake for *men*. Trying to resist the displacement of social and cultural authority, Kemelman ends up displacing Jewish women from the scene of American Jewishness.[36] Jewish women in *Sunday, Monday,* and *Wednesday* are wives, mothers, or, figuratively and literally, children, and Rabbi Small and other Jewish men continually assert their intellectual superiority over them. Jewish women in the Rabbi Small mysteries become visible only as foils to Jewish men, but once visible they tend to be a source of trouble, and so we cannot fully appreciate the collaboration between a Talmudic sissy and a Jewish Dupin unless we consider why it is that Rabbi Small has such *tsuris* from his sisterhood.

SISTERHOOD TROUBLE

In 1977, Dr. Ida Cohen Selavan reviewed the Rabbi Small mysteries for the Jewish feminist magazine *Lilith*. Looking back at her glowing review of *Friday*, written twelve years earlier for the *Pittsburgh Jewish Chronicle*, Selavan sees that the reason for her high praise was that "I had identified with Rabbi David Small, Jewish Scholar, rather than with Rebbetzin Small, Jewish Housewife."[37] Selavan notes that Rabbi Small's status, education, and scholarship make him an attractive figure to readers, despite the obvious "*lacunae* in his Jewish knowledge," but Miriam Small is a stock figure whose physical characteristics never change over the course of twelve years and two pregnancies: she is short and blonde with a "firm, determined chin" and blue eyes that lend her a "schoolgirl ingenuousness."[38] Analyzing her childlike image, Selavan shows that Rebbetzin Small's Jewish knowledge is surprisingly rudimentary, especially for the daughter of a rabbi who is married to a rabbi, and no mention is ever made of her secular education. Rebbetzin Small's primary role in the series is that of Rabbi Small's caregiver, and his attitude toward her "is very protective and paternal, even patriarchal."[39] To Selavan, Miriam Small is outrageously unlike any of the educated and professionally accomplished rebbetzins she knows, and therefore Kemelman's representation of Jewish women reveals the fictional nature of Rabbi Small's teachings: "Some of the material Kemelman is teaching through Rabbi Small is innocuous, popularized, somewhat homogenized Judaism. Some of the material is monolithic, possibly derived by Kemelman from his own rabbis. The material relating to women, however, is pernicious.... Thus Jews and Gentiles who are drinking from the wellsprings of Jewish knowledge via David Small's exploits and explications are also, unfortunately, imbibing additives via Miriam Small's lack of a positive Jewish female identity."[40]

Selavan's review forces us to consider what purpose Kemelman's "patronizing, narrow-minded, and ignorant" representation of Jewish women serves in the Rabbi Small mysteries. If we look at him as an American Jewish Talmudic sissy, Boyarin's work helps us to see how Rabbi Small reflects a particular place and time in the ongoing history of Jewish men's subordination to and negotiation with non-Jewish state authorities. Misogyny is integral to the way that the rabbi makes peace with those authorities. After all, Rabbi Small finds that his bookishness and civility, his defensive strategies, are often considered unmanly and suspicious—this is a key trope in the rabbi's showdown with Rathbone, the angry Black poet. Since we see that Rabbi Small is comfortable in his own Jewishness and well-armed with Jewish historical knowledge, his performance as a Jewish man is never called into question in America, but every time another congregant shows up in temple sporting or professing the latest American trend the rabbi's performance as an American man is. Rabbi Small's misogyny is how Kemelman allays anxiety over doubts about that performance, a "defensive-aggressive move of certifying manhood," according to Boyarin.[41] If we look at Rabbi Small as a Jewish Dupin, Thompson's and Riddel's work helps us to see that the "masculine wish-fulfillment fantasies"[42] that are part of the classical detective formula are integral to how that formula constructs authority. Dupin's quote from Crebillon's *Atreus* at the end of "The Purloined Letter," says Riddel, suggests that Dupin's authority as a detective is modeled on the same kind of filial and fraternal violence that establishes authority in both the House of Atreus and, as Crebillon's translation exemplifies, in literature.[43] In this light, Dupin's masculine fantasies constitute what Riddel calls a "patrilineal myth" about the conflicts and revisions of literary self-construction. Violence against women, such as the brutal murder of Madame L'Espanaye and her daughter in "The Murders in the Rue Morgue," is a part of that myth, and women are both the targets of violence and, as with the queen in "The Purloined Letter," its cause. Misogyny, then, is a kind of violence embedded in the classical detective formula that verifies Rabbi Small's authority as a detective.

But Rabbi Small's manhood and authority are also bound up, in Kemelman's series, with the rabbi's desire to educate. My rough sketch of two possible ways to explain Rabbi Small's misogyny is meant only to situate that misogyny in a cultural and literary matrix, and thus to set the stage for how Kemelman's preoccupation with education finally plays itself out in the Rabbi Small mysteries. For example, it is true that in *Friday* misogyny is what proves that a *mentsch* is still a man, and, in an echo of "The Murders in the Rue Morgue," it is the murder of a housekeeper that sets the stage for the rabbi's authority as a detective. The misogyny in *Friday* also argues, however, how troublesome it is to educate American Jewish women. Lew Wasserman, speaking about the rumors that precipitated the dispute about the defective car, attributes the animosity to the congregants' wives:

> "In all probability when the story comes out it will turn out to be the wives that are behind it. Ben's wife, Myra, she's a regular *kochlefel*, she's got a tongue on her."
> "I know," said the rabbi sadly, "Only too well."
> "Schwartz is a weak man," Wasserman went on, "and in that household it's the wife who wears the pants." (6)

Here, a woman's tongue is like a cooking spoon gone out of control. Unsupervised by her husband, Myra's tongue mixes up social disorder instead of assuming its proper use, as an instrument appropriate to the domestic sphere where it will nourish her family, not embarrass it. As with skirts, pants, and cooking spoons, Jewish women have their assigned functions, and it's up to the rabbi to educate them about those functions. Thus it is no surprise when he lectures his sisterhood "that keeping Judaism in their hearts and a kosher home was more important for Jewish women than campaigning for gifts for the temple" (23). If the desire to graft a masculine gentile corporate culture onto Jewish life is exemplified by the men of the temple board, the desire to transform the temple from a religious center to a social center is exemplified by the misguided, nouveau-riche aspirations of the women of the sisterhood. They must be set straight.

The difficulty with that educational project is that its dimensions keep changing on Kemelman and the rabbi. In the first three books in the series, Rabbi Small concerns himself primarily with educating his sisterhood, the wives of his congregants, and Miriam Small. In *Tuesday the Rabbi Saw Red* (1973), however, Rabbi Small must turn his attention to the world outside Barnard's Crossing, to an instigating source of his sisterhood trouble—the academy. As the opening of the novel makes clear, the shallowness of young Edie Chernow's Jewishness, her crass materialism, and her inability to understand the temple's place in and importance to her wedding plans (she wants to have shellfish served in the temple vestry room, as if the temple were simply a dining hall) suggests that Edie is not only an illustration of the downside of suburban acculturation, but also an example of how badly educated acculturated American Jewish women are. For added irony, Kemelman has Edie marrying a college instructor at Windemere College in Boston, a women's college that went co-educational in the early sixties, but which is described as "still two-thirds women" (20). Kemelman sends Rabbi Small to the rescue, having him fill in at Windemere for a semester as instructor for a course on, naturally enough, "Jewish Thought and Philosophy."

In many ways, Rabbi Small's observations about Windemere echo his points in *The Nine Mile Walk* and *Common Sense in Education* about the baleful influence of the intrusion of politics and the professionalism of the business world on the liberal arts college. The president of the college greets Rabbi Small in his office dressed in golf clothes, and he explains to the rabbi that the contemporary college president "is a combination salesman and public relations man" (35). The dean of faculty, Millicent Hanbury, is not a "scholar of some distinction" (25), as the rabbi expects, but rather a former physical education teacher who is, as Chief Lanigan observes about the new deans populating American colleges, a "forceful executive type who can keep the kids in line" (25). Professor Hendryx, the interim chair of the English department, gives Rabbi Small a cynic's lecture on the irrelevance to Windemere students of the pursuit of knowledge for its own sake, and on the decline of the liberal arts college into a kind of intellectual petting zoo where professors like Hendryx "fritter away our lives while the rest of the world goes about its proper business of making money or children or war or disease or pollution, or whatever the hell they're into" (80). Left to their own devices, it's no wonder that the students get involved in espousing "radical" political causes such as penal reform at a local boys' reformatory, or in demanding that the college give tenure to Larry Fine, Edie Chernow's husband, who, unbeknownst to students, had an affair with a coed. While male students are the primary instigators and leaders of these extracurricular political activities, female students are seen as especially vulnerable to the intrigues and wobbly intellectualizing such activities stir up. When a bomb planted by the campus "Weathervane" group blows up, readers discover that the idea to plant a bomb in the first place was an FBI strategy to flush out the radicals on campus, and that the strategy depended on the Bureau's using a female dupe to infiltrate and betray the group (191).

In Rabbi Small's class, however, it's the feminists who appear the biggest dupes of all. On the first day of class, Rabbi Small tries to quell student disappointment that his course will be a lecture course rather than a discussion course by launching into an explanation of Jewish identity, during which he deflates the significance of women's liberation by pointing out that Jewish identity is traced through matrilineal descent. He is immediately attacked by a student who insists he call her "*Ms.* Goldstein," and by Lillian Dushkin, who both raise questions about Jewish male chauvinism and about why Jewish women are relegated to the domestic sphere and segregated in special women's sections in Orthodox synagogues. The rabbi's response? "This is a very good example . . . of the danger of discussions based on ignorance and limited knowledge," he says, and he answers the women's questions by deploying a lecture, similar to the ones in *Sunday,* about the pathbreaking liberalism of Jewish tradition. He ends with an appeal to domestic common sense: "Think about your own families and then ask yourself if the women, your mothers and grandmothers, your aunts, are registered as inferiors by their husbands or their families" (53). By situating the proof for his position back in the domestic sphere the rabbi is able to make feminism seem like bad advice from women who are strangers to the Jewish family. Poor Lillian Dushkin is particularly susceptible to such bad advice because she is "plain" and, as the rabbi observes, "a pretty girl can develop naturally; a plain one has to look for a role to play, and until she finds one, she never feels quite sure of herself" (134). Given that the mystery in this novel revolves around a number of secret affairs being carried on in a college that seems to be paying a heavy price for its decision to go coed, the real "achievement" of feminism on campus is, as the president's daughter tells her father, the professionalization of sex: "Dad, let me clue you in on the facts of life in the seventies. Sex is a woman's business; it's her specialty, her field of concentration. If any affairs are going on at Windemere between faculty and student, and I'm sure there are, believe me, it's something that the girl has initiated and is managing. And she'll usually be the one who terminates it when she finds someone else or has decided she's had enough" (69–70). It's not surprising, then, that the criminal in this novel turns out to be Dean Millicent Hanbury, a scheming spinster who "terminates" her lover, Professor Hendryx, after he leaves her for the more lucrative career choice of marrying the president's daughter.

The rabbi's pedagogy for teaching his students how to avoid becoming such political and sexual dupes, a pedagogy that echoes the elitism of Professor Nicky Welt in Kemelman's early detective stories, is one with a dynamic of particular import for his female students. This pedagogy can best be described as a combination of a "banking" education, lectures in which Rabbi Small deposits Jewish knowledge into the minds of his students, with a kind of tough love—"It's not my function or the college's to amuse you," he reprimands a student who compliments him on how "fun" a particularly informative class was (144). The rewards of this pedagogy are foundational knowledge for students and an ego boost for the teacher: "You're bound to get a lift to the ego from dispensing information about anything you know better than others. And when that knowledge can change a person's way of living, his lifestyle, it's even more satisfying. It's quite something this—this ego trip, I think the students call it" (54).

Employing this pedagogy at the college once again emphasizes Rabbi Small's authority as a Jew, an American, and a man. His model for how an American Jewish male behaves in the intellectual battle zone of the contemporary liberal arts college provides his male students with a lesson in how to negotiate their acculturation into American middle-class life. *Tuesday* thus reads much like a summary of the ideas Kemelman develops in the first four books in his series. What *Tuesday* shows much more clearly than before, however, is that while the rabbi is a model for American Jewish men (a male student in his class eventually asks his advice about becoming a rabbi), he is simply a stern professor to American Jewish women, insisting that they bank his authoritative interpretation of their place in America and in American Jewish life. In essence, he teaches American Jewish men how to act out their Jewish knowledge in the secular world, while teaching American Jewish women why they ought to honor their Jewish responsibilities at home. This is his formula for an American Jewish success story, as well as Kemelman's and Rabbi Small's formula for containing the rapid changes in women's social status in America.

Such a formula also explains why Rabbi Small's disciplining of American Jewish women is so disturbing. Listen as Jacob Wasserman, the first president of the temple, describes to Al Becker the kind of teacher Rabbi Small resembles: "'What's a rabbi, Becker? A rabbi is a teacher. In the old country when I went to school, the teacher was the boss—not like here. Sometimes if you were maybe fresh, or if you said something stupid, you'd get a slap from the teacher. Believe me, many times I got slapped when I was a boy.' His smile broadened with reminiscence. 'But the mistakes you got slapped for, Becker, you didn't make them again'" (19). So effective were these slaps, we presume, that they helped contribute to Wasserman's success as both a businessman and a temple president, making Wasserman a credit to the old system. Of course, Rabbi Small never slaps anyone in this or the other novels, but the retorts and reprimands he hands out in his class at Windemere recall the verbal slaps that Nicky Welt administers in his stories to one-up his intellectual competition. When Rabbi Small does the "slapping," his competition is seen to be the faulty ideas about Judaism that his students, both men and women, bring to class. Still, when he verbally slaps the "liberated" women—in this murder mystery about illicit affairs gone bad—the implications are not only that they will never best the rabbi in this game of intellectual one-upmanship, but also that these paternalistic "slaps" are in fact kinder than the nasty repercussions they can expect if they subscribe to the sexual licentiousness and political agenda that feminism promotes. Like the president's daughter and Millicent Hanbury, they will, if they fail to heed the rabbi, end up either forlornly free or permanently incarcerated, but single and alone nonetheless.

There is, however, one female student who interacts with Rabbi Small right at the start in a manner congenial to his pedagogical style. Kathy Dunlop, the non-Jewish student having an affair with Larry Fine, comes to Rabbi Small's office and asks about conversion. The civility, intensity, and seriousness with which she asks the rabbi to tell her more about Judaism meet his criteria for the ideal liberal arts college student. As he tells Fine later, a liberal arts college is for "those who really want to be there, who want to know more than they do" (235), and in this exchange readers perceive why Rabbi Small is so gentle with Dunlop and why Fine was drawn to her in the first place: she is both an ideal student and an alluringly empty vessel. Rabbi Small, of course, dissuades her from converting, intuiting that her desire to convert to Judaism (as opposed to her desire for more knowledge about Judaism) is really only a reflection of her desire for Fine. But her visit offers Rabbi Small the opportunity to stress that becoming Jewish is not so simple as declaring one's willingness to accept Judaism. The potential convert must understand that being Jewish is "more a matter of belonging to the Jewish people, the family, than of accepting certain specific beliefs. . . . Judaism is a family religion. It's a set of beliefs, practices, rituals, a way of life, that is peculiar to our people, to our family, to the descendents of Abraham" (229). Converting means Dunlop will have to learn her place in that patriarchal family, a formulation that nicely reflects the collaboration between Kemelman's series and a conservative ethos of the liberal arts college (the pursuit of knowledge for its own sake as a foundation for exploring one's place in the world). That formulation also reflects Rabbi Small's American Jewish midrash, that the way to resolve differences is to convert them into a blessing—in this case, to literally convert Kathy Dunlop into a Jew, an ordeal that, much to the rabbi's relief, she rejects.

What I am arguing here is that Kemelman's and Rabbi Small's educational project of setting American Jewish women straight is all about teaching them to take their place in the American Jewish family. Yes, the misogyny in Kemelman's mystery series is related to Rabbi Small's functions as a Talmudic sissy and a Jewish Dupin, but, more than that, it reveals that Kemelman's emphasis on education plays out as the desire to convert American Jewish women, who must be tolerated anyway, into a blessing. To me, this is a reason why the only book in the series that is not a murder mystery, *Conversations with Rabbi Small* (1981), is both a primer on Judaism and an identity mystery about the conversion of an ostensibly non-Jewish woman.

When Joan Abernathy comes to Rabbi Small's vacation cabin in the mountains and asks him to convert her, he is resistant to the idea for the same reason that he was resistant to converting Kathy Dunlop—she is apparently converting only for the sake of her fiancé. When the rabbi discovers that her fiancé, Aaron Freed, a professor at MIT, considers Judaism "outmoded science," and interprets his parents' disapproval of his marriage to a non-Jew as "completely irrational" (43), Rabbi Small realizes that Joan Abernathy is a terrific opportunity—to reclaim Aaron: "It's Aaron I'm interested in. Him I would like to convert" (57). As it turns out, Aaron really is the only one Rabbi Small has to convert to Judaism. Joan is, in fact, the daughter of a Jewish refugee who married a non-Jewish man, and who died before Joan was old enough to know that she was, according to Jewish law, a Jew (proving the crucial importance of tracing Jewish identity through matrilineal descent). Rabbi Small does convert Joan into a blessing, however. Insisting that Aaron attend their conversations, Rabbi Small succeeds in proving to Aaron that Judaism is an eminently rational religion (even justifying the gendered difference in the status of Jewish men and women as a product of "innate preferences" and as a valid example of the principle of "separate but equal"), and so by the end of the novel Aaron is a proud and firmly self-identified Jewish man working in a research institute in Israel, Joan taking her place at his side as a happy Jewish homemaker. If it hadn't been for the blessing of Joan Abernathy, another American Jewish man would have been lost to the Jews.

The next four books in Kemelman's series rehash the lessons he teaches Joan and Aaron, and reenact Rabbi Small's "conversion" of

American Jewish women. They do so, however, in the context of progressively weaker murder puzzles, as if Kemelman were losing interest in them now that his lecture to American Jews has been perfected. When Rabbi Small finally leaves Barnard's Crossing to take a full-time position as professor of Judaic studies at Windemere College, in *That Day the Rabbi Left Town* (1996), the last mystery in the series, Kemelman manages to bring his murder mystery/lecture series full circle: he returns his protagonist to the American academy where he began. Also, in another kind of circle, *That Day* is essentially *Friday* revisited, for in it Kemelman focuses suspicion for the murder on the new rabbi of Barnard's Crossing, Rabbi Dana Selig (note that he has the same initials as Rabbi Small).

Rabbi Selig is clearly both Rabbi Small's successor and his opposite—he's a Reform rabbi, he's concerned with his body and his physical appearance, and he has a wife who refuses to take on the responsibilities of the traditional rebbetzin, that is, refuses to take her place in the American Jewish family. But he is also seen as more similar, and thus more amenable, to the congregants of the temple. For example, Rabbi Selig is able to bring Lew Baumgold, an unaffiliated, irreligious lawyer, closer to temple life because he can relate to Baumgold in ways that Rabbi Small cannot, although it is still Rabbi Small who once again does the essential work of converting Baumgold's non-Jewish wife and thus guaranteeing the lawyer's reattachment to Judaism. Still, Rabbi Small has done his job of surveying and controlling social change among the Jews in Barnard's Crossing, and Kemelman's need to impress American Jewish men that they ought to be Small has given way to what I think is a subtle admission that it is okay at last for them to be Selig, a last name that translates as "happy" or "blessed."

As the introductory series for American Jewish detective stories, and as the precursor text for affirming male American Jewish detectives, the Rabbi Small mysteries provide a warrant for writers of American Jewish detective stories to take possession of the Jew's closet, of popular cultural formulations of American Jewish identity, and to make it safe for both Jews and Americans. Collaborating with the authority of the classical detective formula, Kemelman's strategy for acculturation, an example of kosher hybridity, enables him to defend the faith by showing that the only secret American Jews possess is a religion compatible with both American law and a conservative ethos of the liberal arts college. Rabbi Small, as both a Talmudic sissy and a Jewish Dupin, disciplines Jewish men living through the social upheavals of the sixties and seventies by arming them with Jewish knowledge and modeling for them how to be American Jewish teachers, either of others or of themselves. If readers, even female readers like Selavan, identify with Rabbi Small they empower themselves to determine how to be Jewish in America.

In theory, Kemelman's prescription for achieving a confident Jewish literacy, as opposed to his proscription about what that literacy entails, seems worthy enough—it underlines the secularizing effect of popular fiction on American Jewish self-construction, although it also sanctions a kind of self-satisfaction and quietism for readers who see themselves reflected in Rabbi Small. As Selavan's review points out, however, the gender of that reflection is male, and the students who remain students in Rabbi Small's classroom are Jewish women. While Jewish men both educate their families and work to ensure that family's secure and successful acculturation to America, Jewish women are simply recirculated in a domestic economy where the payoff is in the continuity of their husband's Jewish identity. Such a classroom is more like a prison, and the power of the Talmudic sissy's midrash and of the classical detective formula is that they not only lend Kemelman a rationale for displacing male anxieties about American Jewish acculturation onto Jewish women (a pattern repeated in James Yaffe's mystery fiction, as I will show), but they also, in their worst excrescences, provide a fictional prison house for those women. What the Rabbi Small mysteries ultimately teach is that for Jewish men to control what it means to be American, Jewish, male and middle-class—and thereby to control fidelity to Jewish culture—they must control American Jewish women, who have become so corrupted by the materialism of the suburbs and the feminism of the academy that they might as well be non-Jews. This gendering of control, and its function as a tool for the "conversion" of assimilated Jews, is a key trope in Faye Kellerman's Peter Decker and Rina Lazarus mysteries—and her inversion of it in service of her explanation of "intermarriage" among American Jews is particularly significant, as I show in the following chapter.

2

UNRAVELING "INTERMARRIAGE"

A really good detective never gets married.
—Raymond Chandler, "Twelve Notes on the Mystery Story"

Although marriage was not included among the ten commandments given to Moses at Sinai, the Talmudic rabbis counted God's commandment in Genesis, "be fruitful and multiply," as one of the 613 mitzvoth (religious obligations), and therefore the basis for making marriage incumbent upon Jewish men and women.[1] In early twentieth-century America, however, the pressures and poverty of immigrant life, as well as the lure of secular interests and non-Jewish partners, enlarged the ranks of Jewish unmarrieds and intermarrieds. Significantly, the most influential American Jewish novel of that period, Abraham Cahan's *The Rise of David Levinsky*, recounts the story of one such unmarried immigrant. Although Levinsky's life is in part a cautionary tale, the story of his investigations into marriage, intermarriage, and "making it" in America helped shape an enduring topos of manhood in American Jewish fiction, a conventionalized description of male individualism that Raymond Chandler would commend, but that Faye Kellerman reshapes in her detective fiction, the Peter Decker and Rina Lazarus mysteries. As a result, the kosher hybridity of Kellerman's series exemplifies a gendered revision of Rabbi Small's misogynist teachings.

For Levinsky, secular America is the crucible wherein traditional Jewish gender roles are upended, and marriage, or the prospect of marriage, tends to magnify his ambivalence about his cultural and economic alliances. On his first day in New York, Levinsky meets a more experienced Russian Jewish immigrant in a small synagogue on the Lower East Side, and the fellow explains what a "topsy-turvy country" the New World is for Jews: "He went on to show [Levinsky] how the New World turned things upside down, transforming an immigrant shoemaker into a man of substance, while a former man of leisure was forced to work in a factory here. In like manner, his wife had changed for the worse, for, lo and behold! instead of supporting him while he read Talmud, as she used to do at home, she persisted in sending him out to peddle" (97). As it turns out, Levinsky himself needs little urging to give up Talmud for the more lucrative garment industry. This is because Cahan models his American Jewish male in reaction to, and in contrast with, an East European Jewish world that, in the novel, represents a far more violent and psychically crippling place. Unlike the unfortunate men whose lives are shaped and lived out in such a harrowing and materially deprived environment, Cahan's American Jewish male takes charge of his economic fate rather than letting himself be its plaything.[2]

Yet once Levinsky absorbs the rules and behavior of American individualism and entrepreneurial capitalism, a congenial mate inevitably proves difficult to find. Dora Margolis, whose seduction by Levinsky comprises the longest section of the novel, is traditional and mothering and equally committed to assimilating American cultural values, but she is already married. Adultery and the breakup of Dora's marriage, though exciting to Levinsky as a kind of corporate "takeover," is ethically repugnant to her. Levinsky can neither return to the orthodoxy embodied by Fanny Kaplan, to whom he is briefly engaged out of nostalgia for Antomir, the Russian town that both he and the Kaplans are from, nor can he cross the political divide that separates him from the socialist Miss Tevkin, his last romantic obsession in the novel, who spurns him not only for his politics, but also because he is simply too old for her. The last chapter, "Episodes of a Lonely Life," underscores Levinsky's ambivalence about his new-found freedom in America—the price of that freedom is eternal bachelorhood. Only when he entertains the thought of marrying a gentile widow do readers glimpse a deep-seated reason for his enforced isolation: "I saw clearly that it would be a mistake. It was not the faith of my fathers that was in the way. It was the medieval prejudice against our people which makes so many marriages between Jew and Gentile a failure. It frightened me" (527). Levinsky, an assimilated, wealthy, irreligious male, is frightened by the private prejudices that threaten to undermine his public successes; because he desires to be a really good success, he never marries. Nevertheless, the bachelor Levinsky is a fruitful literary character, the father of Bellow's, Malamud's, and Roth's alienated protagonists (so often single, widowed, or divorced), and uncle to Kemelman's first influential affirming Jewish detective, all of whom model Levinsky's design for an American Jewish manhood—outsiders in the midst of plenty, and, in the eyes of some, misogynists.

In Faye Kellerman's detective fiction, the character of Peter Decker is Levinsky's literary grandson, but in Kellerman's hands he is also a mass cultural representation of the assimilated American Jewish male who now longs for meaningful spiritual and romantic attachments. The noir-tough, Jewish cowboy image of the orphaned and adopted Peter Decker is meant to evoke how alienated from the traditional Jewish world American Jewish males have become. Like Peter Decker, they might as well have been raised by gentiles. Of course, the attraction that the Orthodox Rina Lazarus has for the apparently non-Jewish Decker is revealing, as well. To her, Decker is the idealized pairing of gentile male virility with Jewish *sechel* (wisdom), an intellectual and spiritual gift that Rina helps him to recognize. In this sense, the relationship between Decker and Lazarus is a cultural "intermarriage," a coded reference—and solution—to the bane of American Jewish life during the 1990s. As her last name implies, Lazarus signifies the contemporary perception that Jewish tradition is being resurrected and embodied by American Jewish women, but her character also perpetuates gender divisions that are part of and a response to assimilation (indicated by Kellerman's consistent use of "Rina" for her female character but "Decker" for her male character, a usage I will maintain in this chapter to foreground those gender divisions). Thus, just how Decker and Rina will accommodate each other and make a home together living in an edgy Los Angeles is one of the mysteries that arises out of the kosher hybridity in Kellerman's series. Moreover, once we read her detective stories as reflective of these social and gender conflicts among the American Jewish middle class, it is clear that the real crime endemic to American Jews is biological merger, the supposed final phase of cultural assimilation. Therefore, in spite of the fact that Decker is the detective and solves all the crimes in Kellerman's stories, Rina Lazarus is the spiritual hero of the series—and thus its real hero—because it is she who saves Decker from biological merger by explaining and adamantly defending the mystifying fences that Orthodox Judaism erects around Jewish women and between Jews and gentiles.

PRIVATE EYES AND PUBLIC IDENTITY

The social function of Kellerman's detective fiction is evidenced in its relationship to the subgenres of American Jewish popular fiction and modernist detective fiction. Arnold Band, citing Neal Gabler's *Empire of Their Own: How the Jews Invented Hollywood,* has pointed out that American Jewish popular fiction (mass-market fiction, musical comedies, Hollywood films, television and radio programs, etc.) is a continuation of the identity-shaping project begun by the early film moguls who articulated the dreams and desires of a burgeoning American Jewish middle class.[3] Like the Zukors, the Foxes, the Mayers, and the Warners, writers of American Jewish popular fiction fabricate an America and a picture of Jews that reflects contemporary middle-class life and concerns, and so help create the basis for an American Jewish identity palatable for mass consumption by both Jews and non-Jews. Appropriately, *The Ritual Bath* (1986), the first book in Kellerman's series, opens with advice on how to make a potato kugel, a clever introduction that uses a kind of ethnic shorthand to signify the identity of this contemporary popular fiction: "'The key to a *good* potato kugel is good potatoes,' Sarah Libba shouted over the noise of the blow dryer. 'The key to a *great* potato kugel is the amount of oil'" (1). This reference to a middle-class "kitchen Judaism" enables Kellerman—aware that the lineaments of Orthodoxy are foreign not only to non-Jews, but also to most American Jews—to begin her fiction about a complex American Jewish subculture by referring readers to a familiar American Jewish domestic context.[4] Using the potato kugel as a touchstone of middle-class American Jewish cultural identity, Kellerman is able to imbue her fiction, from the start, with homey "authenticity." More intriguingly, in light of Decker and Lazarus's impending first meeting, Sarah Libba's qualitative distinction between good and great kugels can also be read as a metonym for the story's theme of a qualitative distinction in American Jewish identity between Jewishness (a good kugel) and "authentic" Judaism (a great kugel), the difference between the two being a matter of cultural/culinary proficiency. Although perhaps fanciful, my reading is meant to illuminate one way Kellerman's popular fiction reshapes images associated with a mass-marketed American Jewish identity. Other aspects of this identity are also reflected and revised, as we shall see.

As a detective fiction, the Peter Decker and Rina Lazarus mysteries represent an interesting improvisation on what journalist and essayist Woody Haute calls "pulp culture," an evocative term for the social and capitalist critiques embedded in modernist detective fiction.[5] The pulp culture detective, according to Haute, is a private detective in public places, and Haute interprets the individualist ethos of the private detective, unwillingly drawn into the mysteries of the public world, as a "hard-boiled" proletariat response to modernization—to the bureaucratization of society, the spread of capitalism, the breakdown of older social norms, the rapid process of urbanization, and the centralization of political power. Think of the famous passage in Raymond Chandler's *The Long Goodbye* where Philip Marlowe gazes out his open window and meditates on the nimbus of light hanging over nighttime Los Angeles:

> Twenty-four hours a day somebody is running, somebody else is trying to catch him. Out there in the night of a thousand crimes, people were dying, being maimed, cut by flying glass, crushed against steering wheels, or under heavy tires. People were being beaten, robbed, strangled, raped, and murdered. People were hungry, sick, bored, desperate with loneliness, or remorse or fear, angry, cruel, feverish, shaken by sobs. A city no worse than others, a city rich and vigorous and full of pride, a city lost and beaten and full of emptiness.
>
> It all depends on where you sit and what your own private score is. I didn't have one. I didn't care. (224)

Neither the powerful nor the powerless are spared in this passage. Yet pulp culture private detectives, whose authors felt the chilling effect of American anticommunism, Cold War censorship, and the moral ambiguity of the atomic era, do not advertise their assessments of the public world as a part of the service or information they provide their employers.[6] A passage such as the one above is always an interior monologue, a private judgment and dismissal. Haute argues that the detectives in pulp culture fiction are subjective critics of capitalism and state power, as well as of human foibles: "Consequently, pulp culture writing retained the basic themes of proletariat writing: the corrosive power of money, class antagonism, capitalism's ability to erode the community, turning its citizens into a disparate band of self centered and alienated individuals."[7] These detectives are men, of course, who privatize the investigative process and its solutions, whose only advertisements are for themselves as the worldly-wise isolates of pulp and noir fame.

When Peter Decker is introduced to readers in chapter 2 of *The Ritual Bath,* the tone of Kellerman's prose echoes the rhythms and wording of the pulp detective fictions, and Decker himself expresses the sentiments of a "hard-boiled" detective:

> Decker dragged on his cigarette, looked out the window, and surveyed his turf. Los Angeles conjured up all sorts of images, he

> thought: the tinsel and glitter of the movie industry, the lapping waves and beach bunnies of Malibu, decadent dope parties and extravagant shopping sprees in Beverly Hills. What it didn't conjure up was the terrain through which they were riding.
>
> The area encompassing Foothill Division was the city's neglected child. It lacked the glamour of West L.A., the ethnicity of the east side, the funk of Venice beach, the suburban complacency of the Valley.
>
> What it did have was lots of crime. (11)

But Decker is a cop, a public detective, and in truth Kellerman's detective fiction is more accurately defined as a police procedural. Still, Decker exhibits some classic signifiers of the pulp culture detective in *The Ritual Bath*—he doesn't want to get involved in this new case (40), he feels alienated (65), he's willing to bend the law when it gets in his way (106), and he has no respect for the callously wealthy and powerful (159). What Kellerman's play on the pulp detective stereotype underscores is the American Jewish male's assimilation into the heart of modern America's state structure. Paradoxically, Decker is a version of the pulp detective who is a part of the machinery of power, a somewhat jaded but loyal insider. As the agent and enforcer of state power he really represents the American Jewish male's successful adaptation of middle-class social values and public behavior. Indeed, what makes the pulp culture detective such a wonderful medium for Kellerman's revision of a longstanding topos of manhood in American Jewish fiction is that both are premised on the ambivalence of professionally successful social loners. Kellerman's fiction therefore profits from the dramatic tension generated between the "private" detective and the "public" detective, and between the private Jew and the public Jew, a tension that Decker's character holds in check. This tension is both attractive and problematical; it is a part of the frisson he brings to his relationship with Rina, but it is also a source of Decker's need for the solace of Judaism.

PETER DECKER

Kellerman develops Decker's character in *The Ritual Bath* through actions and revelations that touch on these tension-building oppositions, playing on the audience's assumption that he is a Gentile interested in Rina and Judaism. Privately, Decker is disturbed by the rape at "Jewtown," the name by which outsiders and the police refer to Yeshivat Ohavei Torah (literally, the "seminary of the lovers of Torah," an undergraduate and postgraduate institution). It is a community of lawabiding citizens, and he "wished he had a city full of 'em" (8). Like

Marlowe, however, he knows that Los Angeles is a city of a thousand crimes, and that the yeshiva cannot remain immune to L.A.'s baleful influence. Decker notes in an interior monologue that, as with other neighborhoods in Foothill Division, the yeshiva is populated by "[p]eople scratching by, people not getting by at all. . . . These people weren't the wealthy Jews portrayed by the media. It was possible that the yeshiva held a secret cache of diamonds, but you'd never know it by looking at its inhabitants. They dressed cheaply, buying most of their clothes at Target or Zody's, and drove broken-down cars like the rest of the locals" (12). The private Decker knows and respects these locals. Yet, urban figure though he is, he owns a horse ranch just a few miles from this neighborhood, in a suburban area that is the border between city and country.

Publicly, Decker plays the tough cop, interested only in upholding the state's laws, suspicious of everyone, even the yeshiva's residents (14). The Orthodox treat this tall, red-headed Gentile warily, and his looks impress Rina as those of a seasoned hunter: "He was a big man, she thought, with strong features and, despite the fair skin and ginger hair, dark penetrating eyes. He looked intimidating yet competent, a man who'd know how to hunt an animal like a rapist. Although she knew size had nothing to do with apprehending a criminal, she was still glad he was big" (17). Unlike the other Orthodox women, however, Rina has looked into Decker's eyes (ultra-Orthodox men and women do not shake hands or look directly into the eyes of the opposite sex, unless they are husband and wife); Rina here signifies her difference from the rest of the community, both by her action and her ability to intuit Decker's "dark," private interior through the windows of his soul.

Rina's initial attraction is reciprocated by Decker, who bends the rules governing the performance of his public duties, to maintain private contact with her. Since Sarah Libba will not submit a statement to the gentile authorities (on grounds of religious modesty), Decker's case is stalled. Rina volunteers to bring Sarah Libba to the stationhouse, but she arrives alone, and, technically, there is no reason for Decker to join Rina for a picnic in the park. Lamely, he offers the excuse that talking with Rina there is preferable to talking with her in a hot interrogation room. While Decker continues to present himself as the concerned public servant, he also impresses Rina with his knowledge of Jewish kitchen culture, the first overt betrayal of his private cultural proficiency. Biting into, yes, a potato kugel, Decker shares a significant moment with Rina:

"You know what it tastes like?" Decker said. "It tastes like a latke. A big, thick latke."

That took her by surprise.

"That's exactly what it is."

"Not too bad for a goy, huh?"

She laughed. "You've picked up an expression or two, Detective."

"Or three or four. My ex-wife was Jewish. But not like you," he qualified. "She and her parents were very Americanized. But her paternal grandparents stayed . . . ethnic. It was her grandmother who used to make me latkes." (53–54)

Decker's comments reveal a private understanding of Jewishness as a kind of ethnicity whose identity is vouched for by certain foods, but whose "authenticity" has been "Americanized," and therefore made different from Rina's much more exacting, and exact, Judaism. This is indeed an impressive observation for a goy, and it, as well as Decker's admissions that he was once married to a Jewish woman (before his devotion to his job led her to divorce him) and that he was a lawyer before he was a cop, signal to Rina that beneath Decker's public persona is a "private" detective capable of reading the subtle clues that describe "authentic" Jewish cultural and religious difference. After this scene, readers know that Decker's romantic desire to see Rina again is bound up with his curiosity about the Orthodox Judaism of the yeshiva, a curiosity for information that goes beyond what is necessary for his case.

Kellerman thus reshapes the figure of a pulp culture detective—and, by extension, the figure of the unattached American Jewish male, for which the detective is an analogy—by giving Decker an education. Decker, the worldly-wise, individualist detective, becomes Decker the student of a Judaism that Rina will reveal (to him and to readers) as multiple and diverse, a revelation that diffuses Decker's single goal-object, solving the case. This transformation of roles is foreshadowed by Rabbi Schulman's remark early in the novel: "You're a wise boy, Detective. You don't mind me calling you boy, do you? I call all my *bochrim*—my pupils—boys. At my age everyone around me looks like a boy" (27). Later, Decker's willingness to learn—to reconsider his preconceptions and his own psychological motives (insofar as readers are made privy to them)—is the key to his transformative relationship with Rina. When Decker meets Rina's parents, he learns the difference between the black-hatted and dark-suited Jews at the yeshiva and modern Orthodox Jews such as Mr. and Mrs. Elias. The Eliases, Hungarian Jews who live in Beverly Hills, are affluent and European, their clothing and manners influenced more by their class than by their religion. Rina also teaches Decker the differences between Misnagdim (the Lithuanian Jewish culture of the yeshiva) and Hasidim, explaining that, among Misnagdim, Yeshivat Ohavei Torah is itself different, being liberal and less restrictive than other Misnagid yeshivas. This prompts Decker to exclaim, "Rina, I wish you wouldn't lump me and billions of other people into one gigantic category. I'm more than just a gentile."

Of course, at this point readers assume that Decker is referring to his private, "pulp" sensibilities, and contrasting them with his outward appearance as a representative of the law. Only later do readers understand that Decker is alluding to his biological identity. Still, it is clear that Decker's willingness to become a student is an attempt to begin interrogating his discrimination between his private life and his public life.

Additionally, "hiding" Decker's private identity enables Kellerman to oppose the image of Decker the Gentile with images of Orthodox Jewish males, thus reflecting and reshaping stereotypes of the Jewish body as well. Decker's size and hair coloring are signs that Kellerman manipulates to fool readers into reading him as a Gentile, and how she clothes his body adds to the deception. When Decker shows up at Rina's house to take her sons to a Dodger game, Kellerman purposely images Decker in casual attire as a way of suggesting that he is more than just a detective but not at all the picture of a Jewish male:

> Rina was taken aback by Peter's appearance. Her image of him until now had been that of a "professional detective" in a shirt, slacks, and tie. This afternoon he wore a white T-shirt, sloppy cut-off shorts, and sneakers, and a baseball cap perched atop his thick patch of orange-red hair. He looked so all-American, so working class. So goyish. . . . Immediately, Rina wondered if she hadn't erred in her judgment. (126)

Decker's immodesty, sloppiness, and "working-class" body validate the middle-class Jewish stereotype of the American goy, and suggest the degree to which Decker is culturally assimilated. Conversely, the Jewishness of Rabbi Schulman, the head of the yeshiva, is imaged through his evidently Jewish body:

> The rabbi was a tall man, not as tall as Decker, but at least six one. Decker put him in his early seventies. Much of his face was covered with a long salt-and-pepper beard, and what wasn't hidden by hair was a road-map of creases. His eyes were dark brown, clear and alert, the brows white and furry. For a man his age he was straight-backed, slender, and a fastidious dresser. His black pants were

razor-pressed, his white shirt starched stiff, and the black Prince Albert coat carefully tailored. Crowning his head was a black felt homburg. (25)

To Decker, whose range of associations are limited by Kellerman to the gentile world, Rabbi Schulman's appearance is "[r]egal, like an archbishop." To many readers, however, his appearance is still that of the typically bearded and wrinkled Jew, whose fastidiousness may recall nineteenth- and early twentieth-century cartoons that pictured such bearded and furry-browed men attired in the clothes of the upper-class so as to satire their ambitions of becoming socially acceptable.[8] Kellerman's point, appropriate to detective fiction, is that these images are indeed manipulable and thus deceiving. In a nice twist, Decker is told by one of his fellow detectives that "Jews, in general, look like Jews," and that despite Rina's "button" nose and Decker's "Jewish" nose, "I can tell that [Rina] is Jewish and you're not" (219). (In another kind of twist, it turns out that Rabbi Schulman really is a sophisticate, a collector of Jewish ritual art and an expert in American jurisprudence.)

Other characters elaborate on Kellerman's point. Shlomo Stein, a student at the yeshiva and a suspect, is imaged as a typical student wearing a white shirt and black velvet yarmulke, but his "Van Dyke" beard gives him away. He is, in fact, a former cocaine dealer who has returned to his Orthodox roots. When, afterward, another suspect at the yeshiva tells Decker, "Detective, Jews don't murder, Jews don't rape. Your people murder and rape, not mine" (187), readers are prepared to accept Decker's moral for Kellerman's point: "If God was so sure that righteous Jewish men and women wouldn't murder, why did He bother with the sixth commandment?" (187). Appearances deceive, but the Jewish God, like all good detectives, is not taken in.

Once readers begin to appreciate that Jewishness is not necessarily signified by public appearances, Orthodoxy's emphasis on private intellectual and spiritual development provides Kellerman a lens that brings Decker's Jewish potential into focus. Granted, Decker has an enlightened, egalitarian relationship with his female partner, Marge Dunn; he takes excellent care of his horses and his dog; he makes his own rough-hewn furniture; and, as Rina asks, exasperated by her own attraction to him, "why did he have to be *so* good with the children?" (137). But this evidence is not as significant in revealing Decker's true potential to readers as are events that demand ratiocination and serious moral judgment. As an adolescent, Decker impulsively defends a Jewish boy against a group of bullies. When he explains his altruism to his Baptist adoptive parents they respond with platitudes about protecting oneself and turning the other cheek. "Who are we to judge the infidels," says Decker's mother. But Decker has already judged the ambivalence of his parents' responses and his schoolmates' avoidance of him after the fight. Thinking it through, Decker "had learned for a brief period what it was like to be a pariah" (65). In another example, in chapter 15, after Rabbi Schulman has warned Rina to stop seeing Decker, the detective twice surprises Rabbi Schulman with his ability to apply "Jewish" reasoning to morally troubling situations. Here is Decker trying to convince Rina not to divulge his list of suspects at the yeshiva to Rabbi Schulman:

> "Rina, you once told me that saving a life takes precedence over everything in Judaism," said Decker. "By talking, you'd be endangering your life."
> The old man's lips turned upward in the hint of a smile.
> "It's a strange world when a gentile enlists halacha for the purpose of persuasion. I give you credit, detective." (151)

Later, trying to convince Rabbi Schulman that he must take in the mentally disturbed yeshiva student found wandering near the murder scene, Decker quotes scripture:

> "Rabbi, this is the twentieth century. If the cup was found on Benjamin, Benjamin is going to be tried for theft. And try as he may, Judah can't do a damn thing about it."
> The old man looked perturbed.
> "Rina has been teaching you Torah?"
> "I learned that in Bible school. That's the Christian equivalent to your place."
> "*Lehavdil.*" The rabbi cranked open the window. (154)

In scenes such as these, Decker reveals his *sechel,* his proto-Jewish "brains." But this word implies more than just intelligence or a reified Jewish essence; it refers to an intellectual/spiritual component in humans that refines and purifies their physical dimension, but that is available only through Torah, only by connection to the wisdom of Jewish teaching and tradition.[9] Kellerman does not mean to suggest that, despite outward appearances, all Jews have an essential, unassimilable nature—an old anti-Semitic stereotype of the Jewish body.[10] Indeed, Kellerman makes a point of having Rina—articulating one theme of the series—tell Decker, "It takes a lot more to be a Torah Jew than just an accident of birth" (200). Only when attracted to the study of Torah (even if, in Kellerman's formulation of this Jewish concept, such attraction is galvanized by a beautiful Jewish woman) can a human being come into possession of the unique spiritual gift of *sechel*. Decker's background and Baptist Bible schooling indicate that even Gentiles have access to this gift. When Decker finally reveals to Rabbi Schulman his biological identity, the rabbi asserts that'"[s]omething pulled you to us" (231), implying not only fate but also that some force was at work bringing the physical to the spiritual—though Decker believes the force is his lust for Rina.

Nevertheless, by the time Decker tackles the rapist/murderer (who turns out not to be Jewish) at the end of *The Ritual Bath*, Rabbi Schulman and many readers are certain that Decker's physicality has been refined by his spiritual education, setting him on the road to religious piety and a better integrated American Jewish identity. Emphasizing this idea of connection (physical and spiritual, private and public, the individual's embrace of community, Decker's literal embrace of Rina), Kellerman has Rabbi Schulman invite a reluctant Decker to join the dance that the men of the yeshiva have broken into in celebration of the capture of the rapist/murderer. Rather than face a news-hungry media alone, Decker elects to be a dancer in the dance: "Okay, Rabbi. Show me what to do" (277).

Most importantly, Kellerman's reshaping of the figure of the unattached American Jewish male gives this figure, as Adrienne Rich would describe it, a "womanly series of choices" (27) that lead him back into a Jewish community."[11] It would have been simple for Kellerman to refashion Decker's gentile male virility into the figure of a "Rambowitz," as Paul Breines calls the "tough" Jew pulp fiction heroes of the seventies and eighties.[12] Indeed, Decker shares a number of traits with that figure; his imposing physique and the fact that he is an exemplary fighter and (inadvertent) agent of revenge in *The Ritual Bath* reflect a "muscular and martial masculinity."[13] In Kellerman's hands, however, Decker never abuses his power to achieve premeditated or political revenge. Decker chooses to use his power, as a man and as an agent of the law, to transform his life and to protect his family. In fact, his desire to serve and protect his family is so obsessive throughout the series that, in *Grievous Sin* and in *Justice,* Cindy Decker, his daughter from his first marriage, eventually rebels against his overprotectiveness. In that light, Decker's power recalls Adrienne Rich's redefinition of power as "not power of domination, but just access to sources"—that is, the power to reclaim and to live out a spiritual and ethical tradition such as Judaism, and to protect those who wish to do the same.[14] Choosing solidarity, education, and faith, Decker's character exemplifies a feminist sensibility of nurturing the world of human beings rather than exploiting dominion over it. The oppositions that Decker's character is able to come to terms with because of these choices—worldly-wise pulp detective *and* "boy" pupil, successful professional *and* religiously committed suitor—are part of Kellerman's fabrication of an American Jewish identity that reflects middle-class readers' desire for a tough "family values" hero who is wise to the mysteries of America (an America that is itself a fabrication of pulp culture detective fiction), but that reshapes this identity by defining toughness as the willingness to embrace an exacting Jewish faith.

RINA LAZARUS

In contrast, the character of Rina Lazarus is more conventional and less developed than Decker, even as late as *Sanctuary* (1994), the seventh installment of Kellerman's series. In *The Ritual Bath,* Rina is introduced, tellingly, as the Bible teacher for the children at the yeshiva. When Decker first sees her, his pulp-flavored observation captures her "traditional" looks: "There was something classic about her face—the oval shape, creamy skin, full, soft mouth, startling blue eyes. Doll her up and she'd blend nicely into high society" (19). With her black hair, Rina's beauty suggests stereotypes of the Jewess's body, but Kellerman, to her credit, undermines that stereotype by periodically focusing reader's attentions on her unexpected and "startling" qualities. Rina is willing to talk to Decker alone at the scene of the crime, an initiative that is considered immodest by the other women at the yeshiva (21), and ultimately she rebukes them for their narrow-minded and judgmental attitudes (273). Although she is in an almost continual state of fear throughout the novel, Rina is still capable of physical force (100) and, because she does not want to be dependent and helpless, still takes chances that place her life in danger (261).

Hence, it is all the more disconcerting that Rina spends the majority of her stage time in the rest of the series cooking, crying, tending to her children, and teaching Judaism to Decker, but we must remember that Kellerman fashions Rina as a standard-bearer of middle-class "norms." Raised modern Orthodox, Rina had her commitment to Orthodoxy deepened by her first marriage and her move into the yeshiva after her first husband's death, but these changes did not make her a fanatic. When she recounts her religious odyssey to Decker, her description of her upbringing iterates both modern Orthodoxy's virtues in maintaining

Jewish identity and its position as the cultural middle ground of Jewish religious practice:

> "We were modern Orthodox. Which is to say I grew up with a strong Jewish identity. My mother was far less strict with the rules than my father. That led to a lot of fights. So in keeping with Freudian psychology, my oldest brother—the *doctor*—married a girl much less religious than he, and I married a boy much more religious than I. We all marry our parents, don't we?" . . . "On the other hand," she continued, "my middle brother—I'm the youngest—was a lost soul. My parents didn't know what to do with him, so he was shipped off to Israel. The Chasidim got to him, and now he's at a Satmar yeshiva, the most religious of the three of us." (117–118)

Kellerman has created in Rina, with her knowledge of Freudian psychology and her frank admission of the personal reasons and rebellions that make one more or less religious, a character who helps to place modern Orthodoxy, considered by many assimilated middle-class Jews a part of the religious right, into a middle position long associated with Conservative Judaism. Given this reading, Rina's brothers seem to represent the movement toward secular or religious extremes. Rina's "norming" of modern Orthodoxy thus clarifies how extreme Decker's own assimilation is, and, more fundamentally, how attractive extremes are to Decker's personality. Rina says as much when she evaluates Decker's potential in *The Ritual Bath:*

> "You know, Decker, you would have made a great yeshiva *bocher*."
>
> He broke up.
>
> "No, I'm serious. You have all the external trappings. You're intelligent, curious, hardworking. You ask the right questions. You're even a lawyer. A yeshiva is like a Jewish law school with ethics and morals thrown in. Anyone who's ever studied both will tell you that Jewish law is much harder and more challenging than American law."
>
> "I missed my calling, huh?"
>
> "You laugh, but I can tell, Peter. If you'd been born Jewish and raised in an Orthodox environment, you would have been a fanatic." (121)

Rina thus represents a middle-class American Jewish culture of religious moderation comparing and contrasting itself with Decker's Southern Baptist, American law-schooled, pulp culture "extremist," thereby revealing the cultural differences between her and Decker.

Throughout the series, Kellerman assiduously develops Rina's "middle" position and her casting of modern Orthodoxy as the normative American Jewish religious identity. Although she used to keep her hair clipped short and hidden under a wig when married to her first husband, Rina allows her hair to grow out, and only covers it with a kerchief when she marries Decker. Rina continues to wear dresses that conform to a rigorous interpretation of feminine modesty, dresses that cover her from neck to ankle, but allows her children to go camping and to Dodger games with Decker, as long as they bring along their own kosher food. Most provocatively, in *Milk and Honey* (1990) Rina sleeps with Decker before they are married. The mitigating circumstances, however, are threefold: Decker is already trying out daily ritual observance; Rina has consented to marry Decker; and both are suffering from severe sexual deprivation. Kellerman here accedes to a pop cultural convention regarding romantic relationships: love—the fact that Decker is clearly Rina's *bashert* (divinely destined partner)—rationalizes their act.

More significantly, in *Sanctuary* Rina's middle-ground modern Orthodoxy is portrayed as coeval with moderate American political values, in scenes where Kellerman contrasts it with the religious Zionism of the Israeli settler movement. Her spiritual appreciation of, and personal attachment to, the sacredness of the *Ma'arat HaMachpelah*, the Cave of the Pairs (Adam and Eve, Abraham and Sarah, Isaac and Rebecca, Jacob and Leah), is made clear when she visits Hebron and prays in the shrine: "Something ethereal came over her, a sense of personal history. As if she were looking through her parents' scrapbook.... These people weren't fairy-tale characters or mythological creatures, they were real people. And like all real people, they had lived, they had died" (310). But as a representative of the middle, Rina is also pragmatic:

> Though Rina knew that Hebron was still a *Jewish Holy City*, would always be a *Jewish Holy City*, it was time to be realistic. Hebron was no longer *Jewish* and hadn't been for fifty years. It was a typical overcrowded Arab village that bred rage and hatred against Jews. It had become such a hotbed of politics, Rina wasn't sure who was securing its borders—the IDF, the Israeli Police, the Palestinian Police, or UN troops. (283)

Kellerman has Rina articulate a very American response to the Israeli-Palestinian conflict (and to Dr. Baruch Goldstein's February 1994 massacre of twenty-nine Palestinians as they worshipped in the mosque above the *Machpelah*), a response that echoes middle-class ideals of moderation and tolerance that readers of Kellerman's series are positioned to accept, and that many would expect to be validated. Later, Kellerman has an Israeli soldier echo Rina's moderate position, as if to paint the average Israeli as a blue-and-white version of middle-class red-white-and-blue sentiments: "Many pray here—Arab and Jew. I don't think you're a crazy fanatic.... Here there has been too much bloodshed caused by small minds. I talk to the settlers, try to tell them that bloodshed and revenge is *their* way, *their* customs, *their* laws. It is not *our* way" (311). Clearly, Rina's embodiment of a normative American Jewish religious identity is based upon a middle-class disavowal of extremism of any kind, cultural or political.

Rina is also an embodiment of spiritual renewal, but in the role of spiritual hero her character reveals its limitations even as it mirrors the contemporary perception that American Jewish women have become agents for Jewish renewal in America. Kellerman addresses this perception in *The Ritual Bath* by first clarifying Rina's attitude toward sex and sexuality. In the beginning of the novel, Decker treats Rina as if she must be sexually naive or prudish, assuming that Orthodox Jews are as puritan about sex as are religious Protestants. Rina first explains to Decker that she abstains from premarital sex and observes the customs of bodily modesty not on moral grounds "but because we believe that the body is private and not some cheesy piece of artwork that's put on public display" (93). Then, in a key passage in *The Ritual Bath,* Rina explains the significance of the mikvah (ritual bath) to Decker:

> "You know what a mikvah really symbolizes, Peter?" She became animated. "Spiritual cleansing. A renewal of the soul. For twelve days, starting from the first day of a woman's menses, she and her husband are forbidden to have sex. When the twelve days are up, if she hasn't bled for the last seven days, she immerses herself in the mikvah, and then they can resume marital relations, renew their physical bond. That means for at least twelve days every month a husband and wife are off-limits to each other. I bet that seems nuts to you, doesn't it?"
> He smiled. "In a word, yes."
> "And yet it seems so *normal* to me." (93)

Rina's explanation of the mikvah suggests that it is the woman's unique responsibility to maintain spiritual housekeeping to renew the soul, and that such renewal is dependant on observing and respecting limits. Rina's explanation—since it completely avoids mentioning when and how men make use of the mikvah—implies that such renewal is domestic woman's work, and it perfectly articulates "the bourgeois gender division that placed religion and the inculcation of religious sensibilities within the female domain."[15] One can't help but be disappointed by Kellerman's missed opportunity (here and elsewhere) to allow Rina a fluid, feminist reading of American Jewish womanhood appropriate to that image of the mikvah. Still, Rina's animation and personal engagement in a religious observance the proscriptions of which she respects offers readers the possibility of a more generous reading. Rina's vital relation—through her body and her sexuality—with her faith, and her use of that vitality in an attempt to teach Decker something important about Judaism and about spiritual healing, evokes, briefly and incompletely, Miryam Glazer's notion of "spiritual romanticism," a feminist spirituality that she observes in the works of a number of contemporary American Jewish women writers.[16]

Unfortunately, Kellerman is not interested in Rina's overturning middle-class American Jewish gender divisions or reclaiming the mystical power of Jewish female spirituality in a way that truly transforms her character. And as a *Los Angeles Times* review of a later book in her series, *Prayers for the Dead* (1996), indicates, many of her readers are more interested in Kellerman's Orthodox explanations of Judaism:

> As always, Kellerman is most fascinating when she's explaining the nuances of Judaism. (I've learned more from her books than I did in 12 years of Sunday school.) For example, "Wiping the dish, Rina thought about the Jewish concept of *shalom bais*, the keeping of marital peace. So important a tenet, a person was allowed to do everything in his or her power to keep home and hearth tranquil, even if it meant slight variations on the truth." Whether this concept justifies Rina jeopardizing her husband's investigation is arguable, but the book is first-rate.[17]

Rina, whose name in Hebrew means "joy," is a character whose primary role is to bring joy and peace to Decker and to teach him the "norms" of Judaism (as Kellerman shapes them for a middlebrow audience) so that *he* may be transformed into a public representative of Judaism. Thus, Rina is referred to by other characters as either Decker's girlfriend or his wife, but Decker's colleagues dub him "Rabbi," a nickname he retains throughout the series. Kellerman underscores the gender division between the two characters by writing "Rina" when designating the female character but using the patronymic "Decker" when designating the male. Additionally, Kellerman uses the symbol of the mikvah in *The Ritual Bath* only to identify Rina as a woman and her place as a woman in the Jewish community. When Rina meets

Decker, Kellerman no longer needs that overt symbol of femininity because Rina has a man; Rina is never seen in a mikvah again in the rest of the series. In short, Rina, as Kellerman has constructed her, is the sort of female popular fiction character whose function is to empower her man, and in that sense Rina needs Decker as much as Decker needs her.

TYING THE KNOT

Rina's relationship with Decker, then, leads inevitably to a kind of "intermarriage," and not only in the sense Kellerman toys with in *The Ritual Bath*. True, Rina and Decker appear to be a coded reference to the overwhelming intermarriage rate among American Jews. Rina and Decker's attraction to each other registers the potential for romantic attractions between Jew and Gentile even among the most Jewishly identified American Jews. Yet the surprise of Decker's biological identity is not simply a "cheap trick," as some students of mine have insisted. If the cultural chasm between assimilated Jew and observant Jew is as wide as that between these two fictional characters, then by analogy any marriage between two such disparate Jews is a kind of cultural "intermarriage." Therefore, the solution to such an "intermarriage," in *The Ritual Bath*, is the "conversion" of the "non-Jewish" partner. Decker's willingness to embrace Jewish practice—to choose solidarity, education, and faith—is that conversion experience. Kellerman, by making Decker's choices and his struggle to understand Judaism and become an observant Jew the central character transformation of her mystery series, thus provides mass cultural evidence that supports Julius Lester's trenchant observation about contemporary American Jewish life. "The convert's experience is becoming a paradigm for being Jewish," says Lester, an African American convert to Judaism, "regardless of natal origin."[18]

Kellerman's mystery series is thus the continuing story of Decker's conversion from unattached individualist to Jewishly identified family man through the loving tutelage of his fiancée, and then wife, Rina. It is a narrative that consequently "intermarries" the individualist pulp culture detective to a middle-class, "family values," American Jewish religious identity. Further, the crime Decker investigates in each mystery is really a pretext for Kellerman to appropriate pulp culture's capitalist critique of America and transform it into a moral critique of secular American society. By doing so, she exposes that society's vapidity as well as the real crime that Rina, the spiritual hero, prevents in this series—biological merger with such a society and the loss of a distinctive identity that provides a moral compass with which to plot one's path through life.

For example, in *Sacred and Profane* (1987), the second book in the series, Decker must learn to balance the separations that Judaism makes between love and lust as well as between Judaism and the secular, public world. These separations are made tangible to Decker when he celebrates the Sabbath and appreciates the haven it provides from the horrors of his case, a double murder of two young girls caught up in a pornography ring. It is the Havdalah blessing marking the end of the Sabbath that provides the title of the book: "Blessed art Thou, Oh Lord, who has made a distinction between sacred and profane" (122). But that spiritual haven does not insulate Decker from his revulsion for the pornographers who steal young girls' lives and the powerful people who keep them in business, or from his confusion about how to resolve his lust for Rina with his love for her. Decker has abstained from sex with Rina because both have not yet resolved their fears and doubts about marrying, but Decker, used to the sexual mores of his assimilated lifestyle, does not yet know how to deal with his carnal desires in a Jewishly appropriate way. So how will Decker balance love and lust as well as his new Jewish life and his public life? According to Rabbi Schulman, Decker must find the answer in faith—not faith in Rina but faith in God. Trying to find relief for his soul through Rina is what is confusing Decker. In that sense, the sexual perversion of the case Decker investigates is a critique of the way sexual desire is perverted in contemporary American society into a substitute for true personal comfort, and the way a woman's body is perverted by pornography into a goal-object. Although Decker considers giving up the religious life he has embarked on (and suggests to Rina that they settle for a "mixed" marriage), Rina helps him understand that balancing his private and public lives, his love and his lusts, means renouncing the professional detective's instinct for "a neat little solution" (239), for a goal-object. Being a really good Jew is not the same as being a really good detective. When Rina and Decker decide to temporarily separate at the end of the novel, Kellerman brings home to readers the message that separation, in Judaism and in this relationship, is not an end, but simply part of an ongoing balancing act that describes the long, spiritual process of creating enduring attachments.

By the time Decker and Rina tie the knot off stage and reemerge in New York on honeymoon in *Day of Atonement* (1991), Decker has learned that spiritual success requires a different standard of measurement than professional success, and that only through faith in God will he be able to balance his pursuit of both. Accepting the separation between himself and his biological mother, Frieda Levine, as well as learning the true meaning of repentance, preoccupies Decker even as he comes to the rescue of his biological family in *Day of Atonement.* He learns that he cannot force Frieda to come to terms with her abandonment of him, and that the only "solution" to what is long past solving is to grant her forgiveness when she asks for it on the eve of Yom Kippur (354). Concurrently, Kellerman continues to portray secular America as corrupted and corrupting. Hersh Schaltz, the megalomaniac serial killer and kidnapper in *Day of Atonement,* is the product of a dysfunctional Orthodox family who finds the secular world murderously liberating, and who does not "steal" Noam Levine, Decker's half-nephew, so much as "trap" him, luring him away from his warm Jewish home in Boro Park by playing on the boy's curiosity about the secular world. In *Milk and Honey,* even Gentiles are affected by this corruption. As Pappy Darcy says about his all-American family farm, "Once it was the Promised Land for me, God's land of milk and honey. Not no more, misters. Not no more" (365). Creating a family in the face of these private and public revelations is difficult at best, as *Milk and Honey* and *False Prophet* (1992), with their respective tales of family skeletons and New Age pagan seductresses, attest.

Therefore, when Rina finally gives birth to Hannah in *Grievous Sin* (1993), the accomplishment seems heroic, spiritually and physically; after all her defenses and explanations of the ritual and spiritual separations that Orthodox Judaism requires, she has, through the birth of their child, guaranteed the continuity of family and identity that redeems the meaning of Decker's life. Rina's heroism does not come easily. Her daughter's birth is a difficult one, and after the delivery she loses her uterus. Giving way momentarily to religious doubt, she calls on Rabbi Schulman to tell her what to do, echoing Decker's action at the end of *The Ritual Bath.* Rabbi Schulman lectures her on what prayer can and cannot accomplish, and on the important understanding that control over human destiny is out of our hands:

> In reality, how much control do we have over our lives? Life is a loan from *Hashem* [The Name]. We are put here by His design; so shall we leave by His design. . . . There are times when *Hashem* is willing

to deviate from His original plans, times when He has forgiven the most grievous of sins. Our prayers are not empty words, Rina Miriam. Though the world may seem very dark now, *Hashem* has an open ear for you. You may ask. You may not get, but you may *ask*. (73)

The point of prayer is that it articulates human hope, weighting the words of prayer with the fullness of human desire, but without guarantee of their fulfillment. Rina, the spiritual hero, is the real hero in Kellerman's series because she brings home to Decker, through the birth of their daughter, evidence of hope's fulfillment, even as she accepts that she has no control over her life. Decker has embraced Judaism, but his detective's instincts still lead him to believe that he can achieve some sort of control over his and his family's Jewish future. As he chases down the nurse/kidnapper of a baby born in the same hospital and at the same time as his own, readers see that the desire for control is what has corrupted the nurse: Tandy Roberts is a control freak who is addicted to body-building as a way of achieving control over herself, but she fails to gain control over her mental illness or the sense of betrayal that fuels her actions. Decker himself must learn to give up his belief that he can control and protect his daughter Cindy, who places herself in danger despite his order that she keep out of his case (265). Hence, Decker may be a success as a detective, solving all of the crimes in the series, but he remains dependant on Rina's heroic example to maintain his hope and trust in the ultimate efficacy of his private conversion, despite his lack of control over past and future.

Kellerman underscores this point in *Grievous Sin* by juxtaposing Decker's desire to be a "successful" Jew to atone for his biological parents' mistakes with the corrupted desires of Tandy Roberts, who thinks of herself as a martyr of the cultural revolution of the 1960s. Like the other "addicts" of that grievous decade—addicted to sex, drugs, Jesus, and now body-building—Roberts justifies her rebellion against middle-class norms as an attempt to rectify and atone for her parents' perceived sins, but this rationalization exacerbates rather than solves her personal problems. In contrast, Rina's example and Decker's experience reveal the wisdom of a Judaism that asks individuals to atone only for their own sins, because, as Decker muses at the end of the novel, "some things are just out of your control" (390). Once Decker appreciates that he is responsible only for his own struggle to avoid biological merger, the grievous sin of American Jews, he discovers that time and God are what heal all his other wounds. Real American Jewish men, in Kellerman's reworking of American Jewish manhood (and in marked contrast to David Levinsky), are consciously aware that, though secular culture promises us the possibility of control over our lives, it fails to deliver. Such men recognize that Judaism makes no promises; it asks only that we trust in God, in ourselves, and—as Decker is surprised to learn when his adoptive, Baptist parents take up Rina's invitation to visit him and his new baby in spite of their initial disapproval of his marriage and conversion—in our families. Thereafter, the books in Kellerman's series read as if, in the words of the Jewish sage Hillel, everything else is commentary.

As an example of kosher hybridity in American Jewish detective stories, the Peter Decker and Rina Lazarus mysteries reflect the current reappraisal by American Jews of the gendered project of cultural assimilation, embraced so wholeheartedly by the immigrant generation and given voice in American Jewish detective stories by Kemelman's Rabbi Small mysteries. Kellerman, along with multicultural writers of both literary and popular fiction, shares in the contemporary project of recuperating and reshaping images and traditions from the past as models for a meaningful hybrid American ethnic identity. Kellerman's audience, however, is not about to embark on a wholesale transformation of their lifestyles, and in that respect Decker and Rina embody a recommitment to the ethical values of those traditions as long as they are compatible with middle-class expectations. Kellerman's series thus reflects the mix of curiosity and unease that many middle-class American Jews have about hybridity and an increasingly multicultural America (I will return to this ambivalence and anxiety in chapter 7). Decker enacts that curiosity and articulates how hard it is to accept that so much about one's life and the life of one's country is beyond one's control. In Kellerman's series, the desire for control is both deflected and indulged. It is deflected in the sense that Decker learns there are limitations to his ability to control the crimes, legal and biological, that threaten him and his family; it is indulged because Decker also learns that for Jewish men to control what it means to be American, Jewish, male and middle-class they must control themselves. Hence, Kellerman's series both reiterates and modifies the inadvertent learning of Kemelman's series, and illustrates how writers like Kellerman revise, though do not necessarily subvert, gender roles in the American Jewish detective story. Kellerman's series may not puncture readers' faith in the future of American Jewish intermarriage, the beneficence of Jewish masculinity, or the comprehensibility of a Jewish place in multicultural America, but it does intrigue them with an American Jewish detective's interrogations of manhood and society in America, and comfort them with Decker's defense of the faith—his validation of Jewish marriage as the solution to the unsettling mysteries of family and hybridity.

3

THE JEWISH WOMAN AS AMATEUR

> Despite the difficulties of my story, despite discomforts, doubts, despairs, despite impulses to be done with it, I unceasingly affirm love, within myself, as a value. Though I listen to all the arguments which the most divergent systems employ to demystify, to limit, to erase, in short to depreciate love, I persist: "I know, I know, but all the same . . . "
> —Roland Barthes, *A Lover's Discourse*

Thus far I have explored the gendering of the male American Jewish detective, and the ways in which the desire for control—over identity, over the Jewish community, and over the crimes that threaten the protagonists and their families—affects the disciplining of gender in American Jewish detective stories. If Rabbi David Small is the patriarch of these stories, and Peter Decker and Rina Lazarus the very model of a modern intermarriage between the hard-boiled masculine detective and his feminine Jewish helpmeet and educator, who speaks for the American Jewish woman detective?

One of the most visible developments in contemporary American Jewish detective stories is the proliferation of female detectives, and so there are a number of writers we might consider here: Carolyn Haddad, Renee B. Horowitz, Susan Isaacs, Sharon Kahn, Kathryn Lasky Knight, Jean Korelitz, Rochelle Krich, Marissa Piesman, Ellen Rawlings, Janice Steinberg, Serita Stevens, and Ayelet Waldman.[1] While it is true that Judaism and Jewishness are merely set-decorations or character flavorings in some of these writers' stories, the detective formulas employed suggest, to me, an interesting line of exploration. In the list of writers I cite, only one, Rochelle Krich, employs the hard-boiled formula, in which the protagonist is a professional detective (by "professional" I mean either a police detective or a private investigator). The rest employ the classical detective formula or the cozy (a mystery version of the comedy of manners), or a variation of the two, and all feature protagonists who are amateur detectives; that is, they are not specifically crime investigators who are paid as such. In contrast, of the male writers included in Lawrence Raphael's bibliography of acculturated and affirming American Jewish detective stories, almost half employ professional detectives as protagonists.[2] Consider, too, that the first American Jewish writer to feature an amateur American Jewish woman detective was a man, James Yaffe, and his protagonist in "Mom Knows Best" (1952) was also, technically, the first American Jewish detective to star in her own mystery series, albeit a short-story mystery series. There is, then, a curious association reflected in the majority of acculturated and affirming detective stories written by American Jewish women: the Jewish woman as amateur.

In this chapter, I will examine that association in James Yaffe's short-story mystery series and in Marissa Piesman's Nina Fischman Mysteries (I will return to Rochelle Krich's work in chapter 5).[3] These series, both of which incorporate aspects of the popular romance and feature single Jewish women who live in New York, manifest the relationship between Jewish women and amateur status as a local trope in American Jewish detective stories. As the date of Yaffe's story evidences, this trope is an outgrowth of postwar, popular cultural images of Jewish women that mirrored anxieties about gender, class, and ethnicity. As such, its presence in American Jewish detective stories deserves scrutiny so that we may consider how Yaffe's and Piesman's detective fiction outline a struggle for control over the image of the amateur American Jewish woman detective who is single and independent.

What I mean by the Jewish woman as amateur is simple: to be an amateur is to be an outsider. The association of the amateur with the outsider is well remarked in detective fiction, in both the classical and hard-boiled detective formula. The works I am interested in, however, model detective outsiders who affirm the value of love relationships in the face of dangers that threaten or challenge those relationships (a convention of the popular romance),[4] and in opposition to the values of the male professional working in a competitive and acquisitive society. In that light, the word "amateur" is suggestive of a particular outsider status. An amateur—from the Latin *amator,* lover—is an agent of love, if you will, and while I don't wish to sentimentalize here or to be understood as positing that all amateur detectives derive their agency from affective relations, I do wish to suggest that Yaffe's Mom and Piesman's Nina Fischman are outsiders as both detectives and Jewish women because they affirm the value of love relationships. As Roland Barthes argued, a lover's discourse is "ignored, disparaged, or derided" by the disciplines and languages that structure and legitimize our knowledge of the world and its workings,[5] and one proof of Barthes's point is surely popular fiction: when in popular fiction that lover's discourse is gendered female (most notably in the popular romance), it is often construed as evidence of that fiction's low worth.[6] Thus the Jewish woman as amateur is as good an example as any of what Barthes calls "the extreme solitude of the lover," which I interpret here as the female amateur's alienation from the intellectual, social, or cultural authorities that provide a warrant for knowledge and for communication. In this sense, the outsider status of the Jewish woman as amateur is that of a protagonist whose agency as a detective is derived from her affirmation of the value of love relationships.

The outsider status of the Jewish woman as amateur is also the outsider status of a protagonist whose identity as a Jewish woman is derived from midcentury popular cultural depictions of American Jewish women. As Sylvia Barack Fishman points out, these depictions, formulated by Jewish men, "described controlling mothers and young women whose parents were grooming them to fit into upper-middle-class norms as they saw them."[7] According to Joyce Antler, the relationship between real Jewish women and these images was, and continues to be, complex, for in "imagining Jewish women in a variety of roles, even those that stereotyped them and constructed false mythologies, American Jews helped establish their own cultural autonomy and became 'true' Americans. In this way images of Jewish women served as reference points for projections of the fears and dreams of American Jews over the course of the twentieth century."[8] Creating a dialogue with these images is Antler's definition of talking back, and in that sense Yaffe and Piesman represent an evocative side conversation in American Jewish literature and culture among amateur American Jewish women detectives who live in New York City. I will argue here that in Yaffe's formulation of the Jewish woman as amateur, Mom's outsider status as both a detective and a Jewish woman reflects and resolves anxieties about midcentury American Jewish acculturation to modern, middle-class New York City society. In Piesman's refiguring of that trope, Nina Fischman's outsider status as a detective and Jewish woman in late eighties and early nineties New York City reflects and resolves anxieties about Jewish women's very representation as a symbol "of the darker side of the Jewish ascension to the American mainstream."[9]

My larger agenda in this chapter, however, is to show how stereotypes of Jewish women inform the Jewish identity of American Jewish women detectives. For in stories where Judaism and Jewishness are merely set-decorations or character flavorings, these stereotypes are what make the stories and the detectives recognizably Jewish. I do not mean to imply that the amateur American Jewish woman detective, as figured by Piesman, fails to reflect the social gains, the successes, that Jewish women have achieved in America. I agree with Naomi Sokoloff that detective fiction by Jewish women generally reflects Jewish women's self-imagination of their own possibilities and potentials—an escape from gender stereotypes, the exploration of new occupations and opportunities for Jewish women following American second-wave feminism, and the improvisation of a distinctly American Jewish feminism.[10] I also do not mean to imply that Yaffe's intent in formulating and promulgating his model of the amateur American Jewish woman detective was nefarious, or that his protagonist is entirely without merit as a representation of the Jewish woman.[11]

What I am positing is that the struggle for control over the image of the amateur American Jewish woman detective is really a cautionary tale about gender and kosher hybridity, about the complexity of imperfect, popular acculturation to American culture. In this case, the imperfect acculturation evident in the trope of the Jewish woman as amateur is rooted in, and is a local example of, American Jewish women's ambivalence and struggle during the last half of the twentieth-century over their images in popular culture as mother, daughter, and wife. One way of taking control over such images is to subvert them entirely, reworking them in ways that completely contradict established generic and cultural conventions. But how subversive can writers of mass-marketed detective stories be? To borrow an observation about feminist subversions of the detective genre from cultural studies scholar Anne Cranny-Francis, the radical avant-garde subversion of the Jewish woman as amateur would similarly result in "a loss of readership so severe as to call into question the whole concept of the feminist appropriation of popular fiction."[12] My intent in focusing on two representative examples of the interplay between stereotype and identity is to show the constraints, a product of the hybrid nature of Yaffe's and Piesman's protagonists, that discipline the subversiveness of both their figurings of the Jewish woman. The struggle for control over the image of the amateur American Jewish woman detective who is single and independent, as acted out by Yaffe's and Piesman's acculturated detectives, evidences not only a masculine interpretation of the amateur Jewish woman detective and how one detective talks back to it; it also reveals, through Piesman's detective, that the trope of the Jewish woman as amateur cannot be subverted without, at the same time, risking the loss of the detective's Jewish identity.

HIS MOM'S VOICE

James Yaffe's "Mom" is a feisty widow and a brilliant detective who can cook and make complicated deductions at the same time, and out of these humorous combinations Yaffe shaped a unique hybrid image of the Jewish woman. Although in 1990 Yaffe resurrected Mom, moved her to Colorado, and made her the protagonist of a mystery series, it is the series of short stories that appeared between 1952 and 1968 in *Ellery Queen's Mystery Magazine,* and was collected in *My Mother the Detective* (1997), that I wish to consider here, because these stories introduced readers to a new kind of protagonist, a detective who is recognizably Jewish because she seems like such a sterotypical Jewish mother. In "Mom Knows Best" (1952), the first few pages characterize her relationship to her son Dave, the narrator: when he was a child she pushed him to become a professional, "something that needs a little intelligence and brainpower" (19), and she is disappointed that he becomes a professional cop; every Friday night she cooks dinner for him and his wife Shirley at her apartment in the Bronx; she is convinced that Shirley, a Wellesley graduate with a degree in psychology and sociology, is "incapable of understanding the practical affairs of life" (20); and she is concerned that Dave be informed about the gossip in the old neighborhood and that he dress warmly in damp weather. Her malapropisms ("Platonic blonde" instead of platinum blonde, "psychoannihilating" instead of psychoanalyzing), her Yiddish vocabulary ("goniff," "meshugenne," "schlemiels") and her Yiddish syntax round out her comical image: "This third degree, it's harder on the policemen than it is on the crooks. If you men would only stop a minute and use your heads, look at all the *tsouris* you'd save. Believe me, there isn't a single one of you that don't need a mother to look after you" (21). By the end of the story, Mom's brilliant solution to Dave's murder case enables her to manipulate him into eating his string beans.

If Mom had been played only for comic effect we could easily read her as a simple version of the postwar stereotype of the Jewish mother. Her bossiness and overprotectiveness, her distrust of Shirley's modern knowledge, and her apparent incompetence with the English language all verify Riv-Ellen Prell's analysis of the stereotype; the Jewish mother is too nurturing, too demanding, too insatiable, too Jewish.[13] According to Prell, the stereotype consists of "comic images of nurturance gone awry" that picture the Jewish mother as "out of place" in postwar America, and as the personification of a family-style Jewishness whose "excesses of difference" are one of the few remaining markers of ethnic difference for American Jews fast acculturating into the suburbs and middle-class life.[14]

Yet Mom is no suburban matron and no simple version of this stereotype. She lives alone in the Bronx, and her fifty-two years of contact with the people, the sights, and the experiences of urban New York have provided her with instructive illustrations of human character. Her Jewishness thus consists not only of the rhetorical props necessary to the stereotype of the Jewish mother, but also of what Dave calls an "ordinary common sense, and her natural talent for seeing into people's motives and never letting herself be fooled by anybody" (20), a sense and talent that are, in fact, Yaffe's shorthand for portraying Mom as the child of Jewish immigrants to the rough-and-tumble world of New York City. Mom is a "New York Jew" in that "her long experience with shifty-eyed butchers and delicatessen store clerks" (20) reflects a lifetime of practical experience with the urban types (to whom she often gives a Yiddish descriptor) who threaten to take advantage of her straitened economic and social circumstances. Indeed, the solution to the mystery puzzle in "Mom Makes a Bet" (1953) depends on Mom's ability to discern a *shlimazel* from a *shmendrick* (43). She recognizes that the delicatessen waiter who served the potassium cyanide–laced noodle soup to the overbearing Broadway producer was simply an unlucky little man (44). His small revenge of serving the producer salted soup instead of unsalted soup inadvertently focused attention away from the real criminal, the producer himself. The producer's guilt becomes readily apparent once Mom points out what an aggravating person he was, and that an overbearing New York producer with a string of flops to his credit is much more likely to hatch a plan for murder, especially one that flops and kills himself instead of his intended victim. Hence, Mom's most egregious Jewish "excess" is not materialism or class ambition, but that she "understands human psychology—a little too well for comfort" (33). Yet this, of course, is what makes her such a good detective, and why Dave's career has been such a success (20, 33).

The hybrid image, then, that Mom embodies is that she is both a version of the Jewish mother stereotype and an amateur armchair detective in the classical detective formula mold, one whose extraordinary powers of observation and analysis put the "professionals" (police, sociologists, psychologists, etc.) to shame. She is the Jewish Miss Marple.[15]

More specifically, Mom is a character both laughable and laudable, and the appeal of her character is that she enables Yaffe to make stereotypes about women a central part of the mystery puzzles in his stories while at the same time entertaining readers with a recognizable Jewish female "type." For example, the mystery in "Mom Knows Best" revolves around the question of who killed the promiscuous platinum blonde living in a seedy "high-class low-class hotel" (21). Dave believes it must be one of the three men who were with her the night of her murder. Mom intuits that Dave, and the other male police detectives, are limited by their belief that murder, and its detection, is a male activity, and she enjoys skewering Dave's masculinist assumptions (and hard-boiled clichés) about police work: "'So now you've got those three men in your police station, is that it?' she said. 'And you're beating them with rubber hoses?'" (25). Of course, Dave protests that the police use modern methods, but it's such masculinist assumptions that blind Dave from seeing that the murderer is Sadie Delaney, the elevator girl. Here, however, Mom's "knowledge" of how women really think returns readers to familiar gendered territory. That is, Mom's ability to read the murder from a gendered perspective is really a product of her superior understanding of gender conventions, so that, once Dave's masculinist assumptions have played their role in misdirecting readers about the murderer, Mom is able to lecture him on the finer points of those conventions. Sadie Delaney, who "fools" Dave because she is not a femme fatale and therefore not the usual female murder suspect as figured in the tidal wave of bad hard-boiled stories written by Yaffe's contemporaries, is the obvious suspect to Mom because the murdered woman wasn't wearing lipstick, meaning that she didn't care how she looked in front of her murderer, meaning that the murderer couldn't have been a man (31). In addition, since Sadie is "a good-natured unmarried Irish girl," and one of the men interested in the murdered woman is a "good-looking unmarried Irish boy," Irish hot-headedness provides an overlooked motive (32), as overlooked as the gender conventions that are on display in this story.

By focusing on character, on Mom's insights into it, and on the fictional possibilities of gender masquerade, Yaffe is able to fashion Mom into a voice critical of her son's and daughter-in-law's acculturation of "modern ideas" about human character. As in "Mom Knows Best," Dave's detecting inevitably goes wrong when he accepts the professional wisdom about how a woman thinks, or, as in "Mom Sheds a Tear" (1954), how a child thinks. But the person Mom really wants to "smother" is not Dave but his wife Shirley (24), whose sociological and psychological insights, gleaned from college textbooks, are repeatedly denigrated by Mom. In a number of stories, the immediate and sometimes nasty conflict is between Mom and Shirley. The bet in "Mom Makes a Bet" is that if Mom solves Dave's case, Dave will have to forbear his Sunday outing to the Metropolitan Museum of Art (Sunday being the day that Shirley "exposes" Dave to culture), and instead put up new wallpaper in Mom's bedroom (41). Naturally, Mom wins the bet, and Shirley's dearth of real knowledge about people is proven by her misunderstanding of her own husband, for Mom knows that Dave doesn't really enjoy his cultural uplift. As he says, the "Metropolitan Museum of Art always ruins my feet, anyway" (46). It's in "Mom Makes a Bet" that Mom castigates Shirley's citation of a sociological study with the amateur's most effective argument: "My knowledge of people don't come strictly out of books. It's the difference between somebody that actually plays in the gin rummy game, and somebody that only sits around and *kibitzes*" (36). In this light, book learning is a passive and self-referential activity, and Mom the amateur distances herself from it through the analogy to a game, quite appropriate in a detective story, where true knowledge is accrued only by those who are players. All that Shirley's Wellesley education adds up to is the annoying propensity to correct Mom's English (38); Shirley, in other words, is an unknowledgeable pedant. Although Shirley's Jewishness is never mentioned, her class ambitions, her pushiness, and her pedantic nature make her the recognizable locus of a negative Jewish femininity. It is, of course, completely coincidental that her name is the one that Noel Airman, in Herman Wouk's *Marjorie Morningstar,* makes symbolic for the Jewish American Princess, but it is evocative, nevertheless, because it suggests that the upwardly mobile, pseudo-intellectual, and pseudo-professional Shirley is a fictional product of her time, a version of the modern young Jewish woman as imaged in popular culture.[16]

Thus, one aspect of Mom's amateur status as a detective is that she defends, even celebrates, her domestic roles as mother and homemaker because as a mother and homemaker her view of the modern, middle-class society in which she lives is clearly more astute than Shirley's view of it through the distorting prism of a modern college education. Such an amateur status enables Yaffe to portray Mom's perspective on that society as authoritative and independent, and even, in a sense, liberated, for she is liberated from slavish adherence to the questionable cultural modes and social norms that Shirley exemplifies and that Dave finds beguiling. Indeed, in "Mom Sheds a Tear," Shirley is sent offstage to visit her parents in Chicago, thereby allowing Mom the freedom not only to press Dave about having children, but also to impress her views upon him without interference. When Dave claims that he needs to save money first, to buy a home in the suburbs, Mom will have none of it: "Young people nowadays, sometimes I think they got checkbooks where their feelings should be" (67). The modern damping down of feelings into economic exchanges and psychological jargon is precisely the theme of the story, a mystery about a five-year-old boy suspected of murdering his uncle. Dave and the rest of the homicide squad do not want to believe such a thing, but they're trapped by their dependence on post-Freudian psychology and terms like "childhood psychosis" and "father fixation," which seem to explain an unusual case. Mom, however, is entirely free of Freud and of bothersome theories about the unconscious. "It's only what you personally think *ought* to go on inside the head of a little boy" (77), Mom says of these theories. Her "real" experiences raising her son provide her with the solution: that the uncle, who wished to marry the boy's mother to get his hands on her money and her house, had in fact been preying on the little boy's feelings—of wanting to be like his father, an Air Force pilot killed in Korea, and so of wanting to fly using only a cape and his father's old uniform. The uncle's plot to kill the boy goes awry, but not Mom's plot to convince Dave that, first, "things have got a simple, obvious explanation—if you only take a little trouble and look at them" (79); second, that all children are sweet and innocent no matter what the psychiatrists say; and third, that therefore Dave and Shirley ought to procreate. In contrast to Shirley, Mom as amateur detective valorizes feelings over intellect, the passion of the *amator* over the bloodlessness of the professional, a valorization given weight by her domestic experiences. Naturally, she is an excellent reader of "old-fashioned" character-driven human dramas, and so it is hardly surprising when we discover, in "Mom Sings an Aria" (1966), that she is passionate about opera. Mom as amateur detective thus reflects a simple typecasting of mothering women as more in touch with their feelings and emotions and therefore free of the obfuscations of social and psychological theorizing.

The ironies of an amateur status in which Mom's domesticity enables her independence are also brought home in two stories where the puzzles revolve around gender and being single, "Mom in the Spring" (1954) and "Mom Makes a Wish" (1955). In "Mom in the Spring" Dave and Shirley try to set her up with Dave's colleague, Inspector Millner, "the oldest and most eligible bachelor on the Homicide Squad" (47). They mislead Millner into believing that "Mom was a poor lonely widow who was sick of cooking for herself and dying to show off her pot-roast to a nice appreciative gentleman," and they mislead Mom into believing that "Millner was a poor lonely bachelor who was sick of restaurant food, and dying to taste one of her home-cooked dinners" (47). To Dave's and Shirley's relief, Mom and Millner hit it off. He comprehends her reasoning and relates to her way of comparing the suspects in a case to characters she's met in the immigrant Jewish community of New York (61), and she appreciates a shy Jewish man with "sad eyes" who, after thirty-two years on the police force, still can't get used to the awful things humans do to each other (47–48). Mom, however, is not lonely and not in any rush to remarry and relinquish her independence, a point she makes obliquely to Dave and Shirley through her analysis of the murder case that Dave and Inspector Millner are working on. The case involves the murder of a wealthy old spinster, whom Mom pegs as a "nice, weak minded woman" because her loneliness has led her to the personals column of the newspaper. Her vulnerability is the key to solving the case: the spinster's nephew and his wife, her only family, murder her out of fear that she will marry the man with whom she's been corresponding, thereby depriving them of her fortune. Her vulnerability is also an object lesson that Mom illuminates for Dave and Shirley; when Shirley remarks how dangerous it is to be a lonely old lady, she's thinking about Mom, but Mom's point is that the real danger to single women like the spinster and herself is that other people will try to arrange things for them and thereby place them in even greater danger. For it turns out that the spinster invented her male correspondent, and was, in fact, writing love letters to herself. "A little bit of love that was strictly her own," Mom says. "This is all she wanted in the world" (65). To Mom, a single woman's vulnerability to those who would manage her life, and thereby make her dependent on them, invites tragedy. Mom's independence is guaranteed precisely because she is a single Jewish mother and homemaker who won't put her life into the hands of "professionals," those who think they know better how to make her happy.

In contrast, the murder case in "Mom Makes a Wish" features a male professor who goes to seed without a wife (86). The professor, whom everyone thinks is a drunk, is accused of murdering the university dean who fired him for ignoring his work and his university responsibilities. As Mom celebrates her birthday with Dave and Shirley, who have once again brought along Inspector Millner, Mom reveals not only that the dean's murder is unrelated to the old animosity between him and the professor, but also that the professor's alcoholism is an act he has developed to maintain his daughter's sympathy and her company so that he will not be all alone in his self-pity. The professor is a weak man who needs his daughter's care to mitigate the loss of "his job, his manliness, . . . his grip on life" (95). In contrast to this professional, Mom the amateur has no such weakness, and again, her firm grip on life is underscored by her amateur's perspective on the modern, middle-class society in which she lives. The opposition between this case and the one in "Mom in the Spring" forces readers to see Mom the amateur detective as an unconventional, passionate woman whose ability to read human character reveals the ways in which certain gendered assumptions about character that are associated with acculturation to modern, middle-class society inevitably skew Dave's—and, by extension, the audience's—reading of mysteries set in that society.

This illuminates an interesting aspect of Yaffe's gender masquerade, for alongside its celebration of domesticity, its employment of gender conventions, and its displacement of a negative Jewish femininity onto Shirley, it also critiques how women absorb and reflect the negative attributes of midcentury Jewish acculturation.[17] Mom complicates the Jewish mother stereotype in ways that force readers to consider that critique and the tensions implicit in aspiring to professional knowledges and mores. In other words, the contradictions that derive from Mom's embodiment of both the Jewish mother stereotype and of an amateur armchair detective in the classical detective formula mold give voice to witting and unwitting anxieties about gender and acculturation. Yaffe's gender masquerade articulates a way to control those anxieties by providing an image of a Jewish detective able to make them evident (because she reveals the gendered assumptions that derive from acculturation) and understandable (because she provides a model for how to address them). This is the image of the Jewish woman as amateur that is put into play in American Jewish detective stories, and it is not so much Yaffe's invention as it is an expression in genre fiction of midcentury images of the Jewish woman. Although he appropriates the image of the Jewish mother in ways undoubtedly problematic, his appropriation is hardly nefarious. Overall, Yaffe's stories are well written, well plotted, and well observed, and I believe we should take him at his word when he says in the introduction to *My Mother the Detective* that, although Mom's traits indeed embody a version of the Jewish mother stereotype, she is also a reflection of a particular time and place: "These traits may be stereotypical, but they are also real; they can be found all the time in women of a certain generation and social group. My conviction is that we are all stereotypical in some ways, and it would be unrealistic for an author to leave that out in struggling to create a character. The point is to show the mingling within people of stereotypical and individual traits, to show the tug of war that goes on between what we are at heart and what the world tells us we should be—with neither side ever completely winning out" (14).

In that light, the "reality" of Mom's traits is that they evidence such midcentury mingling. For Yaffe, the realism of his detective stories is that Mom mirrors the generational and social contradictions of her time, which is another way of understanding the oxymoronic nature of kosher hybridity as a textual strategy and as a strategy of acculturation. Yaffe's figuring of the Jewish woman as amateur is a result of this mingling: the Jewish woman's "excess" is her intuitive understanding of, and gossip-driven fascination with, people and their psychology, which she deploys against the professional knowledges that Dave and Shirley articulate; the Jewish woman's sense of being out of place in postwar America is expressed through Mom's disdain for professionalized book learning as a mode of education about the modern, middle-class society in which she lives; the Jewish woman's personification of a family-style Jewishness valorizes feeling over intellect, and passion for the dramas of a recognizably Jewish family life over professional knowledges about family life; and the Jewish woman's nurturing impulse is evident in her defense of her domestic roles and single status as resources that enable her not only to maintain her independence from the dogma of professional knowledges and mores, but also to nurture her family's, and her own, love life. Mom illustrates that the Jewish woman as amateur opposes love relationships, motherly and familial, to male professionalism, intellectual and economic, an opposition that is apropos to a mystery series that includes many stories incorporating courtship dramas drawn from popular romance.

This opposition is well illustrated in the last Mom short story, "Mom Remembers" (1968), which takes place on Mom's wedding anniversary. In the story, Mom recounts a murder mystery on the Lower East Side that imperiled her fiancé and that Mom's mother solved on the eve of Mom's wedding. At the same time, Dave relates a murder mystery that he's currently investigating, one that involves a young Puerto Rican who represents the new immigrant New Yorkers living on the Lower East Side. In Mom's tale, readers learn that Mom's mother is the original amateur Jewish woman detective, a woman whose intelligence was "wasted on Delancey Street" where she toiled to raise her children in a slum tenement, although Mom is quick to add that "if life wasn't hard for Mama, maybe she never would have developed her wonderful mind in the first place. She had to be smart and think faster and see more than other people—because how else, with no rich relatives, do you keep four daughters from starving and turning into old maids? When it's a matter of life and death to read the butcher's mind, believe me you learn how to be a mindreader!" (137). Love for her daughters (and the desire to nurture them into their domestic roles as wives and mothers) is what motivates her to outwit those who are economically and socially better off. The crimes that Mom's mother solves are petty domestic crimes, but they are also crimes that threaten the marital bonds and familial love of immigrant families. In one case, a wife sells her husband's Hebrew books and the money is stolen; it turns out that the husband stole the money to buy them back. In another, a young girl faints in school from hunger, even though every day her mother gives her a dime for food; it turns out that a group of eleven-year-olds are running a protection racket and stealing many of the children's lunch money. A family's economic well-being is threatened, in the first case, by the misapplied ethos of the professional scholar, and in the second case by the misapplied ethos of the professional gangster. Indeed, the perversity of the husband's crime against his wife is underlined by Mom's observation that he loved his Hebrew books "more than anything on earth, including his wife" (136).

Readers also see love opposed to professionalism in Mom's observations about the Jewish family life of Mom's husband-to-be. Mendel is the son of a strict Orthodox rabbi who is a professional in the sense that he is a pulpit rabbi and a scholar, but also in the sense that he represents a Jewish professional whose Jewishness is his vocation, as opposed to Mom and her mother, who are Jewish amateurs whose Jewishness is a product of the attributes I have described. Mom says of Mendel's father that "nobody was as strict as he was for keeping the old ways, obeying the old laws" (147), but rather than promote observance his inflexibility leads women to resist his authority. Thus, if a woman accidentally mixed a meat dish with a milk dish she would "say a little apology to God and serve the food to her family" and simply not mention the mistake to the rabbi. Secularization is here the amateur's, the lover's, resistance to the professional: "All right, was this such a big sin? Did she do it to save herself trouble? No, she did it to keep her loved ones from going hungry. So wouldn't God forgive one little accident when it's a question of a hard-working husband and growing children who need their nourishment?" (147). Mom loved Mendel because he was his father's opposite, which is to say that he was a Jewish amateur, too, who was no scholar or business professional, but rather a tailor who loved his family more than his occupation. This is why

Mom's mother is able to clear him of the murder of Sadie Katz, a "Jezebel" who is the mistress of the clothing manufacturer for whom Mendel worked. Mendel is initially under suspicion because the police think that, after getting drunk at his bachelor party and then coming home and arguing with his father, he took Sadie up on her proposition that he visit her before his wedding. But during questioning he breaks down and inexplicably declares his guilt to the police and to his father: "'I'm guilty,' he said. 'I broke the law. I deserve to be punished.' And he went up to his papa and got down on his knees. 'Forgive me, Papa, I'm a sinner and a transgressor, just like you called me.'" As it turns out, Mendel's "crime" is the same as that of the Jewish women who resisted Mendel's father's authority: after his argument with his father, Mendel had gone out to a non-Jewish restaurant and eaten pork as an act of rebellion. But, as Mom knows, his love for his family and his passionate Jewish conscience are such that he'd rather be jailed for murder than admit his sin to his father, hoping, as the Jewish women hoped, that God would forgive "one little accident."

In a nice reversal, women behaving like men also helps clarify the opposition between love and professionalism in the story's contemporary murder mystery. Dave thinks he has caught the young Puerto Rican who murdered a cab driver, because he saw the teenager running from the scene of the crime. But the murderer, as Mom reveals, is really the boy's older sister, who has been borrowing his leather jacket and cap to commit a series of robberies around the Lower East Side. Her gender masquerade is in service of her budding career as a criminal, but it's also an expression of her hatred for her authoritarian father, a hatred that the sister stokes in her brother's heart. The brother is described by Inspector Millner as a good boy whose family's difficult economic situation is a product of the tough immigrant life Mom recognizes from her own childhood. The father's harsh attitude and his children's alienation from the family are expressions of how difficult it is for immigrant families to maintain themselves against the economic and cultural difficulties they face. When the brother rebels against the limitations these difficulties place on his career ambitions, his rebellion consists of enrolling in a television repair school and refusing to tell his father about it. Every night he goes to his sister's apartment and changes into a suit, the gendered costume of the aspiring professional, and so, like his sister, his masquerade is in service of a budding career that is also an expression of hatred for his father. Mom's comparison of her murder mystery with Dave's contemporary murder mystery reflects a similar New York immigrant story about the opposition between love and professionalism, but Mom observes one key difference between the two versions: "I was only thinking—the younger generation today, the younger generation in the old days, maybe there is a difference after all. Poor Mendel—he was ready to die so he shouldn't make his father ashamed of him. And this Ortiz boy—he was ready to die so he shouldn't make his father *proud* of him" (173). Behaving like Mom, Mendel is an amateur with the amateur's love for his beloved and for his family, but the Ortiz boy, behaving like his sister, which is to say behaving like a male professional, has wittingly and unwittingly helped to destroy his family.

All these masquerades in "Mom Remembers" exemplify how love relationships are opposed to professionalism, and they both reinforce *and* destabilize various stereotypes about women, men, Jews, Puerto Ricans, New York immigrants, and detectives. It is, of course, outsiders such as women, Jews, and immigrants who embody the lesson this opposition teaches: what Dave and readers learn from Mom is not that one should not become a professional—which is to say, an insider in New York's modern, middle-class society—but rather that one's professionalism must be married to the outsider's insight by the amateur Jew's and the amateur detective's understanding of love and human behavior. Such a combination guarantees social and economic security for the Jewish family. This lesson suggests that Mom's midcentury model for the Jewish woman as amateur is predicated not only on contradictions in the popular cultural image of Jewish women, contradictions that derive from anxieties about acculturation, but also on the image of a Jewish woman whose agency as a detective is derived from her affirmation of the importance of affective relations. According to JoAnn Pavletich, a scholar of early twentieth-century American literature and culture, that image is related to the history of affect as a cultural discourse in twentieth-century America.[18] Using Anzia Yezierska's stories as her proof-texts, Pavletich argues that the figure of the emotionally intense Jewish female immigrant reveals how the "process of seeking and defining 'America' through affective relations imbues [Yezierska's] protagonist with a moral and social authority at the same time that it limits the force of that authority by offering up affective relations as solutions for material problems."[19] In other words, Mom's power is that she enables a Jewish critique of acculturation to a modern, middle-class New York society, but outside of Yezierska's and Yaffe's fictional worlds, love is still no solution for how to pay one's bills—for achieving economic security. Mom is thus an admirable, but also ignorable, critic of acculturation. Like Yezierska's female protagonists, whose subversiveness, as Pavletich argues, is contained because their affective relations are simply a means to achieve the economic and cultural security of the American middle-class to which they aspire,[20] the subversiveness of Yaffe's female protagonist, and her authority, is similarly contained and limited. By affirming love relationships, Mom confirms her own irrelevance. Is it surprising, then, that Mom has been so thoroughly eclipsed by Kemelman's Rabbi David Small?

NINA FISCHMAN

Marissa Piesman did not write her Nina Fischman mysteries with Yaffe's Mom in mind. Newspaper and magazine features about Piesman's balancing act between her writing and her legal practice, and their accounts of her unorthodox writing process (writing 400 words each morning as she commuted by subway to her office downtown) suggest that the person she had in mind when she wrote about Nina Fischman, unorthodox lawyer and amateur detective, was herself.[21] But reading Nina in dialogue with Mom, reading her as another version of the Jewish woman as amateur, reveals one way in which American Jewish women writers of the eighties and nineties talked back to midcentury images of the American Jewish woman. In such a light, Nina Fischman's anxiety about her love life reflects an anxiety about her amateur status—her outsider status as a detective and as an emotionally intense urban Jewish woman.

In *Unorthodox Practices* (1989), Nina's mother, Ida, provides an evocative symbol for New Yorkers like her and her daughter, one that nicely captures the sense of urban angst animating both characters: cockroaches. Ida has spent a lifetime trying to outwit and control roaches, but nevertheless her "attitude toward roaches was a complex one" (49). To Ida, ruminating on her life in New York and on the vulnerable-looking, pastel-clad, automobile-driving newcomers to the city who are changing its look and feel, the tough, shifty-eyed, gray-clad walkers of the city like herself and Nina resemble the tough little cockroaches—they're survivors (50–51). Ida, however, is also ambivalent about the city that is home to both her and the roaches, a conflict reflected in her complex attitudes toward the middle-class women who have left New York City for the suburbs, women whose lives have been shaped by "[d]ependence, timidity, deference" (52), and for whom she feels a "mixture of pity, contempt, and jealousy" (51). Thus it is both funny and appropriate that the murderer in this mystery is using roach poison to kill off single, older New York women whose Manhattan apartments are suddenly valuable properties in a revved-up real estate market: Who is trying to get rid of the native cockroaches/New Yorkers?

The cockroach as familiar inevitably evokes Kafka, and while Ida's rumination may simply be a humorous way for Piesman to characterize Ida's and Nina's anxieties about their self-images, it is hard not to read Ida and Nina as a parodic pair of female Gregor Samsas suffering through a period of confusing metamorphosis. This is, after all, a mystery series where Nina searches New York for a suitable mate to love in order to transform herself into something recognizably "normal" (she is not named Fischman for nothing), only to discover that normal isn't who she is or what she wants to be. In this sense, my reading of Piesman's comic take on New York cockroaches is meant to highlight her struggle for control over her identity and, by extension, over the image of the amateur American Jewish woman detective. Piesman's protagonist is Kafkaesque in that she presents for our entertainment the ambiguities of being an urban Jewish female and an amateur detective, and the absurd choices incited by the comic and emotional intensity of such a composite identity. As Murray Baumgarten points out in *City Scriptures,* Kafka's identity was linked to the intensity of city life, of Prague, wherein languages and cultures collided and where the choice of a language, and the fact of an inhabitant's opportunity to choose, informed identity.[22] Choice, allegiance, ambiguity, and hybridity, in fact, are part of the dynamics informing what Baumgarten calls the myth of the city in modern Jewish literature, "an urban vision of human freedom."[23] The Nina Fischman mysteries provide a popular fictional gloss on the two sets of possibilities constellated in that myth. "If the city is freedom, dignity, activity, and possibility," says Baumgarten, "it is also limiting, and personal experience will surely add potentially imprisoning and degrading to the list of its characteristics."[24] Nina's search for a suitable mate to love enables her to explore these two sets of urban possibilities, and enables, as well, Piesman's urban Jewish parody of the detective genre, making it into an American Jewish romantic comedy about the modern city.[25]

Searching for love, the overweight, loquacious, and emotionally and professionally discontented Nina also tries to find her own definition for what it means to be a normal Jewish woman in New York, which is to say—in light of the myth Baumgarten calls to our attention—what it means to be a free, dignified, and active urban Jewish woman. Like Yaffe, Piesman signals her protagonist's Jewish identity through her association with the intensity of New York City, and, as in Yaffe's detective stories, Piesman's incorporation of courtship dramas drawn from popular romance, and her protagonist's focus on the vagaries of affective relations, help to spring a humorous critique of middle-class society in New York. Nina's search, therefore, entails not only the usual amorous hunting and chasing, but also the reviewing and lampooning of identities and social roles that already define "normal" for Jewish women, a process that in the first novel of the series surfaces the opposition between love relationships and male professionalism.

In *Unorthodox Practices,* the novel that introduces readers to Nina, to her family, and to the social dynamics of late eighties New York City, Nina's mother Ida and her younger sister Laura are two important examples of the putatively normal social roles available for Jewish women. Laura is a model of the young urban professional wife. She has no profession herself, but as a yuppie she exemplifies what it means to be a "professional" at that time and place. The origins of her character clearly lie in *The Yuppie Handbook* (1984), which Piesman co-wrote with Marilee Hartley and that satirized eighties urban culture and its focus on material display and social conformity. Although Laura is not a Jewish American Princess (she doesn't exhibit a sense of entitlement, a disdain for sex, and vulgar taste in clothes and men), her wholehearted embrace of the upper middle-class yuppie lifestyle and, more mildly, but to Nina more surprisingly, of Jewish religious practice, reflects her desire to assimilate professional knowledges about everything from food styling to adult Jewish education. Surveying the Victorian design scheme in her sister's Park Slope, Brooklyn, brownstone, and considering that with Laura's blonde hair and not overlarge nose she could easily pass for gentile (30), Nina wonders in *Unorthodox Practices* whether Laura's lighting Sabbath candles is "simply a design accessory" (29). Like the yuppie renewal of an ersatz Victorianism, the renewal of Jewish religious practice and observance during the late eighties is seen by Nina to be all style and no substance.

In addition, Laura's social role as the quintessential yuppie wife and mother is a manifestation of her desire to achieve the social and economic security of the American middle class. As Nina observes in *Personal Effects* (1991), "Institutions—including marriage, and now, religion—seemed to afford her sister a measure of comfort. That's what institutions were supposed to do" (211). From her roasts to her Shaker furniture to her summer house in Westhampton, Laura exemplifies the upwardly mobile Jewish woman whose social success is evident in her well-groomed children and her conspicuous consumption—and in her ability to land a successful Jewish husband, the dermatologist Ken Rubin. It seems no coincidence that, like Laura, his understanding of what life is all about is only skin deep. Nina describes Ken in *Unorthodox Practices* as being "as content as Laura. He enjoyed his role in the family and never gave any indication that he found his wife narrow or boring" (94). Ken indulges Laura, and treats her well by any standard, but to Nina he simply embodies a kinder, gentler male oppression: "Ken was okay as far as husbands went. He dominated benevolently. The whole setup was pretty seductive. Almost enough to make you want to sell yourself into the Jewish slave trade" (97). As a yuppie, Laura submits to the professionalized social role of Jewish wife and mother, a role that, in the late eighties and early nineties, seems to Nina like self-imposed slavery.

In contrast, Ida seems a more winning, but no less comical, variety of normal New York Jewish woman. Ida grew up on the Lower East Side, attended Hunter College, joined the Young People's Socialist league, raised a family in the Bronx, and was a dutiful New York City schoolteacher. She is a feisty widow whose husband Leo died shortly after they moved to the Upper West Side, an event that Ida shrugs off as an inevitability because "Jewish men of Leo's generation weren't built for the long haul" (14). Strong-willed and possessed of an acerbic wit, she is a version of the Jewish mother, which is why she seems a recognizably normal type at first, but Piesman disrupts the stereotype in *Unorthodox Practices* by giving her, as I have already noted, a number of the same complex attitudes toward New York and its inhabitants that Nina possesses. Thus she is also Nina's precursor, a competent, single, and independent Jewish woman similar to Nina in her pear-shaped body type (19) and in preferring to see herself as a "chronicler of the human spirit" rather than as a *yenta,* a gossip (40). True, she can be excessive, both in conversation and in her concern for her daughters, but her excess is of a piece with her characterization as the embodiment of the socially conscious and left-leaning worldview of a generation of midcentury New York Jews. When she finds out that Nina is dating an Orthodox man, she is horrified because it seems so politically retrograde:

> Ida prided herself on her open-mindedness. While other mothers hocked their kids about choosing the right career, the right spouse, the right piece of real estate, Ida always maintained that she just wanted her girls to be happy. . . . But an Ortho? It made the entire twentieth century seem pointless. Ida's mother in steerage and later in the sweatshop. Ida working to put herself through Hunter during the depression and later to put Nina through law school. Nina pumping herself up every day to do battle with the forces of evil in housing court. So that she could go out with a man who thanked God every morning he wasn't born a woman? (114–115)

Ida is Nina's foil, a partner with whom she can trade witty observations about the New York scene, but Ida is also far more certain of her politics than is Nina. What makes Ida a humorous figure to Nina is that she is ultimately a generational type, an Old Leftie whose liberalism is worthy of respect, but whose Channel 13 tote bag and quite unselfconscious belief that the Upper West Side is "the Holy Land" connotes an attitude toward culture and the "intelligentsia" as faded as Ida's prewar apartment building (14). Ida's political certainties, and her lack of self-consciousness—more accurately, her lack of obsessive self-consciousness in comparison to Nina's—characterize her as out of place in contemporary New York. Ida is an admirable Jewish mother, but also a comical version of a normal New York social role available to competent, single, and independent Jewish mothers of Ida's generation: the retired widow from the Upper West Side, a genius like her fellow widows "at absorbing New York culture at half-price" (15).

Given the choice of playing either Laura's or Ida's social role, Nina prefers neither. After all, the possibility of finding true love while playing those roles is very poor. When Laura suggests that Nina drop her boyfriend, the "tall, thin, painfully shy," and Lutheran Grant Miller (22), in order to date a Jewish professional like her husband Ken, Nina rejects the suggestion:

> Nina had none of the traditional complaints. Miniscule genitalia, princely demeanor, whining voice—that stuff was all nonsense. It existed in all segments of society. It was none of those things. It was this. There she would be, spending the weekend with Mr. X-berg. Saturday would be fine. They'd go to a lively dinner party and both contribute their share of clever conversation. Followed by acceptably enjoyable sex. Sunday morning she would wake up thinking, It's good to be with a Jew again. We understand each other. It would be a rainy day, so they'd decide to get bagels and sit around with the *Times*. There'd she be, complaining about the vapidity of the "His" column, reading the high-end real-estate classifieds out loud for their dramatic effect, scanning the wedding announcements, and commenting on how many Jews were marrying Jews and how many were marrying WASPs. Mr. X-berg would be getting deeper and deeper into the Sports section. And around noon they would look at each other. And suddenly it would be twenty years ago and she'd be locked up in a Bronx apartment on one of those interminable Sundays with Laura and Ida and Leo. Instead of being the stimulating dinner and bed companion of the previous evening, Mr. X-berg would have grown a head of newsprint, just like her father. And she would know what he was thinking behind the paper—that her previously

clever chatter had started to resemble the incessant yakking of his mother, Mrs. X-berg. And to drive the point home, there she would be, slicing bagels. (67–68)

Whether or not readers accept the psychological premises of Nina's critique of endogamous Jewish relationships, the critique itself functions as a witty unmasking of the socially constructed Jewish gender roles that dog Jewish men and women. In place of the egregious stereotypes Nina mentions first, and behind the supposedly enlightened facade of modern, urban Jewish identities, lurk the terrifying roles of the Jewish mother and the Jewish father. Although Laura claims that she and her husband have "worked a lot of this stuff out" (69), Nina can't help but associate commitment to a Jewish man with entrapment in such a gendered and stultifying domestic tableau. Nina's example of the X-bergs makes clear that she can not and will not abide the seemingly inevitable identity of Jewish mom no matter what the guise, a witting reference to her own mother and to Laura, but also one way her character talks back to the popular cultural images of Jewish moms from Yaffe's generation and the Jewish professional moms of her own generation. Both forsake true love in favor of social and economic security.

LOVE, AMERICAN JEWISH STYLE

True love for Nina is the product of uncertainty. Indeed, the pleasure of uncertainty and the imperative to survive are, in *Unorthodox Practices,* the twin themes of Nina's love life, and the twinned allure of detection for her. Could she date, or even marry, an Orthodox Jew? Could she solve a murder mystery? Only if her life depended on it. Of course, since there can be no further mysteries in the series if she doesn't keep exploring such urban unknowns, her fictional life does depend on it. Judah Lev, assistant district attorney and "real" Orthodox Jew, represents a particularly alluring unknown: "Where did these people go on dates? The kosher deli on Seventy-second street? What kind of a date was that? A split of champagne and a side of kasha varnishkes? And would she be able to talk to this man? . . . [S]he couldn't even begin to imagine what his sexual story might be. Did he do it through holes in the bedsheets? Did he do it at all?" (111–112). Nina, "whose curiosity led her around by the nose" (112), discovers Judah's unexpected taste in kosher wine, surprisingly sexy banter, and unpredictable mind to be an irresistible mystery, a connection made explicit in her summation of their first date: "Nina had never encountered this situation before, so it was hard to predict his next move. But she was getting a certain amount of pleasure from the uncertainty. It added a tangible dimension, like a scent. She was enjoying it the way she enjoyed reading a really good Agatha Christie mystery with a lot of lush details about French windows and kippers for breakfast. This romance had atmosphere" (123). Judah Lev deserves further investigation, but what Nina discovers (after indulging in a little self-validating heavy petting) is that, like the mystery surrounding the co-op murders, the mystery of Judah Lev is just another case of people using people to satisfy their base desires. As Judah begins to take over Nina's investigation, she accuses him of being another paternalistic male with a desire to control women (143). When he claims that it is Nina who secretly wants a man to control her, Nina's uncertainty about her life returns in full force. Unsure of whether to see herself as a "successful career woman with plenty of male companionship" or a woman who has nothing—"thirty-five, unmarried, childless, conflicted about her career, ambivalent about her boyfriend, always short of money"—Nina concludes that "her chronic sense of dissatisfaction would always be with her" (144). When she learns that Judah is engaged to marry the very young daughter of a wealthy Orthodox real estate developer, she sees that Judah's Jewish heart (for "heart" is the English translation of "Lev") is really no different from that of the urban professionals who are behind the co-op murders: it too hungers after money. "If you're going to sell your soul," she tells Judah, "sell it for big bucks" (209).

Nina learns here that true love is a mystery, and that there are two kinds of suitors/survivors in New York. Judah Lev, like all professionals, is also a professional survivor. To Judah, the institution of marriage is a means to his survival—an attitude that allies him with Laura; for both, marriage is the professional's strategy for achieving social and economic security. True, Nina also wants to get married. She dumps Grant at the end of *Unorthodox Practices* precisely to look for a viable husband. Piesman figures Nina, however, as, unlike Judah and Laura, an amateur survivor, an emotionally intense Jewish woman who will not tamp down her feelings out of personal convenience, as does Grant, or convert them into an economic exchange, as do Laura and Judah. Nina, despite her self-conflicted desire to be normal like Laura, still finds the pleasure of uncertainty, in love and in her career, a valid guide to domestic and emotional fulfillment.

Like Yaffe's Mom, and in her own way, Nina opposes love relationships to professionalism, although she is as uncertain about the line between the two as she is about everything else in her life. Calling herself a "remarkably good old maid" after ending her relationship with Grant, Nina throws herself into her work, promising herself that she will only date men who are serious marriage material—only to find herself flirting in court with the intelligent, dignified federal judge deciding the case, whom she romanticizes as just her kind of Jewish West Sider (222). One of the key differences between Nina and Mom, then, is that Nina does not believe that affective relations are a solution to material problems, that love will lead to a marriage that guarantees social and economic security. Rather, she believes they are the solution to her specific survival problem: how to transform herself into someone whose life reflects the qualities that she assigns to the Upper West Side—freedom, dignity, activity, and possibility.

In the second book of the series, *Personal Effects*, Nina's anxiety about her survival problem, and about her image as an amateur in love and detection, is tied to feminist social and political anxieties of the seventies, for the book is, in a number of ways, Piesman's rewriting of Judith Rossner's *Looking for Mr. Goodbar* (1975). Susan Gold, the murder victim in *Personal Effects*, is Piesman's Jewish version of Theresa Dunn, the protagonist in Rossner's novel, and she therefore provides Piesman with the opportunity to reconsider the search for autonomy that Rossner's protagonist, and other protagonists in women's fiction of the seventies, acted out.[26] Like Theresa Dunn, Susan embodies the single woman whose contradictory desires for both personal freedom and submission to an idealized mate make her a victim-in-waiting. Like Nina, Susan is an outsider, neither a feminist nor a yuppie by her mid-thirties, and she leads Nina to realize the precariousness and potential danger of Nina's own unconventional identity. Given Susan's pursuit of a yuppie "suit" who could guarantee her a good and comfortable life, and her desire for a normal (which is to say, conventional) identity, her violent end raises the question for Nina of whether the life and fate of a competent, single, and independent New York Jewish woman is really beyond her own control.

That question is one that novels like *Looking for Mr. Goodbar* brought home to women of Nina's, and Piesman's, generation.[27] The social and economic possibilities that second-wave feminism opened up in the seventies for urban women like Nina seemed closed off, by the early nineties, not only, as Elaine Showalter argues, by the specter of male violence and the psychological specters haunting women who grew up amid that violence,[28] but also by the conservative backlash of the eighties and early nineties, a backlash imaged by Piesman as a yuppie takeover of New York City's social and economic "rules." Musing on why she decided to become a lawyer, Nina observes that "she did what all good feminists of the seventies who were born to be social workers did—turned her back on such a traditional woman's career and went to law school—and ended up with a job that was eighty percent social work and twenty percent higher salary" (73). Real social and economic egalitarianism, as Nina tells her mother, is "a lovely sentiment that went out with nosegays and ice skating on frozen ponds," a sentiment that has been replaced by a hard-nosed contemporary sexual politics that offers women who want social and economic security two choices. "My theory is that there are two kinds of women: Women who want what men have—power, audacity, money; and women who want what other women have—protection, a husband, a husband's money. Susan was the second kind of woman.... I'm sort of a hybrid. I want what whoever else in the room has. Even if it's a cold" (135).

Nina's "hybridity" is an accurate expression of her character's feminist situation. By yoking the amateur detective formula to a women's novel of the seventies that itself borrowed elements from mystery fiction, Piesman makes Nina's uncertainty about her identity, and her ambivalence about the social roles available to her, into specific targets of Nina's investigation in *Personal Effects*. The kind of danger such uncertainty and ambivalence places her in is well symbolized by the personal ads that are the key to solving Susan's murder. In Piesman's mystery they represent impersonations, fictions that enable people to escape their social roles to be something they are not, or to "trade up" to a better economic or social arrangement, an apparent freedom that can exact a very high cost. Susan, in fact, met her murderer through a personal ad, and when Nina impersonates Susan's wants in a similar ad in order to track him down, she finds herself, as Susan and Theresa Dunn did, in the arms of a killer. Patrick is exciting and even sexually fulfilling, and Nina can see why Susan, who specialized in "abortive attempts" to find a career and a mate (4), would abort the child she had conceived with a callow previous lover so that she could start over with such good marriage material. Nina, however, knows that Patrick killed Susan because she found out that he is married and had no intention of making an honest woman of her. Returning with Patrick to the hiking trail where Susan was killed, Nina replays Susan's accusation and sees how both Susan's and Patrick's very desire to be something that they were not is what led them to each other and to their fates. It is this unmooring from social reality that made possible the rage that drove Susan to throw a rock at Patrick and that drove Patrick to throttle Susan to death. In Piesman's version of *Looking for Mr.*

Goodbar, Nina's investigation reveals that the irrational forces of evil and violence that frustrate people's control over their lives lie in the socially unmoored self. Given the conservative backlash of the eighties and nineties, and the reduction of an urban woman's choice of identities to two stark alternatives, independent "hybrid" women like Nina are clearly an endangered species of feminist.

This is an object lesson for Nina: "She had a two-year lease and a one-year gym membership and another six months on her New Yorker subscription. And a job that gave her a headache. Were these the ties that bind?" (215). At the end of the novel Nina once again measures herself against Laura, who has just given birth to her third child, a son, and who is planning a *bris* (circumcision) for him. Nina sees Laura as presiding over an "empire," a stable, American Jewish world where her identity and social role are inextricably plugged into the social reality of the yuppie lifestyle. In contrast, Nina is a "free agent," which means that she could easily "slip into oblivion without anyone noticing" (212). Although she restates her plan to date only men who are obvious marriage material, she can't help but find herself drawn to the uncertainty of an affair with the over-fifty Black homicide detective with whom she solved Susan's murder. What readers learn at the end of *Personal Effects* is that Nina cannot square her identity as a free agent with any of the social roles available to her through marriage, and this raises the stakes of her particular survival problem. Instead of transforming herself, she may very well end up like Susan, a fate that, in light of *Looking for Mr. Goodbar* and other women's novels of the seventies featuring violent plots, seems a common enough fear for women of Nina's generation.

Piesman's figuring of the Jewish woman as amateur thus mirrors and disrupts Yaffe's model of the Jewish woman as amateur, because Nina is a character who critiques acculturation to newly ascendant, urban middle-class values *and* takes issue with the limitations of the supposedly normal social roles available to emotionally intense, independent Jewish women. In other words, whereas Mom illustrates how the Jewish mother springs a critique of middle-class values and operates as a guide to economic and personal security, Nina illustrates how the "hybrid" Jewish woman in fact springs a critique of middle-class values *and* of conventional middle-class social roles that require conformity in exchange for economic and personal security.

Critiquing, however, does not equal real transformation for Nina, or complete subversion of the trope of the Jewish woman as amateur, a point that becomes clear in *Heading Uptown* (1993). In this third installment of her series, Piesman takes aim at the image of the Jewish

American Princess (JAP) and of the acculturated, suburban Jewish family in which the JAP thrives. Beverly Hirsch, the Long Island JAP suspected of murdering her husband, shows up at her husband's funeral looking none too mournful in high heels and a black leather miniskirt outfit, and everything about her is big, except her surgically modified nose: "Big black hair, tumbling down her padded leather shoulders. And a big red mouth, outlined in an even deeper red. And big diamond stud earrings, to go with the big diamond tennis bracelet and the big diamond ring and the big gold Rolex watch and the big red nails" (12). Beverly's JAPness is underscored later in the novel when Nina discovers that, true to form, Beverly "wasn't crazy about motherhood" (24), was an indifferent wife whose happiest years with her husband came only after he was able to purchase her a house on the fringes of Great Neck (25), and was already involved with a new and more dependable sugar daddy by the time her husband's body was found in upstate New York (64).[29] Nevertheless, at the novel's end, having used the JAP stereotype to throw suspicion on Beverly's character, Piesman reveals that Beverly, in fact, was really just a pawn in the real estate scheme run by her husband's partners, the wealthy, Jewish, and dysfunctional Silver family whose patriarch, Herb Silver, ordered Beverly's husband murdered. Piesman has Ida address Nina's quickness to suspect and to hate Beverly, and then explain their unwitting sisterhood with her: "Well, I see her as just another Jewish girl, put on this earth without benefit of wealth or privilege, working with what God gave her.... In her case it was a fabulous body and big black hair and an ability to make men want to get into bed with her. In my case, it was being able to pass Latin at Hunter College and to teach thirty-five kids at a time, while raising two of my own.... If I could have ensured my well-being by simply seeing to it that I looked good, I might have skipped the master's degree and gone straight to Elizabeth Arden" (281). For Ida, the JAP image is just another "package," as she calls it, that Jewish women with limited means manipulate in order to ensure their well being in a patriarchal society. According to Ida, survival for women like Beverly, Ida, and Nina—whose independence, emotional intensity, and ambivalence is a package that serves her "pretty well"—is not about transformation but about the ability to manipulate one's image (282).

That assertion makes sense in a novel where Nina realizes that should she never find true love, and so effect real transformation, the best possibilities for manipulating her image are available only in the urban society of New York City. Nina knows that she doesn't "play so well" in the gentile rural towns of upstate New York (where she goes to investigate the Silver's real estate scheme and reignites an old affair with Tom Wilson, her taciturn, marijuana-smoking gentile boyfriend from law school), not so much because of her ethnicity but because "away from home, she was often struck by the fact that it was, after all, a man's world" (98). Out on Long Island, the Hirsches and the Silvers are living out a baleful American Jewish suburban situation: assimilating the deleterious class consciousness and class ambitions of successful middle-class professionals whose families are held together by money, not love. Herb Silver, the family patriarch, rules by ownership, keeping his son Steve in line through his control of the family assets, the kind of tough father "whose idea of a bar mitzvah present was cutting off their kid's balls and having them gold plated" (273). He embodies a suburban American Jewish patriarchy that has turned Long Island into "a place where women seem to be judged mostly on weight and length of nails," a place that is literally killing Beverly's bulimic and psychologically troubled daughter Lisa (301). Outside of New York City, Jewish men like Steve Silver reject Nina as a "chubby feminist" (161) or, like Herb, do not even acknowledge her. "Men like you never listen to women like me," Nina says to Herb; "We're not rich, we're not glamorous, it's like we don't exist" (295). For Nina, that kind of economic, social, and psychological Jewish male violence is mitigated by New York City and the free play it offers to her free agency: "New York City was, in many ways, a woman's town. There the major activities were, as opposed to moving large piles of snow around, shopping, cab-hailing, theatre-going, and negotiating. All things that women were naturally good at. Even the more macho activities, like bond-trading, only required a brain and a mouth, not biceps and deltoids.... Despite all the nuclear family propaganda the magazines were hurling lately, a woman in New York City could still call her own shots" (99–100).

Piesman's gendered and essentialized dichotomy between the city and every place outside it therefore helps to discharge Nina's anxiety about her identity and her social role in two ways. First, this dichotomy clarifies how Nina can square her identity with an acceptable social role. Nina's true spouse turns out to be the city itself: "She was, for all intents and purposes, married to New York. Permanently, like a practicing Catholic; pledged at birth, like a Hindu. All separations had been understood to be temporary" (81). Nina's social and economic security is really determined by her marriage to New York and the social freedom and economic possibilities—the empowerment, if you will—that it offers. In a city in which she can "call her own shots," there is no need to reconcile her identity with an acceptable social role of wife or mother. Second, Piesman's dichotomy, and her defense of Beverly's image as a JAP, displaces the most negative attributes of the powerless and craven JAP (entitlement, class ambition, marital indifference, and the desire for a sugar daddy) onto Kathy Silver, Steve Silver's wife and a convert to Judaism. Kathy's Jewishness is coeval with her JAPness; her new Jewish identity is signaled through the excessiveness of her clothes, accessories, and nails (149), all simply more expensive versions of Beverly's accoutrements. As both convert and JAP, Kathy absorbs (and redirects from Laura) the unresolved animosity that Nina feels for women who forswear true love to benefit from acculturation to the values and attitudes of a conformist and materialistic middle class (258). Kathy exemplifies the JAP's selfish greed even as she functions as a status symbol, the non-Jewish trophy wife (262).

Although Piesman has Nina admit to "shiksaphobia," Kathy nevertheless is the only woman in the novel who accepts and condones the Silvers' economic and domestic rule, because she benefits from the Silvers' patriarchy and from Jewish male violence. As it turns out, Kathy is the one who asked Herb Silver to kill Beverly's husband, in order that she not lose her house and a considerable part of her material comforts. The cost of Kathy's subsuming herself to such patriarchy is made clear when Nina confronts Kathy and tells her that, justice aside, she wants to solve the murder out of pity for Lisa Hirsch. "I don't give a shit," Kathy says (286). A short while later, when she tells Herb Silver that the man he saw as a "business problem" was, in fact, a human being, Herb Silver, too, says "I don't give a shit. I didn't then and I don't now" (294). Such a patriarchy, and subservience to it, inures women to love relationships and to the ability to empathize with other human beings. To Nina, whose image as a Jewish woman is predicated on her affirmation of the value of love relationships, a Jewish woman like Kathy is really not Jewish.

No wonder that, at the end of the novel, Nina feels so strongly that she wouldn't change who she is (282), and that she lives at the right time and in the right place (301). In this sense, Nina's acceptance of herself, and her parental advice to Lisa to accept that she has "a pretty face" (a phrase she once thought of as condescending to overweight girls like her and Lisa), signals not only "middle age" (303). It signals also that the tension between Nina's conflicting desires to remain independent and to marry have been resolved, for neither is necessarily related to the true love that she seeks. Nina doesn't need to transform herself, only make psychic peace with herself—and Piesman no longer needs to spend so much time developing Nina's character. Instead,

Piesman manipulates Nina's image by having the emotionally intense Jewish woman who is uncertain and unplugged mature into middle age and discover that loving herself is the solution for how to survive as a capable and independent urban Jewish woman—and as the protagonist of a mystery series. Nina finds her own definition for what it means to be a free, dignified and active urban Jewish woman: it means being herself. Piesman's character has come to terms with, rather than transformed, the trope of the Jewish woman as amateur because it's precisely that trope that provides Nina with a viable, and recognizably Jewish, New York identity.

Perhaps this is why the next two novels in the series are slack even though they introduce readers to Nina's future Jewish husband. With Nina's anxieties resolved, both *Close Quarters* (1994) and *Alternate Sides* (1995) read like extended magazine columns on New York City life, and Piesman herself acknowledged in 1993, as she was working on *Close Quarters*, "I'm running out of single urban women material to draw on.... I'm reaching the point where I have to hook Nina up with somebody."[30] Although Piesman had Nina observe as early as *Personal Effects* that she felt as if she needed to get married "even if it was only just to move the plot along" (24), the transparency of that assertion as Piesman's literary self-analysis is evident by *Close Quarters*, where Nina observes that "she wanted to get married, even if only to move the plot along. She was getting tired of the same old issues" (146).

Jonathan Harris is Piesman's plot device, but it's no surprise that he resembles Mom's husband Mendel; his qualification for marriage to Nina is that, like Mendel, he possesses many of the attributes of the Jewish woman as amateur. Like Mendel, Jonathan is a different kind of man, which Piesman signals through his clothes. His cotton oxford shirts, khaki pants, and deck shoes make him the most overdressed male on Fire Island, where the male dress code consists of t-shirts, shorts, and sandals. To Nina, he is a vulnerable-looking "alienated preppy" (46), and later in the novel she notes that "Jonathan didn't really look like a type. He looked ... well, the truth was he looked like Nina. Too many clothes, too much hair, too much flesh" (142). Jonathan's alienation, however, is what really makes him Nina's type. He is the son of parents who are both products of intermarriage and, appropriately, he grew up on the border between the borough of Queens and Nassau County. Like Nina, Jonathan is "something in between. In no way did he remind her of the Bronx, with his boat shoes and long-sleeved shirts of purely natural fibers. Yet he had that neurotic New York City homeboy quality, chattily introspective and full of Jewish-mother jokes. Maybe he was a good compromise" (112–113). Equally uncertain about his career and his relationships with his parents and with women, Jonathan finds Nina's loquaciousness sexy and her weight unimportant. He too opposes love relationships to professionalism, seeing his romance with Nina as an antidote to the unfulfilling materialism and competitiveness of his professional life, advertising. Indeed, in a completely unwitting but remarkable echo of Yaffe's "Mom Remembers," the murderer is a woman who acts like a man, who instead of accepting or excusing male violence internalizes it and turns the tables on her victim (262). That the admirable Jonathan acts like a woman is underscored by his role in the mystery: he is the damsel in distress and Nina is the knight who saves him. "You valiantly sought out the truth," he says to Nina when she clears him of the murder of his friend; "You're my hero" (272).

In the interest of moving the plot along, then, Piesman employs the next mystery, *Alternate Sides,* as a vehicle for Jonathan and Nina's decision, at the end, to marry (in spite of the ambivalence each has about marriage), move to Los Angeles, and even consider having a child. Following the irresistible logic of the popular romance, Piesman transforms Nina into an insider, one who adopts the normal social role of Jewish wife. The problem for Piesman, however, is that, unlike her manipulation of Nina's image, her transformation of Nina sentences her to the middle-class conformity she is supposed to find imprisoning and degrading. It cripples Nina's image—and Piesman's series.

It is therefore both surprising and unsurprising that the aptly titled *Survival Instincts* (1997) opens with Nina recounting her separation from Jonathan and her move back to New York after suffering an identity crisis in Los Angeles: surprising because the separation seems to come out of nowhere, unsurprising because it's obvious that Nina, as an amateur survivor, can thrive only in New York. There, in a reprise of her self-recognition in *Heading Uptown,* Nina realizes that others envy her for remaining "true to [her] own self" (206). It's who she is—and what her mother calls "our usual, sticking our noses into other people's business" (199)—that enables her to solve a murder mystery involving the commercial rights to a chemical that controls obesity, a chemical that would enable women to transform themselves in deference to a middle-class and patriarchal norm for women's bodies. So, in *Survival Instincts,* Piesman devises another way to make Nina an insider, another way to portray her as finally plugged in and certain, that is consonant with the author's figuring of the Jewish woman as amateur. Nina becomes a research assistant for an Anna Quindlen/Nora Ephron–type *New Yorker* columnist, and acquiring that job consummates her marriage to New

York because it intimately connects her to the interior life of the city and to other real New Yorkers (during her investigation, doors magically open every time she says she's working for the *New Yorker*). Nina's new job validates and empowers her as a free, dignified, and active New York Jewish woman—which is to say, it symbolizes that she has finally achieved control over her life and fate. We see that she has defended her faith, her interpretation of what it means to be a Jewish woman, in part by interrogating her own identity.

Still, Piesman's figuring of the Jewish woman as amateur remains the basis for Nina's Jewish identity. Without the image of the emotionally intense Jewish woman who affirms love relationships in opposition to male professionalism, and who references herself to the female Jewish stereotypes that constellate around that dichotomy, Nina would not be able to survive in popular fiction as a detective or as a New Yorker or as a Jew. In that light, a trope does bestow control, but is it not also the image of the Jewish woman that is being controlled? In other words, the need for cogent and simple representations in popular fiction, ones that fulfill generic expectations, limits what Piesman can do with the image of the amateur American Jewish woman detective who is single and independent.[31] Since Mom is a widow, her true love is in the past and out of the way; Yaffe can toy with the popular romance without having to transform Mom into a beloved or a wife. In contrast, Nina's single status must be resolved in a manner that satisfies readers' expectations of a protagonist who affirms love relationships; doing so, however, threatens to compromise the love for feminism and for the urban Jewish identity that Nina claims to represent. While self-love seems a reasonable solution to this paradox, the paradox nevertheless is what limits the subversiveness, and the shelf life, of Piesman's detective—who, as of this time, has not survived past *Survival Instincts*.

Piesman's series, however, remains significant. The inadvertent dialogue between Yaffe's Mom and Nina Fischman illustrates that, in spite of Rabbi David Small's claim to the title of first influential affirming Jewish detective, the figure of the Jewish woman detective has been in play since the midcentury beginnings of distinctly American Jewish detective stories—in fact, Mom *is* the first distinctly American Jewish detective. Yaffe's and Piesman's detectives thus reflect the initial struggle not just over the Jewish woman detective, but also over the very figure of the American Jewish detective. Together they represent an important example of the interplay between gender and kosher hybridity. Piesman's series, in its own right, deserves to be remembered and valued as an instructive example of how women's voices shaped, and continue to shape, the detective persona and the narratives of American Jewish detective stories, despite the fact that the series' critique of gender stereotypes is undermined by the very necessity of reproducing them.

In this regard, not only *Personal Effects* but the series as a whole is reminiscent of women's popular novels of the seventies. As Riv-Ellen Prell argues, Jewish writers such as Rhoda Lerman, Gail Parent, Louise Rose Blecher, and Susan Lukas explored the conflict between social expectations and Jewish women's affirmation of the value of love relationships. Like those novels, Piesman's series addresses "the absence of having (love) within a consumer society," and features a protagonist whose dissatisfactions with herself, and whose frustration over her options as a Jewish woman, lead to her anxiety over the middle-class social roles available to her, and over the Jewishness she associates with these roles.[32] And, like those protagonists', Nina's critique is limited "in a way that more overtly feminist statements are not," because "the "talk back art reproduces the stereotype even while using them to criticize what they represent."[33]

But Piesman's comical Jewish outsider, at more than twenty years' distance from the seventies, is no longer a shocking figure engaged in a kind of literary call-and-response with her American Jewish male counterparts. Her critique is of its time and of Piesman's generation, and it remains to be seen how Nina Fischman's legacy and her struggle over the image of the Jewish woman detective will be taken up by writers interested in pushing the limits of generic subversion. Nina Fischman is therefore an acerbic critic of the baby boom generation and its witting and unwitting betrayals of feminism, who becomes, by necessity, a well-recognized and manipulable image from that generation, one whose hyperbolic and comic dramas of uncertainty are, by the last three novels in the series, less a parody of the detective story than the predictable routines of the Jewish woman as amateur.

CASES OF MEMORY

4

TWICE-TOLD TALES OF ASHKENAZ AND SEPHARAD

> The way back is lost, the one obsession.
> The worst is over.
> The worst is yet to come.
> —Carolyn Forché, *The Angel of History*

Stumbling across these lines amid the ruins of people, places, and ideas inhabiting the landscape of Carolyn Forché's book, I heard in them the seduction and the terror of memory, those longings and fears evoked by the remembrance of things past. The seduction of memory, as I experienced it while reading the book, is simple, perhaps even childish: if, from out of the destruction of the twentieth century, we could recover whole our individual and collective pasts, we might then possess the moral conscience and historical consciousness to say with certainty what it means to be human, what it means to be who we are and who we ought to be. The terror of memory is equally simple, though seemingly mature by contrast: individual and collective memories are fragmented and unstable, perhaps even fictions, and therefore such a recovery is impossible. And that impossibility means that we live in an unmoored present where neither remembering nor forgetting the constructions and destructions of the past can protect us against or prepare us for the fearsome unknown of the future.

This is a starkly reductive dichotomy, I admit, one predicated on a brief marginal note written in the heat of reading, but it is a starting place for this section on memory and kosher hybridity and for this chapter's consideration of the interrelationship between the seduction and the terror of memory in American Jewish detective stories. How do detective stories that revolve around the Jewish past reflect that interrelationship? How do they try to possess the past and make it tangible to readers? What reassurances do they provide about our humanity, and about the present and the future?

No one disputes that there is currently an obsession with the past, particularly as refracted through the Holocaust, among Jews in America and around the world. The plethora of books, articles, documentaries, museum exhibitions, educational programs, and so on, all devoted to the recovery and maintenance of the Jewish past, attest to that obsession. So too does the war over the control of Jewish memory that is being waged in the Jewish press and between various communal organizations and educational institutions. The battles over leadership positions within the U.S. Holocaust Museum, over the nature and scope and meaning of Holocaust reparations, over who is a Jew and what is the meaning of Jewish community, over the American Jewish relationship to Israel and Zionism, and among competing museums devoted to Jewish culture are a few noteworthy examples. These battles are often oversimplified, always polemically vicious, and played for such high political (and financial) stakes that all except the most politically driven are dissuaded from participating. In the various subdisciplines of Jewish studies, the scholarship about history and memory is more collegial but is competitive, too, punctuated by the occasional finger wagging at unusual methodologies and, of course, at the simplifications and contradictions of popular culture. Catalyzed by Yosef Yerushalmi's book about the dilemmas of modern Jewish historiography, *Zachor* (1989), in which he asserts that for contemporary Jews "history, not a sacred text, becomes the arbiter of Judaism," such scholarship is now thick with theories and analyses: about the ways Jewish memory was and is constructed; about little-known or marginalized Jewish pasts; about the interdependence of collective memory, myth-making, and historical consciousness (which is to say, the interdependence of remembering and forgetting); about the uses and misuses of culturally and ideologically useable pasts; and about specific Jewish memory sites in Europe, Israel, and the Americas.[1] In short, *Zachor*, "remember," has become more than just a book title, an exhortation, or a slogan. It has become, as Jonathan Webber observed, a "statement of belief" about what it means to be a Jew, a "contemporary Jewish myth" about Jews as "a people of remembrancers"[2] that helps consolidate a secular post-Holocaust Jewish identity attractive to individuals whose Jewish identity is "attenuated, selective, and intermittent."[3] And, I would add, a statement that offers a popular work site for Jewish politicians, journalists, artists, administrators, scholars, and teachers.

Everyone, it seems, now has a story to tell about the Jewish past, or a story about how to tell the story of that past. Like these narratives,

American Jewish detective stories that focus on the Jewish past, and that thrive on the mythologization of Jewish memory, are twice-told tales not only in the sense that they are retellings of stories about the past, but also in that their telling is mediated and revised, and therefore hybridized, by their narrative conventions and generic formulas. As Webber has also observed, "historical memory does not just appear from mid-air but is usually the product, the self-conscious product, of some institutional source that has some motive in delivering a particular rendering of the historical past."[4] Webber is referring to the museums, survivor organizations, and academic disciplines that structure and mediate historical memory of the Holocaust, but his point about the working relationship between memory and its delivery systems is also applicable to the popular arts, and provides another angle on the kosher hybridity at work in American Jewish detective stories.

Taking up the twice-told tales of Ashkenaz and Sepharad—of East European and Iberian Jewish life—that are purveyed in these stories means considering the impact of a particular delivery system on Jewish memory, and the possible motives bound up in detective fiction's rendering of the Jewish past. Is that delivery system primarily suited to entertaining American Jewish nostalgia for a coherent and cohesive Jewish world and Jewish identity, or, through its trivialization of the past, to providing relief and resolution for the traumas, the trauma of the Holocaust in particular, that haunt the Jewish past? We might answer that the seduction of memory in these stories is connected to the seductiveness of the medium in which they appear: the way that the detective genre can reconstruct the complexity of the past into a readable series of clues that are decoded by the detective and offered to the reader as a comprehensible if oftentimes violent narrative about the meaning of that past. Add to this the genre's commodification and spectacularization of the past and the seduction is complete: the past is wholly recoverable and a ripping good tale.

Given the terms of this question and its pat answer, the terror of memory in this case is simply the product of American Jewish cultural anxieties about identity and the traumas of the past. What I want to examine in this chapter, however, are precisely such easy assertions about detective fiction's rendering of the Jewish past—but not to refute them; it is, I believe, important to explain why they are so assertable. Rather, I want to use such assertions as a jumping-off point, for I wish to deepen and widen the significance of the complex of fears and longings the assertions reflect, a complex that we ought to call "Jewish Gothic."

POSSESSION AND THE PAST

To put one's hands physically on the past and take hold of its aura is a compelling desire. It is partly this desire that accounts for why many people collect books, records, photographs, and cultural ephemera from the Jewish past, particularly from the East European Jewish world just before the Holocaust. The past as flea market for the present? That may be too harsh and generalized a description for the current marketing of memory in our computer-aided, information-soaked, and materialist consumer culture, but as I peruse the items on sale in the Judaica category on eBay, the online auction site, it's clear that the past is big business: an 1893 Russian silver kiddush cup; a 1910 postcard of the synagogue in Schlüchtern, Germany; a pre–1948 olive wood letter opener from Jerusalem; a 1912 Manischewitz Hagaddah; an 1870 silver torah pointer from Poland; the November 21, 1938, edition of the *Montana Standard* featuring coverage of Krystallnacht; an 1836 *Mishlei* (Book of Proverbs); and sixteen more virtual pages of "antiques," "vintage" items, and assorted contemporary tchotchkes. Given that this is eBay, the authenticity of these items from the past is not a given: the supposedly late-nineteenth-, early-twentieth-century wood panel depicting a "worried looking" Jewish family from the "scheteyl" (the writer meant "shtetl," not the Yiddish for "wig") is probably a bad investment.

It is also one of the more transparent examples of how these items are totems of what Marianne Hirsch calls "postmemory," which she describes as "a powerful and very particular form of memory precisely because its connection to its object or source is mediated not through recollection but through an imaginative investment and creation."[5] In the case of eBay the investment in memory is not only imaginative—that all Jews in shtetls looked worried—but also monetary, making the cash value of an item proportional to its value as memory. In today's marketplace, for example, memories of East European Jewish life (*Synagogues of Rumania* by Lucian Schwarz, $59.00) are worth more money than memories of American Jewish life (seven issues of *The Menorah Journal* from 1932 to 1938, $39.99). The eBay web site illustrates how the seduction of memory has both a moral and a material dimension that are ripe for criminal mischief and criminal investigation. Purchasing these totems of postmemory turns the buyer, potentially, into a guardian, collector, and manipulator of a past the value of which is subject to the fluctuations of the culture market. The auction items on eBay thus illustrate quite neatly the conflation of postmemory and profit, by the way that the remembrance of the past is affected by commercial forces and the moral stresses that the weight of such forces can produce. The terror of memory, in this case, is how easily the past can be manipulated or fabricated, and that doing so to make a profit is, after all, a kind of second destruction of the past, for the fabricator consigns the "original" to oblivion (because it is forgotten) to make room for the fabrication. But isn't that also the situation of the writer of popular fiction, who is subject to commercial forces, too?

That is the intriguing implication of Janice Steinberg's short story, "Wailing Reed." The murder mystery in her story takes place against the backdrop of the American Jewish revival during the eighties and nineties of klezmer music, the Central/East European Jewish folk music played at weddings and other Jewish celebrations. Margo Simon, Steinberg's acculturated Jewish detective, is a public radio reporter in San Diego whose interest in klezmer was sparked by a story she produced about "Klezmania," a local revivalist band. So when she is summoned to the apartment of Ira Nadler, "a white-haired dealer of rare music" (236) and "one of the pre-eminent klezmer musicologists in the world" (250), Simon quickly agrees to be his "intermediary" and to find a valuable klezmer recording made in Poland during the 1920s and the Klezmania clarinetist whom Nadler suspects stole it. In the course of her investigation, Simon discovers two key relationships between the present and the past. The first is between the ostensibly rebellious youth music of the club scene and the klezmer music that musicians like Jeff Holland, the clarinetist, have rediscovered. Waiting for Holland's rock band to perform, Simon fears that she may be too old to appreciate contemporary rock music, with its pierced and tattooed fans and alienating punk overtones, but listening to the band she is surprised: "Margo actually liked the band's music: they played an interesting if sometimes weird hybrid of rock and jazz, just as Klezmania's music combined traditional and modern influences" (241). Simon does not find Holland (he fails to show up for the gig), but she does find that the appeal of both contemporary youth music and the klezmer revival is their weird hybridity, their mixing of dissimilar but not dissonant sounds from the past and from the present. The result is neither nostalgia nor an over-hip smugness, but rather emotionally accessible music that, in the case of Klezmania, is capable of making Simon cry.

The second relationship Simon discovers is between Nadler and Holland. Holland, in fact, is Nadler's apprentice, learning from the older collector knowledge of the klezmer musicians and recordings of the past. Nadler's knowledge of klezmer is intimate; he himself was a klezmer violinist and the son of a klezmer musician, who played in Lower East

Side klezmer bands just when klezmer was infiltrating and being infiltrated by American jazz. But when klezmer went out of fashion Nadler refused "to waste himself playing in some moldy bar mitzvah band. And he didn't really have the technique for classical or the licks for jazz" (249). What he does have is knowledge of klezmer history and of the recordings that the new klezmer musicians and collectors need. How to use that knowledge turns out to be the conflict that leads to Holland's murder. After discovering Holland's body in Nadler's mountain cabin, Simon interrogates Nadler and uncovers the truth about the missing record—made in Ozorow, Poland, and featuring the famous klezmer violinist Zig Wolinsky—which is that Nadler still has it and that it's not a Wolinsky record. Nadler was going to sell it as a rare recording of the famous musician, in order to profit from the past, and Holland was going to reveal that not only was the record a fraud, but that Nadler had "sold other records the same way, saying they had historical value they didn't" (252). In other words, Nadler was using his knowledge of the past to retail fraudulent memories of it. The pressures of the commercial world to "work every angle" to make a living and to survive are what motivate Nadler and make possible his manipulation of the past and his egregious murder of the musician who, in this story, is the hero capable of bringing back the past as a living art. As Simon notes about Nadler, "What he had given the world was so precious. He had helped save from extinction the musical expression of a culture that was virtually annihilated. What he had taken from the world, however, was so much greater" (253).

By using klezmer as a touchstone for the East European Jewish past, Steinberg's short story asks readers to consider the mysteries of that past's emotional and commercial tangibility. Klezmer, as an example of postmemory about Eastern European Jewish life, and as one of the sales champs of the American Jewish popular arts, is a perfect target for criticizing the romanticization and commercialization of the Ashkenazi culture to which klezmer gives voice, literally. Steinberg's story acknowledges that the klezmer revival, and the opportunity it offers audiences of possessing the past aurally and materially, is subject to a number of scams that well illustrate the seduction of memory: the conning of those who wish to indulge in nostalgia for a lost Jewish music that reflects a coherent and cohesive Jewish world wiped out by the Holocaust; the conning of those who long for an identity as pure as the notes of an expertly played clarinet; and the conning of those who believe that a distinction can be made between the disinterested retrieval of the past and its commodification as collectible entertainment. These are the obvious cons, the ones that make clear how well popular culture can entertain nostalgia, trivialize history, and relieve, without really working through, the traumas of the past.

More troublesome is that Nadler's character suggests that the conning is self-directed to deal with a fear of weird kosher hybridity: the mixing of dissimilar but not dissonant traditions, idioms, and mediums from the Jewish past and the American present. Nadler tells Simon that he put the matter of his outsmarting others or being outsmarted, in business and in murder, "in God's hands" (253)—the question of who is more "clever," as he calls it, is one he passes on to a higher authority. But that only enables him to avoid recognizing that cleverness has nothing to do with his ability not only to control the transmission of the Jewish past but also to direct its responsible grafting onto new musical idioms and sound technologies. Waiting for the police to arrive, Nadler, dealer in old records, "selected a compact disc and put it on the modern sound system he kept in the living room. Jeffrey Holland's clarinet burst forth—passionate, playful, lost forever. Tears stung Margo's eyes. She looked at Ira Nadler. He was weeping, too" (253). Nadler had conned himself so as not to see the demands and the new combinations and connections—aesthetic, cultural, commercial—that the present makes available. Nadler terms his attitude about who is more clever than who a "metaphor" from his old neighborhood, the rough-and-tumble world of the Lower East Side, and his inability to move beyond that metaphor as a way of dealing with others, his incapacity to move beyond that way of thinking about combinations and connections, means that he is still trapped in the past. More, however, Nadler's recognition that the loss of Holland the artist is a profound loss to the future of not only Jewish but also American popular music raises the suggestion that the terror of memory in this story is terror over the human capacity to strand itself, culturally and temporally, in endless, lachrymose nostalgia for what was and what might have been. Fear of weird kosher hybridity, in other words, leads to cultural and temporal stasis.

As the story's official intermediary, Margo Simon takes on Steinberg's investigation of the costs of that fear. Thus "Wailing Reed" is a lesson about how to fruitfully twine memory with entertainment—a weird twinning to some—without falling prey to the self-delusions of postmemory that Nadler exemplifies. If the story uncovers anything, it is that in the popular arts buyers must beware: look to the artist's performance to determine whether the past is being crassly manipulated or is truly being hybridized into a challenging yet emotionally accessible work of art. That advice is underlined by Simon herself, who, having learned to appreciate the weird kosher hybridity of the klezmer revival, is moved at the end of the story in the same way that Nadler is, by her recognition that the greater thing Nadler had taken from the world was an artist able to balance the aesthetic, cultural, and commercial combinations necessary for the maintenance of a living popular art. True, Steinberg's balancing act in "Wailing Reed" is not without its problems, for, in fact, there was no klezmer violinist named Zig Wolinsky, and Ozorow (Ozarow) is famous for its Hasidic rabbis, not its klezmer musicians. Real violinists such as Emil Bruh, Leon Schwartz, and Abe Schwartz, it can be argued, suffer a second death here to make room for the fictional Wolinsky. Yet Steinberg's detective is not out to rescue memory. She is out to interrogate purveyors and shapers of popular culture like Nadler, who, whether aware of it or not, are responsible for conveying memory. Thus another fear that Steinberg's story unwittingly expresses is related to the weird hybridity of its own medium: the fear that the popular arts are born guilty of crimes against the past, and that reconciling the retrieval of memory with entertainment and the commercial forces of the culture market inevitably requires one or another kind of murder, even when the musician or writer appropriates the past with the best of intentions. In other words, the delivery system for Steinberg's story is haunted by the past, both by the past it means to represent and by the past that it has forgotten and made to disappear. The desire to possess the past and make it tangible thus evidences, in and through Steinberg's story, a kind of *possession* by the past—which is to say that it evidences a kind of American Jewish ghost story.

The lineaments of such a ghost story are well illustrated in Ronald Levitsky's short story "Jacob's Voice," where the lawyer/detective, Nate Rosen, considers the extent to which his client has been driven crazy by the voices of the past. Rosen is asked by Max Samuels, a wealthy Jewish entrepreneur, to defend his niece, Judith Arens, in a guardianship hearing that will determine whether she is mentally competent to retain control over the family car dealerships that she inherited from her father. The hearing has been requested by her husband, whom Judith tried to kill. He, in turn, is having an affair with his blond, blue-eyed business manager who, Rosen eventually suspects, is the real power trying to take over the business. The Samuels/Arens clan is a perfectly dysfunctional observant Jewish family. As readers learn, Judith was sexually abused as a child, her parents died in an auto accident, her brother Jacob was murdered collecting back rent for one of Samuels's properties, and Judith's husband is a congenital philanderer. Samuels claims that in his extended family "God always came first, then work" (150), but it's clear that the demands of making it in America have exacted a high cost on his extended family. What's left of the religiosity, the cultural literacy, and the collective memory of Samuels's Polish Jewish past, which in Levitsky's story is synonymous with the word "shtetl," is condensed in the story into three representations: the photographs on Samuels's office walls of "men in black suits and women wearing babushkas and long dresses," the Yiddish that Samuels and Judith are said to speak (aside from a few words like "mamzer," Yiddish is never actually spoken in the story), and the kabbalah (Jewish mysticism) that Samuels, and the story, employs as a metonymy for a putatively authentic Jewishness predicated on Torah learning and observance.

Samuels has chosen Rosen to represent Judith because he knows that Rosen, now a thoroughly secular American Jew, was raised observant in a similarly shtetl-soaked American Jewish environment—he is, at heart, a "real Talmud-Torah man" (152) well versed in Yiddish folk tales. Thus Rosen, since he supposedly understands, as Samuels does, that the Jewish God of the Polish Jewish past "calls for justice" (152), can plausibly argue that Judith is not crazy but is possessed by a dybbuk, the lost soul of her dead brother, who is in search of justice for his murder. Therefore, Judith's possession is, in fact, an idiosyncratic expression of her First Amendment right to freedom of religious belief. Levitsky's story obviously owes more to S. Ansky's classic play *The Dybbuk* than it does to actual Jewish religious practice; Rosen's observant background is less believable after he recollects praying in his tefillin (phylacteries) on the Sabbath, a day on which they are never worn. On the other hand, Levitsky's mystery—is Judith possessed? by what? is she trying to get rid of her husband before he gets rid of her? what is Samuels up to?—successfully engages Rosen in an interesting conflict between the past and the present predicated on the story's multiple meanings of "possession." For, as readers watch Rosen try to discover who wants to possess Judith's business badly enough to want her out of the way, they also observe Rosen's own possession by the memories of his past—he too is hearing voices. Rosen wants to believe that Judith could be possessed by a dybbuk because he wants to believe in the God and in the Judaism of his childhood, wants to believe that the "shtetl tales" he heard as a boy are true and relevant to his present life.

In the end, Rosen discovers that his own possession enabled him to be conned by Samuels into investigating Judith's husband and her husband's mistress so as not to suspect the real criminal—Samuels.

Samuels, he learns, hired a psychologist to hypnotize Judith into believing that she was possessed by her brother, so that Samuels, guilt-stricken over Jacob's murder, could manipulate her into killing him, a scheme based on his own twisted interpretation of biblical justice. Samuels dies and Judith is sent to a mental hospital, but Rosen is left to ponder the meaning of his own choice to believe Samuels. Samuels, like Nadler in Steinberg's story, is a self-centered Jewish con artist who both manipulates the past and is himself possessed by it. Obviously he does not profit from it in the same way that Nadler does. Still, his manipulation of the biblical past, Judith's past, and Rosen's past in order to achieve his own suicide and his own interpretation of Jewish justice is a perverse profitting from the past. It is how he cons himself so as not to see the demands of the present—that he must take care of his ravaged family so that they can survive in the here and now, not destroy it in the hope of achieving otherworldly redemption for himself alone. Unlike Steinberg's story, however, in Levitsky's story being possessed by the past does not lead to stasis and a good cry. It leads to a choice.

Rosen recognizes that, in this mystery, "choice was what it had been all about" (172). Like everyone else involved in the case, in order to validate his beliefs—his beliefs in "God's law" (172) and in the folk tales of his youth—he must choose the right interpretive lens with which to understand the hold that the past still has on him. But how to choose? Levitsky sets up the stakes when he has Rosen and Judith discuss (in a way that oversimplifies the complexity of the subject) the nature of the being that supposedly possesses her. Judith insists that it is not a dybbuk because a "dybbuk is an evil soul. My brother wasn't evil" (157). She insists that her brother's soul is an *ibbur*, a good man's soul who has inhabited a body in order to complete an unfulfilled mitzvah, or religious obligation (158). Judith's argument raises the possibility that, in choosing how to understand the past, Jews like her and Rosen have the power to determine whether the past they retrieve is an evil spirit or a good spirit. Since Judith is Samuels's dupe, however, and since his (twisted) memory of the Polish Jewish God is of a fearful God of justice, readers know that the past that possesses her really is a dybbuk, an evil spirit. So it is Rosen, naturally enough, who provides the moral to this story. When he comes to interpret the hold that the past has on him, the interpretive lens he chooses implies that his retrieval of the past is in service of a future hope: "Rosen's choice drew him closer to that lost soul of his nightmare, which was not a nightmare after all, but a dream. The dream of a young boy on his way to prayers, singing the same prayer that Rosen heard now: 'Thank you, Lord, for giving back my soul which was in your keeping.' The prayer whose melody he still felt with every beat of his heart. A prayer for a God Who, despite what Samuels had said, stood not merely for justice, but for love as well" (172). Rosen's memory of the past is no longer a nightmare about the impossibility of a God of both justice and love. It becomes a good spirit—a dream that is like prayer: an affirming hope that awakening to the past will return to lapsed Jews like Rosen the almost lost belief in a God of both justice and love. The moral of Levitsky's ghost story is that, if we remember only belief in justice, the past will kill us; if we also remember belief in love, the past will sustain us.

It is a simple moral, one appropriate to popular fiction. But the way that it incorporates mysticism, and the mystery of prayer, as a metaphor for the mystery of how to understand memories of the Jewish past, suggests that the motives for the rendering of the past in both Levitsky's and Steinberg's stories go beyond simple nostalgia or the desire to resolve past traumas. There is a weirdness to the past and the present in these stories that is both seductive and terrifying to the detective protagonists. Fascinated by their own emotional reactions to the possibility of putting their hands on the Jewish past, Simon and Rosen interrogate themselves as much as they interrogate the criminals: are American Jews in the process of retrieving useable memories or inventing collectible entertainments, and are those memories an ibbur or a dybbuk, a dream or a nightmare? Klezmer and kabbalah make tangible to Simon and Rosen a past that they desire, but as the subject of Jewish memory klezmer and kabbalah also manifest in each detective something intangible that scares them because of that intangible's capacity to radically alter or to destroy Jewish identity and culture. And, scarier still, what that something is, or what it sets loose, these detectives discover, lies in a dark and potentially criminal part of their American Jewish selves, a part that, in Steinberg's and Levitsky's fictions, enables American Jews to con and kill themselves and others. Where does that dark side come from, and where does it lead?

JEWISH GOTHIC

In the October 1998 issue of the National Foundation for Jewish Culture's online newsletter, *Culture Currents,* a brief, anonymous article on "Reviving the Jewish Gothic" defines Jewish Gothic as "the abiding mystical, sexual, underground, and sometimes sinister facets of Jewish culture."[6] It is a broad definition (as so many definitions of Gothic are) for what the article calls an "undercurrent" and a "counterculture" in American Jewish self-expression, one exemplified by such disparate works as Budd Schulberg's *What Makes Sammy Run?*, Rich Cohen's *Tough Jews*, Isaac Bashevis Singer's *Shadows on the Hudson*, and the films *Pi* and *A Price Above Rubies*. True, these works all exemplify dark sides of American Jewish life, but by lumping them together the article confuses social criticism with nostalgia, cultural representation with genre, and sex with the sinister. More helpful is the article's observation that the most interesting aspect of the Jewish Gothic being revived "is the brooding, shadowy Jewish mysticism that emerged out of the ghettos and shtetls of Eastern Europe," a dark side consisting of Hasids, golems, and dybbuks who represent "a certain authenticity that still resonates today."[7] It is not the obvious trappings of the Gothic (sinister monks, man-made monsters, and the supernatural) or the narrow focus on Jewish mysticism that makes this observation helpful. Rather, the connection made between the shadowy and mystical nature of the Jewish past and "authenticity," and the idea that this connection is mixed up with "the irony and edginess that defines American culture in the 1990's"[8] suggest a line of investigation for explaining the dark side that scares Steinberg's and Levitsky's detectives. Let us look at two examples of Jewish Gothic exhibiting such a connection.

Consider Jewishgothic.com. Opening the index page of Jewishgothic.com brings up two quotes. One is from the *Song of Songs* and the other, and more pertinent, is from Isaac Bashevis Singer's *The Mirror:* "For everything hidden must be revealed, each secret longs to be disclosed, each love yearns to be betrayed, everything sacred must be desecrated. Heaven and earth conspire that all good beginnings should come to a bad end."[9] Ignoring the quote's meaning in the context of Singer's story (and of his fiction generally), the web site appropriates the quote's magus-gaze at these cosmic fears and longings as an explanation of Jewish Gothic. In the site's manifesto, the web author asserts that Jewish Gothic is the "celebration" of a Jewish mystical tradition that (according to the author's reading) understands good and evil, and the contradictory nature of human experience, as bound up in the shadowy oneness of God.[10] Little wonder, then, that the web site is obsessed with origins (of Gothic, of Frankenstein), traditions (of the golem, of Jewish vampires), and the hoary texts that tell stories about good and evil (the Bible, the Talmud, the Zohar, and various non-Jewish texts from the seventeenth through the nineteenth centuries). Its attitude toward Jewish Gothic is pride and certainty that these esoteric and marginalized Jewish origins, traditions, and texts uncover the "eternal realities that afflict the human condition," the intertwining of life and death, stability and instability, pleasure and pain, holy and profane, and meaninglessness.[11] One detects here a compulsion to discover and to understand the verities of a complex and angst-ridden human life; it is not a crank site, by any means. Its author seems convinced that the Jewish past, as documented and memorialized in the sources cited, provides an authentic history of and guide to the "struggle of the human spirit with these realities."[12]

The seduction of memory here is not that retrieving these sources will make one a more strongly identified Jew, but that they will make one a wiser human being, regardless of religion, because they illuminate how the human struggle between, say, the altruistic and the venal reflects a larger cosmic reality. The terror of memory that the site mollifies is that there is no explanation or guiding memory for what it means to be human in a morally corrosive and emotionally disassociated modern society, and that, in the author's words, "all explanations of meaning fail to completely satisfy; all certainty is plagued by doubt."[13] Jewishgothic.com is an interpretation of the confusion of light and dark in human beings and in the contemporary world, a world that, despite the *world*wide web that hosts this site, is really the same as it ever was. History and memory on this site are bound up in the mysterious, eternal, and God-impelled yearning and conspiring toward betrayal, desecration, and bad endings that, according to the author, animate the ghosts and golems of Jewish mystical tradition.

Now consider David Rosenbaum's *Zaddik* (1993). What Jewishgothic.com explains and interprets, *Zaddik* dramatizes. But Rosenbaum's detective story is also particularly significant because it opens a wider and earlier window on the formulation, during the nineties, of a theme for Jewish Gothic, for the connection between the shadowy and mystical nature of the Jewish past and "authenticity." That theme is the uncanny nature of returning and recovery. *Zaddik* revolves around the theft and recovery of a mysterious diamond that has historic significance for a particular sect of ultra-Orthodox Hasidic Jews, the Satmar Hasidim. Dov Taylor, ex–New York policeman and a recovering alcoholic in search of his Jewish roots, is hired by the Satmarer Rebbe to return the diamond to the Satmarers so that he can include it in his daughter's marriage dowry. The rebbe hopes that her marriage to the son of the Lubavitcher Rebbe, uniting the Satmar and Lubavitch sects, will help to hasten the coming of the Messiah. This, however, is only one of two mysteries in the novel, a frame mystery that introduces readers to Taylor and to the cast of characters, who include a Polish aristocrat and Nazi who is the prime antagonist; a Jewish assassin, called the Cutter, who works for him; and the Lubavitch-affiliated rabbi and his daughter, who help Taylor as he investigates the case. Book two of the novel is the mystery within a mystery, which takes place two centuries earlier in Lublin, Poland, "a place of mystery" (200), concerning the Hasidic rebbe and zaddik ("righteous one") Jacob Isaac ha-Hozeh, the Seer of Lublin, "and the great conspiracy he had masterminded unto his death" (189). The hidden connections between the two mysteries convey the hidden connections between past and present, and between returning and recovery, woven into Rosenbaum's detective story.

Taylor the detective explores and enables these hidden connections. His "recovery" in the novel is both of and from his family history and its legacy, as readers learn in the prologue, where they share Taylor's remembrance of the day his grandmother, Rebecca, told the five-year-old Taylor how she and her husband, Sam, fled the Bolsheviks and crossed the Bessarabian border into Rumania. Caught at the border by a Red Army soldier, Rebecca and Sam are brought to a small shed where another soldier is left to guard them while the first soldier goes to find his commanding officer. Rebecca, larger and stronger than the "small, slender" Sam, offers a bribe to the young soldier, and when he tries to collect it she pins him to the wall and throttles him to death. Rebecca tells Taylor, "God will punish me. You hear me, Dov? God will punish me. But if I didn't do it, there would be no Dov because your mother would never be born" (4). Rebecca tells her story as she is bringing Taylor to see his aunt, a Holocaust survivor with a dead eye who is, to the five-year-old boy, old and ugly, and whose apartment he finds dirty and repellent. When he cries and tells Rebecca that he hates his aunt, Rebecca calls him a "murderer," and then promises that if he kisses his aunt she'll take him to Coney Island. Taylor dutifully kisses his aunt, but the confusions and ironies of this episode engender in him a conflict predicated on whether the necessary evils committed in the past produce good (his family's continuity) or simply more evil: "He felt guilty and angry. Maybe someday he would kill all the Nazis in the world, and then God would forgive him for finding Tante Leche disgusting. My grandmother is a murderer, Dov Taylor thought. Maybe someday I'll be a murderer, too" (5). Taylor's matrilineal inheritance, which follows the legal basis of Jewish identity, is power—the physical and spiritual power of his grandmother and, in the wake of the Holocaust and the founding of the State of Israel, the power to take violent action in the political sphere to ensure Jewish survival or to take revenge against oppressors of the past. Taylor does become a murderer—

he accidentally kills a young boy during a stakeout—and his middle-class life falls apart, so the question of how to wield power in a way that is not destructive and does not bring down heavenly punishment becomes Taylor's psychological and spiritual "problem." The hidden sources of the power he inherits, and hence of his problem, are a dark and repressed side of Taylor's Jewish family memory because, if mishandled, those sources threaten the future of Judaism and the meaning of a Jewish identity. But Taylor must recover that repressed memory to return to physical and spiritual health.

First, however, Taylor needs a guide back, and that guide is Hasidism and Jewish mysticism. At the story's beginning Taylor is enrolled in both Alcoholics Anonymous and a *ba'alei teshuva* (returnees to the faith) class run by the Lubavitcher Hasidim. Taylor, trying to make himself over, is at first focused on the outer appearances of ultra-Orthodox Jewish identity, and, looking at himself in the mirror, bearded and wearing tefillin, he sees there a ludicrous and pathetic shade of the Jewish past: "I look like my great-grandfather, he thought, an old man, a ghost out of the nineteenth century, an antique Jew in a dusty photo album. Boo! he said to his face in the mirror. Or rather, he thought, *Oy,* boo!" (36). Taylor shaves off his beard and drops out of the Judaism class, but his teacher, Rabbi Kalman, insists to Taylor that it is his inner "*yikhus,* merit," of a kind "that we call *zekhus avos*" (45), the spiritual merit of his Hasidic forebear, Rabbi Hirsh Leib, the Zaddik of Orlik, that can help him recover from his alcoholism and "his sickness of the heart." *Yikhus,* from the Hebrew for "genealogy," and derived from the root *ykhs,* "relationship," sets the tone for Taylor's return to the Jewish past, for when Kalman enlists Taylor's detective services for the Satmarer Rebbe he is also setting up Taylor for a lesson in Jewish family relationships. Brought to the Satmarer Rebbe's house in Williamsburg, Brooklyn, Taylor is told by the Rebbe that he is a murderer, that the "blood of assassins flows" in his veins (63), but also that Hirsh Leib, Taylor's "great-great-grandfather is in trouble, too. Like you. These troubles of ours, this *tsuris,* has a long, long history. You could help him. You could help each other. That would truly be a great deed, a *mitzvah*" (68). Taylor is the product and living embodiment of all his forebears, a portal between their past and his present. The rebbe's use of present tense, in fact, makes clear that he conceives of Jewish history not only as a series of troubles, but also as synchronous, with the troubles of the past and present happening at the same time, as if past and present were simply two parts of the same family consciousness. When, after meeting with the rebbe, Taylor begins to have mysterious contacts with Hirsh Leib—seeing him in a dream (73), feeling his feelings (99–100), hearing and seeing Hirsh Leib comfort him during a life-threatening moment (173–174)—it turns out that, in contrast to the self-parody in front of the mirror, Taylor is indeed inhabited by a shade of the Jewish past: his forebear's consciousness, a hidden part of his own.

Using Taylor as a "vessel," the Satmarer Rebbe accesses Hirsh Leib's consciousness and plunges Taylor and readers into a mystical past (where Elijah the prophet and the Angel of Death walk about disguised as poor Jews) in order for Hirsh Leib to narrate a memory repressed by history: that Jacob Isaac ha-Hozeh had misused his spiritual power, and that the consequences of his failure to make good out of evil led to his and Hirsh Leib's death. The Seer attempted to bribe Napoleon—after his escape from Elba and in the months before Waterloo—with the mysterious diamond the Seer had found tangled in the roots of a strange plant, so as to bring about the pre-messianic final battle of Gog and Magog. The Seer means to use his power as a zaddik "to unite the upper and lower worlds" (264) and force redemption before "we will all be murdered" (250), a reference to the future pogroms and to the Holocaust that the Seer, with his gift of seeing "from one end of the world to the other" (275), knows is coming. Despite the dangers of his enterprise, both spiritual and physical, the Seer leaps "into the darkness" (215) because he hopes that by wielding his spiritual power he can protect the Jews, in his time and in the future, against the political and physical power of the non-Jewish states in which they live. "This world is not your world," says Prince Adam Czartoryski to the Seer. Czartoryski, the Polish nobleman who helps bring Napoleon to Lublin, warns: "If you play in this world without armies, without power, you and all your people will be crushed" (221). The Seer's conspiracy does indeed go awry, and he is mortally wounded, and Hirsh Leib killed, by Czartoryski's evil, anti-Semitic brother, who steals the Seer's diamond and sends it on its historical peregrinations that eventually terminate in New York City. The Jews, in turn, suffer through a baleful modern history, and the Holocaust happens.

Rosenbaum's recovered and reinvented memories of nineteenth century Lublin and of the second and third generations of Hasidic masters—whose source, as he acknowledges, is Martin Buber's *Tales of the Hasidim*—thus return Taylor and readers to an imagined Jewish past that is a guide to and a lesson about the tellurian and cosmic sources of power. The power of violent action is rooted in an imperfect human body subject to passion and sickness; Hirsh Leib, as Taylor finds out, was also an alcoholic and sick at heart, and despite the physical strength he shares in common with Taylor (Dov is Hebrew for "bear," and Hirsh Leib is Yiddish for "deer lion") Leib cannot save either the Seer or himself from the furies of a tellurian sphere where Jews lack political power. The source of spiritual power is God, and the magnitude of God's strength defies human control: the Seer, for all his spiritual prowess, overreaches himself and fails to bring redemption for the Jews: "I saw too much, and I was fooled. Now I know. The stone cannot purchase paradise; it cannot bring the worlds together until the broken vessel, man, is mended" (284). Given the Seer's insight, the cosmic challenge of *tikkun*, of physical and spiritual repair, needs constant attention; ignoring or repressing the memory of that challenge threatens Jewish continuity as much as or more than do the troubles and pogroms history visits upon the Jews. That challenge, and the human foibles that Hirsh Leib and the Seer are subject to, are what describe the "authentic" and mixed nature of human experience, and, as the characters in the contemporary mystery illustrate, the way that challenge is met describes a family history: the evil Czartoryski's heir is the Polish Nazi who dies unrepentant and greedy; the Nazi's mistress is the descendent of a Polish mistress who, once before, returned the diamond to the Satmars; Sarah, the daughter of Rabbi Kalman (and Taylor's love interest) is a descendent of Soreh, Hirsh Leib's wife; there are even minor Hasidic characters who return with the same foibles they had in Lublin; and Rosenbaum's Satmarer Rebbe (whose forebear in real life, Rabbi Moses Teitelbaum of Ujhely, was a student of Jacob Isaac ha-Hozeh) is the Seer's heir, struggling like the Seer with the desire to speed the coming of the Messiah.

The only new character is the Cutter, a survivor of the Holocaust and a tormented soul who believes it possible that good can come from evil: "So didn't God Himself use evil to achieve His ends? When the Cutter was a child in the camps, didn't the old rabbi tell him that God was testing His people? . . . And all those throats he had cut for Branch 40 of the Mossad, . . . wasn't that blood shed to keep His children safe?" (9–10). The Cutter is a product of modernity and heir to the terror of the Holocaust. He has internalized the violence he witnessed, and he has rationalized that power as a form of justice, when in fact it is an expression of his Jewish self-hate, since he believes that the Holocaust and his victimization are the result of the Hasidim "living up to the worst imaginings of the Christians" (396); the "bad" Jews, like his father the Hasidic ritual slaughterer, got what they deserved. Thinking that he has converted evil into good, he fails to see that he too lives up to these terrifying imaginings, shocking the gentile police as well as the Hasidim by employing the methods of ritual slaughter to kill one of his Hasidic victims. His self-deception leads him to become an assassin for hire, a contemporary golem cut off from humankind and easily recruited by both the Israelis and Odessa, the postwar Nazi organization. As a golem he symbolizes the perverse effects that the violence of the twentieth century and the power to take violent action in the political sphere have had on Jewish identity and Jewish community. The assimilation of a kind of will to thuggishness has created, as Taylor notes, "Jewish Storm troopers...Jews who could watch another Jew murdered and do nothing. There were Jews who would murder other Jews" (375). The Cutter, jealous, ashamed, and enraged at Hasidim, who he imagines think they are "the only real Jews" (396), is a bad return on the Jewish exposure to and investment in the power of physical violence.

Like Jewishgothic.com, Rosenbaum's novel turns to esoteric Jewish traditions and texts—Hasidic ultra-Orthodoxy and Jewish mysticism—to uncover the "eternal realities" of time, space, and identity as guides for understanding the moral chiaroscuro of human experience. Unlike the web site, however, the detective genre offers Rosenbaum the opportunity to explore *how* Hasidism and Jewish mysticism function as avatars of returned memory. Taylor's memories of his forebear's Hasidic world (really countermemories, because Rosenbaum re-narrates a number of Buber's *Tales* and replaces the traditional image of the zaddik with an image of his modern, urban alcoholic) convey knowledge about the irrational and uncontrollable sources of power, memories that produce dread and anxiety: "He had awakened from his dream, or vision, or memory—he wasn't sure what to call it or even how to think about it—to find himself as unprotected, as easily rattled, as a newborn infant. It felt as if his skin had been peeled off" (290). Rosenbaum uses his novel's weird kosher hybridity, its yoking of detective fiction with a Jewish subject and Gothic atmosphere, to tell a story about how what was once *heymish* (homey) for Jews—the Hasidic world centered around the rebbe's courtyard—is *unheimlich* (uncanny) for contemporary American Jews.

It is scary for Taylor to have concealed, obscure, and mystical memories returned to him, but that is not the terror of memory lurking in Rosenbaum's version of the Jewish Gothic. The terror underlying Rosenbaum's story is that without these memories—without what are really postmemories and countermemories that provide an air of Jewish "authenticity" and a fictional moral anchor—Jews will become like the Cutter, golems in the modern world who have power but no real master. Like that figure of terror, and like a number of characters in the novel who work for the Mossad, the Israeli intelligence service, Jews will become collaborators and betrayers capable of killing and conning other Jews, for their own reasons or at the behest of others.

Of course, those postmemories and countermemories have no real claim on authenticity, and this anxiety shows in Rosenbaum's detective fiction through its emphasis on the fallibility and limitations of human agency. For example, Taylor's acceptance of human inability to control either spiritual power or the power of violent action helps Hirsh Leib recover from alcoholism (281), and in return Hirsh Leib helps him recover the diamond (447). Hirsh Leib also helps Taylor to understand that the diamond, as a reflection of the purity and beauty of God, inspires jealousy in human beings who wish to possess that power, and so it must be thrown away (284, 449). That act also symbolizes his awareness that, if it takes almost three hundred years and much generational *yichus* for an unconventional zaddik such as himself to recover from the mistakes of the past—for a zaddik is what the Satmarer Rebbe calls him after Taylor tells the rebbe that he threw the diamond away—then the best that imperfect humans can do is to accept their limitations, as well as the cosmic deferral of redemption, and simply try to reconnect with, and so mend, their families. Once he accepts these limitations Taylor recognizes he must spare the Cutter's life, because doing so will stop the hidden spiritual repercussions of the Seer's mistake, the presumption that one can control the uncontrollable. No good will ever come from evil, Rosenbaum's novel suggests, even if it is to save future generations of Jews, for the evil of taking violent action in the political sphere generates unknown repercussions that are morally corrosive and that harm the Jewish family. To imagine otherwise, to imagine that good can come from evil, is an inauthentic memory that is associated in *Zaddik* with the Cutter's perverted thinking.

The moral of Rosenbaum's detective story thus reflects how the seduction of memory in *Zaddik* satisfies a longing in the American Jewish popular imagination to placate misgivings about the limitations of imaginative re-creations of the Jewish past, re-creations that, like the Cutter, can turn monstrous.

Zaddik's juxtaposition of a Jewish need for postmemories and countermemories against Taylor's recognition of the limitations of human agency suggests that it is not just nostalgia for a *heymish* Hasidic world that is at work. Rosenbaum's reimagining of a mystical East European Jewish past is also a metaphor for Jewishness as something complex and difficult and itself uncanny—something that is and is not available to American Jews. "They think the Holy One, blessed is he, is a friendly, kindly old man whose heart is brimming with love and forgiveness," Rabbi Kalman says of the religious returnees in Taylor's class. "It is hard to serve him. This . . . they don't like" (37). Taylor's experiences with memory posit the possibility of bringing to consciousness a "hard" Jewishness that demands spiritual accountability and personal self-sacrifice in the face of pogroms and political oppression. Such Jewishness was once familiar to Jews, but is now an estranged and strange identity from the past that is extraordinarily difficult to inhabit, and not nearly as cohesive and coherent as the Jewish returnees wish. As a fictional detective, then, Taylor has the functions of negotiating this difficulty and acting as a guide for how to accept and assimilate the terrors and seductions of memory, as illuminated by his recovery of and from the past; this is what makes him a zaddik. As a creative riff on Buber's explanation of the zaddik as a helper, teacher, and guide for his Hasidim (5–6), and as an embodiment of the union of opposites, "of heavenly light and earthly fire, of spirit and nature" (14), Taylor is the character that discharges anxiety about the inability of most American Jews to engage the supposedly unconscious parts of themselves and of the Jewish past that "they don't like." Through Taylor, *Zaddik* provides a convenient mooring for American Jewish readers between recollection and reconstruction of the past, a place where readers can ponder from a safe distance questions about the uncanny nature of return and recovery, about the limitations of human control over power, and about the uncertainties of "authentic" Jewish knowledge. Or, to put it another way, *Zaddik* provides a convenient mooring place between the past and the present where American Jews can ponder the "shadowy, brooding" issues that describe how and why they might kill or save their own Jewishness.

Here we return to the interrogation that so scared Steinberg's and Levitsky's detectives, but better able now to appreciate how the complex of fears and longings in "Wailing Reed," "Jacob's Voice," and *Zaddik* reflects the same anxieties about the instability and ambiguities of history that the British literary scholar David Punter argues is a defining feature of contemporary Gothic in general. If the terror that Gothic incites depends, according to Punter, upon an "awareness of mutability, an understanding of the ways in which history itself, and certainly narratives of history, are not stable, do not constitute a rock onto which we might cling,"[14] then contemporary Gothic, as he notes in another essay, "has discovered, one might say, the impossibility, the undecidability, of discovery . . . that the original 'form of history,' we might say, is not that to be found in social-historical textbooks but that which we overhear, in myths and legends, in half understood tales, in fears and anxieties about the past."[15] Punter notes that this awareness of the instability of narratives, historical as well as psychoanalytical and literary, is constelled in an increasingly prismatic way in the contemporary Gothic, itself undergoing a dizzying array of transformations and mutations.[16]

The terror of memory incited in the Jewish Gothic is one of these transformations, for the Jewish Gothic, as I see it, is a complex of fears and longings about the mutability and instability of time, space, and "authentic" Jewish identities that finds particular expression in postmemories and countermemories of a dark and mystical Jewish past, which is to say in postmemories and countermemories concerning the ghost stories and mystical traditions of the Ashkenazi and Sephardic Jewish pasts. Conceiving of that complex of fears and longings as the dark side haunting the American Jewish popular imagination usefully delimits Jewish Gothic as a descriptive term and suggests why the "brooding, shadowy" cultural legacies of these Jewish pasts have incited a recognizable strain of popular explanation, interpretation, and investigation in the American Jewish popular arts and in American Jewish detective stories. The Jewish detectives sent to investigate and solve the instability of Jewish narratives about identity and the past provide reassurance that there are moral and temporal anchors available to American Jews who take the terror of memory to heart.

No doubt, the need for such anchors in Steinberg's, Levitsky's, and Rosenbaum's detective stories is in part a response to the impact of the Holocaust on the American Jewish popular imagination. The Holocaust, as we have seen, is implicated in all three stories. But having raised the importance of the uncanny as a theme in the Jewish Gothic, let me turn to a scholar of the eighteenth century and her reading of the uncanny in order to mine an insight from her ambitious but intriguing hypothesis. According to Terry Castle, the uncanny is a product of "the profound cultural shift" of the eighteenth century; it was invented as "a kind of toxic side effect," of the "aggressively rationalist imperatives" of the Enlightenment.[17] Freud's essay on the uncanny provides Castle with a model for understanding the cultural legacy of that eighteenth-century invention: an awareness that "the more we seek enlightenment, the more alienating our world becomes; the more we seek to free ourselves, Houdini-like, from the coils of superstition, mystery, and magic, the more tightly, paradoxically, the uncanny holds us in its grip."[18] In other words, the uncanny is an expression of human bewilderment that "the more one understands, the less clear—one finds—things are."[19]

It is a long way from the Gothic of the eighteenth century to the Jewish Gothic of the twentieth, yet in the detective stories I have examined there is, alongside references to the Holocaust, clearly a trace of the "enlightened bewilderment" that Castle sees as a legacy of the Enlightenment.[20] Reading *Zaddik* and "Jacob's Voice," and even "Wailing Reed," it seems as if now that American Jews have unprecedented access—thanks to new museums of culture and testimony, new Jewish studies programs, and new information technologies—to a plethora of histories, documents and artifacts offering new and putatively objective knowledge of the Jewish past, that past is nevertheless returned as more mystifying and terrifying than ever. The postmemories and countermemories of Steinberg's, Levitsky's, and Rosenbaum's stories are the Gothic doubles of those histories, documents, and artifacts: dark reflections of the current expansion of information and understanding about the Jewish past. And so the "enlightened bewilderment" that invites American Jewish detection is not only an after-effect of the Holocaust, but also a product of that much more recent and relevant cultural shift in American Jewish life noted at the beginning of this chapter: the turn to remembrance and to the authority of history as explanation and rationalization for what it means to be a Jew.

Is the Jewish Gothic in the detective stories examined here, then, a kind of toxic side effect of the mythologization of Jewish memory—a toxic side effect of the memorializing imperatives that are spurring the contemporary *kulturkampf* over the Jewish past? I want to close this chapter by offering an opening to an answer: analyzing the place of the future in a tale of the past. Richard Zimler's tale of Sepharad, *The Last Kabbalist of Lisbon* (1998), is set during the Inquisition against the Jews in Spain and Portugal during the fifteenth and sixteenth centuries. Zimler employs the protagonist's memory of the persecution of his fellow Conversos, Jews forcibly baptized as Christians by the Inquisition, and of the Lisbon massacre during Passover of 1506, as a resonant backdrop for his murder mystery. Indeed, what the backdrop immediately calls to mind, as Andrew Furman points out, is the Holocaust. The Conversos' victimization, their secret hiding places and their survivor guilt, and the "elusive truth" that their persecution and slaughter illustrates—that the Holocaust "was not so much an isolated catastrophe as it was the culmination of centuries of European violence directed against the Jews"—bears out Furman's contention that *The Last Kabbalist of Lisbon* can be read as an allusive treatment of the Holocaust.²¹ But it can also be read as more, as is attested by the introductory frame tale about the discovery of a memory secreted for the future.

Zimler begins his tale with an "Author's Note" about the discovery of the manuscript that is Berekiah Zarco's recollection of the murder of his uncle and teacher, the "renowned kabbalist" Abraham Zarco. The author of the note is a graduate student doing research on Sephardic poetry in Istanbul. A remodeling project at the "ancient home at the fringes of Istanbul's medieval Jewish Quarter, the Balat," where he is staying, uncovers a "secret lair" in the cellar that contains "a tik, the small cylindrical chest used by Sephardic Jews to house the Torah," in which is found not a Torah but "a leather-bound set of handwritten manuscripts, nine in all" (11–12). Six of the manuscripts are kabbalistic treatises, and three contain Berekiah Zarco's tale. But the significance here is in Zimler's secularization and manipulation of the *genizah* (traditionally "a room attached to the synagogue where books and ritual objects containing the name of God—which cannot be destroyed according to Jewish law—were buried when they wore out and could no longer be used in the normal ritual"²²) as a metonymy for the space of Jewish memory. Zimler takes advantage of the genizah's similarity to a crypt, and of the lesser-known function of genizahs as hiding places for valuable books and objects and as storage places for heretical texts that the religious authorities have taken out of circulation but not burned, in order to portray the secular genizah that contains Zarco's tale as a resting place, a repository, and a secret annex for Jewish memory of the underground Jewish life of the Conversos. Sealed in the foundation of the Sephardic house, Zarco's genizah is revealed, tellingly, when the new owner of the building decides to remodel. Zimler's point seems clear: the Sephardic Jewish past that interests the author of the note is recovered not through his academic research but through the renovation of a Sephardic Jewish house by new owners for their present needs, renovation that unearths, reanimates, and gives the author a specter-memory from that house's past. Or, in Terry Castle's terms, the student/author, seeking enlightenment, recovers a mystery instead.

Interestingly, the houses and bodies of the Conversos in Zimler's detective story echo the haunted house of Sephardic Jewry in the author's note. They too store and hide information and memories awaiting future recovery. The cellar of the Zarco house in Lisbon—which is the scene of the murder—doubles as a synagogue, contains a genizah, and, like all good haunted houses, accesses a secret passage the existence of which explains a number of clues at the murder scene. The Conversos of Zimler's story also echo such a house, for their ostensibly

New Christian bodies are the storage and hiding places, and, for those who elect to embrace Christianity, the final resting places, of their Jewish memories and Jewish identities. Setting the murder mystery during Passover offers Zimler the opportunity to underscore the evocative relation between memory and freedom and between text and memory for these Conversos, who long for redemption from their present oppression. Abraham Zarco, it turns out, is murdered in the course of selling hidden Jewish manuscripts to redeem them from captivity in Spain and Portugal, and to ensure, despite the Inquisition, the continuity of Judaism and Jewish memory. Berekiah Zarco, whose job as detective in the novel is not only to solve his uncle's murder, but also to investigate how unstable and slave-like a Converso existence is, constantly refers to his "Torah memory," a supposedly kabbalistic concept that connotes the ability to "write" memory in one's mind. Like the genizah, Berekiah's mind is a safe storage place for the kabbalah that his uncle has taught him, and for the clues to his uncle's murder—safe, that is, against the human storm that rages all around him during the Lisbon massacre, which claimed between two and four thousand New Christian lives, and which, like a Gothic storm, reflects the hostile and doleful "natural" world of Converso existence.

As detective, Berekiah investigates ways to understand that world and the violence that describes it. While his response to the Lisbon massacre may well recall how survivors looked for ways to understand the Holocaust, his crisis of faith about the existence of God in particular (127, 165, 199) reflects how Berekiah is also investigating the coming of "a new era . . . a world defined by history texts, not the works of God" (104), an age of rationalism and secularism that looks a lot like both an Enlightenment and a post-Holocaust landscape. In a key passage, Berekiah shares his vision of this new era with a New Christian priest who studied kabbalah with his uncle, but who ultimately remains loyal to the Church. For Berekiah that new era is a refuge from religion, but one in which kabbalah helps inform and reform his understanding of God:

> "Breathe in that darkness, Carlos. Something new is out there between the odor of shit and smoke and forest. A new landscape is forming, a secular countryside that will give us sanctuary from the burning shores of religion. We've only gotten a whiff of it so far. But it's coming. And nothing the Old Christians can do can keep it from giving us refuge."
>
> Carlos answers with a preacherly, skeptical voice: "Pray tell me, what will this new landscape have as a foundation if not religion?"
>
> "I haven't got a clue, Carlos. The landscape hasn't condensed

yet. There'll be mystics and skeptics, of that I have no doubt. But neither priests nor friars, nor deacons nor bishops nor Popes will find a home there. If they take one step on our land, we'll throw them right out on their heads. And no didactic rabbis either. The minute you unfurl your scroll of commandments, we'll slit your throat!"

"You should beg God's forgiveness for that," Carlos warns me.

"Go sing it to the goats! I'm through begging! My God grants neither forgiveness nor punishment."

"Ein Sof?" the priest asks, referencing the kabbalistic concept of an unknowable God without any recognizable attributes. When I nod, he adds: "There's little comfort in a God beyond everything."

"Ah comfort... For that, my dear friend, I want a wife to lie with at night and children to hug, not God. You can keep the Lord written on the pages of the Old and New Testaments for yourself. I'll take the one who's unwritten." (218–219)

Here Berekiah struggles to understand the transition to a landscape where the mystical and the rational, the sacred and the secular, collective memory and self-knowledge share space in ways that are both heretical and informing. True, Berekiah's "secular countryside" can be read as either an Enlightenment or a post-Holocaust landscape, but either reading sets up an implied comparison between Berekiah's tale and the frame tale. To Berekiah the new landscape will be one where God remains unwritten and—as in the *tik* where kabbalah and Berekiah's detective fiction replaced the Torah scroll that should have occupied it—what does get written becomes a counter-scroll whose "true" narrative frees Jews to be family to each other rather than slaves to commandments or to their oppressors. In both Berekiah's tale and in the frame tale, the search for an understanding of the past reveals that the future depends on a mystery and the lessons learned from it: the mystery of an unwritten God in the former, and the mystery of a detective story in the latter.

How apt, therefore, that Berekiah is an illuminator of manuscripts. He certainly sheds light on the counter-scroll and on the seduction of memory in this story: As the last kabbalist of the title, Berekiah, like Dov Taylor, is the helper, teacher, and guide able to bring about a union of opposites—of the past and the present, of the irrational and the rational, of a mystical Jewish tradition and the Enlightenment. He illustrates his uncle's dictum that "a kabbalist should try to live at an intersection of lines—'where two become one'" (165); as the hero of the story, Berekiah recalls both the visionary Dov Taylor and the visionary musician of Steinberg's story, both of whom exemplify how to overcome fear of weird kosher hybridity in order to make a way into the Jewish future. Like them, Berekiah the kabbalist detective is the right kind of hybrid for the future.

Not so the Conversos. The unstable New Christian "masks" that the Conversos must wear to hide their Jewish identity from their Old Christian tormentors block passage to a new landscape because those masks estrange them from themselves and from each other. Unable to assimilate their masks to their identities, or hybridize the two, the Conversos inhabit a landscape without foundation, and so are vulnerable to the worst excrescences, physical and moral, of the Inquisitional storm that rages around them. This is how Berekiah explains the behavior of the murderer (312), for it turns out that his uncle was killed not by Old Christians during the massacre but, ironically, by a Jewish informer and collaborator who used the massacre as a cover. Significantly, Berekiah's uncle had used the murderer's face as a model for the face of Haman, the archenemy of the Jews in the Book of Esther, in a haggadah stolen from his genizah. The murderer's face has become his mask; in the new era Jews like him become "whatever the situation demands. One must be flexible . . . change one's form according to circumstance. A beard and sumptuous clothes for Lisbon. . . . In Constantinople, I may even become a Moslem. It's the same God, after all" (289). Like the Cutter, this murderer, too, has no real master and lives without a foundation, and Berekiah finally sees him clearly as a figure of terror, "the Wandering Jew, a courier not of books or merchandise, but his own soul" (289–290).

We see, then, that Zimler's mystery revolves around the central conceit of recovering foundations in order to remodel and re-anchor literal and figurative Jewish houses for the future, and in so doing exorcise the ghosts that haunt them. Such remodeling is a necessary aftereffect of the fierce storms that force Jews to consider their houses in the light of the landscape their families inhabit. As Berekiah concludes, his uncle understood the true meaning of the Lisbon massacre "when he saw the possibilities which would spring from his death at the hands of the murderer. For better or for worse, he concluded that our family, our people, had reached a terrible impasse, and that only his violent death would compel us to break through" (310). Abraham Zarco's death, and the death of his era of Sephardic Jewry, compels Berekiah to leave Lisbon for Constantinople (the intersection between Europe and Asia) and to write his manuscripts—in essence, compels Berekiah to remodel the haunted house of Sephardic Jewry. Zimler's mystery ends with Berekiah's warning to Jews to abandon Europe because the bloodlust of its kings and bishops is unappeasable. After all, "can you be sure that the Christians won't one day come for you, for all of us? That traitors like Diego won't help them?" (312) Zimler's mystery, of course, assumes that readers will hear the echo of the Holocaust in Berekiah's question and agree that, yes, they did come and they were helped. In that light, the deaths of those victims mirror Abraham Zarco's, and thus the point of Zimler's detective story is that, like Abraham Zarco's death, theirs are the specter-memories compelling a remodeling of Jewish "houses." To me, therefore, *The Last Kabbalist of Lisbon* is an allusive treatment not only of the Holocaust, but also of the connection between the Enlightenment and post-Holocaust landscapes, both of which give shape to questions about how to prepare for a Jewish future that is not quite visible.

Berekiah's tale seduces readers and discharges their anxiety about the future by ending with a peek at his own. Readers learn that after he settles in Constantinople he starts a "family" that includes not only his wife and children, mother and aunt, but also his gay and Arab friend Farid, Farid's companion, and their adopted children. This multigenerational and multicultural family comforts Berekiah and makes his heart glad, and he writes that "maybe I have found that secular landscape I predicted so many years ago" (305). Although Berekiah's family story is pitched at a much lower tone than his almost strident appeal for Jews to leave Europe before something (like the Holocaust) overtakes them, it is the part of Berekiah's tale that, unlike his warning, has not been recovered too late. But it is also the part of Berekiah's tale that reflects the terror of memory: if Berekiah's appeal that Jews leave Europe was written but never heard (and so those memories still could not prepare Jews for the future), perhaps even his example of Jews from a "shadowy, brooding," and mystical Jewish past making a life in a secular landscape still will not prepare Jews for the fearsome unknown of the future. In *The Last Kabbalist of Lisbon,* Berekiah's obsession with memory, and with the recovery of its mysteries, anchors his present and provides a key to securing the future, but conveying this urgent matter to other Jews requires that he return to Portugal to rescue those who still cannot see their inevitable fate and who are unable to prepare themselves for life in a secular landscape. Significantly, Berekiah ends the manuscript with a literal key in hand, the key to his old house in Lisbon, ready to turn away from his own future and return to an unstable place and time to save his fellow Jews. The Jewish Gothic evident in Zimler's detective story thus expresses anxiety and fear not about the future per se but about whether all the memory available to American Jews in the present is well preparing them for it.

And so if Jewish Gothic is a toxic side effect of the mythologization of Jewish memory, in the evidence is the kind of terror given expression by the terror of memory in Zimler's detective story: that the more American Jews remember the past to understand the present, the less clear the future becomes. As Zimler's detective story suggests, this terror is related to the perception that a new era is coming, if not here already.

By turning the possessions of the past over and over, the American Jewish detective stories examined in this chapter challenge readers to consider their passage into the future, and to ponder who or what they are likely to become, or what possessions they will bequeath if they continue on the same path. Conversely, these stories ask, what might happen if readers change paths? Yet, although the recovery of memory in the stories is made to seem an essential task for contemporary Jews who wish to defend fidelity to Jewish culture—who wish to defend the faith as they careen toward a new era—the Jewish future in the tales remains a vague concept, and Jewish identity in the future an even vaguer one. Zimler returns to the Sephardic Conversos as a way of dramatizing his generation's struggle with Jewish memory, a ghost returned unexpectedly and uncannily, and against which that generation's preparation for a Jewish future must be measured—though where that future goes, and what it promises aside from more persecution and violence, is only lightly sketched.

But preparing for the future and predicting it are not the same, of course. Whether the mythologization of Jewish memory is the harbinger of a new era in the Jewish world or, as the cultural theorist Andreas Huyysen argues, evidence of a global new era brought about by "a fundamental crisis" in the human perception of time, space, and identity (as formulated by the Enlightenment and by twentieth-century modernization),[23] preparing for such an era clearly vexes the American Jewish popular imagination. Jewish Gothic is therefore a contemporary popular cultural symptom of the difficult and confusing demands of making a secure Jewish future, a symptom expressed by the weird kosher hybridity of Steinberg's, Levitsky's, Rosenbaum's, and Zimler's American Jewish detective stories.

5

HARD-BOILED HOLOCAUST

> With respect to the victim, the hybridization of fact and fiction creates different problems; the clarity demanded by a story tailored to mass consumption tends to generate simplistic ideological categories to cope with the elusive and spiritually unedifying subject of large-scale physical suffering and submission to death.
> —Sidra DeKoven Ezrahi, *By Words Alone*

As we have seen in the previous chapter, the facts of the Holocaust weigh heavily on American Jewish detective stories that focus on the Jewish past. Janice Steinberg, Ronald Levitsky, David Rosenbaum, and Richard Zimler all see the past through the Holocaust, and the distortions reflected through that lens both trouble and challenge the stories they tell. Trouble them because the Holocaust, whether invoked or evoked, inevitably mobilizes questions that follow each story like a somber cortege: Is the mysticism of *Zaddik* merely a pop-culture sop with which to pacify the persistence of evil in the shadow of the Holocaust? Can American Jews really ever go "home" as Berekiah Zarco does in *The Last Kabbalist of Lisbon,* when all that is left of that home is a genizah full of obscure treatises and old fictions? Have Jewishness and the Holocaust itself become commodities in America, to be retailed in the same way that Ira Nadler, in "Wailing Reed," retails rare klezmer recordings to interested collectors? If, as the literary critic Efraim Sicher observes, Jewish writers of the second and third generations after the Holocaust "must re-member themselves into a past that is fragmented and can be recovered only by painstaking research or in the imagination,"[1] then might not the figure of the Jewish detective be a metonymy for the contemporary American Jewish writer of popular fiction? And so the challenge: in a genre whose stories are both tailored to mass consumption and focused on the desire for justice, can a Jewish detective who seeks justice, and the writer who figures that detective, do justice to Holocaust victims? Or, to state that challenge as a question about kosher hybridity: what kind of narratives about American justice and Holocaust crimes are constructed in American Jewish detective stories?

It is these last two questions that I will explore in this chapter, and Sidra DeKoven Ezrahi's 1980 quote remains a clear and concise expression of the nature of the challenge such stories face. In the chapter "Documentation as Art," Ezrahi surveys what we might think of as the threshold genre into Holocaust literature, "documentary fiction," in which a writer employs the narrative techniques and character development of fiction to tell a true story, one based on diaries or other historical documents. It is, says Ezrahi, "the genre which presents, ostensibly at least, the most faithful historical reconstruction of the Holocaust" because "the assumption is that documentation lends authority as well as credibility to the representation of the unimaginable."[2] Analyzing the differences between the 1967 Soviet edition of Anatoli Kuznetsov's "documentary novel" *Babi Yar* and the unexpurgated edition that he released after his defection to the West in 1970, Ezrahi points out that while the facts in the former excoriate fascism, the same facts in the latter become an excoriation of "all oppressive social systems."[3] For Ezrahi, Kuznetsov's two editions dramatize "the ways in which facts, like fiction, are ultimately cultural constructs," which is not to say that the facts are "untrue," but rather that their interpretation is subject to contemporary social and cultural pressures, needs, and constraints.[4] This is a key part of Ezrahi's argument. She suggests that once we have a particular interpretation of Holocaust victims or of a particular Holocaust event in play in American popular culture, that interpretation should not be thought of as an isolated expression of Holocaust "meaning." The "simplistic ideological categories" that helped to shape popular meanings of the Holocaust in such works as Gerald Green's TV docudrama "Holocaust," Leon Uris's *Mila 18,* or John Hersey's *The Wall*—all "tailored to mass consumption" and transforming the Holocaust experience into pop-heroic epics—became, according to Ezrahi, "a component in the cultural perception" of the Holocaust.[5] They generated in popular culture "stereotypic responses which were compatible with a general avoidance or attempted redress" of the horrors of the Holocaust.[6] In other words, both Jewish and non-Jewish Americans are the heirs of a number of popular cultural constructs of the Holocaust and its meanings, but as cultural constructs these are not inevitable or unchanging or equally malign: like all cultural constructs they are of their time and place and serve particular social and cultural functions.

Hence, teasing out the social and cultural functions of narratives about American justice and Holocaust crimes in American Jewish detective stories, narratives that often borrow facts and tropes from documentary art (and so constitute not historical fiction per se but a kind of meta-historical fiction), means going beyond saying that, with respect to the victims, this story is good or that one bad, or assigning stories to this or that aesthetic category. Judging and assigning has its place, of course. Lawrence Langer brings both to bear on works of the popular imagination in "The Americanization of the Holocaust on Stage and Screen" (1983). He does so in response to Green's "Holocaust," and in order to provide a schema with which to discriminate between entertainment and art in docudramas about the Holocaust: the entertaining "drama of fate" marshals the heroic and so fails as a form of Holocaust art, whereas the "drama of doom" subverts our notions of heroism entirely, and as art enables "fresh insights into the Nazi mind, the victim, the spectator."[7] In contrast, Ezrahi's analysis of popular fiction about the Holocaust anticipates contemporary popular culture criticism—such as the essays in Yosefa Loshitzky's *Spielberg's Holocaust* (1997), Jeffrey Shandler's *While America Watches: Televising the Holocaust* (1999), and Alan Mintz's *Popular Culture and the Shaping of Holocaust Memory in America* (2001)—in that it reminds us that the hybridization of fact and fiction is a fine barometer of ideological tendencies as well as of social and cultural change. Close to twenty years separate "Holocaust" from *Schindler's List*, enough time for us to see that while the writers of American Jewish detective stories that I examine in this chapter have dispatched a similar kind of hero to solve Holocaust crimes, each hero has different social and cultural inflections.

Taking my cue from Ezrahi's analysis, then, my general argument in this chapter is that Ira Levin's *The Boys from Brazil* (1976), Zachary Klein's *No Saving Grace* (1993), and Rochelle Krich's *Angel of Death* (1994) and *Blood Money* (1999) all exemplify how the social and cultural functions of narratives about American justice and Holocaust crimes in detective stories correspond to the changing image of Holocaust victims in the American Jewish popular imagination, and to the changing image of their agent, the "Nazi hunter." That is, Levin's Yakov Liebermann, Klein's Matt Jacob, and Krich's Jessica Drake are "proxies" who, in their pursuit of various fictional Nazis, vocalize and animate attitudes about Holocaust victims that serve as markers of change in the shaping of Holocaust memory. Further, however, the incorporation of conventions and character traits associated with the hard-boiled detective in the stories of all three writers underscores the influence not only of an American popular genre, but also of gender, in determining the meaning of heroism and in meeting the challenge of doing justice to Holocaust victims. One implication that the kosher hybridity of Krich's hard-boiled

Jewish female detective raises is that defending fidelity to Jewish culture in the shadow of the Holocaust—a defense that is the cultural function of Krich's narrative about American justice and Holocaust crimes—is itself heroism of a kind; and down such mean streets an unconventional hero must walk, preferably one who can negotiate unconventional social and gender roles. This implication, appropriate to a character created by the daughter of Holocaust survivors, leads to my final observations about the ability of Krich's Jewish detective to do justice to Holocaust victims: that Krich's improvisation on the figure of the Nazi hunter enables her to investigate the Holocaust and its victims through an educational journey that shuttles back and forth between fact and fiction, the past and the present, and male and female; and that Krich's improvisation on the figure of the hard-boiled detective enables her to ruminate on the meaning of justice as it attaches to current images of Holocaust victims, images being shaped and circulated in the American Jewish popular imagination.

1976: THE VICTIM AS DETECTIVE

The key premise of Levin's *The Boys from Brazil* is that, thirty years after the Holocaust, and thirteen years after Adolf Eichmann's dramatic capture and trial, interest in the victims and perpetrators has waned. Famed Nazi hunter and Holocaust survivor Yakov Liebermann, whom Levin based on famed Nazi hunter and Holocaust survivor Simon Wiesenthal, has become a stale fixture on the temple and Hadassah lecture circuit. He is a fading cause for the Jewish philanthropists whose former largesse enabled his successes during the sixties, and simply a bother to the journalists who used to supply him information and celebrity but who now see his monomania as yesterday's news. Meanwhile, the fictional Dr. Josef Mengele, the infamous camp doctor at Auschwitz, whom Levin based on the real Dr. Josef Mengele, is also a fading figure. Exiled in South America and increasingly irrelevant to the *Kameradenwerk,* the postwar Nazi support network, his diabolical scheme to clone not only Hitler but also the family environment of Hitler's youth (making certain that the civil servant fathers who adopted the clones all die in their sixty-fifth year, in order to replicate the psychological environment and pathologies of the original) is considered by them to be more a liability than a planning priority, though Mengele and the *Kameradenwerk* share the ultimate priority of establishing a Fourth Reich. Both Liebermann and Mengele are two old men whom others see as stuck in the past, blinded by their obsessions, and at odds with their support organizations. Thus Levin predicates his thriller/mystery on a simple irony: with the future in the balance, readers know that Liebermann's detection of Mengele's plot and their climactic duel is of world historical importance, yet both men are consigned by their international backers to the backwaters of current history.

A page-turning premise and irony—both kept *The Boys from Brazil* on the bestseller list for fourteen weeks. While some reviewers admired Levin's facility in cranking out such "terrorburgers"[8] (he also wrote *Rosemary's Baby* and *The Stepford Wives*), others dismissed both the book and the film that followed it in the fall of 1978 as "preposterous" and "pretty silly stuff."[9] The tenor of these reviews, however, along with Levin's premise and irony, are suggestive of wider historical and cultural currents. So, before looking at the implications of Levin's figuring of Liebermann as a detective and a hero, I want to quickly consider the extent to which Levin's novel and the film adaptation reveal the state of American Jewish Holocaust memory on the eve of Gerald Green's *Holocaust,* which aired in April 1978 and is considered "a threshold event in the dynamics of Holocaust consciousness in America."[10]

As Levin's story suggests, the Eichmann trial, too, was a threshold event, and in considering the place of the Holocaust in the American Jewish popular imagination, we must remember that, like Green's *Holocaust,* the Eichmann trial was a televised spectacle. As Ezrahi points out, "The Eichmann trial, coming as it did after a decade and a half of documentation and testimony on the part of scholars and survivors, forcing its entry into the homes of all Americans who committed the minimal act of turning on their television sets, ensued in a spate of literary activity unprecedented at any time since the war."[11] While Jeffrey Shandler acknowledges Ezrahi's conclusion that the event left readily identifiable traces in the work of American writers such as Charles Reznikoff, Denise Levertov, Norma Rosen, Irving Feldman, and Arthur Cohen, he claims that the Eichmann trial telecasts "had a less enduring impact on American Holocaust remembrance in America than have . . . other contemporary phenomena," and that it failed to "become a fixture of American Holocaust memory."[12] Given the impact studies and television histories Shandler cites that document and illustrate American Jewish amnesia about the trial telecasts, his statement is quite accurate, but, as he himself observes, the trial found quite fertile ground in television and popular culture,[13] and in such "stories tailored to mass consumption" Nazis on the run and those who hunted them became very familiar figures, yoked together in various ways. The story of Eichmann and his capture and trial went through a number of popular incarnations: *Engineer of Death: The Eichmann Story* (1960) was a biographical drama that appeared on CBS; Rod Serling's "Death's Head Revisited" (1961) played out the trial as a *Twilight Zone* fantasy; the film *Operation Eichmann* (1961) was a fictionalized version of the capture starring Werner Klemperer as Eichmann; and *The House on Garibaldi Street* was a 1975 recounting by Isser Harel, the Mossad chief who directed the capture, that became a mass market bestseller and a 1979 made-for-television movie. Nazis and Nazi hunters clashed on television shows and in movies: a 1966 episode of the *The Saint,* titled "Locate and Destroy," placed the Bond-like Simon Templar in the midst of a struggle between the two in Peru; the third segment of Rod Serling's 1969 pilot episode of *Night Gallery,* "The Escape Route," is a Gothic fantasy about a Nazi trying to elude his pursuers by escaping into a picture; and Frederick Forsyth's 1972 thriller *The Odessa File,* made into a film in 1974, triangulated a gentile investigative journalist, Nazis, and the Mossad, making the capture of an SS man a family matter for the journalist.

These examples reflect how Eichmann's story captured the popular imagination, as well as the ways in which that story was reworked between 1960 and the 1976–1978 period. In short, a lasting impact of the Eichmann trial has been on how the story of the Holocaust is told in American popular culture: it provided a convenient narrative trope and two handy stock figures. Yet even by 1974 the stock figures of the Nazi and his hunter were overripe and ready for remodeling, not a surprising development given the speed with which popular fiction devours successful figures, plots, formulas, and tropes. In thrillers such as William Goldman's *Marathon Man* (1974), for example, released as a film in 1976, the Jewish figure is remodeled as an innocent bystander and wholly inadvertent hunter. While the Nazi Dr. Szell (played with campy relish by Laurence Olivier) remains a handy symbol for evil, the Jewish "hunter" (played by Dustin Hoffman) becomes a stand-in for a generation of idealistic young Americans sucked into a venal and morally corrupt political world. The aptly named Babe Levy is not a victim of the Holocaust but of Watergate-era American politics. That the covert U.S. government agents of "The Division" have been employing the Nazis as useful collaborators (think Wernher von Braun and the Cold War) makes clear that *Marathon Man* is really a story about American justice itself. The Holocaust is like Dr. Szell's dental equipment—another prop that proves him evil.

Thus, Levin's fading and supposedly irrelevant protagonist and antagonist are, on the one hand, an informative reflection of the distance in time between the Eichmann capture and trial and the changed political, social, and cultural circumstances of the mid- to late seventies. The February 1976 book reviews of *The Boys from Brazil* in *Time* and *Newsweek* describe the Nazis still hiding out in South America as in "retirement," and as "Nazi senior citizens" who have been "rotting in South America for 30 years."[14] The suggestion is that Nazis, the real ones and not the ones on display in Levin's book, really do inhabit the backwaters of current history, and as the October 1978 film review in *Time* observes, "If you stop and think about it, even if there were a nest of Nazis hiding out in South America, most of them would be pushing 80 by now, and quite incapable of the exertions required by this far-flung, not to mention farfetched plot."[15] One has to admit that Levin correctly adduced American conventional wisdom in the mid-seventies about Nazis and Nazi hunters. If their age didn't make them irrelevant then America's preoccupation with a 1975 unemployment rate of 9.2 percent; the developing story of Watergate; the energy crisis; the Cold War; and the political upheavals in Chile, Peru, and Argentina made it unlikely the U.S. would pursue the extradition of aging Nazis. After the killing fields of Vietnam and Cambodia, Nazis and their Holocaust crimes seemed less menacing than they did in 1961–1962 when Eichmann's face was broadcast around the world as the still vital face of evil.

For American Jews, however, Levin's premise is overstated. Other events and issues vied for their attention during the mid-seventies: the 1973 Yom Kippur War; the plight of the Soviet Jews and the arrest of Anatoly Sharansky; the United Nations recognition of the PLO and its declaration of Zionism as "a form of racism and racial discrimination"; and the negotiations, shepherded by President Jimmy Carter, between Menachem Begin and Anwar Sadat that eventually led to the Camp David Accords. But the Holocaust was never irrelevant. As Alan Mintz points out, the publication of Lucy Davidowicz's *War against the Jews* in 1976, and the "selection" of Jews during the highjacking of an Air France plane to Entebbe, Uganda (and their spectacular rescue by Israeli special forces) laid the ground for American receptiveness to Green's *Holocaust*;[16] we should recall, too, that David Irving's *Hitler's War*, in which he claimed that no evidence existed connecting Hitler to the "final solution," and the fight between 1976 and 1978 to stop American Nazis from marching in Skokie, Illinois, were painful Holocaust reminders for many American Jews. What Levin's premise really alludes to in relation to American Jewish life, as Mintz's example of Entebbe illustrates, is that the Holocaust had threaded itself into a wider web of contemporary political, social, and cultural concerns and interests, so that its warp and weft were not always apparent.

On the other hand, Levin's Mengele and Liebermann do reflect how faded those characters had become in the popular arts. Gene Lyons in the *New York Times Book Review* described Levin's book as a fable "constructed to yield meaning as directly and almost as simply as one of Aesop's": Levin's Mengele was a stick figure representing evil, Liebermann a vehicle for delivering the moral.[17] But most of the reviews of Levin's book and its film adaptation focused their invective on the ways that Mengele's character revealed a "de-sinistering" of Nazis in the popular arts, as a 1979 review in *Literature/Film Quarterly* termed it.[18] Nazis had become such convenient and ahistorical symbols for evil in films and popular fiction that critics felt compelled to point out that their diminution into "faintly risible characters, just a step or two away from Mel Brooks creations,"[19] had gone beyond bad taste. Pauline Kael's review of the film in *The New Yorker* is a good example of such criticism, especially since she notes how Lieberman's figure of the Nazi hunter is also diminished by this de-sinistering:

> If the film wants to be taken as a cautionary fable—another one!—about the ever-present dangers of Nazism, then it should leave viewers with a sense of the menace that Mengele's 'boys from Brazil' constitute. Instead we get Lieberman's fuddy-duddy humanism and vague assurances that the boys are not really dangerous. . . . Nazism has become comic-book mythology, a consumer product. Movies like this aren't making the subject more important, they're making it a joke. They're cloning Hitler to death.[20]

Read alongside other reviews with similar arguments, Kael's review suggests that consciousness of the Holocaust and its victims had not so much receded in the popular arts as it had been overtaken by the political, social, and cultural changes of the sixties and seventies, changes that left their imprint on the figures of the Nazi and the Nazi hunter as they were successively appropriated by writers and directors. Knowing this helps us better understand why Green's *Holocaust* had such an impact on America and on American Jews—it revitalized not the Nazi menace itself (as Shandler points out, the sense among survivors and others was that *Holocaust* had trivialized the menace),[21] but rather American and American Jewish discourse about the nature and meaning of that menace and of Holocaust memory.

The figure of the Nazi hunter was also affected by this revitalization. In real life, of course, Wiesenthal, Serge and Beate Klarsfeld, Eli Rosenbaum, and others continued throughout the seventies and long after *Holocaust* to track down Nazis in America and around the world. Although the publicity for their work rose and fell, the work remained the same. In the popular arts, however, what it meant to be a Nazi hunter and to seek justice for Holocaust victims changed—indeed, as *Marathon Man* reveals, was already changing in response to social functions unavailable to the "comic-book" Nazi on the run—because after *Holocaust* how the victims were represented, and how they represented themselves, changed.[22] One way to appreciate the dimensions of that change, insofar as it has been reflected in American Jewish detective stories, is, first, to look closely at the implications of Levin's figuring of Liebermann, the pre-*Holocaust* victim as detective.

Early in the book, Liebermann is described through the eyes of a journalist as a man who "made everyone feel guilty, always. Someone had said of him—was it Stevie Dickens?—'He carries the whole damned concentration-camp scene pinned to his coattails. All those Jews wail at you from the grave every time Liebermann steps in the room'" (49–50). To the journalist, Liebermann's victimhood, his precipitous drop in prestige, and his declining physical strength make him a "loser" (50). Levin's Nazi hunter thus incorporates, as we might expect, a much flattened image of the Holocaust victim: a pathetic, ethnic Ancient Mariner, he induces guilt as he wearily treks around the world lecturing others for a living. Yet it is precisely Liebermann's ability to generate and wield guilt that is his most effective weapon as a detective. It enables him to garner information and funding for his investigation of Holocaust criminals and of the murders that lead to his showdown with Mengele. And it works just as effectively with Gentiles as with Jews, although Liebermann dislikes wielding it on his recalcitrant Jewish contributors: "Inflation, they told him. Recession. Business was awful. He began bringing in dead parents, the Six Million—which he hated doing, using guilt as a fundraiser" (164). This ability to wield guilt is, in fact, a sign of his professionalism, of his long experience in the business of forcing people to do the right thing if there is to be justice for the victims of the Holocaust. That professionalism is tied, naturally, to Liebermann's expertise in questions of life and death, an expertise that is a product both of his own harrowing experiences as a victim (very lightly brushed in the story through a dream and through his reactions while interviewing a female concentration camp guard), and of his experiences as a detective. As Liebermann says to a young German law student who offers to help him investigate the murders of the civil servants, "it's a business for professionals, not amateurs" (93)—it's a line of work where murder is both a hazard and the target of investigation.

Liebermann is no Chandler-esque tough guy, but his professionalism is a striking echo of a character trait in hard-boiled detective fiction. In my reading, then, Levin's victim as detective comes across as a hybrid of the Nazi hunter and of the professional detective who risks his life seeking justice in a violent and morally indifferent world—the knight of hard-boiled detective fiction.[23] Levin, wittingly or unwittingly, transforms a figure derived from the facts of European Jewish history into a recognizably American character through such a hybridization. Aside from identity, of course, the benefit is obvious: the hard-boiled association makes the victim as detective a heroic image, though the nature of such an American Jewish hero is less obvious and deserves scrutiny. Since this hybridization is better evident in Levin's book than it is in the movie adaptation (where Olivier throws the weight of his performance into mining the possibilities of a Middle European accent), I want to focus my analysis here on Levin's book. Looking in, we see that ticking off further attributes of the hard-boiled knight as reflected in Liebermann's character is easy: the world-weary Liebermann, operating out of a rundown office in downtown Vienna, battles evil and embarks on a quest for truth; his opponent, Mengele, is the "mad or evil false priest" whose dark vision reflects the nihilism of modernity and foregrounds Liebermann's idealism and sense of justice;[24] Liebermann's personal courage and ability "to absorb alarming physical punishment" is evident in the climactic scene when, in an attempt to outmaneuver Mengele, he is shot four times—and lives;[25] and though he is helped by both a minuscule staff and amateur volunteers, when it really counts he is a loner, preferring to interview people and plan his course of action by himself, and thinking of himself as essentially an outsider who knows that the gentile authorities, whose help he needs at a crucial juncture, cannot be counted on, leading him to wish for "a Jewish FBI. Or a U.S. branch of Israel's Mossad" (197).[26]

This last attribute of the hard-boiled knight is the most significant in regard to the hybrid figure of the victim as detective. For Liebermann is a loner and an outsider not only in relation to the authorities, but also in relation to other Jews. Most obviously, his outsiderness is related to his faded celebrity and to fading interest in Nazi hunting. But that outsiderness is also evident in his dealings with the Young Jewish Defenders (YJD), a militant Jewish self-defense organization modeled on the Jewish Defense League (JDL), which turns out to be the Jewish

FBI Liebermann needed. Like the JDL, the YJD is a quasi-underground group of tough Jews scornful of the "Jewish establishment" (202). Their sixties-style militancy is how they cope with the crimes of the Holocaust, and how they express their opposition to Israeli compromise in the Middle East conflict, perceived by them to be a new Holocaust in the making. Their leader, Rabbi Moshe Gorin, is a thinly veiled version of Rabbi Meir Kahane, the founder of the JDL, and his admiration for Liebermann sets up an inter-Jewish dialogue—not evident in the film version.

In the book, Liebermann must forge an alliance with the YJD to provide himself with backup. Gorin, at the end of the novel, proposes that the YJD murder the cloned boys, now thirteen and fourteen years old, to make certain that Mengele's scheme never reaches fruition. Gorin thinks that an alliance between Liebermann and the YJD is more than just a matter of convenience—that it betokens a logical extension of, and the next step in, Liebermann's work. It betokens a link, in other words, between witness and vengeance, and Gorin believes it raises him to Liebermann's heroic status. Liebermann will have nothing to do with the plan, however, and destroys the list of boys, whereupon Gorin levels the ultimate insult: "'It's Jews like you,' he said, 'that let it happen last time'" (263). Liebermann's response reflects a contemporary popular judgment of the JDL, equating the YJD with the Nazis: "Nazis *made* it happen. People who would even kill children to get what they wanted" (263). The moral that Liebermann delivers (brought home when he tells his booker that he wants to speak from now on to college and high school groups) is that witness and teaching the young are the appropriate response to the crimes of the Holocaust, not vengeance. As he tells an audience earlier in the book, the way to seek justice for, and do justice to, Holocaust victims is "to remind the world, and . . . you, who weren't even born yet when these things happened," that humanity is capable of such crimes, so that the next generation will make certain the circumstances that permitted Holocaust crimes "shall never again be permitted to arise" (65–66). Liebermann exits the story anticipating a return to his lonely but heroic work, ostensibly neither a part of the "Jewish establishment" nor a part of the Jewish anti-establishment.

I do not mean to suggest here that Liebermann, at the end of *The Boys from Brazil,* is perfectly similar to Sam Spade at the end of *The Maltese Falcon,* when Spade gives up Brigid O'Shaughnessy to the "establishment" in deference to a personal code of honor that keeps him apart from both, or to Philip Marlowe at the end of *The Long Goodbye,* when

Marlowe revokes his friendship with Terry Lennox and remains, as Eileen Wade says, a "self-sufficient, self-satisfied, self-confident, untouchable bastard" (363). But the outlines of such a hard-boiled denouement are sufficiently evident in Levin's book that the similarity of effect is quite evident: Liebermann remains the solitary knight whose ideals are "out of time," to use Chandler scholar Jerry Speir's phrase,[27] operating in a modern world where his knightly ideals are debased by pretenders such as Rabbi Gorin. His social function is therefore best understood in light of Charles J. Rzepka's notion of the hard-boiled detective as a "proxy." Rzepka argues that Raymond Chandler's Marlowe is an agent who reflects "the commodification of desire in late capitalist consumer culture," a broker who enables readers to purchase an anachronistic knightly idealism while still enjoying the vicarious thrill of the knight's adventures in a lascivious and violent wasteland.[28] Levin's heroic victim as detective is also a proxy, but in a different context. Liebermann enables readers to purchase both the victim's witness of, and the tough Jew's revenge for, Holocaust crimes without crossing the moral line that the author draws at the end of *The Boys from Brazil*. That is, Mengele gets his just deserts while the humanity and moral rectitude of the victim is reasserted and reaffirmed.

However, in contrast to Rzepka's assertion that Marlowe, as Chandler's proxy, takes on the sins of a fallen modern world to move readers to recognize their complicity in "America's systemic commodification of sex and violence" (720), it's quite clear that Liebermann, as Levin's proxy, takes on the sins of Holocaust crimes simply to assuage readers. The guilt induced in both Gentiles and Jews by an image of the victim as it was lifted from the "concentration-camp scene" is contained by an image of the detective, dispatched from the War Crimes Information Center by way of the mean streets of America, who works for all humankind, but who prefers to work alone. Thirteen years after the Eichmann trial gave birth to the popular cultural figurations of the Nazi and the Nazi hunter, Levin's book reflects that, indeed, the figure of the Nazi has grown into an adolescent, science-fantasy clone of the original. But it also reflects that the figure of the Nazi hunter has hybridized into a proxy, firmly gendered male, whose implicit message to readers, like Liebermann's to the German law student, is to keep their distance: leave the dirty business of seeking justice to the professional, the victim as detective. Readers can allay their guilt over fading interest in Holocaust victims, or satisfy their conflicting desires for both justice and revenge, by reading Levin's book, or by taking their children to an edifying lecture about humanism and the importance of financial contributions to the professionals. In short, Levin's victim as detective suggests that it is both possible and preferable to purchase justice for the victims of Holocaust crimes—the *American* justice, that is, of the hard-boiled detective story in which the victim becomes a hero by proxy.

Now let us skip ahead seventeen years and consider the first of two ways that the image of the victim and narratives about American justice and Holocaust crimes changed in American Jewish detective stories.

1993: THE DETECTIVE AS VICTIM

Zachary Klein is not a major voice in either American Jewish detective stories or detective fiction generally, but *No Saving Grace,* the third Matt Jacob mystery, is an interesting popular cultural example of the suspicion that some American Jews have toward the contemporary meaning and uses of the Holocaust. If *Holocaust* did signal a change in the representation of Holocaust victims in the popular arts, who now controls that representation—and can they be trusted? This suspicion is given expression, most notoriously, in Norman G. Finkelstein's *The Holocaust Industry: Reflections on the Exploitation of Jewish Suffering* (2000), in which Finkelstein accuses "American Jewish elites" of manipulating and exploiting Holocaust memory as "a potent ideological weapon" in defense of Israel's and their own increasingly right-wing politics and policies.[29] Yet the underlying assumption informing Finkelstein's work, that of a growing disconnect between the Holocaust and what has been called an American "Shoah business" (the organizations, institutes, museums, academic centers, popular and documentary films, literature, and art devoted to managing and interpreting Holocaust memory), is taken quite seriously in mainstream analyses such as Tim Coles's *Selling the Holocaust: From Auschwitz to Schindler, How History Is Bought, Packaged, and Sold* (1999), and Peter Novick's *The Holocaust in American Life* (1999), the study that Finkelstein credits for inspiring his own book. Klein's mystery is a useful text in that it stages that assumption at a time, the early nineties, when it coalesced into the version evident in the works above. And it is staged in such an overblown manner that the question of who is a victim and who is a proxy in *No Saving Grace* becomes a pretext for a question about political and cultural loyalty among American Jews—a contemporaneous anxiety lurking alongside the contradiction of applying American justice to Holocaust crimes.

Klein's mystery revolves around two murders that take place at the outdoor Simchat Torah celebration of a Hasidic sect in Boston: the murder of the sect's rebbe by a member of the White Avengers, a neo-Nazi group whose members are Irish Americans and Irish Republican Army (IRA) sympathizers, and the murder of the murderer by Rabbi Yonah Saperstein, a Holocaust survivor with ties to the Never Agains, Klein's Hasidic version of the JDL, only made up entirely of survivors. Jacob is hired to help defend Saperstein, to find out why the White Avenger was there and what really happened that night. Jacob has no real attachment to the Jewish community or to Judaism, and he is quick to claim that "the measure of my Jewishness had been tossed into a hospital's foreskin container a couple of minutes after my birth" (17). He feels no connection to the Holocaust, and he feels "uncomfortable" around the Hasidim. Jacob, in fact, claims no connection to any belief or ideology, a by-product of his lower-middle-class background and post-Vietnam disillusionment with the "Suits" and "Authority." His alienation and his characterization of himself as an outsider is, of course, essential to his characterization as a hard-boiled detective, albeit one recovering from a very bad sixties hangover. Name-dropping Philip Marlowe and Lew Archer and tucking words like "shamus" into the first-person narration seem beside the point. By the time Jacob discusses Black–Jewish relations with his outlaw African American friend Julius, it's quite clear that Jacob is an outlaw knight, unwilling to be seduced, as his lawyer friend Simon Roth is, by American consumer culture or by the fashionable baby-boomer interest in religion. Indeed, as Julius points out, it is Jacob's refusal of particularist, privileged ideologies of any kind—Jewish, white, capitalist, or other—that accounts for their friendship. When Klein has Julius call Jacob "a nigger turned inside out," the compliment highlights Jacob's knightly idealism: that his refusal of such privilege is a refusal of the system that confers privilege. This idealism makes Jacob both an honorary Black and an authentic American because the two are synonymous with the democratic egalitarianism of the marginalized and oppressed individual; Julius and Jacob, it may be noted, treat each other as equals, sharing marijuana, cigarettes, and Jacob's apartment.

Klein's Julius is obviously an imaginary Black, a foil and racial sounding board whose persona enables Klein to stake out the meaning of Jacob's American identity. Julius is what Toni Morrison calls an "Africanist" character.[30] But equally important in the context of my argument is recognizing that, as an Africanist character, Julius authorizes Jacob's portrayal not as a survivor (as the flap copy on the hardcover calls him), but as a victim: the hard-boiled detective as "nigger," the quintessential American outsider. This is how Klein puts Jacob at odds both with the "authorities" and with a Holocaust victim like Rabbi Saperstein. Saperstein proclaims his victimhood a number of times (even dramatically revealing his tattoed concentration camp numbers to Jacob), but always and only from a Jewish perspective. Saperstein is scornful of Jews like Jacob because they try to assimilate among those who are eternally "united in their hatred of us" (28), and even flings the same charge of Holocaust collaboration that Gorin flung at Liebermann: "I saw you in the camps. You stayed alive by shoveling our dead brothers' and sisters' bones" (291). For Saperstein the next Holocaust is right around the corner, and, as his son Yakov tells Jacob, Jews need to stand up and "feel pride in those who would not die quietly" in the last Holocaust, so that "people will stop pushing us around" (140). Jacob sees this as merely special pleading and an attempt to justify the excesses of the Never Agains who, like the JDL in Levin's book, bear too striking a similarity to the Nazis they claim to oppose. As it turns out, Saperstein had been taken advantage of by the Never Agains in their attempt to infiltrate the Hasidic sect (the rebbe had banned them from his Yeshiva). In order to convince the rebbe that he needed the Never Agains, the group had worked out a deal with the White Avengers to create the Simchat Torah disturbance. The murdered Avenger, who also was an IRA agent, was very much in tune with such particularized and competing victimhoods, and Jacob, as he unravels the mystery, recognizes that the murder and the diabolical alliances among Saperstein, the Avengers, the IRAs, and the Never Agains are "the result of ideology in action" (263).

In Klein's mystery, then, the Holocaust victim is greatly flattened into an image of Orthodox Jewish identity (as if "Holocaust victim" equaled "Hasidic Jew"), an image associated with the desire to use physical force to defend and avenge that particularist identity. Especially disturbing is that Klein figures the Holocaust victim as a kind of double victim: first a victim of Nazism and second a victim of and proxy for those Jews who see fit to manipulate Holocaust memory—to manipulate the victims' "suffering and submission to death," as Ezrahi words it—for their own ideological ends. "Like all vigilantes, like the White Avengers, the Never Agains feed on the fears of its members," Jacob explains to Saperstein. "They created a moment in time which you had spent your life running from. And they manipulated you into helping them do it. Do you really feel any safer now?" (304). Through this diminution and, ironically, manipulation of Holocaust victims, Klein portrays Saperstein the victim as easily preyed upon by Jewish ideologues because of his own unfulfilled desire for power and, ultimately, for revenge.

Jacob's identification of ideology as the real criminal in this mystery helps explain the outrageous solution to the double murder of the rebbe and the Avenger. Behind both the White Avengers and the Never Agains stands Deirdre Ryan, the daughter of Holocaust survivors and now an Israeli secret agent posing as an IRA operative, who has orchestrated the rebbe's murder because Israel "simply won't let American support fade away. Our existence depends on your public and private monies. Anti-Semitism in the United States keeps the money channels flowing" (312). Haunted by her parents' victimhood, Ryan devotes her life to Zionism and to making certain that Jews are never victims again. All the victims and villains in the mystery have been her proxies—agents for a cynical Zionist conspiracy to manipulate Holocaust memory. As Jacob and Ryan face each other with guns drawn, readers are shown a stark contrast: Ryan the true believer, and Jacob the hard-boiled detective, an American hero because "I just wasn't willing to be another walking ideology blinded by commitment to my own dubious vision of right and wrong" (321). Their showdown ends in a standoff, but Jacob sees himself the winner because he remains a free, though vulnerable, individual, a proxy for no one and for no idea, which means that Matt Jacob the hard-boiled detective is the last true victim: the outlaw American knight whose idealism and individualism is not only out of time, it's out of place in an ideologically driven world order of organizational agendas and alliances of convenience. Thus, and given the fascist equivalencies Klein establishes between the Never Agains, the White Avengers, and Zionists, Jacob is also a curious but telling incarnation of the Nazi hunter: his job is to expose, and bear witness against, corrupt ideologues on the loose in America.

Of course, some will argue that to call Jacob a Nazi hunter is to stretch that figure to the point of distortion, but consider: Jacob is a proxy for Klein, who uses the individualism of the hard-boiled detective to split off American justice from revenge for Holocaust crimes, and as a sign of American allegiance. In *No Saving Grace,* American justice is untainted by ideology, and the Holocaust is a European event with a meaning entirely overdetermined by ideology. If part of what it means to be a Nazi hunter is to seek an ideologically untainted justice—the justice of absolute good in opposition to the injustice of absolute evil—then Jacob resembles both Liebermann and Babe Levy, and Deirdre Ryan resembles both Mengele and Dr. Szell. Like Babe Levy, Klein's American hero remains resolutely American. Jacob is respectful of the Holocaust as an international event of great magnitude but convinced that the way to set Yakov straight is to draw his attention away from religion and the Holocaust and toward the urban sport that nurtured Jacob's identity and his understanding of fair play—basketball. Klein thus presents the "Africanist presence" animating his detective as proof of his Jewish character's loyalty to American justice and to his American identity, and this is carried to its absurd conclusion at the end of the novel when Jacob decides to head to his Black girlfriend's mother's house for "more of Mrs. Hampton's, Charlene's, homemade ham" (322).

Matt Jacob is a proxy for readers, too, an agent through whom Gentiles or Jews may purchase an easy and, to many, an offensive answer to the perplexed relations of the Holocaust, Zionism, and America. The social function of Klein's narrative about American justice and Holocaust crimes is to draw a clear line between American and Israeli identity, not a surprising function for an American Jewish detective story written not so much in the shadow of the Holocaust as in the shadow of the Israeli invasion of Lebanon, the expansion of ideological settlements in the West Bank and Gaza (motivated and populated to a significant degree by American Jewish immigrants), the Orthodox revival and Ba'alei Teshuva movement in America, the first Intifada, and the Jonathan Pollard spy case, in which an American Jew was convicted of being an Israeli agent. These events, which precipitated political, social, and cultural changes in American Jewish life during the eighties, find their echo in Jacob's suspicions about the ideological manipulation of Holocaust memory, and they reverberate in Klein's mystery through the image of the Holocaust victim as a proxy for ideologues, the image of the Zionist as spy and conspirator, and the image of the detective as victim.

True, Klein's narrative about American justice and Holocaust crimes, much like Finkelstein's narrative about Shoah business in *The Holocaust Industry*, is an idiosyncratic and marginal one in American Jewish detective stories; it straddles the border between acculturated and assimilated detective stories. But it is important insofar as it sheds light on the changing image of the Holocaust victim, on the transformation of the popular cultural figure of the Nazi hunter (via hard-boiled conventions), and on the anxiety among some acculturated American Jews like Klein about political and cultural loyalty to America in the face of Israel's so-called Zionist excesses. Nevertheless, at the turn of the millennium, the most intriguing and popular narrative about American justice and Holocaust crimes is the one constructed by Rochelle Krich in her novels *Angel of Death* and *Blood Money*.

"DESCENDED FROM VICTIMS": ROCHELLE KRICH'S REWRITE

A few months after the paperback release of Krich's *Blood Money* in 2000, the Amazon.com synopsis described Jessica Drake, Krich's protagonist and Los Angeles Police Department (LAPD) detective, as "driven by the recently acquired knowledge that she is descended from victims of the Nazis."[31] It is a provocative locution that refers to Drake's mother, Frances Claypool, and the extended family Frances lost in the Holocaust. But the statement is also a reminder of the relationship of Krich's protagonist to the image of the victim in American Jewish Holocaust memory, and, in the context of my argument, to the detectives considered thus far. Jessica Drake made her debut appearance in *Fair Game* (1993), but it wasn't until the second book in the series, *Angel of Death*, that Drake was revealed as Jewish. In an interview linked to her internet homepage, Krich describes that revelation as "We (she and I) discovered her Jewishness together."[32] Krich means that the underexplored family trauma that Drake alludes to in the first mystery, which accounts for the physical and emotional abuse Drake and her sister suffered in childhood and adolescence, provided the author an opportunity to mine her own feelings as a child of Holocaust survivors. This is not to say that Krich created a simple bridge between fact and fiction in the character of Jessica Drake, a bridge that somehow solved the problems attending popular cultural representations of Holocaust victims and their experiences, or the complexities of American Jewish political and cultural loyalty in the shadow of the Holocaust and Zionism. There is nothing simple about being a bridge between fact and fiction or between one generation and the next, and Krich's merit in constructing her narrative about American justice and Holocaust crimes lies in her recognition of this difficulty and in inserting that recognition into her series, and thus into the popular cultural shaping of Holocaust memory.

Krich's biography is behind such a recognition. Krich was born in Bayreuth, Germany, in 1947, and was brought by her parents to the United States, where she grew up in Lakewood, New Jersey; Crown Heights, Brooklyn; and Los Angeles, California. Her life reflects a Modern Orthodox trajectory—she attended Jewish elementary and high schools, graduated with a degree in English from Stern College in New York City, a women's college affiliated with Yeshiva University, and received an M.A. in English from the University of California, Los Angeles. She married, became chair of the English Department at Yeshiva University of Los Angeles High School, and raised six children. Her interest in teaching and writing are reminiscent of other literarily-inclined children of survivors, such as Lori Hope Lefkowitz and Kathryn Hellerstein, both of whom are professors, and also of survivor children like Irena Klepfisz, who teaches courses on Jewish women and who has written about herself as a bridge to the *Yidishe svive* (a remnant of the pre-Holocaust Eastern European Jewish world), the Yiddish environment of politics and literature to which she was bound by neighborhood ties and afternoon classes.[33] Although I do not mean to suggest that these four very different writers either constitute a literary school or exhibit some kind of second-generation pathology, I do think that Lefkowitz's self-distance and her ambivalence about inherited memory—that as a child of survivors she bears memory traffic both inherited and imagined, embraced and avoided, so that "I remember and I retreat"—helps illuminate Krich's relationship with her protagonist.[34] Krich's co-discovery of her protagonist's Jewish identity as the daughter of a survivor is a way of simultaneously remembering and retreating, maintaining through the artifice of fiction enough distance so that there remains space in the mystery for Drake to claim memory and then back away to educate herself about its content and its implications for her future. As in Klepfisz's poem *"Di rayze aheym*/The journey home," where the space between Yiddish and English becomes a site of imaginative travel, the space between Krich and Drake, and between Drake and her identity as the daughter of a survivor, enables a form of transit—the ability to shuttle back and forth on a journey, educational for both Drake and the reader, about the Holocaust.

Angel of Death is primarily about that educational journey, even though the passengers are familiar characters. Drake is assigned to investigate who is threatening Barry Lewis, the Jewish lawyer in a "very WASP firm" (18) representing the White Alliance, a neo-Nazi organization seeking legal approval to parade through the primarily Jewish neighborhoods along Pico Boulevard in the Beverly–Fairfax area of Los Angeles. They are parading to mark Hitler's birthday, which, not coincidentally, falls on the same day as Yom Hashoah, Holocaust Remembrance Day. Krich here sets up a symbolic conflict within American space (explicitly modeled on the conflict in Skokie) between Jewish time and neo-Nazi time, and at the beginning of the mystery she drops Drake, who has not yet discovered her Jewish identity, into that space.

Lewis, the son of survivors, suffers the same insults that Liebermann and Matt Jacob endured when they were perceived as working for, rather than against Nazis, and the insults and threats are presumed by him to be the work of the Shield of Jewish Protectors, who are directly compared to the JDL but said to be a "different group" (12). Drake is thus propelled into an investigation of both sides of the conflict. She discovers the diversity of the Jewish community as reflected in the panoply of fictional and real-life groups allied to oppose the march: the Anti-Defamation League, the Organization of Jewish Associations, the American Civil Liberties Union, and, naturally, the Simon Wiesenthal Center. Drake also discovers her ambivalence about the Jewish victims of the Holocaust, hearing in her head her mother's antipathy toward public rehearsals of Holocaust history (46). On the other side, she discovers that the White Alliance is allied with History Is Truth (HIT)—a group modeled on CODOH (Committee for Open Debate on the Holocaust)—an organization devoted to Holocaust denial, whose founder, Emery Kraft, calls himself "a credentialed historian who has presented a highly controversial reexamination of an episode of twentieth-century history" (142).

Drake finds that what draws her into her investigation is precisely the information she is learning about Jews and the Holocaust and the White Alliance and HIT. This being a popular fiction, Krich stacks the deck against the neo-Nazis. The head of the White Alliance, Roy Benning, is a thug and a corrupter of youth. During the march, as the neo-Nazis pass the Museum of Tolerance, he knocks down a little old Jewish lady, a survivor, who later dies of her injuries. And he exploits the troubled and impressionable Gene Oppman, using the adolescent's anger and alienation for his own ends. Emery Kraft, the power behind Benning (Kraft is German for "power"), is a crafty, unctuous, and cynical character who knows quite well that Barry Lewis is good Jewish cover for bad Nazi history, an entertaining spectacle that assures even more media coverage for the march and for Kraft's ideas. To readers familiar with Tom Metzger of the White Aryan Resistance and with CODOH, Krich's portraits of Benning and Kraft are shorthand for the salient characteristics and the danger of American neo-Nazis in the nineties. Unlike the Nazis in Levin's and Klein's stories, who are imaged as corrupting imports, Benning and Kraft are homegrown talent whose racism and lust for power is nurtured and even protected by particularly American situations and institutions: the ethnocentrism and economic grievances of lower-middle-class and working-class whites, the free market of American ideas and entertainment (in which Hitler, the Nazis and fascist ideology circulate freely in the academy and in the mass media), and the legal protections of the First Amendment. As the examples of the free market and the law reveal, Krich re-sinisters the figure of the Nazi precisely by making him the embodiment of American freedoms taken to excess. Although Kraft seems and claims to be the heir to a European phenomenon, he is thoroughly American. His figure is the disfigurement of America's native grounds—he is the enemy within.

Drake's education about Jews and the Holocaust serves a different purpose in *Angel of Death:* it teaches her and readers about Jewish identity. Drake, looking for Joel Ben-Natan, the leader of the Shield of Jewish Protectors, stumbles across his twin brother, Ezra Nathanson, who sent letters of protest to Barry Lewis and who also happens to be a teacher at Ohr Torah, a Jewish outreach program that offers adult education courses on Judaism (modeled on the real-life Aish Hatorah). Ezra, whose Hebrew name means "helper," at first helps Drake to understand why Barry Lewis's collaboration is such an affront to so many Jews. As Drake listens in on Nathanson's class, the teacher explains the relation between memory and Amalek, the biblical "archenemy, and, ironically a grandson of Esau, the twin brother of our forefather Jacob. Esau commanded his son and his grandson, Amalek, to destroy Jacob and his descendents. Amalek, on his deathbed, commanded his children to continue the crusade to the end of the generations" (56–57). Amalek "is the personification of evil" (57) whose memory is preserved in the Bible because Jews must be eternally vigilant for his appearance—Hitler is obviously Amalek—but whose name always invokes the response "*Yemach sh'mo ve'zichro.* May his name and memory be obliterated" (56). Here, the contrast between memory and obliteration, the twinning of good and evil, and the tense question of who qualifies as Amalek (Nathanson is not sure that the neo-Nazis qualify because "We can't jump to conclusions" [57]), all help to inform Jewish identity in *Angel of Death;* Jews are careful and cautious because history teaches them to be. For Drake, Nathanson's lecture teaches that Jewish history is "a heritage of survival" (58) in which Jews always manage to overcome Amalek and to preserve Jewish memory. But it also raises the idea in her mind that some Jews, like Ben-Natan, would not hesitate to obliterate those they suspect of being Amalek or their collaborators. Krich depends on readers to ponder that implication, for it leads to the assumption, evident in Levin's and Klein's stories, that Ben-Natan and Benning are morally equivalent, that they are both ideologues mired in the past and committed to the destruction of their enemies. When Barry Lewis is finally blown up in his car, and Roy Benning found decapitated, Ben-Natan is the obvious suspect.

These issues become personal for Drake when she learns her mother's true history, how as a six-year-old during the Holocaust the young Frances was hidden with a Polish family whose mother abused her physically and psychologically (219–227). Drake sympathizes with her mother's story and sees her in a new light: "So this is where the rage was born, she thought. Pity for her mother flashed through her—it was a strange, unfamiliar sensation" (223). Knowing the source of her mother's rages and abuse of her daughters, Drake suddenly comprehends Frances as a victim. As the heir—or descendent, as Amazon.com put it—of such victimhood, Drake finds herself pulled into the orbit of Jewish history and identity. In short, Drake understands Jewish historical trauma through the personal trauma her mother suffered, seeing also how that trauma perpetuated itself in the victimhood marring her own childhood. Frances Claypool, wife of an Episcopalian husband and a character who "had done a thorough job of erasing her past" (227), offers Krich the opportunity to refigure the image of the Holocaust victim in popular culture, to avoid either the concentration-camp image in Levin's story or the Orthodox and revenge-addled image in Klein's. Krich presents an image of the victim that on the surface does not resemble a Holocaust victim as understood in the popular imagination. Indeed, Frances is a contradictory figure: she exemplifies both the preservation and obliteration of Jewish memory, embodying for her abused daughters both good and evil; her victimization and subsequent victimizing of her daughters makes the question of who may be a contemporary Amalek a deeply unsettling one. As a result, Drake feels both an attraction for and an ambivalence about Jewish identity. After her mother's revelation, the first person Drake identifies herself as Jewish to is Emery Kraft, and she finds the identity a sharp and morally satisfying response to his anti-Semitism. The second person she identifies herself as Jewish to is Nathanson, but she recoils at her motives: "Was she subconsciously attempting to get back at her mother for years of abuse? . . . Or was she searching for an anchor, a system of belief that would fill the void she'd felt during her traumatic childhood and adolescence?" (247).

As the daughter of a Holocaust victim and survivor, Drake is heir to an identity filled with contradictions and confusions, as in her struggle with the distinction between a "victim" and a "survivor." Survival, in Krich's figuring of it, means working through trauma, a long and arduous process accompanied by the sort of confusion that Drake confides to her analyst, Manny Freiberg. Freiberg explains that most survivors feel guilt for surviving, but that some, if faced with a parade by neo-Nazis, may "feel the need to repay the debt of having survived while others didn't, to demonstrate that he won't be a victim again" (320). He points out the difference between Ben-Natan's and Nathanson's choice of patronymic, that the Israeli Ben-Natan "represents victory, assertiveness, independence," whereas the European Nathanson "represents the shtetl Jew, the victim" (321). Drake, trying to see beyond stereotypes and to educate herself about the difference between a victim and a survivor, nevertheless accepts this stereotype of Jews. It fits with the little she has learned about the Holocaust. Visiting the Museum of Tolerance exhibition on the Holocaust, Drake "had no difficulty imagining that she was in a gas chamber, not in a room in a museum" (253); the discovery that her lover doubts the veracity of the Holocaust (154–155) only fuels this imagination. But it is only at the very end of the mystery that readers discover just how far Drake has allowed her imagination about stereotypes to run. Although Ben-Natan and Nathanson *had* been victimized (five years earlier Kraft set a fire that killed their parents and Nathanson's family), their response to it remained within the bounds of the law. Ben-Natan really is just a protector, as evidenced by his fortunate appearance just as Kraft, the real murderer (no surprise), is about to kill another victim and Drake herself. Nathanson, of course, is a teacher, and both brothers enable Drake to see that Jewish survival is a combination of vigilance and enlightenment.

What is Nazi hunting in this mystery, then? It is a far more complicated task than the Nazi hunting in either Levin's or Klein's stories. Indeed, *Angel of Death* reads like a specific refutation of the paranoia evident in Klein's mystery. Nazis are not ideologues but rather Americans bent on perverting American ideals for nefarious ends, specifically, the denial of the Holocaust, the perpetuation of the canard that its memorialization is a Zionist plot, and the fomenting of American anti-Semitism. Krich is responding to a contemporary conflict in America over Holocaust memory, as she explains in her online interview:

> One of my goals in writing *Angel of Death* was to illuminate readers about the veracity of the Holocaust—particularly readers who might not pick up a work of non-fiction. I'm particularly offended and frightened by Holocaust deniers, who title themselves revisionists (à la David Irving, who was soundly defeated in April in his libel suit against historian Debra Lipstadt by a London judge who called him a "liar" and "anti-Semite").[35]

Drake is a Nazi hunter in the sense that she pursues neo-Nazi revisionists and the stereotypes that they promulgate, as well as those cultural stereotypes of Holocaust victims, and of Jews, that play into their hands. As the literary critic Priscilla L. Walton points out, both *Angel* of *Death* and April Smith's *North of Montana* "offer provocative insights into the cultures they examine, at the same time that they work to complicate the ways in which such cultures are stereotypically constructed."[36] Whether readers can also "experience something of the traumas" that beset Drake, and whether, as Walton's argument implies, reading a popular fiction in or out of a classroom will really translate into political action (Janice Radway claims that popular fiction may in fact blunt a reader's desire to take action in the political sphere),[37] Walton's conclusion is still well taken: Drake's social function in the mystery is to be "a bridge" for student-readers "to explore identity politics 'inside' and 'outside' diverse racial and ethnic groups."[38] Krich refigures the image of the Nazi hunter as a hunter not only of Holocaust crimes, but also of the crimes of identity politics, and so it is not surprising that Krich's Nazi hunter is overtly concerned with the hybridization of fact and fiction. Drake exemplifies and investigates the "tension between internal accountability to the imagination and external accountability to the victims," which Ezrahi diagnoses as "the heart of the dilemma of Holocaust literature in America."[39] The justice Drake seeks for Holocaust victims is not justice predicated on the Nazi hunter wielding guilt or exacting revenge, but justice predicated on the Nazi hunter's insistence on working toward just social, cultural, and historical perceptions.

A LIMITED HERO

The kind of heroism that Drake's justice-seeking entails is well illustrated in *Blood Money* and in that mystery's gendering of what it means to do justice to Holocaust victims. For Krich has dispatched a woman to do what in Levin's and Klein's stories was done by men—"Drake" is the perfect name for Krich's odd duck—and that difference, combined with the difference Drake enacts as a hard-boiled Jewish detective, is significant to her role as a Jewish hero. Like Liebermann and Jacob, Drake is a professional detective who risks her life seeking justice in a violent and morally indifferent world (how else could a Benning or a Kraft come to be, and even thrive?). She, too, is a knight whose idealism, whose desire for just social, cultural, and historical perceptions, is contrasted to Kraft's Hitlerian vision, a vision that reflects the cynicism and nihilism of modernity. Her idealism also contributes to the gender conflicts between her and the police force, her family, and her ex-husband, which often leave her feeling alienated and alone, unsure whether she is a colleague or a problem for her fellow officers, whether she can bond with or is really bereft of family. In *Angel of Death,* the allure of remaking a family and a family home is what enables Krich to end the mystery on a hopeful note, constructing a scene where Drake and her ex-husband nail a mezuzah on the doorpost of her house, as if Jessica Drake the hard-boiled detective will finally reconcile with Gary Drake the macho reporter and make a home under a sign of Jewish identity, replete with all the implications that such a reconciliation and such a Jewish home signify—Jessica Drake, good Jew, good wife, good cop.

But again, Krich is not interested in simplifying, whether in relation to American justice and Holocaust crimes or in relation to Drake as a female hard-boiled detective. The beginning of *Blood Money* is a marked contrast to the ending of *Angel of Death:* Krich opens with Drake contemplating "the dilemma of being a female cop" (3), and later contemplating the harasssment and suspicion she endures as a woman detective in the LAPD, confessing that she refused to quit "because she'd been determined not to give her oppressors the satisfaction" (51). Drake even pokes fun at *The Rules* (1993), a briefly popular, anti-feminist book that provided a step-by-step guide showing women how to subordinate themselves to men in order to marry one (37). Indeed, Krich is aware that she is playing with "rules" in *Blood Money:* of courtship, of professional conduct, and of hard-boiled detective identity, evidenced by her figuring of Drake as a single woman, as "a minority in the LAPD" (52), and as a female hard-boiled detective. Jessica Drake should be read, then, not only as a reflection of Krich's awareness of generic limits, but also as a detective who explores what it means to be a limited hero, one who, as a hybrid of the Nazi hunter and the hard-boiled detective, must reconcile her idealism with her limitations.

This conflict is evident in *Blood Money,* once Krich assigns Drake to a mystery about stolen identities and the desire to restore family. The case revolves around the killing of Norman Pomerantz, a Holocaust survivor, found murdered in Rancho Park. The trail leads Drake to an organization run by a wealthy Jewish philanthropist and art collector, dedicated to recovering for survivors the Swiss bank accounts, stolen art, and other valuable assets they and their families lost during the Holocaust. Drake's mother calls these assets "blood money" and she is uninterested in claiming any, telling her daughter, "All the money in the world won't change what happened. . . . All it would do is remind me of everything I've tried to forget. I don't want it, not one dime" (69). Krich is again writing against stereotypes, trying to divorce Jewish identity from the hoary anti-Semitic image of Jews as usurers and moneygrubbers. But she is also using Frances's refusal as a way to instigate, once again, Drake's desire to imagine some connection between herself and the family she never knew, the desire for a family restored. Drake investigates Pomerantz's murder in part because she feels "bereft" of family (160, 191), and in part because she finds herself inexplicably drawn to Pomerantz and to Hilda Rheinhart, a survivor she meets as she investigates a murderous scam being perpetrated on survivors looking to retrieve their assets, a scam related to Pomerantz's death. Frances warns Drake that Pomerantz and Rheinhart are not her grandparents, that they cannot restore the family and the identity that the violence of the Holocaust stole. Nevertheless, Drake continues to involve herself in Rheinhart's personal life, and when she discovers that Pomerantz had made a video testimony, which may provide clues to his murder, she finds it a compelling document.

So does Krich, and the incorporation of video testimony into the mystery reflects another hybridization of fact and fiction that perfectly encapsulates the conflict between idealism and limitations, as well as the issues of identity, memory and gender. Pomerantz's video testimony is, in fact, based in part on Krich's own father's biography and his experiences during the Holocaust.[40] As the voice of truth in the mystery, he occupies a unique position—he is a node between fact and fiction and between father and daughter. As Krich says in her note introducing *Blood Money*, Pomerantz offered her the opportunity to tell her father's tale, and to memorialize a life that she herself only discovered at thirteen, the life of a man who had been married before the war and one of whose daughters was named Yiska, Yiddish for Jessica. Thus the incorporation of video testimony is itself testimony, as I note below, to a current image of Holocaust victims in popular culture, an image culled from both the Fortunoff Archive at Yale and Steven Spielberg's Shoah Foundation and its vast archive of video testimony.

What does this testimony in this medium mean for Drake and for Krich? For both, it manifests another version of Lefkowitz's remembering and retreating. On one level, video testimony reflects the idealism of doing justice to Holocaust victims and survivors. The medium seemingly brings the survivor into a closer relationship with viewers, and so the medium advertises itself as valuable because it supposedly offers a face-to-face encounter between viewer and survivor, and through the survivor a greater appreciation for the survivor's victimization and for victims who cannot speak for themselves. The video subjects are thus honored as witnesses, as living nodes between past and present, bridges who cross the gap between memory and testimony, rather than treated as pathetic figures out of yellowing photographs or disembodied footnotes in a history book. In this manner, Pomerantz represents the testimony of the father lovingly preserved by his daughter, an homage relevant to the plot of *Blood Money* in that it reinforces Frances's point about the misplaced interest in the memory of violence rather than in the memory of the victims.

On another level, however, video testimony reflects the limits to the idealism of testimony as homage, for video *is* a medium, and as such manipulated by framing, lighting, editing, and so on. These distance the video subject from viewers and undercut the video's air of immediacy and transparency, lending it a televisual appearance.[41] In a work of popular fiction like *Blood Money*, video testimony therefore boldfaces the hybridization of fact and fiction, the yoking of an homage to victims and survivors with a reimagination of them consequent to the very manipulatability of the medium of popular fiction. In this regard, Pomerantz, with his warmth and humor, reshapes popular imagination about Holocaust victims in a manner reminiscent of Krich's reshaping of Frances as a victim who does not look like a victim. Pomerantz enables Krich to have a survivor speak in his own words about his experiences as a victim and as a survivor. Krich's act of fiction is to present a fact speaking for himself—an act of homage and reimagination.

My point here is that the video testimony of *Blood Money* provides the key to understanding Krich's hard-boiled female protagonist and Drake's educational journey. In the patriarchal hard-boiled formula, Krich also prefers both homage and reimagination. Putting Jessica Drake in the hard-boiled detective's shoes is both an act of admiration and an act of redirection that refigures the detective in service of Krich's popular cultural reshaping of Holocaust memory without doing violence to that figure, without disfiguring the detective and hobbling her literary and social utility. Walton, writing with Manina Jones in *Detective Agency*, borrows a term from Michel Foucault to describe such co-optation as "reverse discourse" of which the "efficacy depends on the reader's recognition of differential intertextual relationships. It also depends on the genre's ability to signify in alternative ways, to accommodate ideologically contradictory practices without ceasing to be recognizable."[42] The "differential intertextual relationships" in *Blood Money* are the contradictions between the hard-boiled detective and the Nazi hunter, between detective fiction and video testimony, and between father and daughter that describe the kosher hybridity at work. Drake, an unconventional, hybrid female detective, is therefore the detective best qualified to thread these contradictions together to solve the unconventional mysteries embedded in Krich's narrative and provide a bridge between American justice and Holocaust crimes.

Drake's self-education about Jewish identity in the shadow of the Holocaust also operates on the principle of homage and reimagination, as witness the co-optation in *Blood Money* (albeit in a loving way and under the gaze of a male teacher) of two traditional, patriarchal Jewish texts about guilt and justice. The first text is the Torah, "in the portion called *Shoftim*—Judges," where, according to Ezra Nathanson, it is recounted how the all-male Sanhedrin, "the Supreme Court of that time," determined moral responsibility for "an unwitnessed, unsolved murder of a traveler whose corpse is found lying in an open field" by measuring the distance between the field and the cities nearby and then assigning moral responsibility to the nearest (96). The implications of the guilt-cleansing ritual required of the elders of that city suggest that, even though they did not witness the murder, they still bear responsibility for the sinfulness present in their town; as Drake notes, they are their brother's keepers (97). If the body is moved or hidden, however, the ritual is not required, for it betokens a murderer with a conscience, and thus a community not wholly sinful. Drake takes on the Sanhedrin's role of trying to assign moral responsibility for Pomerantz's murder, and for trying to determine the sinfulness of her community. Thus one of her cultural functions in the mystery is to be a female proxy for Jewish tradition, an example of reverse discourse that does not subvert tradition so much as widen it and provide space in *Shoftim* for a brother's keeper who is a sister, and so for yet another educational journey that shuttles back and forth between past and present, male and female.

The second text is a Hasidic tale from the Bobover Rebbe, a tale that Krich found in a book in her father's library, and that is related by Pomerantz in his video testimony.[43] The tale concerns the murder of Bellievsky, a Polish peasant, and the arrest of a Jewish bar owner for it. The bar owner's son travels to the rebbe and tells him that his father is innocent and that three other peasants had wanted to murder Bellievsky, but the son has no way to prove it. The rebbe immediately devises a way to prove the Jewish bar owner's innocence, and tells the son to convince the Polish judge to agree to this plan: the three peasants and the Jew should be taken to the funeral home and made to grab the hand of the dead man, and the one who refuses is the murderer. Naturally, the plan works and the bar owner goes free, but, more important, we see in this tale the reappearance of the first Jewish detective in Jewish literature, Rabbi Eleazar son of Rabbi Simeon. Like Rabbi Eleazar, and like Kemelman's Rabbi Small, the Bobover Rebbe brings his training in Jewish law and textual analysis to bear on discerning the innocent from the guilty, and although his relation to the authorities is different from that of his Talmudic forebear, the lesson his tale teaches is the same: Jewish detectives are defenders of the faith and of the faithful.

Drake takes on this role, a conspicuous example of the regendering of Rabbi Eleazar and Rabbi Small in American Jewish detective stories, but in *Blood Money* it's a role that goes beyond her obvious incarnation as the Jewish detective who solves Pomerantz's murder. As it turns out, the Jewish philanthropist, Maurice Steele, whose organization helps Holocaust survivors recover their assets, is really a Gentile who had been a political prisoner at Auschwitz and who stole Pomerantz's brother's identity. Steele had befriended the brother, who died in his arms, but he stole his identity nevertheless, partly because the money and art that Pomerantz's family had hidden in a Swiss bank were so alluring, and partly because he wanted inclusion in the Jewish "family" whose bitter fortunes he had shared in Auschwitz. During the explanation of the solution to the mystery, Drake concludes that Steele's two sons had colluded with the con artist whose murderous scam she was investigating, and that together the three of them had planned Pomerantz's murder to keep him from finding out that the brother he thought was still alive was, in fact, someone else. The sons believed that the Steele family would be ruined—and of course they are, but what Drake proves is that no real Jewish family could have committed such heinous and self-deceiving crimes. Drake's cultural function in this respect is to be a female proxy for the Jewish "family," defending that family from the charge, leveled in Klein's story, of cynically manipulating Holocaust memory for its own ends. Krich's hard-boiled Jewish female detective is a hero, finally, because fidelity to Jewish culture in the shadow of the Holocaust is itself heroism of a kind. And only a character such as Drake, herself both in and out of the Jewish family, both a hard-boiled detective and a woman, is able to achieve such heroism.

But here I must pause before concluding. I fear that my analysis makes Krich's mystery seem transparent, and makes the reverse discourse of Drake's character seem an easy way of claiming both a Jewish and a feminist identity without really challenging the whole notion of stealing identities. What is the difference between the heroic Drake who dresses up as a survivor in order to trap a suspect, even having a fake concentration-camp number "tattooed" on her arm, and the morally culpable Steele who simply wants to trap a better life for himself? What is the difference between Drake "dressing up" as a male-modeled detective and Matt Jacob's "dressing up" as an American? Can these inconsistencies and contradictions really be fully explored, much less resolved, in a popular fiction? If we expect or demand the same formal experimentation and fictional brooding over identity and memory as in a work by Norma Rosen or Thane Rosenbaum or Cynthia Ozick, or as in Philip Roth's masterful *Operation Shylock*, our answer is likely to be no.

Yet, since *Blood Money* asks readers to make connections between the mystery and video testimony, Alan Mintz's insight about the uses of video testimony must serve as our guide for judging Krich's narrative: for those mediums pressed into memory's service that are still in the process of being troped and shaped, it is important to first map the master narratives that are emerging, before determining these mediums' relative worth.[44] In the narratives about American justice and Holocaust crimes constructed by the writers examined in this chapter, Krich's narrative, described by its remembering and retreating, homage and reimagination, is the only one that makes a space in which to ruminate on the meaning of justice as it attaches to images of Holocaust victims—or rather to those images circulating in the American Jewish popular imagination—and in which to ruminate on the image of a female Jewish hero. *Blood Money* is also the only Holocaust-themed mystery with this sort of conclusion: unable to elicit a confession from Steele's sons, Drake must settle for an untidy solution to the crime, letting both go free, and recognizing that the story of the family "restored"—a story she first hears from Nathanson, a story that led to Pomerantz's death, a story that Drake herself desires, and a story that lies behind the story in Pomerantz's video—is only a story, a fiction that Drake describes as a "tease" (339). Here is another instance of Lefkowitz's remembering and retreating, a concluding example of the self-distance that Drake embodies as proxy for second-generation writers. This is also, of course, a hard-boiled conclusion, because it illustrates what a tease the hard-boiled detective's idealism really is. It's a convention that underscores limitations, and Krich makes good use of it. Her narrative, through an illustration of its own limitations in providing justice for Holocaust victims, gently prods readers to recognize limitations in the popular imagination, and through these limitations to feel, even if only in an oblique manner, the weight of "the elusive and spiritually unedifying subject of large-scale physical suffering and submission to death," as Ezrahi puts it. By doing so, Krich, unlike Levin and Klein, meets the challenge of doing justice to Holocaust victims, providing as her proxy a female model of the hard-boiled hero cognizant of the responsibilities and limitations that attend the shaping of Holocaust memory.

CASES OF ALTERITY

6

UNDERCOVER GENTILES AND UNDERCOVER JEWS

> The word *Jew* is no longer a mirror in which I seek my self-portrait, but where I look for everything I'm not, everything I'll never be able to glimpse by taking myself as a point of reference.
> —Alain Finkielkraut, *The Imaginary Jew*

Problematic for all American Jewish artists, writers, and intellectuals is the lure of idealizing some aspect of Judaism or Jewish culture as authentic Jewishness, a problem I have briefly noted, or noted in passing, in a number of places in the previous chapters. It is a temptation that Alain Finkielkraut describes as "bringing back to imaginary life what prior generations had experienced in reality"—for instance, by borrowing a born-again Orthodoxy gleaned from images of pre-Holocaust Europe, or making a fetish of midrash and kabbalah.[1] This idealization is the act of "spectators who project their desires, their frustrations into a panting plot they will never live."[2] Finkielkraut's critique of such "imaginary" Jews exposes the inauthentic modes of claiming Jewish identity after assimilation and acculturation has changed the relationship between Jews and the societies they live in, and after the Holocaust destroyed a truly multicultural Yiddish culture that encompassed more than just Orthodoxy. *Yidishkayt* was a secular Jewish culture grounded in living memory that offered a vibrant and transformative engagement with Jewishness, a culture, as Finkielkraut observes, that was not dependent on the self as a point of reference.[3] As Finkielkraut points out, without a sense of Jewishness as a living culture in mortal danger (a sense that helps forestall idealizations of Jewishness), Jewishness becomes just another metaphor for the self.[4]

One way to avoid the narcissism of "the imaginary Jew" is by defining Jewishness as other, a strategy that enables Finkielkraut's awareness that "[t]he Judaism into which I was born is increasingly acquiring the status of a historical object, marked by a sudden distance making it both a painful and desirable object of reflection."[5] The drawback to that strategy, however, is that even a self-aware observation of such an object of reflection does not necessarily lead to an understanding of Jewishness as a living culture. That is, considering Jewishness as an Other whose difference and incomprehensibility thoroughly distance it from the self may also impede critical investigation or a meaningful accounting of Jewishness as a living culture. From that perspective Jewishness becomes so other, so radically different and distant that it may appear fruitless to bother with at all. Finkielkraut's critique of imaginary Jews, which dissected the political and polemical uses of Jewish identity, is important precisely because it foregrounds this complex relation between spectatorship and identity, but in such light is there really a profound difference between *Jew* as mirror and *Jew* as object of reflection, or do they evocatively frame two problematic aspects of spectatorship? True, the reflection in Finkielkraut's mirror refers to an image, and the reflection of his self-reflection refers to thought. But if one worries the word "reflection," if one tugs at and is troubled by the word's denotation of "folding back" or "throwing back" in *visible* form an image or a thought, then one may wonder not only at the variety of selves in Finkielkraut's mirror, but also at what kind of other is thrown back as a replacement for these selves. Thus one implication of the quote that opens this chapter is the necessity of exploring the visibility of Jewishness and of Jewish alterity, and how that visibility folds back on Jewish identity. What sorts of collaborations occur between *Jew* and *non-Jew,* and between viewer and object of reflection, when Jewishness is mediated in terms of spectatorship and visual representation?

This is an important question for American Jewish detective stories because these stories are not limited to written texts, a fact I want to acknowledge in this chapter. By exploiting insights from the study of film, in combination with Finkielkraut's observations, I also want to explore in greater depth (in this chapter and in this section) the problematics of viewer/reader positioning in American Jewish detective stories—the point of view that readers are asked to collaborate with in these stories. The involuntary or insubordinate embodying of Rabbi Eleazar, the original Jewish detective from the Babylonian Talmud, in the figures of Rabbi Small, Rina Lazarus, Nina Fischman, Dov Taylor, Berekiah Zarco, and Jessica Drake has pointed our attention toward cases of gender and cases of memory. Thinking about the involuntary or insubordinate embodiment of Rabbi Eleazar in Sidney Lumet's *A Stranger among Us* (1992) and David Mamet's *Homicide* (1991) points our attention toward cases of alterity, sites of struggle over spectatorship and the meaning of Jewish difference to American Jews. In this chapter, I consider the visibility of the Jewish body and its uses as a public symbol for borders and border crossings between Jew and non-Jew.

Once again, I am indebted to Daniel Boyarin's analysis of Rabbi Eleazar in *Unheroic Conduct* for opening up a line of thinking about detectives and Jewish bodies. In chapter 2 of that work, Boyarin ponders the implications of a story that follows the story of Rabbi Eleazar's collaboration with the Romans.[6] In this subsequent aggadah, Rabbi Eleazar sentences to death a man who insults him, reasoning that such a disrespectful fellow must certainly be a criminal. Gazing at the hanged man, Rabbi Eleazar is struck by powerful feelings of remorse and guilt that he may have sent an innocent man to his death, simply out of spite. Despite the fact that he is assured the dead man was indeed a sinner and a criminal, he still feels the need to see his own innocence embodied. So the corpulent rabbi has his stomach ripped open and the considerable fat therein scooped out and placed in the sun. Only the wonder of his bodily fat remaining uncorrupted after long exposure under the sun's rays reassures him, for it symbolizes his own moral incorruptibility. Boyarin's insight into this tale is that feelings of guilt about collaboration with the non-Jewish authorities of male-dominated political regimes enables and incites the self-feminization and deformation of the Jewish body.[7] That is, if the political power and violence associated with male-dominated political regimes is symbolized by the impermeable body, and body politic, then "the correction of having participated in this violence would require a self-feminization,"[8] would require that Rabbi Eleazar make his body permeable as a repentance for that collaboration and as a challenge to such political power.[9]

Boyarin, though quite careful to note that he is not "claiming any utopian (or even protofeminist) moment for rabbinic and early Christian culture through this analysis,"[10] goes on to make a provocative claim about the "diasporization" of Rabbi Eleazar's grotesque body:

> This body can be taken, then, as an ideal representation of Jewish culture in the Diaspora as a site where the confines between the body of Jewish culture and other social bodies are overcome, not forgetting, of course, the frequently violent response from many of those other bodies. Paradoxically, however, this diasporization of the body is also a pursuit of purity, of a moral pristineness that engagement with power seemingly would preclude. This paradox of Diaspora as the site of purity and cultural interchange is inherent in postbiblical Jewish culture.[11]

Boyarin's claim that Rabbi Eleazar's body stands for a particular kind of power relation between Jewish and non-Jewish bodies, and for a particular kind of paradox, helps bring into focus a contradiction of kosher hybridity attending the spectatorship and visual representation of the Jewish body in *A Stranger among Us* and *Homicide:* the desire to penetrate and be penetrated by the dominant culture, and the concomitant desire to remain pure. Such a contradiction is appropriate to, and instigates, a consideration of the ways film audiences insert themselves into Jewish identities on the screen, because it mimes the paradox of cinematic point of view, the subjective viewpoint that offers audiences both a bridge and a border between themselves and the film they are viewing.[12] How does cinematic point of view in the two films mentioned establish the Jewish body as both pristine and penetrable, as the site of purity and cultural interchange? How does point of view help viewers construct imaginary Jewish others? In *A Stranger among Us*, where the point of view follows a gentile detective who goes undercover as a Jewish woman and who falls in love with a Hasid, the quintessential diasporic Jew, viewers are positioned to see themselves as such an undercover Gentile, and thus to see the Jewish body as an other who is the site of a moral purity so desirable that desire itself becomes the fulcrum for cultural interchange. Nevertheless, though viewers are invited to "penetrate" the Jewish body as they watch the gentile detective's masquerade and attempt to seduce her Hasidic love interest, the permeable/impermeable diasporic Jew is finally positioned as an other lying beyond a boundary that must not, and cannot, be crossed. The film is thus a lesson on the need for and usefulness of borders between Jews and non-Jews, a lesson that brings home Finkielkraut's observation about the desirability of Jewishness as an object of reflection—and that flatters Jewish viewers—since the film is an idealization and romanticization of everything the undercover Gentile is not.

In contrast, the point of view in *Homicide*, though primarily anchored in Detective Bobby Gold, is often shifted and played with, so that the separation between self and other, Jew and non-Jew, blur. As Gold, the thoroughly assimilated hence "undercover" Jew, investigates his own social and ethnic collaborations, viewers are positioned to see themselves as such an undercover Jew, and thus to see, through the abrupt shifts in point of view, the kinds of violence that accompany Gold's and their "penetration" of the other. Interestingly, the critical material on the Jewish aspects of *Homicide* have focused almost exclusively on Mamet's language, yet a visual analysis of the film, and of the image of a gut-shot Bobby Gold, helps us to understand better the ramifications of that violence: such an opening of the Jewish body reveals neither moral corruptibility nor moral incorruptibility, but merely the vulnerability of bodies as they negotiate the politically and socially charged spaces of postmodern America. The film is therefore an object lesson about the vagaries and dangers of borders and border-making that brings home another of Finkielkraut's observations, this time about the painfulness of Jewishness as an object of reflection—one that frustrates both Jewish and non-Jewish viewers—since the film is a thorough deconstruction of the imaginary Jewish identities that the undercover Jew might adopt.

EMILY EDEN, UNDERCOVER GENTILE

A Stranger among Us is the story of New York Police Department (NYPD) detective Emily Eden (Melanie Griffith), an independent and unconventional cop, who investigates the disappearance of a Hasidic diamond worker. When the Hasid turns up dead, Eden intuits that the murder must be an inside job, and so she insists to the rebbe of the Hasidic sect (Lee Richardson) that she must go undercover as a Hasidic woman to find the murderer. Chaperoned by Leah (Mia Sara), the rebbe's dutiful and chaste adopted daughter, and advised by Ariel (Eric Thal), the rebbe's independent and unconventional adopted son and spiritual heir, Eden falls in love with Ariel, learns about the ethics and values of Hasidic Judaism, discovers that a *ba'alat teshuva* (Tracy Pollan), a returnee to the faith, is the murderer, and realizes that to be a truly fulfilled woman she must give up Ariel and her machismo masquerade.

The film, with a screenplay written by Robert J. Avrech, is essentially a revision of *Witness* (1985), in which Harrison Ford goes undercover in an Amish community. It is also a revision of a familiar theme from the police procedural, the travails of the lonely/alienated cop, in this case Eden's search for love and community. Lumet and Avrech's twist on both is that the detective is a woman, and so the film is also about the travails of the modern, urban woman who is free to work in a man's world but who finds no fulfillment in trying to be one of the guys. *A Stranger among Us* was savaged by critics, who thought it a "halfwitted crime movie" overly focused on (and misrepresentative of) the Hasidim, poorly acted by Melanie Griffith, and an insult to feminists and, indeed, any single woman uninterested in "conventional patriarchal life styles."[13] Most critics, however, recognized that, whatever Avrech's intention, Lumet was not so interested in the murder mystery as in exploring the Hasidic community, and if we begin with that premise the film can be read as yet another of Lumet's New York stories. According to film scholars David Desser and Lester D. Friedman, Lumet "may lack the immediate personal style or obsessive set of themes critics isolate with satisfied glee,"[14] but the director of such disparate films as *Twelve Angry Men* (1957), *Fail Safe* (1964), *The Pawnbroker* (1965), *Bye Bye Braverman* (1968), *Serpico* (1974), *Dog Day Afternoon* (1975), *Network* (1976), *Prince of the City* (1981), *Daniel* (1983), and *Q & A* (1990) does exhibit a number of motifs and characteristics that identify his works, many of which reflect a deep and abiding interest in the social fabric of New York City (168–169).[15] One of the most important of these recurring motifs, in Desser and Friedman's view, is the exploration of family loyalty, in regard to both actual and surrogate families.[16] *A Stranger among Us* exemplifies a particular kind of voyeurism that recurs in Lumet's work, the desire to look into the private life of the "families" that inhabit the public spaces of New York City in order to observe how they engage outsiders and/or strive to protect their close-knit communities. This theme is especially evident in, for example, Lumet's controversial films *The Pawnbroker* (which treats the Holocaust as both a Jewish family story and a universal fable) and *Daniel* (which treats the Old Left in America as the Julius and Ethel Rosenberg family fable), as well as in the director's police trilogy (*Serpico*, *Prince of the City*, and *Q & A*).

A Stranger among Us is also a simplified investigation of the oppositions Lumet explored in these earlier films: insiders versus outsiders, heroes versus villains, "real" men versus "real" women. It is a "melodrama," as Lumet himself called it in a 1991 interview in *Film Comment*. "The thing is that melodrama is built on a very simple level," Lumet explained. "What was tough about *Stranger* is that the melodrama was sort of the hanger on which I wanted to hang another set of clothes, sort of the excuse for doing the rest of the picture."[17] The simplicity of the film is evident in the way Lumet elected to dress and shoot the sets for the two communities, the two families, that are at odds in the film. The Hasidic community "was very color-controlled—clothes in relation to wall colors and so on. Primarily because it was Old World, the color scheme in both the art direction and gelling of the light was based around the whole range of amber colors—russets, browns, deep reds—because they're autumnal. There were no blues in the Hasidic world."[18] There are, of course, very sharp blues in the police world; Lumet used an exceptionally sharp, ungelled Primo lens for those scenes, and no color control at all; "We just let it be haphazard," he noted.[19] As a template for the other oppositions in the film, and for determining which side viewers might choose to identify with, this opposition between the autumnal and the haphazard makes clear just how unambiguous a choice Lumet has fashioned for his melodrama, as well as the seductiveness of the Jewish "Other" on display. Both the melodrama and murder mystery are simply pretexts for staging such a choice and seduction.

The film opens with a series of crosscuts that establish the contrast between cops and Hasids and that create the expectation that Eden's and Ariel's "families" will somehow intersect. The opening helicopter shot, the establishing shot, of Brooklyn from the Verrazano Narrows and of the East River, in beautiful golds and russets, ends at the Manhattan Bridge, the viewers' bridge into the Hasidic world of Ariel. The film then cuts to a shot from Ariel's point of view of the children in his cheder (elementary religious school) singing the *birkat hamazon,* the grace after meals, and the reverse shot reveals Ariel's pleased reaction to their performance. As spectators, viewers are positioned to see these Jewish characters as the Others of the film, but the cuteness of the children and Ariel's Hollywood-handsome face are cues that these Jewish bodies, though different, are recognizable as versions of characters viewers know from other Hollywood films. It is a wholesome, family-values grouping (perhaps reminiscent, for some viewers, of a children's choir or Sunday school recital) in which the characters are dressed in Hasidic garb. The crosscut is to Eden and her partner outside Club Zap as they reminisce about their "rogue shit," their youthful, cowboy-cop pasts. Both have their backs to the camera so that viewers are looking over Eden's shoulder, an evocative metaphor for how they are being positioned to identify with Eden. Visually, Eden's world is, ostensibly, familiar, a world of clubs and American teenage rituals that establish Lumet's protagonist as the typical American Adam—except that she's an Eden whose wistfulness in this scene ("Are these kids getting younger or are we getting older?") makes it obvious that she feels expelled from such an American teenager's Garden. The contrast between the two worlds in this opening crosscut is manifested in the contrasts between Jews and Gentiles, innocent children and cocky teenagers, community and alienation—between private spaces shared by adults and children and public spaces demarcated by age and shadowed by violence.

The bridge between Eden and Ariel, and thus between these two seemingly incompatible worlds, is suggested in the next crosscut. A close-up of Eden's stricken face after her partner is shot (an event for which she is partly responsible) dissolves into a stained glass Star of David in the study/prayer hall where Ariel is caught by his friend reading a book of kabbalah. Although the camera avoids shooting from Ariel's point of view in the scene that follows (dissuading viewers from identifying with his character), the dissolve suggests that both Ariel and Eden are alike in that they push at the boundaries that describe their respective worlds. The gentile, female cop and the Jewish kabbalist are both adventurous and somewhat rebellious by nature, an interior quality not apparent if people judge them by their bodies. Eden's performance as a cop in the opening scene is meant to portray her alienation, rebelliousness, and sexually aggressive, hard-boiled attitude, but, as reviewers noted, Melanie Griffith's little-girl voice, her slight physique, and her projection of a modern but fairly conventional femininity undercut the belief that she embodies a cowboy-cop with a hyperactive libido. While that contradiction was treated as a humorous flaw by reviewers, it nevertheless works quite well as a visual analogy between Eden as played by Griffith and Ariel as played by Thal, for Ariel too is supposed to look conventional but act unconventionally. His wholesomeness, earlocks, and black-clad body reference popular cultural images of Hasidic Jews, and Lumet plays with this image of Hasidim as a uniform(ed) Jewish Other, icons of Jewish purity (in the sense of both authenticity and morality) whose studiousness and gentleness make them a child-like and naive people who deny their carnal appetites.[20] Indeed, one of the "evil" attributes of the murderer is that she takes advantage of this naiveté by playing on the fact that her fiancé sees her body, which she treated like "trash," as one that is "lost" rather than as a sexual object. But Ariel, the beefcake Hasid who will help Eden, is supposed to represent and to undermine the image of the Hasid—he is both an *ilui*, a scholarly prodigy, and a real man capable of shooting a gun (though not without fainting). The dark clothes that cover Ariel's body hide his interior qualities, not all of which have been revealed at this early point in the film, just as effectively as Eden's femininity hides her interior qualities, not all yet revealed, either. Both embody secret bridges.

It is no surprise, then, that investigating bodies is the raison d'etre of the film: the dead body of the murdered Hasid, the overheated and overexposed body of Eden, and the cool, mysterious body of Ariel. After the introductory crosscuts depicting the protagonists, viewers are introduced to the russet-and-gold-colored Brooklyn home of the Hasidic "family" and its families. As spectators to a montage of Hasidic businesses, strolling men, and mothers with scores of babies and toddlers—all presented from Eden's point of view through the windshield of her car—viewers are clearly positioned to see themselves in Eden's place: a

Gentile observing fruitful and multiplying Jewish bodies, and a Jewish space so different from other New York spaces that instead of traffic or other city noises there is, on the soundtrack, klezmer music. As Eden (and viewers) enter the rebbe's home and office, the contrast between the covered-up bodies of the Hasidim and Eden's immodestly dressed form—white tee-shirt and short black skirt, and a camel-colored coat that she removes before going into the rebbe's study—becomes a running gag, with Leah struggling to keep Eden wrapped in shawls that slip off at awkward moments. The idea of Eden being "under cover" thus starts out as a joke, but the scene establishes visual cues for viewers who are going undercover with her. Eden's masculine aggressiveness, the way she blithely insults the rebbe and Ariel with her questions and her manner in this scene and later in the precinct ("I guess you're not used to a woman like me, huh?" she asks Ariel. "Is anyone?" he responds) is mediated by the visual inconsistency between the Eden character and Griffith's body. That inconsistency suggests that the real Eden is "undercover" disguised as a male cop, and that this cover will also slip off eventually. More obviously, Eden the undercover Gentile in the Hasidic world will be introduced to the Hasidim and the Hasidic way of life, putting on what at first seems a comical disguise, but one with significances and attractiveness that will be explained by Leah and Ariel as they slowly allow Eden, and viewers, to penetrate their family and their world.

And how good that penetration feels; witness Eden's barely containable enjoyment in initiating verbal foreplay with Ariel (Ariel: "We are not quaint or exotic. We are not cute little characters." Eden: "You are . . . cute." Ariel: "Please do not say things like that to me") Witness, too, Eden's visible admiration for the strength and depth of attachment the community members feel for one another, for the rebbe, and for the traditional gender roles that it is Leah's function as a character to explain and defend (of her aspiration to be a wife and mother she asks rhetorically, "What could be more important?"). Eden and viewers find themselves inside a very attractive social body indeed. But there is also a kind of tease at work here: how far can Eden and viewers really go as they go undercover as Jews? Lumet continues to use crosscutting to play out this tease, developing Eden's and viewers' desire for Ariel and his world, but flipping back to the haphazard world of the cops to throw a little cold water on that desire. So, for example, after Eden makes her first rounds of the Hasidic community dressed as a Hasidic woman, Lumet crosscuts to Eden playing a card game of "War" with her injured partner, reminding viewers that her professional relationship with her world, and her relationship with men, is combative: the "independent woman," as she describes herself, is a woman who behaves like a man, and the costs of such gender undercover work is what ails contemporary women like Eden. In the scene following, Eden arrives at a meeting back at the precinct to discuss her case, and when she enters the room dressed as a Hasidic woman, the reactions from her male colleagues reveal both the seductiveness of Jewish bodies (even her fake one) and the price Eden is paying for her acceptance into this police "family." All the men ogle Eden, and they tell her she looks "radiant" and like a "lady." Her new, "Jewish" body, covered in a modest dark blue dress and topped by a wig-like hairdo, is glowing and attractive, and, ironically, this identity is a big turn-on for the self-hating, secular Jew Levine. "You still got a great ass, Eden," he tells her before launching into a comic rant about the Hasidim and their sexual mores. In this scene the attractiveness of Jewish bodies is portrayed as an unwanted accompaniment to modesty—as if in the police world anything covered triggers in cops the desire to uncover it. The salaciousness, crassness, and disrespect of such "penetration" is disturbing to Eden, and she discovers through Levine that self-hate is the price of acceptance into the police "family" for non-Jewish Jews and nontraditional females. To be police, she and Levine must police themselves and any desire they may have to be different—to be modest, respectful, and self-aware, traits that here are deemed "feminine."

When it comes to Ariel, however, squelching desire—for him and for the "feminine" traits that he exemplifies—proves quite difficult. Eden prefers to be in his and the other Hasidim's company, and the conflict between her "family" and the Hasidic "family" is made literal when she visits her father, a retired cop, and realizes that their relationship is mediated through police work and its material rewards, whereas for the Hasidim family relations are mediated through communitarian work and its spiritual rewards. Scenes of Hasidic women crowded into a kitchen helping to prepare the Sabbath meal, and of Hasidic men and women rushing to the aid of the injured *ba'alat teshuva*, prepare viewers to see Eden's ostensibly inappropriate desire for Ariel as both a sexual and a moral longing. Loving him would make her both a better person and a better woman, a point brought home as viewers watch her watch him dance and teach young children during a multigenerational and multicultural Sabbath meal (as if one fantasy required another as its vehicle). The power Ariel and the Hasidic community possess, in contradistinction to the physical power of the police (which viewers witness when Eden and Levine face down a pair of bad guys in the Diamond District), is that not only of a higher-order morality, but also of self-knowledge. And that power of self-knowledge is, finally, what separates Eden, the undercover Gentile, from "real" Jews, that is, from Hasidim. In a scene that begins with a dissolve from the face of the self-hating Levine to the face of the rebbe, Emily tries to apologize to the rebbe, a Holocaust survivor, for inadvertently suggesting in a previous scene that he knows nothing about evil. "Compared to you I haven't seen that much," she admits. "You and I have a great deal in common," the rebbe says. "We both are on intimate terms with evil. It does things to your soul, doesn't it?" "I wouldn't know about that," Eden responds. The rebbe assures Eden that she has a soul, but her uncertainty about what really lies inside her—whether it's a soul or not, and whether that interior can be made congruent with her exterior—reveals both her non-Jewishness (real Jews are in touch with their Jewish souls) and a part of her that needs to be opened up. Eden's desire thus foregrounds the limits and the lure of cultural interchange.

It is both apt and logical, therefore, that, in a key scene in the film's rising action, Eden and Ariel perform a kind of cultural interchange that plays fast and loose with limits and lures. Entering the courtyard of the rebbe's house late at night after the Sabbath meal, and after it has been announced that Ariel is to marry the daughter of a French Hasidic rebbe, Eden discovers Ariel reading a kabbalistic text on sex, a lure she can't resist. Ariel drapes his black coat over Eden's shoulders, ostensibly to keep the bathrobe-clad Eden warm in the chill night air, but wearing the coat Eden transparently becomes the male pursuer and Ariel the feminine pursued and champion of limits. As they spar with each other, Ariel wondering at Eden's power to kill people and she wondering at his power to read the spiritual into the sexual, Eden's conversation reflects her frustration and anger at being denied what she really wants: Ariel and true love. He, on the other hand, wants only worthiness to be the next rebbe, and to maintain his purity. As for Eden, he just wants to be friends. Besides, his French fiancée is his *basherte*, his destined mate. In a statement that is a perfect expression of limits that *are* lures, Ariel tells Eden: "Everything is predestined, but everybody has freedom of choice." Well, not really. By this point in the film the choice that Eden and viewers have been positioned to want is an easy one: we want the Jewish Other who offers the heroine sex *and* spirituality—we want the angry and unhappy independent woman to fulfill her domestic potential and to be fulfilled, and for the limits between Jew and non-Jew to fall away. When Ariel finally enters her world, going to her apartment for no other apparent reason except to provide a climax to their relationship (and to provide unmotivated exposition about the solution to the case), he finds her watching an old Fred Astaire and Ginger Rogers movie, symbol for the kind of traditional and aesthetically pleasing secular couple they would make. As with Astaire and Rogers, Ariel would bring class to their act and Eden would bring sex. With those arch-gentile bodies dancing in the background, a half-dressed Eden tells Ariel how miserable she is in her secular gentile life. She desperately wants Ariel because then she won't be angry anymore. "You made me feel soft on the inside," she says, and when they kiss it appears as if the two will indeed trespass their limits and quite literally reveal themselves to each other.

But Ariel breaks away and remains dressed and closed-off to Eden, and he runs cold water over his wrists as if to imply that the Jewish Other may neck with an undercover Gentile, the Gentile who wants to break down the boundaries between Jew and non-Jew, but will draw the line there. Why? And what is Lumet's rationale? As the cultural critic Edward Norden observed in his *Commentary* review, perhaps "Lumet wished *Stranger* to be a fable," for so much of his portrait of Hasidim and of Eden strains credulity.[21] The scene undoubtedly reflects Lumet's idealization and romanticization of both the Hasidim and of women, in that both are imbued not only with an unbelievable sweetness, but also, as Norden points out, with one last, great desire: to remain in their place, safely positioned as traditional and obedient urban citizens.[22] Or perhaps Ariel's explanation that he has been promised to another, and his disquisition on predestination and choice, is an attempt to mobilize the idea of the Jewish people's "chosenness"—that the Jew is already a partner in a long-running act that can't be broken up. Ultimately there does not seem a well worked-out reason, and the scene is an anticlimactic climax, in both senses, signaling that the long tease of the film's rising action is finally over. Having shown viewers the limits to "penetrating" the Jewish body, Lumet focuses the rest of the third act on reestablishing boundaries and underscoring why Jewishness is so desirable.

Lumet therefore takes care to visually distance Eden and Ariel in most of the scenes at the end of the film, scenes that illustrate the two characters taking sides and recognizing which side they are on. For example, in the scene in which Eden lies in a hospital bed, crying, while Ariel stands over her saying goodbye, the camera visually places him above her and out of her reach. Lumet then cuts from that shot to one where she, crying, is framed in her bed by the doorway to her hospital room as Ariel meets his fiancé and discovers that she is indeed his long-awaited *basherte*. And during the wedding scene, filmed in beautiful, glowing golds and antique whites, Lumet fashions a significant shot–reverse shot sequence that images their final separation. Ariel is framed in a tight shot looking at Eden, who is framed in a long shot at the edge of the crowd, and, in one of the only shots from his point of view, he watches her as his bride circles him, passing in front of the camera. When his bride steps out of the frame and the long shot reappears, Eden is gone, visually disappearing from Ariel's life and from his view of the social fabric of New York City.

In the final scene, viewers find themselves back in Eden's world—which is to say, back in their world. She arrives at the precinct house and turns down Levine's offer of a trip to Aruba, telling him that she's waiting for her *bashert*. She is still a part of the police "family," but Levine is the wrong family man and the wrong kind of Jew since he doesn't even know what the word *bashert* means. When Eden, dressed modestly now but more fashionably than her previous disguise, utters the film's final line, "Ask your rabbi," she is a changed woman; she is a "real" woman who knows that true happiness equals domesticity, and who is not a Jew but is nevertheless more "Jewish" than Levine because she has discovered the power of "real" Jews: she knows who she is and what she wants, and she knows whom viewers should ask if they wish to achieve the same thing.

It is easy to see why Lumet's film received the reviews it did, but in fashioning Hasidim as Jewish Others who function as modern urban touchstones of authenticity—authentic Jews, authentic family life, authentic self-knowledge—Lumet also fashions a lesson about the need for and usefulness of borders between Jews and non-Jews. The Jewish body, both literal and figurative, is open to outsiders, but if it is to retain its putative mystique, power, and purity it can only open so far. Jews like Levine have squandered that power and are clearly so open to the outside world that they fail to be Jews anymore. For Ariel to remain the desirable Other, he must be unattainable, and if this means that people in Eden's world and in her police "family" misread him, then so be it. In Lumet's film, Ariel and the Hasidim are the melodrama's unattainable objects of desire. They are ideals of authenticity that need not be possessed (though they incite the desire to possess), and the boundaries that Lumet establishes around them through Eden's point of view, and through crosscutting and color matching, in fact make them very safe objects of desire. They do not require that viewers actually engage real Jews or real Hasidim. They function as Others who validate a simple character transformation: from unhappy urban professional woman to happy urban traditionalist.

In this respect, Eden is a reflection of late eighties and early nineties New York urban society, a yuppie looking for amorous, ethical, and social fulfillment. The kosher hybridity of Lumet's film, which is one part melodrama, one part police procedural, and one part Hasidic family fable, models the need for an "us" and a "them" in order that viewers may better define "us" as a product of the clear distinction between the discomfort of independence and the fulfillment of belonging. In other words, the film's lesson is that boundaries enable comprehensible and safe social groupings, amorous couplings, and personal identities. No boundaries, no identities. Further, viewers of the film are clearly "us" because they experience the need for boundaries from Eden's point of view. Hence, *A Stranger among Us* is a film from the dominant culture's perspective that, wittingly or unwittingly, sutures viewers within the boundaries of that perspective by inserting them into the position of the undercover Gentile. Perhaps this accounts for the confusion of the title. As the web site *Jabootu's Bad Movie Dimension* notes, from Eden's point of view the title ought to be *I among the Strangers*. But if, to viewers who identify with Eden, the stranger is, and remains, the Hasidic Ariel, paragon of the Jewish Other, then, despite any ethnic or religious affiliations, allegiances, or knowledges that Lumet may claim, the film is narrated from a *non-Jewish* perspective. Therefore, the title makes sense as an unwitting admission of who is reflecting on whom in Lumet's film. As an object of reflection and desire, Ariel flatters Jewish viewers, but in the end Lumet's film throws back a distorted Jewish Other who is no more than a stick figure in a melodrama about urban social conformity and its masquerades.

BOBBY GOLD, UNDERCOVER JEW

In David Mamet's *Homicide,* New York police detective Bobby Gold (Joe Mantegna), a talented police negotiator, and his partner Tim Sullivan (William H. Macy) are assigned to find Randolph Sims (Ving Rhames), an African American drug dealer and murder suspect wanted by the FBI. On their way to investigate a lead, Gold gets sidetracked by a variety store murder and robbery. A number of things seem curious to Gold: the murdered owner was an old Jewish woman who had stayed in what had become a primarily Black neighborhood; a group of children claim she was murdered for the fortune she kept hidden in the basement; and the woman's relatives claim that her murder was an act of anti-Semitism. In a fluke of circumstance, Gold is peremptorily reassigned to the murder/robbery case by his superiors. As he investigates the woman's background and the family's insinuations, and, at the same time, tries to stay involved in the NYPD/FBI manhunt, Gold finds himself drawn into a mysterious, covert conflict between neo-Nazis and Israeli secret agents that forces him to consider his ethnic and social allegiances as an American Jew. Asked by the Israelis to pass them confidential police information, Gold complies, but realizes too late that he has been double-crossed by them and that his inattentiveness to the manhunt has cost the life of his partner. Finding himself trapped with the Black drug dealer whom he is trying to convince to surrender, Gold understands that he and the dealer have both betrayed and been betrayed by their "families." At the end of the film, when the wounded Gold discovers that the Black children had indeed killed the old Jewish woman for her hidden fortune and that he has been kicked off the homicide squad, he appears to belong nowhere, professionally, socially, or ethnically.

Mamet's film did not do very well at the box office (its byzantine plot, lugubrious pacing, and unsatisfying solution to the murder mystery inevitably rankle my students when I screen it), but it continues to draw critical analysis. Two excellent essays on the film, Ranen Omer's "The Metaphysics of Lost Jewish Identity in David Mamet's Homicide" and Adam Zachary Newton's "Homicide: Kike on the Streets or, Chicago PD Jew" (in chapter 5 of *Facing Black and Jew*), exemplify two competing views about the Jewish aspects of *Homicide,* and how both these views focus almost exclusively on Mamet's language.

Omer's essay takes its cue from Hayim Nahman Bialik's 1915 essay "Revealment and Concealment in Language," in which Bialik, echoing the sentiments of other modernists of his time but employing biblical and kabbalistic allusions that speak to the situation of the Jewish writer, argues that language conceals a radical void, a nothingness, that lies outside or behind what he calls "man's atmosphere of knowledge."[23] Language, however, also periodically reveals that void through the cracks of worn-out tropes, *topoi,* and systems of knowledge, thereby revealing itself as a human construct meant to mollify the terror incited by nothingness. Omer's argument is that Mamet is the postmodern American Jewish writer who "has most compellingly returned us to the stark terms of Bialik's disturbing confession about the desperation that wears the mask of Jewish art. But Mamet's disturbances transcend even the frightening radical metaphysics described by Bialik in 1915, juxtaposing the modernist preoccupation with poetic language with the ambiguities that thwart the formulation of ethnic identity and self-construction."[24] Citing interviews, a pair of critical essays on Mamet's "Jewish" language, and Mamet's previous dramatic and nonfiction writing about Jews and Jewishness, Omer reads *Homicide* as a skeptical take on the "self-deceptions of Jewish exile" and of American Jewish cultural assimilation.[25] In Omer's view, the dialogue and wordplay in Mamet's film reveals ethnic identity as a construct very much like the suit of armor that Bialik conjures as a symbol for how language shields humans against the void. The links in that armor, however, are loose and coming apart, and the instability of those links is reflected by the instability of language in the film: GROFAZ, an acronym for Hitler ("Grossten fur alle Zeiten," "the greatest [leader] of all time"), seems an important clue to uncovering a neo-Nazi conspiracy, but turns out to be the incomplete name for a pigeon feed—GROFAZT. To Omer "the story's conflicts are defined not through action or even conventional narrative resolution, but through language,"[26] and ultimately Omer sees Mamet "very much in the tradition of Benjamin and Kafka, a radical skeptic of both language and absolutist identities."[27] If in the end Omer concludes that Mamet offers no substance to Jewish identity "outside of victimhood" and no other strategy in the face of alienation than withdrawal into "Kabbalistic games with language,"[28] Omer's conclusion still places Mamet in very notable company, situating Mamet's *Homicide* as a postmodern Jewish film that plays out an important line of influence in Jewish literary modernism.

Adam Zachary Newton's essay, on the other hand, identifies *Homicide* as "a very American movie"[29] in the way that Mamet pushes language and characters around like postmodern stage props to signify, but not investigate or challenge, ethnic and social identities. Newton sees the language of Mamet's film as neither concealing nor revealing but, like the gun that Gold keeps losing throughout it, operating "indexically": pointing attention to itself as a locus of meaning that never resolves into *a* meaning. Newton grants the postmodernism of Mamet's film, but not its kabbalistic or even its modernist pedigree. For Newton, *Homicide* is another take on "the signature world of Mamet's antinaturalism,"[30] a world in which cops, Jews, Blacks, Zionists, and Nazis seem like so many floating signifiers, and in which "words have the same effect as other mobile modes of signification—detachable fragments, the junk-shop of Mamet-talk: swagger, epithet, iambic rattle."[31] Gold's rootlessness is "diasporism as unmoored solipsism,"[32] and the use of the epithet "kike" at the film's beginning does not frame any real issues of Jewishness but rather enacts a form of diasporism (becoming a verbal allegory that serves no purpose) and invokes the appearance, later in the film, of the obvious social partner, "nigger." The two epithets together (and Gold's scene with the drug dealer) ultimately mobilize, to no apparent purpose, "blackjewishrelations," Newton's neologism for the social trope that has become an easy label and a perilous blinder for the vexed relationship between Blacks and Jews in America.[33] The very gratuitousness of the "character changes ... the tiered levels of paranoia and parallel-tracked conspiracies, the recycling of words and objects, and last but not least, the collision of Jewish-identity and black-outlaw plots"[34] suggests to Newton that the word "job," a word that Gold and the other policemen constantly banter about, is the axis around which the film turns.[35] In Newton's reading, this word seems to have two implications for the film, one overt and the other slyly implied: first, that the characters, plot, and language in *Homicide* are constantly "at work" and their meanings not allowed to come to rest; second, that the film itself is just another job for Mamet—that it has, in fact, no ulterior purpose or meaning. Newton's conclusion is blunt: "Either *Homicide* is postmodern reflexivity made so superfine as to be ultimately tendentious, or it is just out of control."[36] Obviously, neither view is complimentary, but, in both, Mamet's language speaks for itself.

Omer's and Newton's essays stake out the critical positions on *Homicide*, and to a large extent agreement with a version of one or the other becomes a matter of personal taste; one either admires the postmodernism on display in *Homicide* or one does not. But whether the film is heir to Kafka or a space for the floating signifier "kike," the proof-text for either position remains the film's screenplay. Looking at the bodies on the screen, however, and at the shifting point of view from which the film is narrated and those bodies seen, provides a different perspective on the Jewish aspects of *Homicide*. That is, if the range of references granted to the film is enlarged beyond literary theory and hermeneutics to include film theory and the anti-detective story (also known as the metaphysical or analytic detective story, in which the conventions of detective fiction are parodied, deconstructed, or allegorized),[37] the question of pedigree or purpose becomes less important than the question of violence in relation to bodies both Jewish and non-Jewish.

For example, consider the film's opening sequence of shots, a sequence not analyzed or even mentioned in either essay. The first shot reveals a deep diagonal line running from the top left of the frame to the bottom right. As the lighting in the shot brightens, viewers see that the line divides black and white, and then that the line is a staircase, the camera tracking down until the guns and helmets of the police SWAT team, on its way up, come into the frame. In the next couple of tight-framed shots, the camera situates viewers in front of the police phalanx as it advances up the stairwell and down an apartment house hall, their faces hidden behind protective helmet shields and their guns seemingly drawn and pointed at the audience. In a quick cut, the camera then situates viewers behind and to the side of the phalanx as it arrives in front of the apartment door. The faceless lead policeman then points his finger directly at viewers, as if they were now among the police officers, and silently signs an order for viewers to take a position next to him. Consequently, the violence of their storming of the apartment—a policeman shot by someone inside, a woman and man shot in their bed, the tension as the officers realize that their suspect, the drug dealer Randolph Sims, has escaped through a secret passage out onto the rooftop—is witnessed from the police point of view. This opening sequence sets up a visual tension between black and white, not just in the sense of Blacks versus Whites, but also in the sense of right versus wrong, good guys versus bad guys. These tensions are all a product of the opening scene, in which viewers are directed to find a point of view from which to understand what is happening onscreen—that is, to resolve what at first appears a gray field into a clear picture of sharp divisions. The violence of such division and resolution is brought home by that first, abrupt switch in point of view from in front of the police guns to beside/behind them. Viewers are forced into choosing, and choosing quickly, to identify with the police, to being on the side behind the guns and acceding to the officer's instruction to take their place at his side.

Thus, in the first sequence in *Homicide,* viewers are positioned to find the safe identification in the film, to collaborate with the point of view that offers a defense against the violence that lurks behind closed doors, against the violence of guns hidden from sight. This sequence initiates a "gun" motif that, in addition to its sexual and gendered connotations, foregrounds the very real danger and dread that attends the violent social world of the film. True, Mamet may also be improvising on Jewish literary modernism, extending Bialik's insight that the protection identity affords is indeed a construct, a bulwark against the metaphysical void behind the social world, but it is not the metaphysical that wields the firearms here. And no doubt, identity is offered viewers as a spectator insurance against physical harm—imaginary insurance and imaginary harm, to be sure—but the stakes involved are familiar to the genre: as befits a detective story, this is a film about life and death choices in the social world, of bodies and social bodies threatened by guns. Putting aside Omer's and Newton's arguments about this film, let us consider the way the detective genre illuminates the interplay between spectatorship and collaboration.

To begin, as the images in the opening sequence suggest, bodies without an identity or out of "uniform" (like the bodies caught in bed, a literal deathbed) are highly vulnerable. For Gold, as for the police in his precinct and the FBI agents they have to work with, that uniform is the coat and tie. Differences between the police and FBI bodies are not only signaled by the FBI agent's Black anti-Semitism, which raises the divisiveness of race in a way that seems unwarranted to Gold's racially and ethnically mixed comrades, but also by the *differences* in the coats and ties (the FBI agent is dressed in a natty suit, whereas the cops reflect a motley of cheap department store fashions). As the conflict with the FBI agent illustrates, Gold is an assimilated Jew, one whose uniform betokens his allegiance to the police; as the audience is presented the story from his point of view, viewers are positioned at first to identify with him, with this undercover Jew working for the police defenders. This positioning is made apparent when Gold stumbles into the variety store murder/robbery; viewers see the murdered woman and examine the evidence from Gold's point of view. What they see is that the Jewish woman was apparently reaching for a pistol hidden in a cigar box, another example of hidden firearms, and that she and her family were outsiders in what had become a Black neighborhood. These Jewish others are said to be Gold's "people," but as viewers can see by Gold's uniform, they are not. Once he is reassigned to the murder/robbery, however, Gold's uniform slowly begins to unravel: in a precinct scuffle with a murder suspect, his holster is knocked off; he takes his tie off in order to seem more sympathetic to Sims's mother as he tries to convince her to betray her son; and in some scenes he is the only cop with his sport coat off.

Gold finds himself a body alone, cut off from his partner because of his reassignment, and the confusion this isolation engenders is reflected in the scene where he visits the dead woman's family in their luxury apartment. The family claims that someone has fired shots at them, and Gold, hearing them speak what sounds like Yiddish and feeling their otherness as a combination of class, ethnic, and linguistic differences, refuses to believe them. As he talks to the dead woman's son, the camera literalizes this conflict between subject-psychological points of view (the family's point of view that Jews are being threatened again, versus Gold's point of view that the Jews are fantasizing a conspiracy and buying protection) by shifting the scene's cinematic point of view. As the woman's son asks him if he'll do his job, and Gold insists that this is why he is there, the camera circles the pair and cuts back and forth between the son's point of view and Gold's. Which is the "right" point of view? Which is the "safe" point of view?

For Gold and for viewers, the moment of decision comes after this scene during a phone conversation he has with his partner. As he twiddles with a magnifying glass, Gold catches up on the Sims case, and, although told that he was the "linchpin" who helped turn Sims's mother against her son, he sees himself as out of the loop:

> I would've been there. I'm stuck here with my, my Jews. You should see this fuckin' room. No fuckin' bullshit, bunch of highstrung fuckin' bullshit, they pay so much taxes, fuck 'em. Yo! She did? Fan-fuckin'-tastic! What? Oh some bullshit, somebody's takin' shots at 'em. Hey, fuck 'em. Don't tell me. Don't say the old lady worked down there and tell me how you're so surprised. Fuck 'em and the taxes they pay. You tell me, ten more bucks a week they're making lettin' her work down there. Hey, not my people baby, fuck 'em. [*Here Gold moves out of the frame to reveal the granddaughter whose presence in the background had been hidden by his head.*] There's so much anti-Semitism the last four thousand years we must be doin' something to bring it about.
>
> [My transcription.]

Visually, the film suggests here that what Gold does not see is the imaginary Jewish Other *in* his head and the real Jewish Other *behind* his head, who is in the room with him. Once again, subject-psychological point of view is spatially symbolized, and Gold's point of view looks shameful from both the viewer's and the granddaughter's perspective. She tells Gold that her grandmother "was a fighter. She wanted to die there," and that the family wants his respect, not his sympathy. Caught in this moment of apparent Jewish self-hate, Gold recognizes that he is in a precarious spot: he cannot do his job if he is not trusted and respected by the Jews, but to be trusted and respected he will have to venture out of the safety of his police "cover." He will have to expose himself. When Gold hears what he calls "backfire," but now thinks might be a gunshot, he and viewers take off to find the hidden source of the sound, and so viewers are once again positioned to choose the defender, to get behind him.

Gold himself chooses to defend a Jewish perspective. But what does he find when he penetrates that perspective? Not authenticity or purity, to be sure; he finds himself in an anti-detective story. For me, that reading is triggered in the scene where he lingers for a moment in front of a photograph of the dead woman as a happy young pioneer in pre-state Palestine. As he reaches out to adjust the photo, another photo falls from the back. It pictures the dead woman holding a rifle, obviously a picture of her as a fighter with the Jewish underground. This picture within a picture once again images the violence hidden from sight, but Gold reads it as verifying the dead woman's place in the Jewish conspiracy that takes root in the imaginary Jewish Other in his head. While the postmodern constructedness of such a conspiracy is clearly being signaled, the conspiracy is also an indirection appropriate to the anti-detective story. For it helps instigate Gold's investigation of GROFAZ, and lands him in the Jewish library that Newton interprets as "the film's allegorical ground zero,"[38] a place where language folds back on itself to no apparent purpose, but a place that also bears a far closer relationship to the library of Dr. Marcel Yarmolinsky and the "Jewish" clues in Jorge Luis Borges's classic anti-detective story, "Death and the Compass." Erik Lönnrot, Borges's detective, investigates Yarmolinsky's murder at the Third Talmudic Congress, and, noting the many Jewish books that Yarmolinsky had brought there, Lönnrot announces, "I should prefer a purely rabbinical explanation" to the murder, not a prosaic one that admits the "reality" of wholly unmotivated violence.[39] "Maybe this crime belongs to the history of Jewish superstitions,"[40] Lönnrot conjectures, but it does not. It belongs to the history of Red Scharlach, the criminal who has invented the entire mystery—planting within it a Hasidic conspiracy and murdering Yarmolinsky for no cause—as a ruse to lure Lönnrot to his death. Even as he is about to die, Lönnrot continues to spin out the sort of abstract reasoning that describes the classical detective figure, but one of the amusing and instructive ironies of Borges's fiction is that in the end Scharlach's retort to such reasoning is a straightforward bullet fired from his non-abstract gun.

Similarly, Gold prefers a "rabbinical" explanation to the dead woman's murder, and he duly finds the evidence in the library, in the variety store's basement, in a schoolroom, and in the back of a print shop. Gold's decision to buy into the "rabbinical" explanation ("I want to be a part of it," he tells the Israelis, though he has no real idea what "it" is), his decision to take the perspective of the Jewish Other in order to assume a Jewish identity that he will not be ashamed of—he is even dressed like the bodies of the Israeli secret agents, in a leather jacket and dark shirt, so that sartorially he is no longer a cop but a "Jewish" body—inevitably leads to the violence that Borges's fiction illustrates. Pocketing his police badge, Gold blows up the print shop, a front for a neo-Nazi group. But the action "blows up" in Gold's face when the Israelis blackmail him into handing over the list of names he found in the dead woman's basement. And because he tarried investigating this mystery, he fails to arrive in time to help spring the capture of Randolph Sims, and so Gold is responsible for the death of his partner. As viewers follow Gold down into the coal cellar where Sims is hiding out, the two together image a tableau of two bodies trapped by the indirections that have been planted for them; in Sims's case those indirections had been planted by Gold himself, so that one irony in the scene is that Gold, like Lönnrot, is a victim of his own reasoning. Both men have also been betrayed and victimized by their "families," seduced by the indirections of partisan explanations that divided "us" from "them," but that in the end leave them alone and vulnerable. Sims's reaction to the news of his mother's betrayal, shooting Gold a second time in the gut, illustrates that despite all the language in the film, "the labyrinth made of the single straight line which is invisible and everlasting," as Borges's character describes a bullet's trajectory,[41] remains the most dreadful mystery of all. Gold is no longer a defender or a negotiator but a victim, illustrating that the violence of opening the Jewish body (a body that is Jewish, in the end, only by dint of assertion) reveals the vulnerability of all bodies as they try to negotiate, and to negotiate their way out of, the politically and socially charged spaces of postmodern America.

Let me clarify here that it's not, or not only, that Mamet cannot imagine any other Jewish identity but that of the victim, as Newton claims, or that the film simply advertises violence as "a lovely and legitimate expression of Jewish identity," as Leon Wieseltier argues.[42] Like other anti-detective stories, *Homicide* is responding to the chaos of the contemporary world, a chaos that, as Borges's fiction suggests, is both metaphysical and quite physical. Victimization leaves its mark on both the mind and the body. Michael Holquist, the literary scholar who brought psychology and myth to bear on detective fiction when he dubbed Borges's fiction a "metaphysical" detective story, was concerned with only the metaphysical, as is Omer when he brings Bialik and Benjamin to bear on Mamet. The physical violence signified by the gun motif of the film, however, and brought home by the deaths of the variety store owner, Gold's partner, and Sims, and by the twice-shot Gold himself, is the violence that accompanies physical attempts to re-impose order, identity, and meaningful division on the chaotic world. The implication in the film is that the expression of any identity, of taking one's place at the side of any group, is itself a kind of collaborative violence and potential victimization that is both metaphysical and physical. The price paid by Gold for his collaboration with a suspect point of view and for placing himself in harm's way is high. His body, clothed in the film's final scene in jeans and a letterman's jacket, and thereby marked as both "juvenile" and "civilian," is crippled, and whatever his Jewishness may consist of, it remains deeply undercover, to both the audience and to Gold, its authenticity an indirection and its visibility a moot point.

In respect to spectatorship and collaboration, the price paid by Gold and viewers for the collaborative violence of subject-psychological and cinematic point of view is evoked in the final sequence of shots at the film's close. On its most obvious level of meaning, that final sequence provides closure for the "relationship" between Gold and a murderer he meets at the film's beginning, a man who killed his own wife and children with a deer rifle. In their first meeting, where the murderer tries to grab Gold's gun, both Gold and the killer are similarly clothed, two men in professional attire, and like the "uniforms" of the police and the FBI, the difference between Gold's and the murderer's is a minor difference in sartorial emphasis: the murderer wears a staid business suit. In that first meeting, the camera frames both men in an eye-level shot, visually implying a kind of equivalency. Here, the film deploys a convention of detective fiction, the similarity between the detective and the criminal and the struggle between two great minds, except that in this scene, as in Borges's anti-detective story, when the murderer offers to tell Gold "the nature of Evil," Gold refuses the offer, wryly noting that if he accepted he'd be out of a job. Gold, in keeping with the anti-detective story, prefers to develop his own explanations and to choose his own perspectives. As the film progresses, the murderer's uniform, like Gold's, unravels, so that in their next shared scene, where Gold refuses to press charges against the man for assaulting a police officer, Gold is half-undressed and the murderer, though still in his suit jacket and pants, is seen with his shirt untucked and unbuttoned, and his tie is missing. In this shot, Gold is in the foreground and the murderer is in a holding cell in the background, as if to suggest that Gold's shadow is the criminal, a caged man coming undone. When the camera cuts to a shot of Gold as he looks into a mirror, it's appropriate that his gaze comes to rest not on himself or the killer but on a neo-Nazi flyer asserting that "Crime is caused by the ghetto," which is, again, another indirection that references Gold's preferred explanation to his case, in spite of the fact that an answer to what causes crime has been offered by the criminal sitting behind him. In both of these scenes, viewers are positioned to see the murderer from Gold's point of view, both psychologically and cinematically, and the price for this point of view is indifference to the murderer and his perspective despite any acknowledged or unacknowledged similarity between the two men.

In the final sequence of shots, then, both Gold and viewers are prepared to see the murderer as a kind of commentary on that indifference, a commentary made evident in how the man is clothed. Gold catches sight of the murderer being led by a trooper down the corridor toward where Gold stands framed in a doorway. The killer is dressed in prison garb, a gray-blue uniform, and he is shackled hand and foot. As he nears Gold, Gold is handed a file that reveals GROFAZ is really GROFAZT (signaling that he himself is the "pigeon," the dupe), and so as viewers watch the murderer pass Gold from Gold's point of view, the eye-level shot of the two men locking eyes makes clear that this is a recognition scene: psychologically and cinematically, how one views a murder locks one into a perspective that is like a cage or like manacles.

It is not that point of view is a prison—that is too facile a conclusion—but that, in respect to the physical violence of the social world, the postmodern observation that all perspectives and identities are social or philosophical constructs imprisons us in a kind of indifference toward the Other. This makes Gold and viewers dupes, complicit in seeing the Jewish other in the same way that the murderer viewed his family, as if they were something to be hunted. Like the murderer, Gold and viewers have voluntarily handed themselves up to the authorities and allowed themselves to be hauled away as spectators, so that in taking their place at the side of the "safe" point of view, in becoming accomplices in the creation of a division between "us" and "them," they have in fact become prisoners within that perspective and lost sight of the murder at hand. *Homicide* is, after all, a film about murder, and the way the film delivers its lesson about spectatorship and collaboration, about the painfulness of border-making and of Jewishness as an object of reflection, reminds us that, as in Borges's fiction, the ultimate cost of such voluntary self-indirection is death. Gold, therefore, is lucky—he's only been wounded. He and viewers have a second chance to learn that lesson.

SEW AND TELL?: SUTURE AND KOSHER HYBRIDITY

Looking at the film language in *A Stranger among Us* and in *Homicide* we see some of the properties of the Other who takes the place of the self, and therefore some of the properties of Jewishness as an object of reflection. Film provides a venue both for spectator identification with others and for taking pleasure in a coherent world of coherent others objectified for spectator gratification. But while Mamet's film reiterates Finkielkraut's argument that Jewishness can be an eminently useable fiction, it also reiterates film theorist Kaja Silverman's argument about the relation between film and the psychoanalytic concept of "suture." In her use of the term, "suture" describes the positioning and inscribing of viewers into a cinematic discourse that formulates and lends them social identities.[43] In other words, film provides viewers with understandable perspectives on social and political arrangements, and through cinematic point of view it positions viewers within those arrangements and provides them with coherent and safe social identities, albeit ones that support the dominant ideologies. Discussing Hitchcock's *Psycho* and its disruptive shifts in cinematic point of view, Silverman asserts that despite such disruption, which ought to undermine viewer positioning, the film "obliges us to understand . . . that we want suture so badly that we'll take it at any price, even with the fullest knowledge of what it entails—passive insertions into preexisting discursive positions (both mythically potent and mythically impotent); threatened losses and false recoveries; and subordination to the castrating gaze of a symbolic Other [the symbolic "father figure" policing viewer perception of social reality]."[44] The "want" within individual viewers that Silverman refers to is a psychological need for wholeness and coherence in spite of the oppression or repression that inevitably accompanies such willing submission to a dominant ideology.

I think that a similar kind of "want" enables and feeds off the pedagogical function of the kosher hybridity in American Jewish detective stories. That "wanting" is to locate borders between Jews and non-Jews, and thereby to manifest one or another kind of "authentic" Jewishness, in the stories. Borders give shape to the perceived values of Jewishness; they gratify a desire for understandable perspectives on American Jewish social and political arrangements, and so they give shape to the bridge-building possible—or not possible—between Jews and non-Jews, between Jewishness and Americanness. As my reading of *A Stranger among Us* suggests, non-Jewish viewers and readers of American Jewish detective stories are lent this particular desire as part of the general desire for suture that Silverman describes—a desire for "the solving of emotion," as Muriel Rukeyser put it—that film and popular cultural texts provide. As a result, non-Jewish viewers are positioned as cultural tourists for whom Jewishness is an idealization, one that functions as a coordinate, enabling them to find their place in the American terrain that the Jewish detective investigates. As my reading of *Homicide* suggests, Jewish viewers and readers of American Jewish detective stories are positioned as both the penetrated and the penetrators for whom Jewishness is idealization and mystery, self and other, riddle and solution. In a dark film like *Homicide*, suture with that identity is seen as something for which Gold is willing to pay any price, though Silverman's concept of suture helps us to see just how high that price really is. The inadvertent learning in *Homicide* is a painful lesson, not only about the difficulty of making and achieving secure borders between "us" and "them," but also about the very advisability of doing so. Gold's desire ultimately condemns him; hence his recognition scene with a condemned man. Both are at the mercy of the "authorities," and, taking Silverman's view, so are audiences who give themselves up to narratives that promise coherent and authentic perspectives on Americanness and Jewishness.

Or are they? The concept of suture, as employed in film studies, enables us to see how the opening of the Jewish social body in American Jewish detective stories, and the use of the Jewish body in these stories as a public symbol for borders and border crossings between Jews and non-Jews, is linked to a specific desire to give shape to Jewishness in America, and to the way popular cultural texts in general incite and satisfy a desire to be situated in a clearly demarcated and comprehensible social order. More difficult to gauge, however, is the intent of the "authorities" in positioning audiences, and audience reception of their positioning. My employment of suture raises a number of questions, which I believe attend the inadvertent learning of kosher hybridity in American Jewish detective stories. Is the positioning of an audience as spectators to border-making always a suspect activity? How does the relationship between self and other resolve into a view of American Jewish life about which we can be sure an audience is cognizant? In what ways do readers and viewers assimilate such inadvertent learning? Clearly, the pedagogical function of kosher hybridity is not a simple one, for even in stories that are far simpler than *Homicide* we cannot make assumptions about how viewers respond to their positioning. That is, the gap between what may be taught and what may be learned is fraught with problems. Not the least of these are problems associated with the purported dominance of dominant ideologies and narrative discourses, and the supposed passivity of viewers and readers. As Stuart Hall noted in respect to race and mass media, "neither a unifiedly conspiratorial media nor indeed a unified racist ruling class exist in anything like that simple way."[45]

In respect to my study, I do not mean to assert that the kosher hybridity in American Jewish detective stories is all of a piece, that there is a conspiratorial or unified ideology lurking behind those stories and analyzing the inadvertent learning in them is a simple matter of sew and tell. Even granting the use of the Jewish body in Lumet's and Mamet's films as a public symbol for borders and border-making, such popular cultural symbols (like all popular cultural texts) are shaped by and sustain a multiplicity of meanings and readings, as witness Omer's and Newton's essays. In the following chapter, I take up how confusing and confused the ideology of a detective fiction can be. Even though certain choices are made inevitable in such stories, the implications of choosing still raise questions for readers, even those readers amenable to the choices offered. As in the two films examined here, the confusions arise out of the contradiction of positioning Jewish identity as both different from and the same as American identity.

7

AM I MY BROTHER'S DETECTIVE?

> Anyone who has ever thought about
>   the difference between himself
>   and the figure he cuts in the world
> begins to understand
>   the Jewish position.
> Anyone who looks on that figure
>   as a brother
> and laughs like a brother
> could put the Jews out of business
>
> —Rodger Kamenetz, *The Missing Jew*

The brotherly sympathy for the double-consciousness of "the Jewish position" in Kamenetz's poem is, appropriately, a double-edged one. Such sympathy is available to "anyone" who is capable of recognizing the difference between how one sees oneself and how others see one. On its face, that assertion seems a reasonable foundation for human brotherhood (and, of course, sisterhood): recognize the Other in one's self. But when in the second stanza Kamenetz observes that the absence of that difference would obviate the difference of Jewish identity, the observation spins the poem into a complex and ironic insight into identity. For while understanding is ostensibly not the same as being, in Kamenetz's poem, Jewish identity is clearly related to the business of being in a middle position: Among the poem's indented lines, "the Jewish position" is indented to a space past "the difference between himself" but before "and the figure he cuts in the world." Jews are professional middlemen and middlewomen whose social job is to model what it means to be a bridge between self and other—to be the exemplar *par excellence* of self-conscious alienation. Yet the figure to which "anyone" might relate as a brother, yet laugh at, is not the Jew, but rather "anyone's" public self. Is this a Jewish, ironic version of W.E.B. Du Bois's concept of African American double-consciousness ("always looking at one's self through the eyes of others . . . an American, a Negro; two souls, two thoughts, two unreconciled strivings; two warring ideals in one dark body, whose dogged strength alone keeps it from being torn asunder")?[1]

What kind of collaborations define brotherhood—might "anyone" in the same business be considered a Jew, or only *like* a Jew? How should we read the conditional "could put" of the last line? Kamenetz, by vexing "the Jewish position" and the apparently simple relationship between Jews and "anyone," vexes how a reader might insert her or himself into his poem. For to align oneself with "right" conduct, that is, with brotherly or sisterly conduct, would be bad for the Jews because such conduct would obviate the social function of the Jewish position, whereas aligning oneself with "wrong" conduct would be good for the Jews, would help to maintain the social meaning and purpose of the Jewish position, though it would not bode well for the quality of Jewish life. The implicit questions that the poem raises for "anyone" are thus ethical ones: Where do *you* stand in relation to the ironies of "the Jewish position"? What are *your* sympathies?

I begin this chapter with Kamenetz's poem because its implied questions about "brotherly" collaboration—between people and between a text and its readers—are also entertained in Stuart Kaminsky's Abe Lieberman mysteries, although at first glance these mysteries seem a straightforward exploration of the ethics of Jewish power in America during the last decade of the century. Lieberman is the "Hebraic" detective, the ethical detective, whose job it is to police wrong conduct and protect families in the "Hellenic," the chaotic and fate-driven, American urban environment. Kaminsky himself says that the Abe Lieberman mysteries "take their story conception from Greek tragedy. The families, religion, problems, ills, and ethnic backgrounds with which the Chicago police must deal are endless and lead them to consistently tragic conclusions."[2] Lieberman is a kind of hard-boiled Jewish *coryphaeus,* chorus-leader, both a model of and a commentary on the ethical action in the mysteries. He even sleeps with the key to his gun drawer tied around his neck; one might say that he is the key to understanding how and why Jewish men wield physical, social, and cultural power in hopes of forestalling tragic conclusions, and so is one more example of the tough Jews we have encountered in American Jewish detective stories—Peter Decker, Dov Taylor, Yakov Liebermann, Jessica Drake, and Bobby Gold.

In this chapter, however, I'm interested in pursuing a different, though still related, reading of ethics in the Abe Lieberman mysteries, one less concerned with the references to Greek tragedy and more focused on "brotherhood" and the gendered meaning of Jewish difference in the series (hence my use of the fraternal referent, a usage I shall maintain in this chapter to foreground the patriarchal nature of the

Abe Lieberman mysteries and of the collaboration they promote). In my reading, the interrelationships among right conduct, Americanness, and Jewishness in the Abe Lieberman mysteries describe a borderland where the ethnicities and races that inhabit Chicago's multicultural streets work out their boundaries and bridges. To be more precise, Jewishness is reduced to ethical behavior, and so helps to distinguish between good guys and bad guys, good Americans and bad Americans. And though it is the family, biological and social, that benefits from the brotherly collaboration that describes the Jewish position in Kaminsky's series, buying into that position is an individual choice. Jewishness thus becomes the right conduct of the American individual (who is modeled male). The result is a wobbly and confused fictional multiculturalism, a brotherhood of difference in which everyone is the same, that echoes the paradox of Kamenetz's poem: brotherhood may be good for American Jews but it's bad for a particularist Jewish identity.

The Abe Lieberman mysteries are instructive, therefore, because they reflect the ambivalences and anxieties that arise when ideology, ethics, gender, and identity are threaded into popular cultural texts such as Kaminsky's, texts that thrive on intended and unintended contradictions. Border-making and bridge-building in the Abe Lieberman mysteries are ultimately the product of each character's subjective choices, reinforcing the individualist ethos of the detective story. Yet these choices, in many cases, also question that ethos and its effect on right conduct in society and within ethnic cultures; some individuals, after all, are simply loose cannons whose choices threaten the stability of their communities and of urban society.[3] Fittingly, Abe Lieberman is a detective who models and defends individual choice as a self-fulfilling collective good. Lieberman embodies a "Jewish" figure who, as in Kamenetz's poem, inhabits a middle ground between "us" and "them," who laughs at the disparity between himself and the figure he cuts in the world, and who promotes brotherhood among the diverse "families" and individuals who live on the mean streets of Chicago; he *is* his brother's detective (literally and figuratively), but one who leaves it up to his brothers—all the varied families and individuals—to define their own borders and bridges. He respects their autonomy. That means that they can believe anything they want about their own identity; the detective's job (as I have been arguing throughout this study) is to defend the faith, however variously defined "faith" may be. This characteristic of the Jewish detective is a constitutive feature of American Jewish detective stories, but in his series Kaminsky takes this feature to its logical conclusion: Lieberman defends the faith that everyone is free to define "faith." The irony of this laudable position is that Lieberman's libertarian "law"—believe what you want but don't act on that belief in a way that harms people who just want to raise a family or get on with their lives—treats all identity as equivalent individual choices.[4] In the interest of promoting urban civility, Lieberman defends delicatessen Jewishness and Orthodox fundamentalism as equally valid forms of individual Jewish difference that confer a voluntary corporate Jewish identity.

These two formulations describe the gamut of Jewish identity in the Abe Lieberman mysteries—as well as how American Jews can be Other to each other—but they also beg the question, wittingly and unwittingly entertained in *Lieberman's Law* (1996), of why Jewish identity is important or even necessary in America. If individuals are free to define their own faith, why be a particular kind of Jew, or Jewish altogether, especially if Jewishness is only a flavor or an ethnocentric preference, or if particularist Jewish identities inevitably provoke social and cultural conflict? To borrow an insight from a recent anthology about Jews and multiculturalism, the individualism and libertarianism of the Lieberman series reflect a struggle over how to acknowledge "the multifaceted nature of identity without abandoning the importance of identity altogether."[5]

As that quote implies, the larger concern of this chapter is with the relationship between American Jews and multiculturalism.[6] An important aspect of the inadvertent learning of contemporary American Jewish detective stories is how these stories situate Jews and defend the faith within the context of a multicultural America and within the fabric of an increasingly multicultural detective fiction genre (see chapter 2). Nevertheless, it is not that the phenomenon of American Jewish detective stories, and the current popularity of affirming and acculturated Jewish detectives, is explained by the happy coincidence between the contemporary theorizing of American Jews as "insiders who are outsiders and outsiders who are insiders,"[7] and a genre where such a position is essential to the role and personality of the detective hero. There are specific historical and cultural factors that helped shape such a "coincidence," as we saw in the Rabbi Small and the Mom mysteries, as well as in the detective stories from the seventies, eighties and nineties analyzed in subsequent chapters. What I wish to suggest in this chapter is that a prime concern of the defenders of the faith in these stories, and in the Abe Lieberman mysteries in particular, is making sense of how and why anyone, whether a fictional character or a reader, may be a brother to Jews, and in trying to quell the ambivalences and anxieties produced by the specter of unregulated individual autonomy and by the irony that a multicultural brotherhood could very well put the Jews "out of business."

BROTHERHOOD IN THE HOOD

Abe Lieberman is a world-weary but compassionate character who illuminates the traits and "families" that help unpack the "brotherhood" described by the collaborations within the Abe Lieberman mysteries. In this section, I want to extend the connotations of "brotherhood" to include the intergroup and interpersonal dynamics of the patriarchal "families" that inhabit the various neighborhoods of Kaminsky's Chicago.

Abe Lieberman first appears in *When the Dark Man Calls* (1983) as the Chicago policeman who helps the protagonist, a radio call-in host, solve her parents' murder. Lieberman is short and thin with gray curly hair and a preference for suspenders, and he is portrayed throughout the series as a fatherly little Jewish man with a self-deprecating and sometimes sarcastic wit who is tougher and more capable with a gun than people expect. He looks "about sixty" and " more like the pop of a mom-and-pop neighborhood grocery than a cop" (77). In a telephone conversation that takes place during the scene that introduces him, readers overhear Lieberman as he advises a fellow officer to book or not book a suspect, but either way, "I'm not going to make the decision for you so you can say 'Hell, Abe Lieberman told me to do it this way.' You're a big boy, Bart" (76). "Brotherhood" here is obviously a police brotherhood, one of shared duties and individual responsibilities, but Kaminsky's "mom-and-pop" simile and Lieberman's treatment of Bart also yokes the brotherhood of one's "neighborhood" with the brotherhood of one's "family." That is, Lieberman is both a neighborhood anchor and a family patriarch who listens to his customers/children as they tell him their problems, and, while he sympathizes, he will not tell them what to do; they may act like children, but he will not treat them like children. He is a facilitator and protector who is willing to listen, but who also has a respect for healthy boundaries among adults. This characterization is underscored in the series by the nicknames that Kaminsky gives Lieberman and his partner, Bill Hanrahan: "Rabbi" and "Father Murphy." Lieberman's identity is that of the paternal guardian of an urban neighborhood: facilitator, protector, judge, and mentor.

While Kaminsky claims that Lieberman is modeled on film director Don Siegel, a former boss and mentor, Lieberman is more obviously a type of tough Jew and a version of the idiosyncratic, hard-boiled detective of the police procedural.[8] Lieberman as a hybrid facilitator and protector—as a local institution, if you will—possesses the traits necessary for someone navigating the varied, porous borders and the rapidly changing demographics that describe the city's ethnic and racial turfs. For example, in *Lieberman's Folly* (1991), the first book of the series, Kaminsky's exposition of the shifting Jewish neighborhood of Chicago gives voice to the ethnic, class, and personal displacements, and the "false memories" generated by these displacements, that compose the interrelated themes of the mystery:

> They were parked in front of Hinky's Bike Shop. Hinky, like most of the Jews in the neighborhood, including Lieberman, had migrated north from the West Side to Albany Park thirty years earlier. The poor southern whites and East Indians had driven them further north to Rogers Park and now Rogers Park was starting to show signs of change. East Rogers Park, from Lake Michigan to Ridge Road, was already given up as lost to Russian immigrants, Vietnamese, Hispanics, and white dropouts. West Rogers Park, where Lieberman lived, was holding on. The Chinese and Koreans had helped to stabilize the neighborhood, but the Jewish migration continued. Skokie was still the place to go if you couldn't afford to go even further into Wilmette or Highland Park.
>
> With each move, false memories of the good old days in Lawndale, "Jew Town," before the blacks moved in were evident in small ways in Rogers Park. The small white lettering on Hinky's sign said, "Formerly on Roosevelt and Central Park." Sam and Harry's Hot Dogs on Western Avenue had topped that. In the middle of the store was a replica of a street sign from the old neighborhood. (20–21)

All the characters in the mystery are similarly displaced, pushed into or moving out of various "homes," and lugging around or constructing "false memories" even as they try to get along with the denizens of their new "neighborhoods." Bill Hanrahan, Lieberman's partner, is an alcoholic whose wife has divorced him and whose grown-up children no longer speak to him, and who keeps his house spotlessly clean in the anticipation that she will one day return, to a home whose perfect arrangement is a false memory of a marriage in shambles. In the meantime, he tries as best he can to accommodate himself to his new circumstances, and in the course of *Lieberman's Folly* he meets and begins dating a Chinese woman five years older than himself. Lieberman's daughter leaves her husband, a classics professor at the University of Chicago, and moves with her two children back into her parents' home.

Lisa Lieberman thinks that by doing so she will reclaim her identity and her independence, but Lieberman sees her move as a simple case of domestic and personal dissatisfaction. The murder mystery itself concerns the regional and class displacements of the Madera sisters from Corpus Christi, Texas, who relocate to Chicago after murdering their pimp and stealing part of his fortune. Life was definitely not better in the old neighborhood for the sisters, but their fates reflect how hard it is to set memory straight: one of them remains a prostitute, and because she brings a bit of the old neighborhood along with her she enables her own murder, whereas the other sister marries a police captain and tries to escape the past, though she inevitably drags the captain down with her when she tries to kill a witness whose memory of the Texas murder threatens to ruin her future.

Despite Kaminsky's use of "Madera" and "Corpus Christi," it is not the inability of the sisters to make wine out of blood, or the Christian mystery alluded to in that word play, that focuses the meaning of brotherhood in *Lieberman's Folly*. It is the various social and biological "families" that inhabit the shifting geography and demographics of Kaminsky's Chicago. These families facilitate interactions with other families (sometimes innocently, sometimes nefariously), and they protect the individuals within them as best they can. They dispense advice and counsel, although individuals are free to make choices and mistakes. The police are one such group, and so are the aptly named Tentaculos (the tentacles), a Latino gang led by Emiliano "El Perro" Del Sol; the Alter Cockers (the old farts), a group of retired Jewish men whose Jewishness consists primarily in gathering at the T&L Deli, owned by Lieberman's brother, Maish; Temple Mir Shavot (the name is either an inadvertent corruption or simply meaningless),[9] whose leadership is divided among Rabbi Wass, Ida Katzman (the resident wealthy widow), and Bess Lieberman, Abe's wife, who becomes temple president at the end of *Lieberman's Folly;* and the gangs, extended biological families (like Lieberman's and Hanrahan's) and community service organizations that appear throughout the series. Lieberman, the Jewish detective/middleman, is able to negotiate his way around and into all these groups, and Kaminsky often uses this ability as Lieberman's trump card in solving a crime.

The Tentaculos are a particularly good example of the meaning and ironies of brotherhood in the series because, as their name indicates, they are all about reaching out to others, in both bad and good ways. Lieberman often uses the Tentaculos as a source of information and as "muscle" during the course of an investigation. In *Lieberman's Folly*, he agrees to drop charges against El Perro's brother and cousin in exchange for information on a suspect (156), aware that El Perro likes to think of himself as the *patron* of his neighborhood (27). Indeed, El Perro is similar to Lieberman in that he too is a patriarchal neighborhood anchor, the local institution that keeps his community protected and in line, though primarily for his benefit. In *Lieberman's Thief* (1995), the similarity between the two is given an overtly familial spin:

> *"Bueno,"* said El Perro. "My family. I take care of my family. You know that. I take care of you. You're like an uncle to me, a crazy uncle, *Tio Loco."*
>
> Lieberman had developed a reputation for recklessness on the streets when he worked out of the North Avenue before being transferred to Clark Street.
>
> Part of the reputation was earned. Most of it was calculated. But Emiliano Del Sol had believed all of it as a kid and respected the old Jew policeman who was every bit as wild as El Perro himself. (171)

In *Lieberman's Day* (1994), when Lieberman needs muscle to help him track down his nephew's murderer, it is El Perro and the Tentaculos that he turns to in order to locate and mete out justice to a murderer who encroached on Lieberman's turf, ruptured the fabric of his family life, and upset the truces and alliances of convenience among Haitian, African American, Latino, and Russian gangs. Brotherhood, as the Tentaculos evidence, is not a starry-eyed belief in human equality or a desire to forge human solidarity against the forces of intolerance, but rather something much more pragmatic. Improvising on the "familial" relationship between detective and criminal that is a convention of the detective story, on the "family" motif of the gangster story (Kaminsky wrote the dialogue for Sergio Leone's film *Once Upon a Time in America*), and on the hard-boiled detective story's atmosphere of moral ambiguity, Kaminsky predicates intergroup and interpersonal relations on the willingness to extend help to others to check any danger that might upset the status quo or lead a family member to serious harm. Such help often requires the exchange of some benefit that will keep relations between families reasonably peaceful (because each is allowed to pursue its own agendas without interference). The ironies here are that such brotherhood is self-serving and that the agents of brotherhood are not the families per se but their male leaders, or the strong male individuals authorized to make deals on the groups' behalf.

Brotherhood, as I am defining it, is therefore contingent not only on the willingness or need to help others, but also on the quality of the male leader, or strong male individual, of the family. This is well illustrated in *Lieberman's Choice* (1993), where the main plot concerns the revenge fantasy of a rogue cop who wants to destroy his police family and the subplots concern the dialectically opposed methods that Lieberman and the "borderline psychotic" Frankie Kraylaw employ to keep their biological families together. Bernie Shepard, the rogue cop, shoots his wife and her lover and then barricades himself on top of an apartment building, sending word that he wants his ex-partner, Alan Kearney, who is the new precinct captain, to meet him there so that he can exact revenge on the man he thinks turned first his wife and then the rest of the precinct against him. His barricade is well planned and well stocked, reflecting his expertise and skill at police work. And yet, as readers find out in the book's climax, the qualities that ought to have made Shepard a good leader and dependable partner (to his wife and fellow officers) are obviated by his inability to understand, to use Kamenetz's terms, "the difference between himself/and the figure he cuts in the world." Because of his childhood upbringing, Shepard sees himself as a man barricaded against the baleful changes of the world around him, a man of right conduct who followed the rules and whose "neighborhood" has changed while he himself has not. He feels betrayed by his wife, by his police family, and by life. But that is not how Kearney or others see him. "She did what she did because you're a cold, self-righteous, unbending asshole," Kearney tells him. "You treated her the way you treated everyone else, by the book. You weren't a husband. You were a keeper. You never listened to her, me, anyone in your life" (197).

Conversely, both Kraylaw and Lieberman are quite aware of the difference between who they are and the way the world sees them. Kraylaw, however, employs his self-conscious alienation as cover that enables him to use people and abuse his family, rather than employing it, as Lieberman does, as a gift that enables him to understand, and so potentially benefit from, others. Kraylaw knows that he is perceived as just another street evangelical with a "little-boy smile" trying to save souls by bringing them back into the Lord's family. Watching a news report about Bernie Shepard, his empathy with the rogue cop's desire to exact revenge for his wife's adultery makes clear that Kraylaw sees himself as a patriarchal "arm of the Lord":

> The family, yes, he thought. The family is the only salvation for civilization. The husband must hold the family together. It is God's way. Always was. His own father had held his family together with a strong hand and a mighty heart.

> Frankie Kraylaw loved his wife, loved his little boy, loved the Lord and the memory of his own mother and father. But the Lord knew best and the Lord had told Abraham to get rid of his wives and sacrifice his son, Isaac. (50)

Kraylaw's seemingly harmless evangelism is cover for his violent self-interest, and his religious mania is such that there really is no way in which he can be made to get along with other people and groups. He is totally at odds with the urban brotherhood described in the Abe Lieberman mysteries. That is why Lieberman and his partner end up running Kraylaw out of town, which Lieberman admits to Kraylaw isn't legal, but "is right" (149), for, if they do not exile him, his wife and child "would not live out the year" (130). It is also why, in *Lieberman's Day,* Bill Hanrahan must kill Kraylaw rather than arrest him, for Hanrahan "had seen too much in his life as a police officer to take any chances" (205–206), in particular, that Kraylaw might kill his family and anyone else who does not submit to his form of religious "civilization."

Lieberman, by contrast, has no conflict between his religion and his ability to collaborate with other denizens of urban life. As Kaminsky's introduction of him in *Lieberman's Choice* illustrates, he knows how others see him:

> Lieberman was well aware that he was not an imposing figure at five seven and hovering around 145 pounds. He looked, even to himself, a good five years older than his sixty years. Bess thought his best features were his curly hair and his little white mustache. Lieberman could never see anything in his mirror except his own long-dead father in disguise. (10)

The unimposing old Jew that others see is, of course, at odds with the quick-witted, strong, and strongly opinionated Jew he knows himself to be. Lieberman is quite capable of using his power in blunt fashion, whether by using his gun to intimidate Frankie Kraylaw (145) or in telling a fellow officer to keep the fact that he slept with Bernie Shepard's wife to himself (118–119). But Lieberman, whose favorite character in Greek tragedy is Cassandra, primarily uses his self-conscious alienation as a gift for listening to others, making him uniquely suited to advise people about the right choices available—though, of course, they rarely listen.

Lieberman, in other words, is the leader as middleman, whose ability to see himself as others see him gains him insight into how others think and into the advantages of collaborating with others; Lieberman, who is told by Shepard to "get your kosher ass out of here if you're so goddamn concerned about your family" (197), intuits that Shephard's barricades are a perverse expression of his thwarted desire to protect his family, and so Shepard ought to cooperate with his fellow officers and give himself up quietly because that will preserve rather than further harm their families (196–197); Lisa, who sees her father's marriage as a better model than her own (when in fact he almost had an affair with his partner's ex-wife), ought to stay in her marriage because "I don't think walking away from your husband with two kids is going to make you happy, but who knows? . . . People go around looking for happy and not finding it when they should be looking for content" (214). Lieberman is the good father, an insomniac who patiently listens to everyone—his daughter, her husband, Shepard, Kearney, etc.—and solves all the standoffs in the book. When bad things happen to misguided people like Shepard and Lieberman's daughter, it is a product of fate and choice (as the mystery's epigraph from Euripedes' *Iphigeneia in Tauris* implies), though this fact does not make Lieberman, the good father, feel any better at the end of *Lieberman's Choice*, where Kaminsky closes with the detective crying in bed (216). Lieberman's choice is for family and brotherhood, and taking that position imposes certain responsibilities on him, and on anyone who makes the same choice. And here is where, in the series, ethics, gender, and Jewishness meet.

A JEWISH POSITION

In *Lieberman's Folly,* Lieberman retrieves evidence, a lamp, from Raw Izzy's pawnshop where he and Izzy engage in a telling negotiation. Lieberman offers to buy the lamp for three dollars, but Izzy asks for five. When Lieberman responds that he could simply take the lamp as evidence, Izzy, "who had a Ph.D. in philosophy and another in theology from the University of Chicago" (89), retorts that he could call his lawyer:

> "For a two-buck lamp?" Lieberman said.
> "For a principle," said Izzy.
> "Four," said Lieberman.
> "Compromise is moral defeat," said Raw Izzy.
> "All right, five," agreed Lieberman, pulling out his wallet.
> Izzy remained in his chair to receive the five singles and then handed Lieberman a key.
> "The case you were looking at, the harmonicas. Take one, a premium. Goes with the lamp. Special today." (90)

Their negotiation exemplifies the brotherhood established between two principled individuals for whom compromise "is a moral defeat." As the negotiation illustrates, Lieberman accedes to the correct principle—that among lawful, if not always law-abiding, citizens no one has the right to expropriate property or information from another; cooperation and collaboration must be purchased in some way (even Frankie Kraylaw was offered his life in exchange for leaving town). Listening to the other and paying the right fee gains Lieberman a little truth and a little beauty: he will not only have a lamp with which to shed light on his case, but also a harmonica as a free personal benefit. The relation of this "principle" to Kaminsky's mystery series is drawn in Raw Izzy's philosophical statement that closes the scene: "'Life,' said Izzy, 'is a series of strange and seemingly pointless stories. Meaning is derived from a relationship of story, storyteller, and listener, but by far the hardest task is that of the listener'" (91). Given the negotiation, one interpretation of this statement is that listeners have the hardest task because to understand the meaning of a story they must investigate and then negotiate the purchase price of that meaning. What are the story and the storyteller asking of them? What kind of brotherhood do the two call forth?

Without belaboring this reading into arcane levels (after all, the exchange can also be read simply as Izzy's oracular advice to Lieberman that, whatever case he may investigate, he will have to make sense of "seemingly pointless stories" to solve it), I believe this scene underscores the responsibility to listen to and respect others, a responsibility that, in Kaminsky's story, implies brotherhood and the taking of a principled position. Kaminsky is signaling to readers of this first book in the series that there is more to his mystery than just the mystery at hand, that the purchase price is not only what they paid for their copy, but also their willingness to negotiate their relation to Lieberman's principles. In return, the readers will receive not only light but music—they will get both an expected and an unexpected benefit. Kaminsky is asking for active readers, active collaborators—one of the attractions of the Abe Lieberman mysteries. (I will return to this point later.)

Lieberman's principled position, which readers are asked to be spectators of and to collaborate with, is a "Jewish position," but one not exclusive to Jews, for the unexpected benefit of collaborating with it is a keener understanding of how to achieve brotherhood with others. This position, as already shown, is grounded within a "family" and the responsibilities of its patriarch. Lieberman is a responsible family man: he is faithful to his wife, successfully resisting the impulse to have an affair with his partner's ex-wife, and he accepts his daughter's life decisions despite his misgivings about them—and because he loves his grandchildren. Lieberman is also a family man in the sense that he stands by his urban Jewish identity and his neighborhood's remaining Jewish "family" even though most of the urban Jews from his neighborhood have moved to "safe, new one-bedroom" condominiums in Skokie (36), and despite his ambivalence about Judaism. Lieberman "had stopped fighting his tradition, though he was still not sure what he made of the universe" (38). He has come to terms with Jewish worship as a kind of "meditation" that he finds personally "comforting" (38) in that it provides a ritual that binds him to others in both a voluntary and communitarian way. The congregation is a shared space where the inscrutable liturgy and apparently pointless stories of old Rabbi Wass serve, as Raw Izzy's statement helps us see, to create a collaborative community whose diverse members stand by each other out of loyalty and, more prosaically, convenience:

> Upon old Wass's retirement, Lieberman and Bess had considered moving to Temple Beth Israel, whose rabbi was young, smart, and progressive and whose congregation included many families with small children, but loyalty prevailed, and even when the new Rabbi Wass revealed himself to be no brighter than his father, they stayed because it was familiar, because it was convenient, because they didn't want to abandon their friends and they didn't want to hurt the new rabbi. (39)

Such "Jewish" right conduct is exemplified, too, in Maish Lieberman and the Alter Cockers, all of whom embody a literal delicatessen Jewishness that is, similarly, a collaborative community of convenience and loyalty that welcomes any non-Jewish customer who does not disturb the peace. Gathering every morning at the "T&L deli," which Lieberman often employs as a second office, the Alter Cockers provide a running commentary on life and the Chicago Cubs, rib Abe Lieberman when he comes in for delicatessen, provide solace and support for Maish after his son is murdered, and generally look out for each other. Except in *Lieberman's Day,* Maish fulfills the same function, a reminder of Abe's past and his community ties. By feeding his brother and sending him home with bags of bagels or pastrami or other deli food, Maish, the Alter Cockers, and the deli symbolize how such a Jewish collaborative community sustains Lieberman, though as the series progresses Kaminsky comically highlights Lieberman's weariness and old age by revealing that, for reasons of health, his character must cut down on the high fat and stomach-churning food he so loves. But the difficulty that Lieberman has in adhering to the bland and tasteless diet he is reduced to, only confirms his deepseated taste for Jewishness and, thereby, his attachment to his position.

Since that position is coeval with delicatessen Jewishness, it is no surprise that one need not be Jewish to love or exemplify such a "gut" identity. The T&L, after all, is not kosher; it is an ethnic Jewish space indebted to but not dependent on Judaism, a place where the proof of one's voluntary Jewish identity is in the noodle pudding.[10] The Alter Cockers include Howie Chen, who used to own a Chinese restaurant and who, in *Lieberman's Thief* (1995), is said to speak "the best Yiddish of all the Cockers" (83). As an extension of jokes about urban Jews' proclivity for Chinese food, Howie Chen underscores the comic relief that the Alter Cockers provide, but he also verifies that Lieberman's principled position, his "Jewish position," is not so much about ethnicity or religious belief as about a certain kind of behavior. Ethnic difference and group identity go no deeper than food or a second language, which anyone can master. Therefore, although their food and their second language may differ from Lieberman's and the Alter Cockers', any of the other characters who relate in the same way to their collaborative communities and who choose family and brotherhood are arguably just as "Jewish" as Howie Chen. Obviously, this is how Kaminsky identifies the good guys/good Americans: Alan Kearney is a "Jewish" American, Iris Chin, Hanrahan's Chinese girlfriend, and her father are "Jewish" Americans, and even El Perro is a "Jewish" American in his own imperfect way.

Consider as well the two Abe Lieberman short stories in Lawrence Raphael's anthologies of Jewish mystery and detective fiction. In *Mystery Midrash*'s "Confession," Arnold Sokol, a convert to Catholicism, confesses to Lieberman not only that he killed a mugger but also that his mixed marriage is shaky and that he is confused about his identity—is he a Jew, a Catholic, or nothing? When Lieberman discovers that the mugger is not dead, only injured, the scene in the hospital where Sokol and his assailant confront each other reveals that both are dangerously adrift from their families. Each still wants to kill the other, and when Sokol grabs Lieberman's gun, their showdown seems headed toward a violent conclusion. Only a selfless act by Rabbi Wass helps avert disaster and illustrates to Sokol that cooperation yields a more satisfying resolution than rash individual actions. Sokol's willingness to accept Rabbi Wass's suggestion to go home to his family and to come back for Friday night services—to accept, in other words, Wass's point of view (which mirrors Lieberman's principled position)—proves that Sokol, as Lieberman asserts earlier in the story, is essentially a Jew with "dual citizenship" (112). In *Criminal Kabbalah*'s "The Tenth Man," also a story about vengeance, a stranger wandering the halls of Temple Mir Shavot is roped into being the tenth man for morning services, ten being the number for a minyan, a prayer quorum. Mr. Green makes a lucky addition to the group: when the brother of a criminal that Lieberman and his partner killed during a robbery comes looking for Lieberman and revenge, Mr. Green, a retired cop, manages to pass his gun to Maish who passes it to Lieberman who pulls it on the brother and thus saves himself and the rest of the minyan. As it turns out, Mr. Green is not Jewish (he had been invited to a bar mitzvah), but when Mr. Green's daughter appears and claims that, for minyans, he "doesn't count," Maish quickly replies, "I think he does" (138). Green enjoys, and exemplifies, the brotherhood of the minyan—it is, after all, a policeman's minyan—and so asks if he can come back the next day. "Anyone's welcome," replies a congregant (138). Like Howie Chen, Green has proven himself essentially "Jewish."

In these stories, doing the right thing is how an out-married Jew retains an attachment to a collaborative community that may help him to save his marriage, and how a non-Jew finds a place where he feels at home. Behavior, as constituted by the choices an individual makes, trumps belief, and results in a dual citizenship benefitting all the families involved.

Criminals, on the other hand, are almost always portrayed as anti-"family," and therefore they are disruptive of brotherhood and clearly not "Jewish." They are bad guys/bad Americans. This distinction is made in *Lieberman's Thief*, where Harvey Rozier kills his wife so as to be available to the much older and more socially advanced Betty Franklin when her wealthy but cancer-ridden husband finally dies. The adulterers are only interested in themselves—Harvey in improving his class standing and Betty in denying that her once beautiful body is aging—and so collaborate only in order to destroy their families. In addition, the WASP-y, private-club Franklins are portrayed as old-school Chicagoans so haughty, emotionally remote, and self-centered that their physical decay seems a fitting commentary on their decaying Americanness. Conversely, the subplot concerning the pathetic Rabbi Nathanson, who tries to buy Lieberman's house because, significantly, it "has a history, a family, the aura, if you will, of Jewish culture" (95) (but whom Lieberman thinks is trying to scam him for either his house or his money), illustrates the desire to collaborate so as not to be destroyed. As Nathanson's lawyer explains, the rabbi's congregation is trying to remove him (begging the question of just how "Jewish" a congregation it is); in response,

Nathanson has "been going around giving thousand-dollar checks and trying to make deals on houses all over the neighborhood" (227). The symbolism is straightforward, yet it also underscores how Jewishness, in the series, helps differentiate between ethical and unethical behavior, between those who enable brotherhood and those who undermine it.

Lieberman's Day works similarly to draw such boundaries, and it also makes clear that the boundaries are patrolled by men. The murder mystery in *Lieberman's Day* revolves around an interracial affair gone awry, one that affects Lieberman deeply because it leads to the murder of his nephew, Maish's son David Lieberman. David is a high-powered TV executive whose wife, Carol, has an affair with Raymond Carrou, a Trinidadian immigrant. When she finds herself pregnant, she is warned by Raymond that she must carry the fetus to term or he will expose her to her husband. Of course, if she follows Raymond's wishes and gives birth to a child of color she will be exposed anyway, and the mystery opens with Raymond's murder of David, planned by him and Carol, and the mistaken shooting of Carol by Raymond's partner, George DuPelee. The rest of the mystery follows Lieberman as he unravels this back-story and hunts for David's murderer, but the obscenity of the crime (of killing a husband, not of having an interracial affair) is such that Carol's betrayal must be countered forcefully and permanently, a lesson brought home not only by the mystery's main plot but also by its subplot, Hanrahan's showdown with and murder of Frankie Kraylaw.

Raymond and George are not inherently evil, and they are not crudely drawn stereotypes of amoral immigrants of color out to abuse America for its wealth, but they are unmoored individuals who have no family, biological or social, to support and guide them. As such, they inevitably descend into the sort of unethical behavior that is neither Jewish nor American, despite their potential to be good Americans (Raymond is "smart" and wants to be a lawyer). Both Raymond and George represent the problem of "unsupervised" immigrants left on their own in Chicago's urban landscape. In addition, what makes things worse for Raymond is that he has an affair with the self-centered Carol, and (as in *Lieberman's Thief* as well as in the Kraylaw subplot) the desire for a woman triggers crime and self-destruction. Carol, like Betty Franklin, is a bad influence. She is a Jew who does not behave "Jewishly"; an early clue to her true identity is provided in the first few pages of the mystery when David voices his disapproval of his boss's philandering:

"What a man," David said. "Everyone knows he's shtupping Betty the

>receptionist, who's young enough to be his granddaughter. And there he stands. Big-city Gothic."
>"Maybe he needs to be appreciated as a man," Carol said.
>"Carol. Wrong is wrong. Family is family."
>"Bertrand Russell, Immanuel Kant?" Carol said.
>"You O.K., Carol?" David asked, taking his wife's arm as she tottered backward a step as the elevator dropped. (8)

Carol is not O.K., and no matter how many philosophers she can name whose work analyzes how humans construct reality, there can still be no excusing her crossing the boundary between right and wrong conduct—and taking two men down with her. Carol's behavior may be human behavior, which Lieberman, talking about his daughter, describes as "stubborn, confused, directionless, and self-destructive" (23), but it is not "Jewish" behavior, which is to say it is not behavior that sustains urban brotherhood. Carol, like Frankie Kraylaw, is a destroyer of families, who cannot be trusted, and like him her case must be "solved" once and for all.

For Lieberman, as for Hanrahan, that means pushing at the boundaries of ethical behavior, for the sake of that ethical behavior that will protect the family from further hurt. As readers might expect, Lieberman makes Carol and Raymond offers they cannot refuse. In return for giving Carol a "walk" on the murder charge, he tells her to leave Chicago and never come back (245), so that Maish and Yetta will never find out that their grandson is a bastard. When she asks what he will do to Raymond, Lieberman responds, "Raymond Carrou has disappeared" (245). In fact, Lieberman, at this point in the mystery, has, with the help of the Tentaculos, captured Raymond as he was sneaking into the hospital to see Carol, leaving readers to wonder if Lieberman will kill Raymond or not. Lieberman seems to anticipate that, by negotiation or force, he will make both Carol and Raymond "disappear." As it turns out, his deal with Raymond is that he will help him avoid the death penalty if he "keeps Carol out of it" (248), again in order to protect Maish and Yetta from the truth about their daughter-in-law. Raymond, unable to agree, commits suicide by jumping off the hospital roof and so disappears, just as Lieberman predicted.

Lieberman's defense of his principled "Jewish position" thus encourages readers to see gender as an important delineation of its responsibilities. Following the inexorable logic of modeling a collaborative community on the middle-class family and its conventional gender roles, Kaminsky figures women in *Lieberman's Day* as nurturers in need of protection from themselves and from others. He figures Lieberman as the model of patriarchal "Jewish" right conduct, which sometimes must include violence, for that is how men like Lieberman protect the defenseless and shield those who simply cannot handle the truth. Lieberman's wife may be the president of their synagogue and an intragroup leader, but hers is at heart a nurturing job; Lieberman is "rabbi," the responsible patriarch of the family who listens, advises, protects, exhibits loyalty, and is authorized to make deals with other groups and individuals on the family's behalf. Jewishness therefore underscores the gendered nature of brotherhood, in Kaminsky's conventionally gendered series, because "Jewish" fathers, which is to say good fathers, exemplify the qualities that foster brotherhood with others, and so model the right way to shepherd families into American spaces. For example, Lieberman, at the end of the mystery, dreams that he takes his daughter Lisa and his nephew David, "as they were as children," along with his grandchildren to a Cubs opening game, and, catching a fly ball, he lovingly hands it to David "who took it gently in two hands as if it were a fragile treasure" (259). Baseball's field of dreams is the perfect setting for Lieberman's sentimental gesture of "catching one" for David. It helps foreground that Lieberman the "Jewish" American father not only promotes and polices brotherhood by promoting team play and team spirit among his children, but also that he desires to gift these children with the pleasures and rewards of American life.

LAYING DOWN THE LAW

Lieberman is his brother's detective because he works for anyone who shares his "Jewish position"; he models for other characters, and for readers, what it means to be a good American. The limitations of such brotherhood for understanding differences in Jewish identity, however, are evident in *Lieberman's Law*. The fifth mystery in the series was written in the shadow of the nascent Oslo peace process and Dr. Baruch Goldstein's February 1994 massacre of twenty-nine Palestinians as they worshipped in the mosque above the *Ma'arat HaMachpelah,* the Cave of the Pairs (also called the Tomb of the Patriarchs), in Hebron. It opens with a recounting of the massacre of the Mohammed family one night in 1973 by "the half-mad fanatic" physician of a West Bank kibbutz, and of the rescue of two of the Mohammed children by the physician's cousin, a border guard who kills his relative "to save the lives of Arabs" (8). Kaminsky's mystery plays out the repercussions of that night twenty years later in Chicago, thus providing an object lesson about crossing the border between ethical and unethical behavior. It also illustrates the consequent cycles of violence that are propagated through, and thereby threaten to destroy, the children that families are supposed to protect. The triggering irony, of course, is that in this mystery the danger to border guards comes not from across the line in "enemy" territory, but rather from within, among the border guard's family, a recognizable irony to readers of *Lieberman's Day*, where one of the criminals is Carol Lieberman. As in that mystery, brotherhood between the wary and feuding families in *Lieberman's Law* —Palestinian Americans, American Jews, African Americans, and the mystery's generic White Americans—depends on the right conduct associated with Lieberman's principled "Jewish position." Getting at the root of what impedes individuals from accepting this position is the "peace process" of the mystery, but is also why Jewish identity is less important than "Jewish" behavior.

Lieberman is pulled into the mystery when neo-Nazi thugs supposedly vandalize Temple Mir Shavot and steal a four-hundred-year-old Torah made, significantly, "by Spanish Jews during the reign of the Moors, when Jews were allowed not only to hold office in Spain but to worship as they chose" (40). Over the course of his investigation, Lieberman discovers that not neo-Nazis, but the Arab Student Response Committee (a Palestinian American student group at the University of Chicago) vandalized the temple, to mark the anniversary of Goldstein's massacre of Palestinians in Hebron. The student group includes Jara and Massad Mohammed, the two survivors of the West Bank killings. From there the plot weaves an improbable (and suspiciously paranoid) conspiracy between Massad and the Hate Mongers, a White neo-Nazi group, to attack an "African Muslim church" and leave the Torah behind in order to blame the Jews and incite a race war in America, and possibly a regional war in the Middle East. Unbeknownst to Lieberman, the leader of the Hate Mongers, William Stanley Berk, is working for the pseudonymous Mr. Grits who is a "dispatcher" for a nebulous worldwide conspiracy against Jews, Arabs, and people of color. Once Mr. Grits is introduced, the reason why individuals cannot all just get along is easily solved: the shadow government that Mr. Grits works for enforces an intolerant, murderous worldview that vividly contrasts with that of the government that produced the Golden Age of Spanish Jewry and Temple Mir Shavot's Torah. Kaminsky's fictional totem of *convivencia*, the cooperative and collaborative spirit that characterized Muslim medieval Spain, is really another expression of Lieberman's "Jewish" position, and thus of the worldview of a good American government.

Brotherhood is thereby further developed in *Lieberman's Law* as a kind of *convivencia* where every group or family has the right to make a book of teachings and propagate those teachings as long as those teachings are not acted upon in a murderous way, or in a way that permanently upsets the social status quo, such as by inciting a racial war. The content of the teachings is beside the point; belief in them is a matter of personal choice. Thus Lieberman has no real animosity for the Arab Student Response Committee. Jara Mohammed, who reminds Lieberman of his daughter (139), is simply an all-too-human child, and, as she tells Lieberman, her motives are political, not genocidal, because she remembers the kindness of the Israeli border guard who saved her life: "'I don't believe in killing,' she said. 'Attacks on American Jews are not the answer. That will only make it worse. Innocent Jews will suffer and then innocent Arabs'" (225). Similarly, Mustafa Quadri is a well-educated man who can quote the Bible on the folly of hearkening to the words of a false prophet (234), and who recognizes Massad Mohammed as such a false prophet because he advocates violence. Hanrahan is surprised that Lieberman likes Quadri and Jara: "'They tear up your church, crap on your prayer shawls, and you like them.' 'A paradox,' said Lieberman" (235). Lieberman also finds himself drawn to Detective Ibrahim Said, a former member of the Arab Student Response Committee assigned to the case as the "specialist in Arab terrorist and hate groups in Chicago" (67), who is, as his name makes obvious, a Muslim Lieberman—pragmatic, ethical, loyal, cooperative. Through Ibrahim/Abraham Lieberman, readers are positioned to accept the sometimes grudging, but nevertheless brotherly, collaboration of the mystery's Arabs as a warrant for their American identity, and the conclusion that, despite differing religious affiliations and politics, despite different "dual citizenships," Muslims and Jews are really more the same than different.

These good Arab Americans also reveal to readers another paradox, that particularist identities informed by belief, whether Palestinian, Jewish or other, can become both less important and more dangerous. This paradox is reflected in the curious elision between "Arab" and "Palestinian" in the mystery. "Palestinian," which appears only once (178), is less important because it is descriptive of a family member more than it is a family in its own right (as witness Mohammed's family name), and it is only one of the many variations on "Arab." It is "Arab" that defines the family and that enables brotherhood, in this case because Kaminsky relates such a "family" to the libertarianism and individualism that Lieberman represents and to the Jewish and Christian monotheistic "families." "Palestinian" is more dangerous because it mobilizes the passions of politics in the same way that "Zionist" and "Israeli" do:

"I hate Israelis. I do not hate Jews," Jara tells Lieberman (225). And at an Arab Student Response Committee rally at the University of Chicago, the words "Palestine" and "Zionist" accompany the fists and stones hurled between the brawling Arab and Jewish partisans of those antagonistic politics. The word "Palestinian," in other words, mobilizes hatred of others, and, as Massad illustrates, it describes the enemy within the family who threatens the family from within its own borders; Massad, in the service of the evil conspiracy orchestrated by Berk and Mr. Grits, ends up killing three Arabs, one of whom is his own cousin, but, ironically, no Jews.

The paradox of particularist identities is especially embodied by the Jews in the mystery. Charles Kenneth Leary, "Pig Sticker," calls himself half-Jewish, but since his mother was Jewish and his father was an Irish cop, the ironically named Pig Sticker is technically Jewish according to matrilineal descent, and technically "Jewish" according to the series's definition of Jewishness as right conduct that enables and polices brotherhood. But Pig Sticker, growing up a troubled young boy with no friends, and alienated from both his mother and his father—and therefore another example of the vulnerable child—really does believe in the Hate Mongers' political ideals, and Kaminsky explains Pig Sticker's individual choice as motivated by the desire to "spite his father, shame his mother, and feel that he belonged somewhere" (110). Nevertheless, Pig Sticker's very desire to be part of a family, and his aversion to mortal violence (as opposed to simple mayhem) gives him away to Hanrahan and Lieberman, who use him to gain inside information on the Hate Mongers. When Pig Sticker does the right thing and tips the detectives about the date of an upcoming attack, Hanrahan and Lieberman joke about why he volunteers the information:

> "Charles Kenneth Leary," Hanrahan sighed, watching the young man hurry between two cars and into the darkness. "You think he's straight on this Monday business?"
> "Yes," said Lieberman, putting away his weapon and buttoning up.
> "The Irish in him," said Hanrahan.
> "The Jew in him," said Lieberman.
> "We are truly blessed to belong to the two best ethnic groups in our free country," said Hanrahan. "And that's an objective truth."
> "You hear me arguing, Father Murphy?" (186)

Readers are obviously not supposed to take this banter seriously, but the unwitting implication of it, in light of Kaminsky's mystery about identity and violence, is that Pig Sticker's specific identity is less important than his embodiment of the right conduct that allies the Irish and the Jews as the "best ethnic groups" in America. Indeed, his very awareness that he possesses a kind of "dual citizenship" makes him a brother to Hanrahan and Lieberman.

Conversely, the appropriately named Eli Towser ("My God" Towser) illustrates why a particularist Jewish identity is more dangerous, for Towser's political beliefs, modeled on those of the Jewish Defense League and the fanatical religious Zionism of Rabbi Meir Kahane, pose a threat to the Jewish "family" and thus to the possibility of brotherhood with others. Lieberman hires Towser to tutor his grandson Barry in preparation for Barry's bar mitzvah. When Lieberman finds out that Towser spends much of that time teaching Barry about "driving Arabs out of Israel, a return to war against the PLO" (20), Lieberman, the patriarchal protector of children, fires him, for it is precisely those views that propagate violence through and to children. Towser argues that there "is no line between the politics of Israel and the process of being a Jew" (20), and that Barry is now old enough to be part of both a minyan and a war against Israel's enemies, but Lieberman the border guard will have none of that logic:

> Lieberman was far more familiar with what twelve-year-old boys are capable of than Elie Towser was. That was Lieberman's point. He knew how ready they were to follow a leader into violence and their own sense of group respect, survival, and often a creative or idiotic sense of honor or territory. A minyan, a gathering of ten adult, bar mitzvahed Jews needed in order to pray, required no political posture. "I don't want my grandson to be taught hate," said Lieberman. (21)

Lieberman here divorces politics from religion, an obvious reaction to contemporary events in Israel, but we must also remember that for Lieberman Jewish worship is a ritual, not a belief, that binds him to others in both a voluntary and communitarian way. Judaism for Lieberman simply inculcates ethical behavior, whereas Towser's particularist Jewish identity, like Massad's Palestinian identity, is political and fosters hatred of others. Towser is not an entirely lost cause, however, and his membership in the Jewish family is telegraphed by the fact that he enjoys deli food as much as Lieberman does—albeit, for Towser, only kosher deli. Towser is therefore useful to Lieberman later in the mystery, for his familiarity with the politics of hatred enable him to predict that Berk's conspiracy will target an "African Muslim church" because it is a "perfect target for a partnership of Arab terrorists and neo-Nazi skinheads" (244). Towser helps Lieberman protect the Jewish "family" and the other Chicago families threatened by Berk's conspiracy.

Another example of the danger of a particularist Jewish identity is Towser's favorite book of Jewish thought, *Rejoice O Youth: Comprehensive Jewish Ideology* (1965) by Rabbi Avigdor Miller. The book, written when Orthodoxy in America was on the defensive, is a touchstone of mid-century Orthodox fundamentalism: Rabbi Miller attacks evolution, modern Bible criticism, the Reform movement, Jewish cultural nationalism, libertarianism, and Zionism in order to argue for the superiority of strict Torah observance and for a Jewish ethics isolated from the perversions of modern thought. The book's near-livid animus toward modernity, and its often sarcastic and dismissive tone, its intolerance and chauvinism, well illustrate the negative attributes of particularist identities. But its promotion of an Orthodox Jewish ethics where right conduct is the expression of a true understanding of God and of renewed awareness of Jewish community, also telegraphs its membership in Lieberman's Jewish family, as well as its usefulness as a pedagogical prop: Jews, like anyone, are free to believe anything they want about their identity as long as they do not act murderously on these self-interested beliefs—which is to say, as long as they continue to exemplify "Jewish" ethical and communitarian behavior. As long as Towser behaves "Jewishly," through behavior that guarantees the security of the family and the protection of children, his self-interested political and religious beliefs are his own personal affair, a lesson none too subtly conveyed at the close when Lieberman and Said, the Abrahamic brothers, send Towser a copy of Miller's book (he conveniently does not own one). The inscription reads: "To Eli Towser, and all his children yet to be. Shalom. Peace. Salaam" (306).

The lesson is underscored for readers in the epilogue of the mystery, where the border guard who saved the Mohammed children is seen in present-day Israel, a lawmaker in the Israeli Knesset trying to improve "the education of Arab children in Israel" (308). Rather than appeal to his fellow lawmaker's sense of morality, he recognizes that these "men of diversity would be moved only by a chain of logic that convinced them that the bill would best serve Israel and its continued sovereignty" (309), that is, by logic that would appeal to the self-interest of the state. Like Towser's gift, the lawmaker's strategy exemplifies the pragmatic negotiation of brotherhood in Kaminsky's series; cooperation and collaboration are purchased with the coin of self-interest in return for expected and unexpected benefits—you have to give something to get something.

Oddly, though, the Israeli border guard ends up the same kind of Jew as Lieberman, and, furthermore, he seems a very American lawmaker, so that as a fictional character we might say that he too exemplifies "dual citizenship," Israeli and American. This is yet another irony of a "family" identity based on individual choice, but it also reflects how confusing and confused the fictional multiculturalism of the Abe Lieberman mysteries is. Brotherhood, as I see it described in these mysteries, reflects the ways the various ethnicities and races inhabiting Kaminsky's Chicago maintain "dual citizenship," but they all do so in the same "Jewish" American way. And so, as in *A Stranger among Us* and *Homicide*, the Jewish position that, in this series, is the desirable object of reflection—a mirror in which to seek both the self and the other—is riddled with contradictions: brotherhood is predicated on willingness *and* coercion; it is a collective endeavor *and* an individual choice; it is achieved through negotiation *and* a principled aversion to compromise; it requires a payoff *and* promises a payback; it is "Jewish" behavior *and* non-Jewish behavior. Like Kamenetz's poem, the Abe Lieberman mysteries reflect not only the difficulties of trying to acknowledge the diverse allegiances and ambivalent collaborations that describe identity without doing away with identity altogether, but also the difficulties of positioning Jewish identity in a multicultural America—where it is, what it is, and how to determine one's perspective on it.

These difficulties return us to the negotiations and collaborations among listeners, stories, and storytellers that Raw Izzy pointed out in *Lieberman's Folly*. By suggesting that the Jews are both in business and out of business, that America needs "Jewish" ethical conduct but not particularist Jewish identities, and that bridges and boundaries between Jews and non-Jews are a matter of individual choice, the Abe Lieberman mysteries, and Kaminsky, seem to take the easy way out of the difficulties waylaying story and storyteller. It would be simple enough, then, to say that the contradictions I cite reveal how the ideology of the Abe Lieberman mysteries tries to, but ultimately cannot, resolve the mysteries' ambivalence about multiculturalism and American Jews. I believe, however, that the confused fictional multiculturalism of the series is only half the story, or rather, only one half of this American Jewish detective story's meaning. While the mysteries offer a Jewish position, and no doubt gender it and reduce it to ethical conduct that leads to right choices, they also reveal, as shown, a self-conscious awareness—reflected in Raw Izzy's philosophical statement about life and stories, and in the quandaries (which Kaminsky takes great care to illustrate) of individuals struggling to negotiate the choices they face—that active listeners are going to fashion and negotiate their own collaborations with Lieberman's Jewish position. Indeed, part of the purchase price of these mysteries is listeners' willingness to negotiate their relation to that position. By floating the idea that listeners, too, must be paid off for their investment in a popular story about brotherhood, Kaminsky signals his recognition of their participation in the narrative design of his series. Equally important is that the emphasis of the fictional multiculturalism of the series on bridges and boundaries, right and wrong conduct, good and bad Jews (and Americans), also seems a recognition of how unpredictable listeners can be—that they may pocket a mystery's delight and only counterfeit what Lieberman teaches. Free to interpret the series in their own way, why should Kaminsky's listeners be any different from all the characters who fail to hear what Lieberman has to say?

Once we are aware of Kaminsky's presumption that unpredictable listeners help shape the meanings of stories and of life, we are able to see how the series' anxiety about the freedoms of an open and often uncivil contemporary American society is reflected in and related to anxiety about the freedoms of an open and often uncivil detective text. In short, the Abe Lieberman mysteries draw an analogy: the open society is like the open text—both promise (but do not necessarily deliver) freedom of belief. Given the variety of social, cultural, and text-mapping choices available to a listener, and the freedom to choose between competing interpretive communities, the question becomes not *what* a listener should choose but *how*.[11] In this light, Raw Izzy is right: the listener does have the hardest task. As a model listener, Lieberman is meant to help the reader discover how individuals choose, but in a detective story where he defends the faith that everyone is free to define "faith," the perils of the open society and the open text undercut his lessons in right conduct and right choices. "When reinforced by the growing sense of individualism and loss of respect for the general paradigm of the civil society," says Rabbi Irving Greenberg, addressing the open society's threat to American Jewish solidarity, "[the] release from pressure to homogenize can lead to rejection of outside faiths and to 'othering' even of groups inside one's historic inner circle. This is especially likely when there is less feeling for the need to self-limit for the sake of a collective good—because there is reduced fear that outsiders may intervene."[12] Greenberg's diagnosis of the uncivil open society that erupted out of the newly asserted individual and social freedoms of post-sixties America voices precisely the anxiety about "out-of-control autonomy and freedom"[13] that is symptomatic of the open society and the open text in the Abe Lieberman mysteries. Lieberman's law is applicable to both; one can believe whatever one wants to believe about a story or one's social "family" as long as one avoids doing violence to either. His law is the hard-boiled "ethical view of life" (as Heta Pyrhönen, a scholar of narrative and the detective story, terms the "beliefs about life and human fate" embedded in detective stories) that regulates individual autonomy and enforces social and interpretive civility.[14] This hard-boiled view legislates a kind of ethical solidarity that is the lowest common denominator of collective good for all interpretive communities. Brotherhood reminds self-interested listeners of their responsibility to pay attention to "others," that they are part of an interrelated network of associations (connective and corporate) giving meaning to stories and to life. No interpretive community is an island, entire of itself. Lieberman's Jewish position helps bring this into focus, and his anxiety about the fractiousness within his family—conflicts between the out-marrying Lisa Lieberman and her in-married parents, between Rabbi Miller and "Rabbi" Lieberman—becomes a Jewish prooftext for anxiety about the interpretive anarchy that haunts contemporary American social and literary multiculturalism.

Hence, to the question at the end of the previous chapter—is the positioning of an audience as spectators to border-making always a suspect activity?—I answer no. Parsing the intentionality of the inadvertent learning in American Jewish detective stories, or treating the positioning of readers, and of Jewishness, as always a suspect activity, obscures an important aspect of kosher hybridity that is acknowledged in the Abe Lieberman mysteries: readers help shape the meaning of Jewish difference and of Jewishness as a desirable object of reflection in American Jewish detective stories. They are the "missing Jews" who may return a more worrying iteration of this chapter's title: am I *really* my brother's detective? Thinking about them leads inevitably to a consideration of kosher hybridity and audience reception.

8

THE FAITHFUL DEFENDED

> Our masters taught: He who sees hosts of Israelites should say, "Blessed be He who discerns secrets," for the mind of each of them is not like the mind of any other, nor is the countenance of each of them like the countenance of any other.
> —Babylonian Talmud, Berakhot 58a

In November and December of 2001, I ran advertisements in the *Forward* and the Los Angeles *Jewish Journal* seeking respondents for an online survey of Jewish detective fiction fans. The ads directed respondents to a site on my university's server where they were asked to answer twenty-five questions about themselves and their reading preferences (see Appendix). I knew from the start that my self-selected survey was more anecdotal than scientific evidence, and that, in relation to the rest of my study, which is primarily a series of close readings, the survey might be seen as a useful mixing of methodologies at best, a superfluous exercise at worst. My reasons for going ahead in spite of these weaknesses, however, are intimately connected to my rationale for this study's analysis and illustration of kosher hybridity, and especially to the inadvertent learning bound up in my organizing concept. After all, if Jewish detectives defend the faith(s), defend the diversity of what it means to be Jewish in America, and if their stories present sites of struggle in the American Jewish popular arts over border-making and collaboration, how do the faithful feel about being defended? Who are these others to the detectives working on their behalf—and to textual studies such as this? Thinking about kosher hybridity in terms of audience reception thus provides the springboard for my closing thoughts about readers, modern midrash, and further exploration of the complicated and imperfectly understood intersection between American popular culture and Jewish literature.

Throughout, I have tried to show how the detective texts examined are contradictory, how they exemplify generic and cultural hybridity, how they try to establish both borders and bridges between Jews and non-Jews, and how they insist on both the similarity and the difference between Jewish and American identity. Such an analytical focus reflects my original and still prevailing attitude toward this study. When I began work on what I thought of as only an initial examination of American Jewish popular literature, I felt it was important to begin with the text and follow the trail from there. As I read detective stories one after another—some old acquaintances, others new and unfamiliar—the relationship between a text's social or cultural function and the readers who might or might not use a text according to that function seemed less important than the dynamics of the text and the relationship between it and its author. I was, at that time, more interested in the American Jewish popular arts as a kind of side show in the broad history of Jewish cultural tradition, and in how writers of American Jewish detective stories might negotiate that periphery and perhaps even use it to their advantage. For this was a paradox I began with: writing formula fiction in English ostensibly places its writers in the margins of Jewish literature and culture, yet through these stories many of them speak to more Jewish readers than writers who work in the more rarified world of "serious" literature. So at first I saw the writers of American Jewish detective stories, and not their detectives, as modern Rabbi Eleazars, collaborators who ran the risk of working for the wrong authorities or who were unaware, in ways that their more literary colleagues were not, about the ambiguities that their collaborations set loose in their texts. As I began to appreciate just what those ambiguities were (not the least of which were the dividing lines between center and margin, highbrow and middlebrow), and the skill with which a number of writers handled these ambiguities, I recognized that their detective stories, in general, spawned precisely the sorts of contradictions that all popular cultural texts spawn—tremendous complacency and deep misgivings, awful entertainment and sometimes art, a slackening or even corruption of tradition and tradition's renewal. In other words, I recognized the obvious—that texts and writers were only two points on my literary compass. More and more I wanted to know: what were readers, Jewish readers in particular, making of all this?

When I finally sketched out the last section of my study, and the questions that followed from my interest in audience positioning, I realized that kosher hybridity as a textual phenomenon demands some accounting of audience reception. How does the relationship between self and other in American Jewish detective stories resolve into a view of American Jewish life about which one can be sure an audience is cognizant? In what ways do Jewish readers and viewers assimilate their inadvertent learning? The anxiety about interpretive anarchy that worries the Abe Lieberman mysteries attests to the need for an understanding of the interests and expectations that Jewish readers bring to the stories, and of the social and cultural functions such readers assign to them. Yet I did not want to remake this work into another version of Janice Radway's *Reading the Romance* (1984, 1991). In her ground-breaking study, Radway took an ethnographical approach to the romance formula by first examining the institutional matrix of the formula (business data on, and the hows and whys of, acquisitions, editing, and publishing) and then running a series of in-depth interviews with a romance reading group whose responses were analyzed as expressions of the social and cultural context of romances. What deeply impressed me about Radway's study was her recognition of "the essentially human practice of making meaning," that "mass-produced literary texts are selected, purchased, constructed, and used by real people with previously existing needs, desires, intentions, and interpretive strategies."[1] While ideology certainly informs interpretive practice, I think it an overstatement to insist, as the cultural theorist Tania Modleski has, that as readers and critics we are "all victims, down to the very depths of our psyches, of political and cultural domination (even though we are never only victims)."[2] Readers are both seduced by and resist mass culture, and critics both celebrate and denigrate it, for each is no less a part of this culture than is anyone else with access to televisions, newspapers, films, radios, books, and computers. As Modleski's own argument about women and popular culture rightly notes, American popular culture, and the study of it, is described by contradiction:[3] readers are both like and unlike each other, just as they are both like and unlike the academic critics who study them, and recognizing the contradictions and interrelationships among racial, gender, ethnic, and class differences (and factoring in personal idiosyncrasies) does not invalidate that we are all familiar, on one level or another, with many of the same interpretive cues and values that circulate generally in our society.

But I am not an ethnographer, only a literary critic with an appreciation for how methodologies from other disciplines can enrich my readings. So, rather than pursue a study that would engage what seems an already tired intra-feminist and intra-psychoanalytical debate, I felt that treating my audience reception survey simply as anecdotal evidence for how kosher hybridity is received could serve two important purposes: one, getting at least some sense of who reads American Jewish detective stories; two, seeing whether my interpretation of American Jewish detective stories resonated with or was contradicted by the reading experiences of other American Jews. While my questionnaire was by no means perfect, and the respondents were, socioeconomically, a relatively homogenous group of Jews (as one might expect given the left-of-center, Jewishly literate, and consumer-friendly publications in which I advertised), the results, juxtaposed against the host of detective stories I spent time with over the course of this study, brought to mind the epigraph that begins this chapter, and in particular the line "for the mind of each of them is not like the mind of any other." No, there were no working-class respondents, and by no means did those who did respond reflect the entire diversity of American Jewish "faiths." Yet the differences in the respondents' attitudes about American Jewish detective stories, specifically their comments about what they did or did not learn from the stories and about the stories' social and cultural functions, evoked for me Irena Klepfisz's definition of *Yidishkayt* in her poem "*Etlekhe verter oyf mame-loshn*/A few words in the mother tongue." In that poem, Jewishness is like a play of voices, the voices of students, conversing about the collective memory of *Yidishkayt*, "a way of being/Jewish always arguable."[4] What I heard in the survey was an upper middle-class play of voices that, in a limited way, bore witness to American Jewish diversity and to disputations among American Jewish readers.

THE MIND OF EACH OF THEM

There were forty-one self-selected respondents to the survey, 68 percent of whom were women and 85 percent of whom were married. The respondents were spread out among fourteen states, with the most responses from California and one response from Quebec, Canada; the vast majority said they lived in either an urban area (44 percent) or a suburb (46 percent). The median age was 55, and they were predominantly middle class and upper middle class: only 4 percent reported a total household income of $0–$11,999 or $12,000–$24,999, but 29 percent reported a total household income of $50,000–$99,999, and 41 percent reported a total household income of $100,000 or more. Almost half described themselves as Conservative Jews, and 68 percent claimed to attend synagogue from once a week to several times per month. Further, 41 percent had a master's degree, and as a group they reported voracious reading habits—the majority found out about new Jewish detective fiction at either a bookstore or a library, and they near-unanimously reported themselves as regular readers of both general detective fiction and Jewish detective fiction. The only literature categories read for pleasure by less than 40 percent of the respondents were poetry (10 percent), inspirational (17 percent), romances (17 percent), westerns (5 percent), and horror stories (12 percent). Altogether, these facts provide an unsurprising picture of the readers of the *Forward* and the *Jewish Journal*. The respondents seem representative of those successful, highly educated American Jews who maintain a strong affiliation with Judaism and Jewish cultural tradition, the kind of Jews who would search out and read affirming and acculturated American Jewish detective stories on a regular basis. While there were not enough responses to draw any conclusions about the demographics of regular readers of American Jewish detective stories, one would be hard-pressed to find a better demographic than the one intimated here to illustrate the potential profitability of niche-marketed detective stories with Jewish perspectives and interests.

Also unsurprising was the variety of middle- and upper-middle-class occupations that respondents reported, although here the picture that the survey painted began to suggest some challenges of assessing how even such relatively homogenous readers process and assign meaning to Jewish detective fiction. While a quarter of the respondents were retired, and over a quarter were librarians or educators of some kind, three-quarters reported present or former occupations ranging from prison guard to president/CEO of a Jewish nonprofit organization to homemaker/community volunteer. Doctors, musicians, and accountants all claimed an abiding interest in Jewish detective fiction. Since I had assumed that there would be some similarity in socioeconomic background, and a concomitant diversity of middle-class occupations, I was curious about the relationship between my respondents' gender, their jobs, and the kind of detective, amateur or professional, they preferred to read about. This was a logical extension of questions that my section on cases of gender raised, since my textual analysis took its cue from the values and attitudes reflected in the stories of professional and amateur detectives. In particular, I was interested in the reception of the Jewish woman as amateur, the image of the Jewish woman as an outsider first put into play by James Yaffe and other midcentury American Jewish male writers. Was that image familiar to readers? What meanings, if any, did readers assign stories featuring such amateur detectives? After I had completed a number of chapters, my questions about gender and class were followed by questions related to representations in the stories of middle-class Jews and non-Jews generally. Did the middle-class environment of the stories resonate with the middle- to upper-middle-class environment in which the majority of my respondents lived? In what ways?

Naturally, I was also interested in the reception of inadvertent learning, which, as we have seen, is often not so inadvertent. When analyzing the Peter Decker and Rina Lazarus mysteries, the twice-told tales of Ashkenaz and Sepharad, *A Stranger Among Us,* and the Abe Lieberman mysteries, I noted that the texts often appealed to the audience's recognition of being, in fact, taught something about Jewish identity; I noticed, too, that there was a presumption in the texts that their audiences were aware of the choices they could or might make in yoking their Jewish identity with their American identity. Did audiences find their attitudes and self-images confirmed (a result I thought likely, given my concept of kosher hybridity and given the generally homogenous nature of my self-selected respondents), or did they have a more pragmatic take on the fictiveness of the stories? Finally, I was obviously curious about audience reception of the involuntary or insubordinate midrash of the stories, the popular cultural midrash that describes and defines the intersection between American popular culture and Jewish literature. I assumed that this reception would prove most difficult to adduce. Was any aspect of Rabbi Eleazar's situation—his struggle over the meaning of fidelity to Jewish culture—recognizable to these readers in the actions and "solutions" embodied by the detectives in these stories?

The questions that articulated my first set of interests about gender and preference yielded some meaningful, and some not so meaningful, responses. Faye Kellerman was by far the most popular "favorite author," even for respondents outside Los Angeles, and seeing that result underscored for me the power and reach of Kellerman's reshaping of American Jewish manhood, her portrait of Rina Lazarus's normative Orthodoxy and "resurrection" of Jewish tradition, and her moral critique of American secular society. "Intermarriage" as one of the clearest formulations of kosher hybridity is also perhaps one of the best expressions of the contradiction between the desire for borders and the desire for collaboration that animates American Jewish detective stories. Still, it was not clear that my respondents read the Peter Decker and Rina Lazarus mysteries in the way I did, nor was it entirely clear that Kellerman's hybrid pulp-culture detective or narrative style reflected a favorite subgenre. True, two writers in the hard-boiled tradition, Stuart Kaminsky and Rochelle Krich, were the second and third most popular authors, but they were followed in no particular order by writers such as Sharon Kahn, Harry Kemelman, Marissa Piesman, Ayelet Waldman, Robert Rosenberg, Janice Steinberg, Joseph Telushkin, and Batya Gur (a preference that raised the problem of translation, both linguistic and cultural, but one that is outside the scope of this study). Given this mix of writers, it followed that the majority of my respondents reported no preference for either an amateur or a professional detective, and no preference for either a male or a female hero—and it occurred to me that Kellerman's popularity among my respondents might be partly explained by the intermarriage in her series between a male professional detective and a female amateur detective, that the series appealed to a very wide readership by entertaining a number of formula preferences.

Among readers who did prefer one or another kind of detective, the choices often revealed an awareness of subgenre and gender differences. For example, for the 15 percent of respondents who had a preference for a professional detective the reasons cited were plot-related—that professionals and their hard-boiled stories are more realistic. "I prefer professional investigators for series novels because it is totally unrealistic for amateurs to become involved with crimes," said one respondent, adding that for a "one-shot story, an amateur would be okay." Another asserted that professional detectives "don't require any convoluted plot machinations to be involved in crime solving," while one respondent observed that professionals "just seem more credible to me." For the 7 percent who preferred amateur detectives, the reasons cited were character-related. "An amateur is usually more stumbling," noted one respondent, making the story "more interesting, especially if you are ahead of the detective." One of the respondents who preferred professionals admitted that "the amateur sleuth can be funnier than the professional." Only two responses directly echoed observations that I would make, about the amateur detectives analyzed in chapters 2 and 3. "You can more readily identify with an 'amateur' rather than a professional," said one, and another added that amateurs "are usually more involved in Judaism . . . which adds an interesting element." Similarly, only the few respondents who had a preference for either a male or a female hero acknowledged that gendered self-identification was part of their reading experience. "As a woman, I'm usually more interested in the point of view of women," said one, and another noted that "I appreciate the unorthodox, pardon the pun, approach of the female hero." "Maybe because I am male I prefer male protagonists," admitted another, "but I do read mysteries with both male and female leads." And while one respondent with no preference did observe that there are currently "more females than males to read about," another who preferred male heroes seemed to write himself into an awareness of his gendered self-identification: "Typically the male hero has greater access to 'Jewish' activities than does the female (e.g. morning minyan), and so there's a greater probability of introducing 'Jewish' content into the story. (Perhaps also it's because I'm a male.)"

Some of the more surprising responses to the survey were those that considered the "realism" of the stories' representations of Jews and non-Jews. I expected that many respondents, in their answers to the questions "In general, do you think Jewish detective fiction reflects a realistic portrayal of Jews? Why or why not?" and "In general, do you think Jewish detective fiction reflects a realistic portrayal of non-Jews? Why or why not?" would object that fictions are not real, and that the two questions on the subject were thus beside the point. In fact, only a handful of respondents replied in such a pragmatic vein. Among respondents who felt that Jews and non-Jews were not realistically portrayed, a few complained that non-Jews are depicted as overly ignorant of Judaism and Jewish culture, while others took aim at specific lapses in depictions of contemporary American Jewish life, making comments that touched on cultural faultlines: "No, religious people are depicted as crazy in their practices or as 'ultra-orthodox.' Observant people are normal!"; "No, there usually isn't as much interaction among religious groups as the authors would like us to believe." The overwhelming majority felt that the characters encountered in the stories did reflect people or ethnic traits (in particular the infighting within synagogues) that resonated with their experiences. However, a quick look at some affirmative answers to the question of whether Jewish detective fiction reflects a realistic portrayal of Jews and non-Jews shows how varied were my respondents' understanding of "real" Jews and non-Jews: "Yes I believe we are as a people as varied as anyone and the detective fiction is a reflection of our diversity including the ditsy females, and their mothers, the female Mossad agent of Jon Land, and Batya Gur's Israeli detective"; "Unfortunately, I do—there's all too much ignorance and assimilation, and it seems as though none of the Jewish protagonists ever have Jewish love interests"; "We are a clever people in general and like to solve a good mystery"; "The Kellerman books seem very realistic in their portrayal of non-Jews, both the curiosity about Jewish life and the awkwardness when confronted by limitations in it"; "Yeah, oy the goy!"; "The books I have read reflected a realistic portrayal of non-Jews while sometimes leaning toward being non-realistic to Jewish families" (no examples were provided for this last judgment in which the Jewish self appeared less real than the gentile Other).

Obviously, some of these responses suggest that my respondents are indeed aware that there is a pedagogical function to American Jewish detective stories, and recognize these stories as sites of struggle over fidelity to Jewish culture. This was verified in their responses about whether the respondents had learned something new about Judaism and Jewish history when reading Jewish detective fiction, and about what made Jewish detective fiction enjoyable. The majority claimed that they did learn something new—that the stories often "present another perspective or interpretation," "stimulate thought about Judaism and/or Jewish history," or illustrate "a new tradition" or "details of observance." One respondent averred that "that's the main reason I like it," while another, who did not learn anything new, reported that a non-Jewish friend "says everything she learned about Judaism before she met me was from Faye Kellerman." For those who claimed to be culturally literate, or who learned something new only "sometimes," the stories "spark some other learning after research," or put "something I already knew into a different context." "I get my memory refreshed," said one. Clearly, these respondents are engaged with Jewish detective fiction in ways that verify Rabbi David Small's (which is to say, Harry Kemelman's) enduring influence over American Jewish detective stories. The responses illustrate that the pedagogical function of these stories continues to be integral, and intimate that at least some American Jews (and non-Jews) get much of their information about Judaism and Jewish cultural tradition, however contradictory or imperfect, from these stories.

As for what made Jewish detective fiction enjoyable, the near-unanimous response was self-identification and "a sense of connection" to the detectives and their mysteries. "Sometimes the characters are like someone in my Jewish family," a respondent observed; "they resonate with my life." Some respondents did acknowledge Jewish detective fiction as simply escape fiction, or noted that they find all mystery fiction enjoyable: "It works better than a valium to relax me and take my mind off real-world worries. I can get involved in the lives of nice Jewish folks and not have to worry about them"; "Mystery fiction of all types is my love—it fills a need I have for order in a chaotic universe—and when the books combine other interests of mine (Jewish, Hawaiian culture), that makes the books all that much more interesting to me." For those who could "relate to the characters easier in Jewish detective fiction," however, seeing their own "concerns and problems" reflected was a large part of why they enjoyed the stories. One respondent's concern was to feel connected to Jewish culture: "Jewish detective fiction adds an element of feeling in touch with my cultural background, giving me characters I relate to." Another's was ethical: "It allows you to bond with the detective because some of the same values underlie the fiction. Some of the dilemmas are those that we as Jews face. We know what is right but then???" One respondent appreciated that Jewish detective fiction addressed the problems of acculturation —"it can provide some, albeit fictional, examples of an integrated Jewish life lived in modernity." Another saw in Jewish detective fiction a solution for how to continue learning about Jewish culture, and to maintain a Jewish identity: "As a recent convert to Judaism, I suppose I have a need to learn more about my faith, my culture and my people. This is a very enjoyable way to keep learning. I seem to have a fascination with things Jewish: music, art, customs, food, Israel, etc. I also teach courses . . . so that affords me an opportunity to learn more and more, especially Torah, the Holocaust, Jewish Values, etc. It all helps me to identify with who I am and where I am going." While no responses used the term "modern midrash" (i.e., the way that Jewish writers figure and refigure the meanings of Jewish memory and Jewish experience to make a space for themselves within Jewish cultural tradition), the replies did reflect an appreciation of how detective stories authorized a place for concerns about, and interest in, Jewish identity, and of how they provided solutions to the challenges of keeping in touch with Jewish cultural tradition.

The survey also made clear that there were differences between how I read these stories and how the respondents read them, and one difference in particular ought to be emphasized. While a number of respondents recognized that there are more female than male detectives featured in contemporary American Jewish detective stories, and a number did acknowledge that gendered self-identification affects their preferences, their responses did not echo my analysis and interpretation of the struggle for control over the meaning of gendered American Jewish identities. No doubt, a more in-depth interview might provide better insight into the respondents' attitudes about gender, and the complex ways their attitudes are consciously and unconsciously woven into their social selves. But I point out this difference in order to reiterate part of my argument in the first section of this study: in the struggle over the meaning of Jewish identity in American Jewish detective stories, gender issues are implicated at the stories' foundational level, and so are deeply implicated in the narratives, tropes, and topoi that have come to describe these stories. If subverting the gendered characteristics and images of the stories proves difficult (at least without distorting the genre in ways that undermine the goals of such subversion), so is ascertaining audience reception of gender issues in the stories. Yes, I found some respondents' comments about Orthodox Jewish women detectives highly evocative of a point I made in regard to Faye Kellerman's mysteries, that Rina Lazarus reflects the perception that Jewish women, and Orthodoxy, are helping to resurrect Judaism and Jewish tradition in America; however, although I believe that such a perception is indirectly verified by some respondents' comments, no single respondent overtly articulated such a belief, or indicated that they read detective stories for anything other than educational or self-fulfilling reasons.

In and of itself, this difference between my reading and my respondents' readings of the stories is self-explanatory: I am a critic with a thesis, they are fans with a habit. However, if we take into account changes in the gendering of the stories (the hybridizations of both American Jewish male and female identity), the demographics of my respondents, and the pedagogical function of kosher hybridity, it is quite clear that our different perspectives about the importance of gender boldface how the detectives in the stories are avatars of American Jewish social and cultural contradiction. The detectives' very existence, as I have been arguing throughout this study, depends on their ability to sustain generic imperatives and the self-fulfilling desires of readers—their ability to sustain the witting and the unwitting, the advertent and the inadvertent, the conscious and the unconscious. The difference between the way I read Jewish detective stories and the way my respondents read them indicates not an interpretive gap between me and them, but, rather, how wide a range of reception there is for the inadvertent learning attending the kosher hybridity of these tales. The difference reminds us again of Rabbi Eleazar's situation, in that it underscores the need to recognize the impact of a variety of unwitting collaborations, not only in the texts but also in the readers. This fact very much complicates the significance of kosher hybridity as a textual phenomenon. Taking, as I do in this chapter, a final measurement of Jewish detective stories by measuring them against reader responses, even in an anecdotal way, usefully opens up the intersection between American popular culture and Jewish literature, because it asks us to consider: if 76 percent of my respondents also read literary fiction, if 49 percent also read historical fiction, if 44 percent also read biographies, is such reading affecting how they process and assign meaning to detective stories? In what ways?

What I am getting at here is the need, in studies of American Jewish popular literature, to ask questions such as who is reading this literature and why? In what contexts and venues are people reading American Jewish popular fiction? What else do they read? What other popular arts do they consume or invest time in? How might that bigger picture help us to grasp better not only the specific issues of this study—the dynamics of kosher hybridity in American Jewish detective stories—but also larger, knottier issues related to modern Jewish literature? For example, I am not aware of any study or article that employs audience reception as a tool with which to address the definition of Jewish or American Jewish literature, or the formation of a modern Jewish canon. Only by spending time thinking about the intersection of American popular culture and Jewish literature, and the implications of gender within that intersection, did it occur to me that much of the theory and criticism on Jewish and American Jewish literature proceeded on the assumption that readers were ancillary to, or synonyms for, writers, book reviewers, and academicians.

Let me be clear about my point here. I am not suggesting that textual studies of American Jewish popular literature are somehow invalid without audience reception surveys, or that we ought to have American Jewish book clubs compile their own modern Jewish canon, or a list of the hundred best Jewish books ever. In my introduction, I asserted that taking American Jewish detective stories seriously leads us to the recognition that the textual language and thematic concerns of those stories are a part of, and not separate from, the canon of Jewish literature and the process of modern Jewish self-definition and self-explanation. So, for example, in chapter 5, I showed how the image of the Nazi hunter engaged the concern in Holocaust literature over the meaning of witness and the limits of doing justice to Holocaust victims, and at the same time responded to changing images, in the American Jewish popular imagination, of those victims. Jessica Drake, as an agent of American justice within Jewish time, is a limited hero who must recognize that the story of the family restored is a tease and a fiction. When I consider that one respondent read Jewish detective fiction as populated by characters from "my Jewish family," and that some readers even employ that fiction as a way to restore their Jewish "family," I want to know more about the relationship between readers and an unconventional, popular cultural Jewish hero like Jessica Drake. I want to know, from the reader's perspective, how the desire for Jewishness as an object of reflection creates feedback loops between narrative and popular culture, and how that feedback blunts or incites the casting and recasting of a modern Jewish cultural tradition. Textual studies from a host of critical perspectives that are augmented and leavened, even if only in a peripheral way, by audience reception surveys can provide a far richer matrix for understanding the progress of, and the traffic among, Jewish literature, American Jewish popular literature, and the American Jewish popular arts as a whole.

Without taking into account the unknowns attending the evolving diversity within texts *and* among American Jewish readers, we risk making incomplete judgments about these literatures and this popular art, and about the larger significance of kosher hybridity. Two critical articles and a quick look at American Jewish children's mysteries will help me to illustrate the inadvisability of such judgments—of trying to police kosher hybridity. They will also help to emphasize how kosher hybridity as a textual phenomenon reveals the unflagging creative energy that continues to drive American Jewish literature and culture, as well as the stakes involved in future study of the intersection between American popular culture and Jewish literature.

POLICING KOSHER HYBRIDITY

Impressed by the immense popularity among Reform and Conservative American Jewish women of Anita Diamant's *The Red Tent,* Simone Lotven Sofian decided to take a closer look at Diamant's feminist retelling and refiguring of the biblical stories about the patriarch Jacob's family.[5] Aghast at what she found, Sofian, a university lecturer and member of the editorial board of the UAHC (Union of American Hebrew Congregations) Press, published "Popular Fiction and the Limits of Modern Midrash," a review essay in which she argues that Diamant's popular fiction does not deserve to be called modern midrash, feminist or otherwise, and ought not to be accepted as such by educators and readers. For Sofian, the term "midrash" must be reserved for Jewish texts that reflect "an awareness of the sacredness of the original biblical text which confers a sacredness to the creation of the midrash. It is not simply a literary exercise."[6] In Sofian's definition of midrash, God remains in the text, and any attempt to write God out, or to refigure the meaning of "basic Jewish monotheism," is a corruption of Judaism and a danger to American Jews' identity. After explicating exactly how Diamant's narrative and characters deviate from their originals—and so allow goddess worship, a condemnation of circumcision, and "the language of the romance novel" to infiltrate Jewish cultural tradition—Sofian sounds a warning for those who think their students and congregants are simply being entertained:

> *The Red Tent* leads women to question the truth of this monotheistic Judaism for themselves. Rather than searching for a fuller Judaism which incorporates the female in God as well as the female Jew's relationship with God, we are faced with a Sara, Rebecca, Leah and Rachel who worship Innana, Asherah, Anat, Ilat. . . . Finding meaning in this reading of our matriarchs' story implies that Judaism as we have inherited it is meaningless to women, for it is the descendent of a singularly male religion. Thus, rather than finding meaning in Judaism, its covert or perhaps overt message is that women should be re-establishing the separate but parallel women's religion which is the true inheritance from our foremothers.[7]

Sofian accuses secularizing and disestablishmentarian popular fictions like Diamant's of highjacking the social and cultural functions of midrash. Based on her observation of the novel's wide circulation among Reform and Conservative reading groups, and on the glowing notices it received from the UAHC (but not on any kind of audience reception survey), Sofian concludes that the reception of Diamant's popular fiction is indicative of "an intellectual and religious sloppiness which has to be challenged."[8]

Sofian's article, published in the spring 2002 issue of *Conservative Judaism,* is followed in that issue by a reply from Naomi Graetz, a feminist critic and also a university teacher. Graetz defends the project of feminist modern midrash, explaining how the gendering of God as male marginalizes the feminine attributes of God, and disempowers modern Jewish women because it marginalizes the importance of their "changing needs."[9] Sofian's charge that goddess worship threatens the very foundation of a Jewish monotheism, Graetz argues, is evidence that the call to "oneness" in monotheism is often a ploy to smother theological differences within Judaism itself, and to stifle independent thinking: "If God is non-gendered and incorporates both sexes (as we're told Elohim does), why is it so difficult to accept the need to include language and metaphors about the female aspects of God, as well as male, in worship? Why not? Perhaps because when viewed from the other side, it exposes the imbalance and makes us uncomfortable, forcing us to think!"[10] For Graetz, the real issue under debate is not monotheism and the inclusion of female aspects of divinity in worship of the Jewish God (which Sofian seems willing to accept), but rather modernity and the inclusion of Jewish women as equals within Judaism. Traditional midrash and its misogynist attitudes must be countered by modern midrash that, by striking a transgressive attitude, opens up a needed space for women within Jewish cultural tradition. And, in a move that means to defend the kosher hybridity of texts such as *The Red Tent,* Graetz ends her reply to Sofian by challenging her, and critics like her, to recognize that modern midrash is reader-responsive: "I do not think the only function of midrash is to preserve a reading of Torah in which teachings about a male God are center-stage. I believe midrash is and should be reader-responsive and thus I view all text-based interpretation as legitimate."[11]

What is interesting at this point in her argument, however, is not the challenge itself but that immediately following her challenge, Graetz provides a list of eight provisos—rules, really—for what feminist midrash "should consciously do." Once again it becomes clear that "readers" is a synonym for "writers." Granted, one implication of this move is that all readers are writers in the Barthian sense, that they help to "write" a text's meaning, but the provisos are very much pitched to storytellers. Feminist midrash must "strike an equal balance between men and women in talking about God," must "deal with typically female concerns," must "find and develop biblical role models" with whom Jewish women can identify, must "attempt to depict the loneliness and ambiguities of women's leadership in a patriarchal society," must "imaginatively rediscover" a women-centered biblical history, must "flesh out gaps" in the Bible where women are eclipsed or missing, must "be constantly eisegetical [subjectively biased]: if you view violence as wrong, don't hesitate to depict zealotry as bad," and must "never regard male behavior as normative and identify against oneself."[12]

I see both Sofian's and Graetz's arguments as well-intentioned but incomplete judgments about modern midrash and kosher hybridity, because once each argument moves beyond a definition and textual analysis of modern midrash (and I am obviously inclined toward Graetz's definition here), each elides the difficult issue of trying to compose the larger picture: sketching out *how* to see the feedback loop between texts and readers that either incites or blunts the advertent and inadvertent learning attending kosher hybridity. For those who wish to pursue further questions about the social context of this textual phenomenon, there needs to be some instrument with which to determine the audience reception of kosher hybridity as modern midrash. What we need—and what I am calling for from those more qualified to take this up—is a sociology of American Jewish popular literature and the popular arts. Instead of recognizing that need, both Sofian and Graetz return us to an either/or proposition about kosher hybridity as modern midrash—either it is good or it is bad, either it has a legislatable poetics or it is unregulated, individualistic speculation. They return us to what is too often a fallback critical position: policing kosher hybridity—policing the intersection between narrative and popular culture rather than engaging the complex and troubling questions that the intersection raises. Sofian proscribes what readers should read and educators should make available, and Graetz prescribes what writers should write, and how they should write it, if they wish their work included under the rubric of feminist modern midrash.

But if my study has shown anything it is that over the course of time, from midcentury to the last decade of the twentieth century, the kinds of collaborations and border-makings that describe kosher hybridity are highly dynamic and vexingly unregulatable. And creatively fruitful. We hear critics today debating the relative achievements and worth of contemporary American Jewish literature, and much attention is paid to whether the ethnic revival of the last few decades can sustain Jewish writing in America, or whether the mainstream of Jewish imaginative genius lies in Hebrew literature and in the revival of Yiddish as a post-Zionist folk culture.[13] Yet here are American Jewish detective stories with contradictions and sites of struggle that are witness to a restless and anxious creative energy that continues unabated in American Jewish culture. These stories speak to and articulate the lively and conflicted contemporary Jewish experience in America: the value and meaning of a Jewish education; the vexing issues of intermarriage and multiculturalism; the challenges of, and to, Jewish feminism; the obsession with the Jewish past; the unease about tough Jews and about the right use of Jewish political and physical power; ambivalence about the burden and responsibility of Holocaust memory; the spectre of anti-Semitism; the question of authenticity and Jewish identity; and (as we have seen again and again) the worry over the vulnerability and breakdown of the American Jewish family. Should we be surprised that, as the cultural critic Morris Dickstein has noted, Jewish writers fail "to give up the ghost, especially now that the ghost, the past, has taken on new flesh and blood"?[14] Further, if we expand the horizons of American Jewish literature, we find popular fictions like *The Red Tent*, whose production and controversial reception suggest that we take a closer look at American Jewish romances, science fiction, inspirational books (self-help books, Hasidic hagiography, *mussar*, etc.), or cookbooks—perhaps even American Jewish comic books, graphic novels, and other visual culture texts—as examples of kosher hybridity. Where we might expect to find no meaningful or fruitful collaborations, witting or unwitting, we may find, upon closer examination of these texts, their writers, and their audiences, an unexpected window onto the American Jewish popular imagination and onto sites of struggle in the American Jewish popular arts.

CHILDREN AND POLITICS, HEARTS AND MINDS

Let us take, as my final example of such an unexpected window, the Devora Doresh and Bina Gold children's mystery series (the former written by Carol Korb Hubner, the latter by various authors). At first glance, these popular fictions seem well within the limits of a sacralizing modern midrash. They both represent an Orthodox modern midrash for girls in which God and traditional monotheism is central, yet which makes a place for "the female Jew's relationship with God." Even the names of the two detectives reflect a woman-centered biblical history and the female aspects of God: Devora is named after the biblical prophet who led the Jews in their victory over the army of the Canaanite king Sisera, and Bina means "intelligence," a name for one of the kabbalistic *sefirot*, divine emanations, with a feminine connotation. Devora "Doresh," Hebrew for "investigator," constantly cites *aggadot*, tales, from the Talmud, and very self-consciously applies midrash to the mysteries she solves. In "The Whispering Mezuzah" (1979), the Doresh family is on its way to the country to visit Mrs. Doresh's sister and her family, and to deliver four new mezuzot to them. After a none too subtle discourse by Devora's father, Rebbe Doresh, on the halacha, the laws, of mezuzot, the rebbe relates first one *aggadah* about the sage Onkelos and how a mezuzah enabled him to convert a host of Roman soldiers to Judaism, and then Devora relates another about the sage Rav and his gift of a mezuzah to the sultan Artaban that results in Rav's appointment as the sultan's chief advisor. Mrs. Doresh offers a tale, as well, but hers is really a mystery: she received a mezuzah key ring, in the mail, that makes a funny sound when pressed, and she invites Devora to discover what the mezuzah is trying to say. Is it simply broken? "'I don't know,' Mrs. Doresh said, smiling. 'But at least you'll now have a mystery to solve while we're away from the excitement of city life. And once you've solved it, you'll have a fresh new *mezuzah* story to tell in addition to the ones about Onkelos and Rav'" (14). Devora's story, that of a young armchair detective, ends up being about how a Jewish girl's knowledge of Hebrew and the Torah enables her to read and to hear clues, unreadable and unhearable to the police, that reveal the secret treasures hidden in "rooms"—the antique gold mezuzah cases hidden in the basement of her aunt's summer house, and the mezuzah's commandment to "Hear O Israel" that reminds Jews, in every room of their homes, of

God's protection over the Jewish people. Like Onkelos, Devora illustrates the lure of Judaism's protectiveness. Like Rav, she becomes a valuable advisor to the gentile authorities. And like Devora the prophet, this Jewish girl makes a place for herself within tradition by being unafraid to lead when her people need her.

This is the formula for every story in Hubner's Devora Doresh series, as well as for the Bina Gold mysteries. In *The Real Megan* (1996), written by Batya Swift Yasgur, Bina Gold has the dual task of recovering a stolen challah cover and the "Jewishly lost" Megan whose terrible home life has led her away from Judaism. By the end of the story Bina solves the mystery of the challah cover (stolen by another family so hard-pressed by circumstances that the theft is more a cry for help than a crime), and her acts of lovingkindness have so impressed Megan's stepparents, and Megan herself, that they decide to become better Jews. The real Megan, readers discover, is Malka, a newly enrolled yeshiva student. "The best mystery to solve is how we can be better people," Bina's mother opines, to which Bina's younger brother replies "Just do lots of *chesed*—give *tzedaka*, visit sick people—you know, stuff like that." (190) As good students (both Devora Doresh and Bina Gold are described as the best and brightest students in their respective Jewish high schools for girls), these young detectives teach the merits of what they have learned, and the applicability of Jewish learning as a key to, and shield against, the hazardous secular world of robberies, murders, kidnappings, and political intrigue. A Jewish girl's relationship to God is therefore imaged as like the one between the most gifted student and her teacher.

Even in their very resistance to collaboration with the non-Orthodox world, these stories about intelligent and independent Jewish girls, stories that champion the power of Jewish women and yet are still fit for Orthodox Jewish consumption, already betray a number of unwitting collaborations that fail to be regulated by all their Talmudic citations and out-and-out lecturing. When we read the *Hadassah Magazine* quote on the back of *The Whispering Mezuzah and Other Devora Doresh Mysteries*, "[Devora Doresh] puts even Rabbi Small to shame," and "Nancy Drew addicts will become hooked on her," we recognize that through these precursors Devora Doresh is hybridized twice-over. Watching Devora take her place in Rabbi Small's classroom reminds us again that his was the first model of an American Jewish classroom in Jewish detective stories, one that reflects anxiety over how to have *naches* in a world of *goyim naches,* and over the place of Jewish religious practice and Jewish identity in America. Reading Devora, and Bina Gold, in the shadow of Nancy Drew also blurs the limits of modern midrash, for that precursor threatens to set loose exactly what, or whom, the "solutions" of these stories aim to control: Orthodox Jewish girls. Nancy Drew is no feminist, but, as Sara Paretsky argues, she embodies a very American kind of heroism that girls need at just the age when they may encounter her. Nancy Drew "rises above fear and despair and finds herself a lever," Paretsky says, and that self-reliance is indispensable for girls who "still grow up without a strong sense of themselves as people or of their right to play active roles in adult life."[15] Devora Doresh and Bina Gold are Jewish Nancy Drews whose Jewish faith is hybridized with Nancy Drew's self-faith. Cornered by the gun-toting daughter of a Nazi in the Holocaust-themed *The Secret of the Grandfather Clock* (1998), also written by Yasgur, Bina Gold finds herself in a perilous situation because she had struck out on her own, "convinced that she held the key that would unlock the entire mystery" (140). She did hold the key, although Yasgur takes care to set up Bina's rescue as a modern-day "miracle." Like the Jews pursued by Pharaoh's army, like Abraham and Daniel, Bina "[seemed to have] no place to go—they were doomed. But Hashem found a way to rescue them at the last minute" (153). However, it was Bina's note to her mother that she would be back in time for dinner that started the chain of events leading to her "miraculous" rescue, and, as in the Nancy Drew stories, it is such self-reliant talents and self-impelled coincidences that make Bina the successful detective she is. And Devora Doresh's faith in her own abilities makes her unafraid to venture into the spooky and potentially dangerous synagogues in "The Haunted Shul" (1981) and "The Twisted Menora" (1981). The synagogues' hauntings and secret passages, and their centrality to the communal conflicts roiling the Jewish communities they serve, only highlight Devora's right to play an active role in the adult life of the communities. Could independent and intelligent leaders like Devora and Bina grow up to demand a right to study for the Orthodox rabbinate?

Add to Devora's and Bina's sense of self-reliance the ideological contradictions in each series, and it becomes even more apparent why these examples of American Jewish children's literature demand greater analysis in light of their kosher hybridity. Devora Doresh ostensibly works for only one authority, God. Her investigations reveal that, in the words of a character who is a Holocaust survivor, in "all destruction, there is renewal. In all despair, there is hope, for Hashem is always with us." Only God has the ability to restore the Jewish family, miraculously bringing together fathers and children separated by Stalin's KGB ("A

Purim Mystery" [1981]) or by the Nazis ("The Tattered Tallis" [1979]). Yet Devora's investigative skills are enlisted by the FBI and the CIA in their cold war against communism ("The Gold Bug" [1979]), "The Tattered Tallis," "The Russian Connection" [1981]) and in their adventures in third world countries ("Message From Tangiers" [1981]). The implication of these modern, youth versions of Rabbi Eleazar's ancient situation is that learning how to negotiate political collaboration begins early, even among Orthodox Jews. The contradictions of collaboration, however, remain hard to control: Does God really work with and through the CIA? Isn't this question also a part of general American political discourse? The kosher hybridity of American Jewish children's literature as a whole brings forward another project worth investigating: How are political collaborations threaded into Orthodox, Conservative, and Reform children's literature? How does that literature reflect a site of struggle about the political affiliations of American Jews?

I find especially troubling the way the Israeli–Palestinian conflict is imported into both the Devora Doresh and Bina Gold mysteries. Given the recent uproar over the corrosive and anti-Semitic ideology of the textbooks used by Palestinian schools in the West Bank and Gaza, it seems only fair play that we examine American Jewish children's literature and textbooks, too, even if we have to acknowledge at the start that there is no moral equivalency between the two sets of texts. *The Secret of the Hotel DelaRosa* (1996), written by Ruchama King Feuerman, is a particularly heavyhanded Bina Gold mystery. Bina is in Jerusalem trying to save another wayward Jewish girl from a broken home, and finds herself saving the girl from the more serious crime of collaborating with the Palestinians and converting to Islam. Bina helps to illustrate how the Jewish relationship with Jerusalem is a spiritual one, how the "Jerusalem magic" (144) infuses Jewish worship with a spirituality that brings it a step closer to God than does Jewish worship in America. In contrast, the Palestinian terrorists who have brainwashed Lisa Marks— two cackling hags whose villainy is of the crudest and most melodramatic kind—help to illustrate the absolute disregard that Palestinians have for the sanctity of Jewish Jerusalem and of human life. After capturing Bina, the two terrorists strap explosives onto her and Lisa (Jews as suicide bombers!) and force them to walk to the Western Wall, in an attempt to blow it up with a maximum loss of life. The dichotomy is a stark one, and the portrayal of Palestinians in this mystery is distasteful and disturbing. The site of struggle here is over the hearts and minds of American Jewish youth, and in this respect the book compels our attention as a popular fiction with meanings and import having deep resonances for American Jewish culture.

This becomes clear when we measure this volume against an earlier Devora Doresh mystery. In "Kidnapped" (1983), Rabbi and Rebbetzin Pollack, along with an American congressman and his wife, are kidnapped by Palestinians as they tour Hebron. The congressman refuses to be used as the voice of the terrorist's demands, so Rabbi Pollack voices them instead. As a political unknown, Rabbi Pollack is allowed to send a message that identifies him to the Americans. The Pollacks are friends of the Doresh family, and since Rabbi Pollack knows that Devora is a first-rate detective, his identifying statement is in fact a coded message to her about where they are being held. Working with the State Department representative and an Israeli agent, Devora recognizes that the clue to the code is Rabbi Pollack's oblique reference to a comment he had made to Devora before he left: "G-d gave us the Torah in the Sinai, but every city of Israel is a Torah city, with its yeshivos and students learning, studying, and praising G-d's name" (66). As Devora thinks about where Rabbi Pollack might be in relation to Hebron, a daydream about the city reveals the solution:

> The map of Israel flashed in front of her and then, as if by a miracle, she felt herself deposited through time and standing in Hebron, the city that Abraham called *Chaver Na'eh*—the agreeable friend of G-d.
>
> Her eyes focused on a group of yeshiva students praying there with piety and awe before the graves of the four couples buried there: Adam and Eve, Abraham and Sarah, Isaac and Rebecca, Jacob and Leah. Hebron, one of Israel's four holy cities.
>
> In the year 1929 the Arabs had turned on the Jews living there and massacred them. The Synagogue of Abraham lay in ruins, its builders destroyed.
>
> Suddenly it was 1967, and Devora saw the builders return. They were singing and praying in the city again. It was, once again, a city of Torah.
>
> A city of Torah, she murmured. Suddenly, she shot out of bed, her eyes aglow. (83)

Naturally, everyone is saved and the terrorists killed, and the Israeli agent is so impressed by Devora that he decides to become a more observant Jew. But, more important in a story about secret codes, the message transmitted is about the meaning of "Israel," not only as a Jewish state, but also as a geographic entity. *Hebron is ours*, say Rabbi Pollack and Devora Doresh, *a city of yeshivas and synagogues that is no different from Jerusalem or Safed or Meron*. Or Boro Park for that matter.

Theirs is a message from American Jews to Israel, and the Israeli agent gets it. So does Bina Gold thirteen years later.

Taken together, then, these two American Jewish children's detective stories are a final and compelling example of the meaning and function of kosher hybridity, and of the stakes involved in future study of the intersection between American popular culture and Jewish literature. Whatever the future may hold for American Jews and American Jewish culture, I have no doubt that it will be reflected and affected by that intersection, and that even now that intersection testifies to how well-founded are a number of the anxieties American Jews have. As a teacher, however, I know that, while I can influence others, I cannot legislate what my students read and what writers write. I know, too, that celebrating such an intersection is as inappropriate as denigrating or policing it. What I hope is that, by recognizing it as an indicator of a still very dynamic, imperfectly acculturated, diverse, and constantly surprising American Jewish culture, we can better understand the contemporary need for inspecting Jews. We can better appreciate how our children, those we bear and those we teach and mentor, take hold of what they are given and what they find, make these theirs, and do their best to negotiate a world in which cases are never closed.

Appendix: Audience Reception Survey

Question 1: True/False
I am a regular reader of detective fiction.

Question 2: True/False
I am a regular reader of Jewish detective fiction.

Question 3: Multiple Choice
How often do you discuss Jewish detective fiction with others?

- never ___
- rarely ___
- sometimes ___
- often ___

Question 4: Multiple Choice
Where do you get most of the Jewish detective fiction you read?

- bookstore ___
- supermarket or drugstore ___
- library ___
- borrow from friend ___
- borrow from relative ___
- other ___

Question 5: Multiple Choice
How do you find out about new Jewish detective fiction most often?

- I see them at the bookstore ___

- I see them at the supermarket or drugstore ___
- Someone at the bookstore tells me about them ___
- I learn about them from friends ___
- I learn about them from relatives ___
- Other ___

Question 6: Short Answer/Essay
Who are your favorite authors of Jewish detective fiction? Please list no more than five, and please list them in order.

Question 7: Multiple Choice
Do you prefer Jewish detective fiction that features an amateur detective or a professional investigator?

- amateur ___
- professional ___
- I don't distinguish ___

Question 8: Short Answer/Essay
If you do have a preference, briefly explain why you prefer either an amateur detective or a professional investigator.

Question 9: Multiple Choice
Do you prefer Jewish detective fiction that features a male hero or a female hero?

- male ___
- female ___
- I don't distinguish ___

Question 10: Short Answer/Essay
If you do have a preference, briefly explain why you prefer either a male hero or a female hero.

Question 11: Short Answer/Essay
In general, when you read Jewish detective fiction do you learn something new about Judaism and/or Jewish history? Why or why not?

Question 12: Short Answer/Essay
In general, do you think Jewish detective fiction reflects a realistic portrayal of Jews? Why or why not?

Question 13: Short Answer/Essay
In general, do you think Jewish detective fiction reflects a realistic portrayal of non-Jews? Why or why not?

Question 14: Multiple Choice
What books do you read for pleasure besides Jewish detective fiction?

Please check as many as you like.

- none ___
- literary fiction ___
- poetry ___
- nonfiction/journalism ___
- history (general) ___
- inspirational (general, hasidic, *mussar*, etc.) ___
- romances ___
- biography ___
- historical fiction ___
- westerns ___
- horror-stories ___
- other ___

Question 15: Multiple Choice
What is your gender?

- male ___
- female ___

Question 16: Short Answer/Essay
What is your age?

Question 17: Multiple Choice
What is your total household income?

- $0–$11,999 ___
- $12,000–$24,999 ___
- $25,000–$49,999 ___
- $50,000–$99,999 ___
- $100,000 or more ___

Question 18: Multiple Choice
What is your current marital status?

- single ___
- married ___
- widowed ___
- separated ___
- divorced ___

Question 19: Multiple Choice
How many years of education have you completed?

- less than 8 ___
- K–8 ___
- high school ___

- some college ___
- completed college ___
- some postgraduate work ___
- master's degree ___
- Ph.D. ___

Question 20: Short Answer/Essay
In what state do you presently live?

Question 21: Multiple Choice
Do you live in:

- an urban area ___
- a suburb ___
- a rural area ___

Question 22: Short Answer/Essay
If you have a job, what is your occupation or job description?

Question 23: Multiple Choice
Which of the following would you call yourself? (Choose one)

- Orthodox ___
- Conservative ___
- Reform ___
- Reconstructionist ___
- Just Jewish ___
- Christian ___
- Muslim ___
- Buddhist ___
- other ___

Question 24: Multiple Choice
How often do you usually attend any type of synagogue, church, or organized religious service?

- daily ___
- once per week or more ___
- once or several times a month ___
- a few times a year ___
- not at all or only on special occasions (a wedding, bar mitzvah, etc.) ___

Question 25: Short Answer/Essay
Could you briefly describe what makes Jewish detective fiction enjoyable?

Notes

INTRODUCTION: INSPECTING JEWS

1. Lawrence W. Raphael, *Mystery Midrash*, 13. Variations of that argument appear in Andrew Furman, "The Secret Jews of Sixteenth-Century Lisbon," *Midstream*, September/October 1998; Naomi Sokoloff, "Jewish Mysteries: Detective Fiction by Faye Kellerman and Batya Gur," *Midstream*, October 1997; Richard E. Sherwin, *Menorah Review*, spring/summer 1997; and Margo Kaufman, *Los Angeles Times*, 22 September 1996.
2. Laura Brahm, *Pakn Treger*, fall 1998/5759, 34.
3. Jon Thompson, *Fiction, Crime, and Empire*, 8.
4. Muriel Rukeyser, *The Life of Poetry*, 103–104.
5. Philip Roth, *Operation Shylock*, 196.
6. "Taking it seriously" also alludes to Donald Weber's discussion of acculturation and American Jewish parody, desire, and ambivalence in his excellent article, "Taking Jewish American Popular Culture Seriously: The Yinglish Worlds of Gertrude Berg, Milton Berle, and Mickey Katz."
7. The appellation "the new Jewish cultural studies" is borrowed from the title of Jonathan and Daniel Boyarin's groundbreaking critical anthology, *Jews and Other Differences: The New Jewish Cultural Studies*. Representative scholars associated with the appellation include Jack Kugelmass, Ann Pellegrini, Daniel Itzkowitz, and Naomi Seidman, all represented in the Boyarin anthology, but the increase in scholarship on the American Jewish popular arts has also been spurred by the work of Stephen J. Whitfield, Joyce Antler, Jonathan Sarna, Sylvia Barack Fishman, and others in what I call the "Brandeis school" of American Jewish studies, and by the work of such diverse scholars as Jenna Weisman Joselit, Michael Rogin, Riv-Ellen Prell, Jeffrey Melnick, Laura Levitt, Andrew Heinze, Hasia Diner, and Jeffrey Shandler.
8. See, for example, Matti Bunzl's review essay, "Jews, Queers, and Other Symptoms," for a discussion of the intervention of queer theory into Jewish studies.
9. In Edward Said's formulation of the first hypothesis, "all cultures impose corrections upon raw reality, changing it from free-floating objects into units of knowledge" (*Orientalism*, 67). The second hypothesis is predicated on Clifford Geertz's definition of "culture"; see Geertz, *The Interpretation of Cultures* and "Blurred Genres: The Refiguration of Social Thought." The modifications that I note of these two hypotheses all underscore the political nature of the word "culture," so that many scholars I mention may share common ground, but not a common politics, with John Fiske, who defines culture as "a way of living within an industrial

society that encompasses all the meanings of that social experience." Fiske, *Literary Theory,* 305.
10. Mark Bauerlein, *Literary Criticism,* 30; Arnold Eisen, "In the Wilderness: Reflections on American Jewish Culture," 28.
11. This interpretation is also predicated on Ray Surette, *Popular Culture, Crime, and Justice,* xiv–xxiv, and Stuart Hall, *Gender, Race, and Class in Media,* 18–22.
12. Kosher hybridity reveals how American Jewish detective stories fashion identities out of the multiplicity of American Jewish popular culture. As Ray Surette points out in his prologue to *Popular Culture, Crime, and Justice,* "popular culture will remain a dominant social construction engine, so that influence in the popular culture realm will remain highly important" (xxiii).
13. Quotation cited is from Booker, *A Practical Introduction,* 480; and see Mikhail Bakhtin, "Discourse in the Novel" (from *The Dialogic Imagination*). In addition, Robert J. C. Young's *Colonial Desire: Hybridity in Theory, Culture, and Race* is a valuable reminder that "the property of being informed" also refers us back to the biological aspects of hybridity—i.e., sexual relations between colonizer and colonized, something too often glossed over in the critical material on hybridity (26–28).
14. Stephen J. Whitfield, *American Space, Jewish Time,* 45.
15. Jonathan Sarna, "The Cult of Synthesis in American Jewish Culture," 52.
16. American Jewish popular fiction, as Arnold Band points out, is a continuation of the identity-shaping project of the Jewish film moguls in the first part of the twentieth century. See Band, *Jewish Identity in America,* 217.
17. John Fiske calls such popular cultural texts "producerly texts," and he sees them as occupying a middle ground between what Roland Barthes called the "readerly text" (one that packages meaning for easy and unconscious consumption) and the "writerly text" (one that incites a reader to participate consciously in shaping the text's meaning). See Fiske, *Understanding Popular Culture,* 103–106. My use of "idioms" is indebted to Jean François Lyotard's study of the generative aspect of disputation as a linguistic activity in *The Differend: Phrases in Dispute.* For Lyotard, pluralism is the disputation that gives rise to *differends* between "phrases," units of grammatical signification about reasoning, knowing, describing, recounting, questioning, showing, ordering, etc. One cannot translate one phrase into another; one can only link phrases together. Intellectual freedom, the freedom to disseminate new idioms for phrasing, is the result of differends, the disputations within pluralist societies. "What is at stake in a literature, in a philosophy, in a politics perhaps," notes Lyotard, "is to bear witness to différends by finding idioms for them" (13).
18. Sylvia Barack Fishman, *Jewish Life and American Culture,* 11.
19. Sarna, "The Cult of Synthesis," 74.
20. Fishman, *Jewish Life and American Culture,* 10.
21. Larry Landrum, *American Mystery and Detective Novels,* 1.
22. Robert Ray, *The Avant Garde Finds Andy Hardy,* 30 and 32.
23. See Stephen Soitos, *The Blues Detective,* and Adrienne Johnson Gosselin, *Multicultural Detective Fiction* and "The Psychology of Uncertainty: (Re)Inscribing Indeterminacy in Rudolph Fisher's *The Conjure-Man Dies.*"
24. Soitos, *The Blues Detective,* 28.
25. Gosselin, *Multicultural Detective Fiction,* 3–4.
26. Ibid, 4.
27. Yaffe, "Is This Any Job for a Nice Jewish Boy?" 19.
28. Ibid.
29. Ibid, 30, 31, and 32.
30. Raphael, *Mystery Midrash,* 11–12, and "Assimilated, Acculturated, or Affirming: The Jewish Detective in America," 124.
31. Whitfield, *In Search of American Jewish Culture,* 20.
32. Ibid, 22–27. By "logocentricity" Whitfield means not only the privileging of reason and what Jacques Derrida calls the "invisible," but also, and simply, a love of language and books.
33. Colonel Prentiss Ingraham, *The Jew Detective; or, The Beautiful Convict* (New York: Beadle's Dime Library, 1 July 1891). As far as is known, the second Jewish detective in American literature is the protagonist of Charles Norton's comedy tabloid drama *The Hebrew Detective* (Chicago, 1914), extant only in a typescript edition held by the University of Chicago and the Library of Congress Manuscript Division.

34. Sol Liptzin, *The Jew in American Literature*, 91. See also Whitfield's discussion of Henry Harland in *In Search of American Jewish Culture*, 18.
35. Hayim Nahman Bialik and Yehoshua Hana Ravnitzky, eds., *The Book of Legends: Sefer Ha-Aggadah*, trans. William G. Braude (New York: Schocken Books, 1992), 654:161. In other collections, "detective" is translated as "officer of the king," and there is also another version of Rabbi Eleazar's tale in Bava Metzia 84a that substitutes as the protagonist Rabbi Yishmael son of Rabbi Yose, who runs away rather than collaborate with the Romans. Rabbi Eleazar is a fascinating figure. His father was the celebrated Rabbi Simeon bar Yohai who reviled and defied the Roman authorities, but his grandfather Yohai occupied the same position in the Roman administration as would his grandson. This technically makes Yohai the first professional Jewish detective in Jewish literature, but, unfortunately, we have only the mention in Pesahim 112a, and, therefore, none of the material that, in contrast, makes Rabbi Eleazar a usable model. See also Rabbi Israel V. Berman, ed. and trans., *The Talmud: The Steinsaltz Edition*, vol. 5, Tractate Bava Metzia, Part 5, 111–119; Shmuel Safrai, "Eleazar ben Simeon (tan.)," *Encyclopaedia Judaica*, CD-ROM Edition; and Gershom Bader, *The Encyclopedia of Talmudic Sages*, trans. Solomon Katz, 641.
36. As Arnold Eisen points out, "the commitment to pluralism" among American Jews is a reflection of the Jewish passage into modernity ("In the Wilderness," 35). What I am trying to make clear is how Rabbi Eleazar's model of a defender of the faith describes an ancient situation that lends itself to, and is refigured by, the imposition of a modern Jewish situation and modern Jewish sensibilities and syntheses.
37. I use "site of struggle" here in its commonplace meaning, derived from reader-response criticism, of those places in a text where there is a struggle over the text's interpretation, and also as an allusion to a theoretical point in Bakhtin's "Discourse in the Novel" (from *The Dialogic Imagination*). I note the allusion only to provide an heuristic angle on my point about kosher hybridity. For Bakhtin, internally persuasive discourse "enters into interanimating relationships with new contexts. More than that, it enters into an intense interaction, a *struggle* with other internally persuasive discourses. Our ideological development is just such an intense struggle within us for hegemony among the various available verbal and ideological points of view, approaches, directions and values. The semantic structure of an internally persuasive discourse is *not finite*, it is *open*; in each of the new contexts that dialogize it, this discourse is able to reveal ever newer *ways to mean*." Bakhtin, "Discourse in the Novel," 346.
38. Hartman asserts that the secular Jewish writer "is caught between a poetics of quotation imitative of midrash and so remaining in the field of force of these canonical texts, and the need to make room for a supplementary modern scripture—still, perhaps an 'écriture du désastre' (Maurice Blanchot), yet based on a reanimated and circulating language that seeks to purge itself of inflated or sacred phraseology." Geoffrey Hartman, "On the Jewish Imagination," 210.
39. Norman Finkelstein, *The Ritual of New Creation*, 3. Finkelstein's title is an homage to Gershom Scholem's essay "Tradition and New Creation in the Ritual of the Kabbalists," and Finkelstein acknowledges in his introduction that his book is an improvisation on Scholem's essay.
40. Ibid, 9. "Ritual," in Finkelstein's use of the word, signals the taking over and reworking of the rituals of Jewish faith, not so much a secularization of ritual as a sublation of ritual: "In modern times, ritual and the investment of faith which stood behind it have been cast radically into doubt. If ritual remains, it is preserved in the act of new creation itself. Contemporary Jewish writers ... honor the past *through* rupture because, as Yosef Hayim Yerushalmi tells us, their past has been a tradition *of* rupture" (3).
41. My terminology in this sentence is borrowed from John Cawelti, *Adventure, Mystery, and Romance*. Cawelti identifies the balance between ratiocination and mystification as a particular "problem of proportion" in the classical detective formula, but I see it in a more general way, as expressive of the challenge that faces all writers of multicultural detective fiction, for whom "reasoning" is a perplexed and culturally marked element.
42. See, for example, Charles Norton's *The Hebrew Detective*, as well as Claire Booth Luce's Jewish detective, Moe Finkelstein, in her 1940 play *Margin for Error* (a detective that James Yaffe thought was the first significant Jewish detective in American literature, one that "paves the way for the Jewish detective of the postwar years"; see "Is This Any Job for a Nice Jewish Boy?" 23). Diana Arbin Ben-Merre, in her article "Murdering Traditional Assumptions: The Jewish-American Mystery" in *The Detective in American Fiction, Film, and Television*, cites Lesley Egan's Jesse Falkenstein and Richard and Frances Lockridge's Nathan Shapiro as Rabbi Small's

contemporaries (57–58), but, as she observes in a footnote, Egan and the Lockridges use Jewishness simply to characterize their detectives' concern with justice and morality (66). Much as I argue of Alvan Judah, Ben-Merre asserts that these detectives say more about the image of the Jew in American literature (Ben-Merre cites John Updike's Bech). Although they are the protagonists of their mysteries and not merely local color, they are not contenders for the title of first affirming or acculturated American Jewish detective.

43. For an in-depth discussion of both formulas see Cawelti, *Adventure, Mystery, and Romance*, 80–105 and 139–161. See also Heta Pyrhönen, *Mayhem and Murder*, 21–22.

1. TALMUDIC SISSY OR JEWISH DUPIN?

1. On the "tough" Jew, see Paul Breines, *Tough Jews*. Breines's quick definition of tough Jews is "Jews who fight, who are violent in the public political sphere" (ix). In contrast to the stereotype of gentle or "weak" Jews (which Breines connects to images of Holocaust victims), images of tough Jews in popular fiction reflect a newfound Jewish nationalism engendered by Israel's military victory in the 1967 Six Day War: "What occurred in the Middle East in early June 1967 transformed the way American Jews thought not only about Israel but about the Holocaust, politics, their parents, grandparents, children, Jews, non-Jews, and, not least, themselves and their bodies" (58). On the "weak" Jew in popular culture see Maurice Berger, *Too Jewish?* 97–107. For a discussion of the "feminization of Jewish men" see Naomi Seidman, *Judaism since Gender*, 40–48.
2. Daniel Itzkovitz, *Jews and Other Differences*, 193. Itzkovitz explains his appropriation of the term: "Eve Kosofsky Sedgwick's useful differentiation between homophobia and anti-Semitism notwithstanding, and without claiming any absolute similarity in these two oppressions, there are many ways, as this article has attempted, in part, to show, that American anxieties concerning the secrecy of the homosexual closet have been mapped onto popular perceptions of American Jews. In marking only the clear separation (between 'Jewish' secrecy and 'distinctive gay' secrecy), Sedgwick's analysis examines neither the popularly constructed contents of the Jew's closet nor the reactive relation these cultural fantasies have on the construction of actual and queer identities" (193).
3. Ibid.
4. I cite these two literary works to telegraph how Itzkovitz's work leavens my own thinking about American Jews and American literature. My scholarly concerns in general, and in this study in particular, are not the same as Itzkovitz's and Boyarin's, but rather congruent with them. I borrow from and build on their insights about the social construction of sex/gender identities, aware that I am open to the charge of hijacking queer theory for my own ends, and aware of the controversial nature of Boyarin's project. Matti Bunzl, in "Jews, Queers, and Other Symptoms," has pointed out that Boyarin's linking of Jewish "self-feminization" first to Roman masculinity and then to European romantic masculinity is "a great analytic leap" (328), and I know that I am extending that leap even farther by applying Boyarin's queer theorizing to an American Jewish context and literary production. I believe, however, that Boyarin's and Itzkovitz's work provide particularly appropriate and useful tools for understanding the performance of American Jewish masculinity within a non-Jewish, heterosexist political state, and especially within the gendered tropes, topoi, and narratives of detective fiction.
5. See Priestman, *Detective Fiction and Scandal*, 5–6, and Thompson, *Fiction, Crime, and Empire*, 43–45.
6. I do not mean to underestimate Kemelman's Jewish background. Kemelman's grandparents were Orthodox, and, though his parents were not religiously observant, they were concerned to give him a Jewish education. His father, Isaac Kemelman, a diamond merchant, sent him to a number of afternoon Hebrew schools. In an interview a few months before his death in 1996, Kemelman recalled that he first began studying Talmud in an evening class at the age of eleven or twelve, and that the class was in Yiddish: "I became fascinated. We sat around this long oval table. We would read a passage and talk about it in Yiddish and argue about it, toss it back and forth. We might spend two or three days discussing a single item. My father was very pleased." Irene Sege, *Boston Globe*, 21 May 1996. For general biographical information on Kemelman, see Sheldon Hershinow, *Dictionary of Literary Biography* 28, 127–133.
7. Kemelman, *Common Sense in Education*, 20.
8. Ibid, 7.

9. For a discussion of the challenges and struggles of Jewish academics during the early twentieth century to be accepted in Ivy league literature departments (Columbia University, in particular), see Suzanne Klingenstein, *Jews in the American Academy, 1900–1940*, 83–198. Klingenstein claims that the 1939 appointments of Lionel Trilling and Harry Levin at, respectively, Columbia and Harvard, "are generally taken to be the first appointment of Jews to tenure-track positions in American English departments" (98). But Jonathan Freedman argues in *The Temple of Culture* that universities in the Midwest tenured Jews "much earlier.... The University of Michigan English Department was chaired by a Jew in the early thirties; Ruth Wallerstein was teaching at Wisconsin later in that decade" (176).
10. Jonathan Webber, "Modern Jewish Identities: The Ethnographic Complexities," 255. Embourgeoisement is itself one aspect of modernization.
11. S. T. Meravi, *Jerusalem Post*, 17 March 1989.
12. Sege, *Boston Globe*, 21 May 1996. The story of the origins of *Friday* is told by Kemelman in his introduction to Hershinow's *The Nine Mile Walk*; by Hershinow in the *Dictionary of Literary Biography* 28; by Hershinow and King in "Judaism for the Millions"; by Janet Rudolph in her unpublished dissertation, "The Kemelman Capers: A Religio-Cultural Study of Harry Kemelman's Detective Fiction"; and by numerous newspaper, magazine, and journal articles.
13. Louis Harap, *In the Mainstream*, 21–51.
14. What we might think of as Jewish bildungsromans about success are also evident in pre–World War II American Jewish literature. Writers such as Abraham Cahan, Mary Antin, Ludwig Lewisohn, Anzia Yezierska, Israel Jacob Schwartz, Muriel Rukeyser, and Daniel Fuchs also wrote about the vagaries of "making it" as a middle-class or wealthy American, a point that Margaret J. King and Sheldon J. Hershinow make in their essay, "Judaism for the Millions: Harry Kemelman's 'Rabbi Books,'" and which Hershinow repeats in the revised version of that essay in the *Dictionary of Literary Biography* 28. See also Harap's discussion of the second generation's acculturation, in *In the Mainstream*, 1–19, 25.
15. Cited in Chametzky, Felstiner, Flanzbaum, and Hellerstein, eds., *Jewish American Literature: A Norton Anthology*, 581.
16. Philip Roth, *Goodbye, Columbus*, xiv. The contradictory yearnings Roth mentions exemplify the kind of creatively fruitful dynamic that Stephen J. Whitfield explores in *American Space, Jewish Time*. Whitfield argues that, when Jewish writers, artists and musicians made their way at midcentury into the "democratic marketplace," the popular culture of American arts and letters, they drew upon their awareness of Jewish and gentile high culture and created "something different, something fresh and vibrant and compelling" (45). Whitfield sees such straddling—of high and popular culture as well as the tensions articulated by Roth—as a distinctively American Jewish expression of cultural assimilation. American Jewish expression "constitutes an effort to bridge the chasm between the fashionable and the transcendent, the ephemeral and the exalted. It is a hybrid, composed both of some high cultural memories and pretensions and of the commercial necessities and ambitions of popular culture" (45). Thus, the publication date and setting of Kemelman's first Rabbi Small mystery help to place the genesis of his series at a moment when American Jewish expression was reaching one of its high water marks, a moment when American Jewish writers yoked Jewish memory to American popular culture in surprising and fruitful ways.
17. In other words, there were, in the literary scene, still writers who could imaginatively recall a lived Judaism, the Jewish life of Eastern Europe or of the immigrant ghettos, or, as in the case of Rukeyser, the legacy of the German Jewish Reform movement in America (reflected in her memory of the classical Reform temple of her childhood, which emphasized social justice and the Judeo-Christian "tradition" of the Bible). Such vivid memories enabled these writers to explore, analyze, and criticize Americanness, or to abjure Jewish identity, but not necessarily to abjure the middle-class life that most Jews and Americans aspired to. Just entering the literary scene, however, were a younger generation of American Jewish writers to whom the suburbs were a much more vivid and fresh experience. The contradictions of middle-class life backlit in the suburbs by a highly developed consumer economy provided new and provocative material for a new and provocative literature.
18. Deborah Dash Moore, *The American Jewish Experience*, 314.
19. Arnold Band, *Jewish Identity in America*, 224.
20. See Steven J. Zipperstein, *Imagining Russian Jewry*, 37–39. Irving Howe, in *Celebrations and Attacks*, reflects on this moment of transition, though without naming a specific date and in the context of describing an end rather than a beginning; he describes a process of loss, "the

break-up of Jewish community and the crumbling of Jewish identity" (19), accounting for what he perceived as the exhaustion of American Jewish fiction and the sense of displacement among American Jewish fiction writers. Only American Jewish poets were exempt from this fate—because, according to Howe, they were free to mythologize Jewishness, to renew and reinvent it, in ways unavailable to fiction writers weaned on Russian realism. David Roskies, in *The Jewish Search for a Useable Past*, argues that the loss of memory is in fact the precondition for its renewal. Roskies specifically points out Kemelman's detective story as an example of how the loss of the Yiddish literary image of the rabbi enabled an author's American Jewish reinvention of the rabbi (88).

21. Zachary Klein, *No Saving Grace*, 17.
22. See, for example, Ida Cohen Selavan, *The (Pittsburgh) Jewish Chronicle*, 28 May 1965 (I will return to this review later in the chapter); Allen J. Hubin, *The New York Times Book Review*, 2 March 1969; William David Spencer, *Mysterium and Mystery*, 35; John Boland, *Books and Bookmen*, September 1972; Daisy Maryles, "Harry Kemelman: Creator of the World's Best Known Rabbi"; Hershinow and King, "Judaism for the Millions," 90–91; Ruth Wisse, "Reading about Jews", 47 ("Kemelman's failings are merely artistic"); and Ben-Merre, *The Detective in American Fiction, Film, and Television*, 66.
23. The phrase is from Naomi Sokoloff, "Sleuths and Sages: Detective Fiction by American Jewish Women," 37.
24. Boyarin, *Unheroic Conduct*, 2.
25. Ibid., 78.
26. Ibid., 45–48.
27. Kenneth Barker, "One Day the Rabbi Speculated," 428. See also Spencer, *Mysterium and Mystery*, and Hershinow and King, "Judaism for the Millions."
28. Wisse, "Reading Jews," 47. On redirection, effeminacy, and the "feminine" see Boyarin, *Unheroic Conduct*, 96–98.
29. C. August Dupin seeks to know and control his world. Hence, for both Priestman and Thompson, Poe's detective, and the classical detective formula, are best understood in light of Foucault's analysis of the "disciplinary society." Rather than punish the body, as in pre-industrial France, the newly industrialized modern society Foucault theorizes extends the technologies of observation and control into schools, factories, the military, and prisons in order to discipline the modern "soul" by snaring it (a political construct) in a web of post-Enlightenment knowledge and power relations (Foucault, *Discipline and Punish*, 102–103, 130–131, and 227–228). Foucault argues that we police ourselves—we collaborate with the prevailing definition of what is normal—when we voluntarily see, and agree to be seen, through the interpretive methods and technologies that mediate and organize our understanding of modern society. According to Thompson, the classical detective formula, which emerges at the same time as the disciplinary society, articulates that society's desire for a complete form of knowledge, for a totalizing interpretation of the world that can survey and control a confusing and forbidding modernity (Thompson, *Fiction, Crime, and Empire*, 44). Priestman, on the other hand, reads the disciplinary society's desire for order and control as evidence of the nineteenth-century embourgeoisement of political life, in which crime and punishment, detection and guilt, are no longer public spectacles but rather private dramas (Priestman, 2–5). The detective in the classical detective formula is a means to survey and control the private scandals of the lower and upper classes that threaten the social order, and detective fiction itself surveys and controls the scandalous introduction of public crime reportage into the privacy of literature, inviting "real, or realistically squalid, crime into the house of fiction in a schizophrenic formula which then comes to constitute a new kind of scandal within the walls of literature itself: the scandal of indifference" (6). The classical detective formula, in which patterns are tightly controlled and controlling, provides a medium through which the emerging ambivalence about the social meaning of real crime (covered by literary meaning and uses) can be resolved, and in which the ambiguities of the modern social order, and what Thompson calls the "maelstrom of modernity" (8), can be stabilized. The classical detective formula makes fictional boundaries that discipline society, that survey/surveill(er) the line between the normal and the deviant. (I review this line of criticism about the classical detective formula only to underscore how closely related that formula is to the needs and pressures of transition periods both great and small.)
30. Thompson, *Fiction, Crime, and Empire*, 49.
31. Ibid., 56–57.

32. Ibid., 51.
33. Andrew Furman, *Israel through the Jewish American Imagination*, 11.
34. Ibid., 49.
35. Joseph Riddel, *Purloined Letters*, 144.
36. My wording is borrowed from Ann Pellegrini, *Judaism Since Gender*, 51. I have kept her essay in mind as I write this chapter, a caution light for my thinking about Rabbi Small and the Talmudic sissy: "If all Jews are womanly, are any women also Jews? The collapse of Jewish masculinity into an abject femininity appears to 'disappear' Jewish women. . . . The displacement of Jewish women from the scene of Jewishness seems to me an unfortunate and frequent side-effect of some pathbreaking studies of race, gender, and Jewishness."
37. Ida Cohen Selavan, "Friday the Rebbetzin . . . A Feminist Look at the Rabbi Small Series," 39.
38. Ibid.
39. Ibid., 40.
40. Ibid., 41.
41. Boyarin, *Unheroic Conduct*, 98.
42. Thompson, *Fiction, Crime, and Empire*, 45.
43. Riddel, *Purloined Letters*, 146.

2. UNRAVELING "INTERMARRIAGE"

1. Rabbi Yitzchak Etshalom, *Rambam's Hilkhot T'fillah*, http//www.torah.org, March 1996. In his online commentary on Maimonides' "Laws of Prayer," Rabbi Etshalom explains: "The Torah commands a general Mitzvah without defining those actions which we must do to fulfill it. The Rabbis create a structure through which we can fulfill this command of the Torah. By mandating that we visit the sick, for example, the Rabbis have given us a vehicle for fulfilling the Torah's command of 'Love your fellow as yourself'" (Part II). Similarly, by mandating marriage the rabbis have given Jews a vehicle for fulfilling the command "be fruitful and multiply."
2. Consider the character of Reb Sender in Cahan's novel, or even the way passivity is made a female trait, as in the Russian Jewish immigrant's lecture to Levinsky. Another way to understand the contrast that Cahan imagines, for example, is illustrated by S. Anski's roughly contemporaneous play *The Dybbuk*, which features a type of Jewish male derived from East European Jewish folklore. Khonnon, a poverty-stricken Kabbalist and disappointed bridegroom, "wins" his bride by dying at the end of the first act after fate has seemingly stolen his intended from him (38). In the second act, he responds to his circumstances by transforming himself into a dybbuk, a ghost, as if to suggest that the only "action" available to a Jewish male is in the spiritual and not the material realm (39–68).
3. Band, *Jewish Identity in America*, 217.
4. On "kitchen Judaism," see Jenna Weissman Joselit, *The Wonders of America*, 171–218. Joselit notes that in American Jewish recipes "what counted was not the authenticity of the recipe but its symbolic power and presentational value as a touchstone of authentic Jewish culture" (217).
5. Woody Haute, *Pulp Culture*, 9.
6. Ibid. and 72–73.
7. Ibid., 10.
8. See, for example, Sander Gilman, *The Jew's Body*, 65.
9. See Rabbi Shaya Karlinsky, *Maharal Derech Chaim*, http//www.torah.org, 1996. Rabbi Karlinsky, in his online translation of and commentary on Rabbi Judah Loew's sixteenth-century exegesis of the *Sayings of the Fathers*, words the Maharal's discussion of *sechel* thus: "A human being who lacks Torah has two characteristics. First, he is empty and void of wisdom. He lacks the element of 'sechel' (the intellectual/spiritual component) that should be found in the human being. Secondly, his human physicality is less perfect due to this lack of wisdom. (While he could have a more purely physical strength, which would appear to indicate a superior physical dimension, this aspect of his physicality is really animal physicality, since it [is] built purely on physical strength. If we focus on what is unique in the human being, even his material dimension is more perfect when it is imbued with 'sechel.'). . . . When man's physical dimension is connected to the 'sechel' (imbuing the material human being with a spiritual/intellectual reality), then that physical body is refined and purified. It is clear that the body of an animal is of a more material nature than the body of a human being, for the

animal has no 'sechel' (spiritual/intellectual dimension). The more connected man's body becomes with this 'sechel,' the more refined that physicality becomes. And the more refined and elevated the physicality becomes, the more piety it will manifest, with this person doing acts of kindness to all" (chapter 2, Mishna 6, part 1).

10. Gilman, *The Jew's Body,* 194–209.
11. Adrienne Rich, *Your Native Land, Your Life,* 27. A "womanly series of choices" refers, in part, to choices that reflect feminist revisions of patriarchal traditions.
12. Breines, *Tough Jews,* 58.
13. Ibid., 176.
14. Quoted in Terrence DePres, *Praises and Dispraises,* 205.
15. Paula Hyman, *Gender and Assimilation in Modern Jewish History,* 36. In chapter 1, "Paradoxes of Assimilation," Hyman explains how the project of assimilation helped shift responsibility for educating Jewish children from fathers to mothers, and notes that the outcome "permitted Jewish men to pursue success in the worlds of commerce and civic affairs and to assume leadership positions within the Jewish community while relegating the transmission of Jewish knowledge and identity to the domestic sphere and to women, who, incidentally, had fewer educational and material resources to accomplish the task" (48).
16. Miriyam Glazer, *People of the Book,* 439. "Spiritual romanticism" is her term for Jewish women's imaginative spiritual exploration and re-vision of a rationalist, egalitarian American Judaism. The writers Glazer refer to—Anne Roiphe, Nessa Rapoport, Tova Reich, and Rhoda Lerman—write narratives that "are evolving a new spiritual romanticism, rooted at once in the experience of Jewish womanhood and in a mystically imaginative Judaism" (443). Glazer's essay is useful in suggesting what Kellerman might have done with the character of Rina, not in identifying Rina's putative feminism.
17. Margo Kaufman, *Los Angeles Times,* 22 September 1996: Book Review, 8.
18. Julius Lester, *Commentary* 102, 2, August 1996, 64.

3. THE JEWISH WOMAN AS AMATEUR

1. There are also a number of ways to close-read and theorize these diverse writers. After all, discussions and criticism about women, feminism, and detective fiction have ranged over a variety of issues germane to American Jewish detective stories. Much of the early critical material in the late seventies and early eighties focused on recovering the history of women detectives in detective fiction, reflecting the general trend among academic feminists of recovering and recuperating women's writing and history. In the late eighties and the early nineties, following the appearance of mysteries by writers such as Valerie Miner, Carolyn Heilbrun (writing as Amanda Cross), Sara Paretsky, and Sue Grafton, there was a great deal of debate over the feminization of the classical detective formula, and whether the hard-boiled detective formula was ineluctably "male" or open to regendering and revision, debates that mirrored wider concerns about androcentricity, the female reader, and the literary canon. These debates gave rise in the late nineties to further investigations into the roles of irony, parody, politics, drag and gender play, the male and/or female gaze, feminine subjectivity, and the social generation of meaning in detective fiction by and for women. I review this history to situate my own reading of the Jewish woman as amateur within a clear line of feminist and cultural studies explorations of gender and genre performance. See Kathleen G. Klein, *The Woman Detective,* and Kathleen G. Klein, ed., *Diversity and Detective Fiction;* Sally Munt, *Murder by the Book?;* Glenwood Irons, ed., *Feminism in Women's Detective Fiction;* and Priscilla L. Walton and Manina Jones, *Detective Agency.*
2. The number of writers surveyed (41) and their division into professionals (18) and amateurs (24) is based on the 5 June 2000 version of Raphael's bibliography, "Jews and Jewish Identity in American Mystery Fiction: A Selected Bibliography," then at http://www.jewishwhodunit.com. The current internet address of the bibliography is http://www.jewishmystery.com/bibliography.html
3. Since Krich's most well-known detective, Jessica Drake, is primarily concerned with women's issues as they relate to memory and crimes of the Holocaust, I believe it makes more sense to triangulate Krich's use of gender, the Holocaust, and the hard-boiled formula in my later section, "Cases of Memory," where I will focus on the gendered reinvention of Jewish memory in American Jewish detective stories.

4. See John Cawelti, *Adventure, Mystery, and Romance,* 41–42; Jean Radford, *The Progress of Romance,* 11; and Janice Radway, *Reading the Romance,* 64–85. Radway makes it a point to let the Smithton women whom she studied define the genre. All her respondents "admitted that they want to identify with the heroine as she attempts to comprehend, anticipate, and deal with the ambiguous attentions of a man who inevitably cannot understand her feelings at all" (64).
5. Roland Barthes, *A Lover's Discourse,* 1–9.
6. See Andreas Huyssen, *Studies in Entertainment,* 193–194, where Huyssen relates that attitude to a modernist perception of mass culture as "feminine."
7. Sylvia Barack Fishman, *Talking Back,* 157.
8. Joyce Antler, *Talking Back,* 2. See also Riv-Ellen Prell's outstanding study of Jewish gender stereotypes and cultural anxiety, *Fighting to Become Americans.*
9. Ibid, 7.
10. Naomi Sokoloff, "Sleuths and Sages," 39. Sokoloff amply demonstrates in her essay that "a new tradition in Jewish imaginative literature" (36) has come into view, although the number (a half dozen or so) of writers she covers seem to contradict her assertion that the tradition "exists in abundance" (36).
11. Joyce Antler, in "From Molly Goldberg to Sophie Portnoy," a paper presented at the Association for Jewish Studies Conference on 18 December 2000, historicized and theorized a scale of difference between the progressive and benevolent radio and television character and Philip Roth's malevolent literary creation. Molly Goldberg is a version of the *Yidishe mama,* an early twentieth-century stock character who exemplifies strength, nurturance, loyalty, and a desire for success. Sophie Portnoy reflects Roth's parodic and misogynistic improvisation on that character as well as Alex Portnoy's anxieties about midcentury acculturation. Both images, once entering circulation in American popular culture, reveal how artists wield power over their creations and hence over gender representation, illustrating that literary power is also cultural power. I believe that Mom is closer to Molly Goldberg than to Sophie Portnoy, in both time and temperament, although she is by no means a duplicate of Goldberg or a *Yidishe mama.* As I show, Mom is a competent, independent, and single Jewish woman whose observations sometimes undermine or question stereotypes of Jewish women.
12. As quoted in Walton and Jones, *Detective Agency,* 39.
13. Prell, *Fighting to Become Americans,* 142–176.
14. Ibid.; quotations cited are from, respectively, 151, 150, 163.
15. Reviews of the collected "Mom" short stories were quick to note the comparison. See the reviews collected on the publisher's web site, http://www.crippenlandru.com/reviews/momrev.html.
16. See Prell, *Talking Back,* 125–127 and *Fighting to Become Americans,* 222–227.
17. In this respect, Mom does resemble Miss Marple, who at times seems nearly subversive and at others seems a guardian of the social and cultural status quo. For a discussion of Miss Marple's contradictions, see Marion Shaw and Sabine Vanacker, *Reflecting on Miss Marple.*
18. JoAnn Pavletich, "Anzia Yezierska, Immigrant Authority, and the Uses of Affect," 81. According to Pavletich, "as state and corporate powers moved toward containment and regulation, so too did the country's dominant emotion culture move from expressive toward contained" (83), a move that marginalized emotionally expressive Americans such as women, Jews, and immigrants.
19. Ibid., 94.
20. Ibid., 98.
21. See the *New York Times,* 13 January 1993; *Cosmopolitan,* November 1993; *New York Law Journal,* 15 August 1995; *New York Times,* 11 July 1999.
22. Murray Baumgarten, *City Scriptures,* 125.
23. Ibid., 12.
24. Ibid., 2.
25. Sally Munt sees parody as the woman writer's strategy for transforming the detective genre from the inside. Munt is arguing against Kathleen Gregory Klein, who claims in *The Woman Detective* that parody simply reflects masculinist norms and values in detective fiction, and who advocates opposing those norms and values through a far more disruptive revisioning of the genre (191). Munt feels that detective fiction is not so easily divided into subversive/nonsubversive texts or masculine/feminine texts, and that the parodic mode has a long history in the work of women writers working in the genre (26–27).

26. See Elaine Showalter, "Rethinking the Seventies," 157–159, and Riv-Ellen Prell, *Talking Back,* 134–135, and *Fighting to Become Americans,* 212.
27. Showalter argues that Rossner's novel reflects a concern not only with the social reality of rape during this decade, but also with the psychological interplay between "feminist fantasies of the liberated will" and male violence (170). Novels such as Rossner's, and others by Muriel Spark, Gail Godwin, Diane Johnson, and Marilyn French implicitly ask these questions: "What are the irrational forces of evil and violence that collide with control of one's life? Are they outside the self, in male society? Or are they also within the self, in fantasy, guilt, and hate?" (159).
28. Ibid., 170.
29. On the JAP stereotype, see Prell, *Fighting to Become Americans,* 180–185.
30. Interview with Thomas Clavin, *New York Times,* 6 June 1993, Sunday, Late Edition, Section 13LI, 17. Earlier that year, Michele Ross, in the *Atlanta Journal and Constitution,* wrote, "A hint for author Marissa Piesman: Forget the novel. Write a column instead" (14 March 1993, Arts, Section N, 11), and the 1 June 1994 *Kirkus Reviews* critique of *Close Quarters* suggests that Piesman "ought to forget the mystery angle and just use her ironic gifts to go to town à la Nora Ephron." Considering that Nina ends up as a research assistant for a famous New York columnist much like Nora Ephron, and that Piesman did write a number of columns after the demise of her series, it seems the author took the reviews to heart.
31. Piesman's series thus seemingly lends credence to Kathleen Klein's argument about the inadequacy of parody as a subversive strategy in detective fiction by women writers. Still, I see the main difficulty that Piesman faced as an aspect of talking back, a point I make in the next two paragraphs.
32. Prell, *Talking Back,* 138.
33. Prell, *Fighting to Become Americans,* 211.

4. TWICE-TOLD TALES OF ASHKENAZ AND SEPHARAD

1. For recent discussions of the scholarship and theorization of Jewish memory, see Oren Baruch Stier, "Memory Matters"; Steven J. Zipperstein, *Imagining Russian Jewry,* 3–14; David Roskies, *The Jewish Search for a Usable Past,* 1–16; and Jonathan Webber, *Modern Jewish Mythologies,* 108–113. For discussions of gender and Jewish memory, see Gil Anidjar, *Jews and Other Differences,* 360–396; Sarah Silberstein Swartz and Margie Wolfe, eds., *From Memory to Transformation;* and Sara R. Horowitz, "Gender, Genocide, and Jewish Memory." For a discussion of the globalization of memory, see Andreas Huyssen, "Present Pasts: Media, Politics, Amnesia."
2. Webber, *Modern Jewish Mythologies,* 108.
3. Ibid., 128.
4. Ibid., 122.
5. Marianne Hirsch, *Family Frames,* 22.
6. *Culture Currents,* http://www.jewishculture.org/publications_cult_curr_9810.html.
7. Ibid.
8. Ibid.
9. *Jewish Gothic* (index page), http://www.jewishgothic.com/index.html.
10. "A Gothic Manifesto," http://www.jewishgothic.com/manifesto.html
11. Ibid.
12. Ibid.
13. Ibid.
14. David Punter, *A Companion to the Gothic,* x.
15. Punter, *The Literature of Terror,* vol. 2, 179.
16. This is the gist of both chapter 7 and chapter 8 of *The Literature of Terror,* vol. 2. Thus in chapter 7, Punter tracks that awareness in works as different as Salman Rushdie's *Shame,* Thomas Harris's *Red Dragon,* and Brett Easton Ellis's *American Psycho* (just a few of the novels he cites). Although it may seem from these examples that Punter, like the *Culture Currents* article, overapplies the term "Gothic," he takes aim at the Gothic through a far cleaner siteline (psychoanalysis from Freud to Slavoj Zizek) than does the article.
17. Terry Castle, *The Female Thermometer,* 8.
18. Ibid., 15.
19. Ibid., 19.
20. Ibid.

21. Andrew Furman, "The Secret Jews of Sixteenth Century Lisbon," 40.
22. S.v. "genizah," *Encyclopedia Judaica,* 1971 ed.
23. Andreas Huyssen, "Present Pasts: Media, Politics, Amnesia," 36. Huyssen argues that the Jewish obsession with the past, particularly as refracted through the Holocaust, is only one part of a much larger phenomenon, "a fundamental crisis" in the human perception of time, space, and identity, a perception formulated by "the age of high modernity—with its trust in progress and development, its celebration of the new as utopian (as radically and irreducibly other), and its unshaken belief in some telos of history" (36).

5. HARD-BOILED HOLOCAUST

1. Efraim Sicher, "The Future of the Past," 70.
2. Sidra DeKoven Ezrahi, *By Words Alone,* 24 and 25.
3. Ibid., 30.
4. Ibid.
5. Ibid., 35.
6. Ibid., 36.
7. Lawrence Langer, *Admitting the Holocaust,* 176.
8. Quotation cited is from *The New Yorker,* 1 May 1976, 130. See also book reviews by Gene Lyons, *New York Times Book Review,* 14 March 1976; Valentine Cunningham, *New Statesman,* 16 April 1976; and T. J. Binyon, *Times Literary Supplement,* 11 June 1976.
9. First quotation cited is from Peter S. Prescott, *Newsweek,* 23 February 1976, 83. See also book reviews by Gerard C. Reedy, *America,* 1 May 1976, and R. Z. Sheppard, *Time,* 23 February 1976. The second quotation is from Richard Schickel, *Time,* 9 October 1978, 100. The film received generally good reviews, not for its screenplay or direction but for the acting of Laurence Olivier, Gregory Peck, and James Mason. See Jack Kroll, *Newsweek,* 9 October 1978; Harold C. Schonberg, *New York Times,* 6 November 1978; and Vincent Canby, *New York Times,* 3 December 1978.
10. Jeffrey Shandler, "Schindler's Discourse," 153.
11. Ezrahi, *By Words Alone,* 205.
12. Shandler, *While America Watches,* 128–129.
13. Ibid., 122, 127. Shandler cites Michel Foucault's argument in "About the Concept of the Dangerous Individual in Nineteenth Century Legal Psychiatry"—the argument that industrial society's interest in the "psychiatric" bases of crime led to the investigation of "motive" in modern crime and to the expectation of a confession by the criminal—as explanation for the success of television dramas about the Eichmann trial (121–122). The popular dramas about Eichmann or an Eichmann-like character, according to Shandler, satisfied viewers' desire "for psychological insight into his crimes" (122). But the nature of popular cultural "insights" about the motives of Nazis and Nazi hunters changed over time, as I show.
14. The first quotation cited is from Sheppard, *Time,* 64; the next two are from Prescott, *Newsweek,* 86.
15. Schickel, *Time,* 101.
16. Alan Mintz, *Popular Culture and the Shaping of Holocaust Memory in America,* 25.
17. Lyons, *New York Times Book Review,* 4.
18. Robert F. Willson, Jr., "From Novel to Film: De-Sinistering *The Boys from Brazil,*" 322–324.
19. Schickel, *Time,* 101.
20. Pauline Kael, *The New Yorker,* 9 October 1978. The Yakov Liebermann character was renamed Ezra Lieberman in the film.
21. Shandler, "Schindler's Discourse," 155.
22. Ibid. For example, consider the difference, within Holocaust scholarship, between the sources and conclusions of Terrence Des Pres's *The Survivor* and Lawrence Langer's *Holocaust Testimonies.*
23. This definition of the hard-boiled detective is from Philip Durham, *Down These Mean Streets a Man Must Go,* 79–98, and George Grella, *Detective Fiction,* 113–116. Both focus on Raymond Chandler's Philip Marlowe as the example of the relation between the hard-boiled detective and the European romance tradition.
24. Grella, *Detective Fiction,* 114.
25. Ibid., 107.
26. Ibid., 109–110.
27. Jerry Speir, *Raymond Chandler,* 105–116.

28. Charles J. Rzepka, "'I'm In the Business Too'" 698.
29. Norman G. Finkelstein, *The Holocaust Industry*, 11–38. Henry Feingold, in a 1999 *Congress Monthly* review of Peter Novick's *The Holocaust in American Life*, suggests that this suspicious view of how Jewish leaders manage Holocaust memory, echoes, and may be related to, Hannah Arendt's negative judgments in *Eichmann in Jerusalem* on the perceived vacillation of Jewish leadership during the Holocaust.
30. Toni Morrison, *Playing in the Dark*, 6–7. Morrison defines "Africanism" as "a term for the denotative and connotative blackness that African peoples have come to signify, as well as the entire range of views, assumptions, readings, and misreadings that accompany Eurocentric learning about these people. . . . American Africanism makes it possible to say and not to say, to inscribe and erase, to escape and engage, to act out and act on, to historicize and render timeless" (7).
31. *Blood Money* page, http://www.amazon.com, 8 March 2000.
32. Rochelle Krich, "The Holocaust in Her Soul, Romantic Comedy in Her Heart," interview with Reed Andrus, http://www.rochellekrich.com/Rochelle%27sBio.htm.
33. Irena Klepfisz, *Dreams of an Insomniac*, 145.
34. Lori Hope Lefkowitz, *Shaping Losses*, 226.
35. Krich, "The Holocaust in Her Soul, Romantic Comedy in Her Heart."
36. Priscilla L. Walton, *Diversity and Detective Fiction*, 132.
37. Janice Radway, *Reading the Romance*, 212.
38. Walton, *Diversity and Detective Fiction*, 143.
39. Ezrahi, *By Words Alone*, 216.
40. See Krich's introduction to *Blood Money*, where she recounts her discovery of her father's pre-Holocaust life and family, and her interview, "The Holocaust in Her Soul, Romantic Comedy in Her Heart," where she relates how personal *Blood Money* was for her: "Writing about my father's experiences was difficult, because they were real, and because I had to try to obtain a certain objective narrative voice. But I felt honored to have been able to write about his experiences (a small part of them), and especially gratified that readers and reviewers love the Nathan Pomerantz character who is based on him."
41. Geoffrey Hartman claims in *Visual Culture and the Holocaust* that the "unsophisticated" techniques of the Fortunoff Archive videographers—employing a sparsely furnished and simply lit set, filming only the witness and not the interviewer, and using only a medium shot—undercut the televisualness of the testimonies. "In short, our technique, or lack of it, was homeopathic: it used television to cure television, to turn the medium against itself, limiting even while exploiting its visual power" (117). I am not certain that the "talking head" format is as subversive of spectator positioning as Hartman assumes it is. Video testimony is only now resolving into a recognizable and "readable" genre, and at present there exist no reception surveys of its viewers, whoever they may be. As Alan Mintz observes in *Popular Culture and the Shaping of Holocaust Memory in America*, there is a vast storehouse of video testimony, and not many scholars, much less ordinary, interested lay people, have seen most of it—or even know what questions to ask of it (182–183). Most of what the public has seen is in the form of documentary films that anthologize the interviews (183), a format that only complicates the issue of spectator positioning and audience reception. Lawrence Langer's analogy between viewers' position and that of a Jesuit priest who witnessed the deportation of his neighbors through a knothole in the fence around the train station is evocative of one kind of positioning currently being formulated: "The fence and the knothole blockade and invite us simultaneously, excluding us from terrain where we dare not venture and do not 'belong' while offering an apparently secure post of observation for our role as witness. But as 'what' we witness makes inroads on that fragile security, as 'distance' provides less and less defense, we are sucked through that knothole and forced to find our moral bearings shorn of prior visions of the noble human spirit under duress" (*Holocaust Testimonies*, 32).
42. Walton and Manina Jones, *Detective Agency*, 92–93.
43. The book is *Ner Ma'aravi* by B. Goldman and A. B. Biegel. Related in an e-mail post from Rochelle Krich, 21 January 2002.
44. Mintz, *Popular Culture and the Shaping of Holocaust Memory*, 184–185.

6. UNDERCOVER GENTILES AND UNDERCOVER JEWS

1. Alain Finkielkraut, *The Imaginary Jew*, 178.

2. Ibid., 15.
3. Ibid., 179.
4. Ibid., 173.
5. Ibid., 176.
6. Daniel Boyarin, *Unheroic Conduct*, 89–94; and Rabbi Israel V. Berman, *The Talmud: The Steinsaltz Edition*, 117–118.
7. Boyarin, *Unheroic Conduct*, 92.
8. Ibid.
9. Ibid., 91–92.
10. Ibid., 91.
11. Ibid., 93. Boyarin, in a note appended to the first sentence cited here, acknowledges a debt to Mary Douglas for his analogy of the individual body to the social body politic.
12. On point of view and spectatorship in film, see Nick Browne, *Narrative Apparatus, Ideology*, 102–119; Laura Mulvey, *Narrative Apparatus, Ideology*, 198–209; Kaja Silverman, *Narrative Apparatus, Ideology*, 219–235; Julia Kristeva, *Narrative Apparatus, Ideology*, 236–243; and Robert B. Ray, *A Certain Tendency of the Hollywood Cinema, 1930–1980*, 25–69.
13. The first quotation cited is from Roger Ebert, *Chicago Sun-Times*, 17 July 1992, and the second is from Elayne Rapping, *The Progressive*, October 1992. See also Edward Norden, *Commentary*, November 1992; Michael Sragow, *The New Yorker*, 27 July 1992; and Stanley Kauffmann, *The New Republic*, 17 August 1992.
14. David Desser and Lester D. Friedman, *American-Jewish Filmmakers*, 161.
15. Ibid., 168–169.
16. Ibid., 163.
17. Gavin Smith, *Film Comment*, September 1992, 52.
18. Ibid., 51.
19. Ibid.
20. As Jack Kugelmass has pointed out, photographs of Hasidic Jews now serve as icons of Jewish identity and authenticity, icons that have been made into a metaphor for Jewishness: "But if this iconization works as metaphor, the Hasid represents not one facet of the family of American Jewry but a differentness that for most of us has passed and is therefore no longer part of a lived reality." Jack Kugelmass, *Jews and Other Differences*, 50.
21. Norden, *Commentary*, 52.
22. Ibid. In the psychoanalytic model of subject formation current in film theory, this "desire" to remain in place can also be interpreted as the desire for unity and coherence symbolized by the pre-Oedipal relationship between child and mother. The body in a film becomes a "relay," as Linda Williams calls it, that routes spectators' desire "to figure a unity and coherence in [themselves] that has long since been lost in the spectator-subject's entrance into the symbolic of difference" (*Narrative, Apparatus, Ideology*, 508). From a feminist perspective on this model, Eden's containment follows the logic of "a discourse which circumscribes woman in the sexual, binds her (in) sexuality, makes her the absolute representation, the phallic scenario," according to Teresa de Lauretis, who concludes, "It is then the case that the ideological effects produced in and by those concepts, that discourse, perform, as dominant cinema does, a political function in the service of domination including, but not limited to, the sexual exploitation of women and the repression or containment of their sexuality" (*Narrative, Apparatus, Ideology*, 365). What Lumet's film ultimately exemplifies from that perspective is what Laura Mulvey calls the pleasure of male "scopophilia" (*Narrative, Apparatus, Ideology*, 200), looking at women as objects, which she describes as an act of power and narcissism.
23. Hayim Nahman Bialik, *Modern Hebrew Literature*, 134–135.
24. Ranen Omer, "The Metaphysics of Lost Jewish Identity in David Mamet's *Homicide*," 38.
25. Ibid., 39.
26. Ibid., 46.
27. Ibid., 48.
28. Ibid., 49–50.
29. Adam Zachary Newton, *Facing Black and Jew*, 143.
30. Ibid., 148.
31. Ibid., 147.
32. Ibid., 148.
33. Ibid., 10–11 and 146.
34. Ibid., 149.

35. Ibid., 150.
36. Ibid.
37. On the anti-detective story see Michael Holquist, *The Poetics of Murder*, 149–174, and Patricia Merivale and Susan Elizabeth Sweeney, eds., *Detecting Texts*.
38. Newton, *Facing Black and Jew*, 144.
39. Jorge Luis Borges, *Crime Classics*, 286.
40. Ibid.
41. Ibid., 295.
42. Leon Wieseltier, *The New Republic*, 24 April 1995.
43. Kaja Silverman, *Narrative Apparatus, Ideology*, 219–222.
44. Ibid., 227.
45. Stuart Hall, *Gender, Race, and Class in Media*, 20.

7. AM I MY BROTHER'S DETECTIVE?

1. W.E.B. Du Bois, *Three Negro Classics*, 215.
2. Quoted in *St. James Guide to Crime and Mystery Writers* and reproduced in *Biography Resource Center*, http://galenet.galegroup.com/servlet/BioRc.
3. Heta Pyrhönen, in *Mayhem and Murder,* argues that such a paradoxical link between the ideology of individualism and the choices that characters are forced to make between right and wrong social behavior is precisely how hard-boiled detective stories situate ethics (189–190). While her point is that, as a consequence, these stories fail to imagine anything other than individualism, there are, as shown in chapter 3, limits to how subversive the writers of mass-marketed detective stories can be, since the cost of radical subversiveness is a loss of readership so severe it undercuts the point of such ideological combativeness. Given the constraints of the genre, asking readers to question their relationship to "the Jewish position" rather than to take it for granted is perhaps as "subversive" as the inadvertent learning of mass-marketed American Jewish detective stories can be, and *Homicide,* as we saw, is a good example of the furthest limits of such subversiveness. Given, too, that the ideology of American individualism suffuses almost all the stories analyzed thus far, it is evident that what lends these Jewish detective stories an American imprimatur is precisely that the kind of hybrid identity that audiences (Jewish or non-Jewish) bring to or take from these stories, and especially the kind of kosher hybridity each American Jewish detective story fashions for itself, is always made to seem a matter of individual choice for audiences, detectives, and authors. My comments here indicate the submerged dialogue between this chapter's argument and Pyrhönen's argument in her chapter 5, "Putting Together an Ethical View of Life." I am indebted to her study for my understanding of the relation between the way readers process the narrative designs of detective texts and the social dimensions of hard-boiled detective stories (as my argument at the end of this chapter makes overt).
4. I use the term "libertarian" here, and in the rest of the chapter, in reference to this articulation of an absolute individual right to self-government. It is a version of a comment quoted in a story about Kaminsky in a libertarian electronic newsletter: "I believe that people should have the right to do as they wish as long as they do not violate the rights of others. Thus, I do not believe in the initiation of force, though I believe in strong response if one is attacked or a nation is attacked." James W. Harris, *The Liberator OnLine,* 21 August 1998.
5. David Biale, Michael Galchinsky, and Susannah Heschel, *Insider/Outsider*, 9.
6. A well-worn term, "multiculturalism" has been appropriated by tepid scholars and critics of American literature simply as an academic brand name for the study of African Americans, Hispanics, Native Americans, and Asian Americans, but not for American Jews. (For an extended critique of this trend, see Andrew Furman's *Contemporary Jewish American Writers and the Multicultural Dilemma.*) At worst, the word has become pejorative, employed to vilify a "politically correct" ideology of difference, an ideology often described as the Orwellian assertion that, although all cultures are different, some cultures are more different than others. At best, the word refers to the contemporary re(dis)covery of diversity within and among hybrid American identities, and, used in that sense, "multiculturalism" helps underscore the continuing effect of cultural assimilation on American Jewish literature and culture. For detailed analyses of the history, meaning, and implications of the term for American Jews and

American Jewish cultural studies, see Biale, Galchinsky, and Heschel, eds., *Insider/Outsider*, and Marla Brettschneider, ed., *The Narrow Bridge*.
7. Biale, Galchinsky, and Heschel, *Insider/Outsider*, 5.
8. In an online magazine interview, Kaminsky says that, in the Lieberman series, "I also wanted to bring my former boss and another mentor, Don Siegel, the film director (*Dirty Harry, Invasion of the Body Snatchers, The Shootist, Two Mules for Sister Sara, Coogan's Bluff, The Beguiled*, etc.), to life as a character. Lieberman is Don. He looks like Don, talks like Don, thinks like Don." Donna Andrews, *Crescent Blues E'Magazine*, February 1999.
9. "Shavot" appears a number of times in the series as a corruption of *Shabbat*, the Sabbath, while "Mir" remains a mystery to me. It's unlikely that it refers to the town in present-day Belarus that was the prewar home of the famous Mir Yeshiva, though it could be a corruption of "ner," candle or light. Temple "Sabbath Light" seems a euphonious and reasonable name that would underscore the temple as a domestic space and ethical illuminator. As sheer fancy, however, I also offer the Yiddish/Hebrew possibility of Temple Mir Shabbat, Temple "My Sabbath," which would underscore the paradox of a Jewish communal identity as the product of individual choice.
10. On consent relations and ethnic identity, see Werner Sollors, *Beyond Ethnicity*. For an overview of the delicatessen as an ethnic Jewish space, and in relation to food and Jewish identity, see Jenna Weisman Joselit, *The Wonders of America*, 171–218. On the delicatessen as a memory site, see Eve Jochnowitz, *Remembering the Lower East Side*, 212–225; on the delicatessen as "a metonym for the American Jewish diaspora," see Michael Galchinsky, *Insiders/Outsiders*, 205–207.
11. I am taking liberties here with Stanley Fish's term "interpretive communities"—groups of readers who share similar strategies for assigning meaning to a text—by suggesting that the Lieberman mysteries invite us to consider whether one "reads" a society or a culture in the same way that one does a text. The meaning of life and of stories inhere in a reader's interpretive act, not in the text itself (see Fish, "Interpreting the *Variorum*"). In this regard, the Lieberman mysteries open up the vexed social dimensions of reader-response criticism. For a discussion of narrative, reader-response, and detective texts in light of contemporary literary theory, see Pyrhönen, *Mayhem and Murder*, 3–28.
12. Rabbi Irving Greenberg, *One Nation under God*, 41.
13. Ibid., 56.
14. Quotations cited are from Pyrhönen, *Mayhem and Murder*, 163; see also Pyrhönen, 20.

8. THE FAITHFUL DEFENDED

1. Janice Radway, *Reading the Romance*, 221.
2. Tania Modleski, *Feminism without Women*, 45.
3. Ibid., 44. Modleski argues that Radway's treatment of the Smithton women "as if they were natives of Bora-Bora rather than middle-class housewives from somewhere around Kansas" (43) promotes condescension toward the Smithton women. Their interpretations of romances are inadvertently made to seem different from and less sophisticated than Radway's, and this interpretive contradiction, rather than deepening critical inquiry into, and bridging the gap between, the feminist critic's subjectivity and "the subjectivity of 'the others'" (44), ends up blunting the inquiry. Critiquing Radway's methodology, Modleski observes: "In general, the crucial element missing here is the sense of the various ways a notion of contradiction must be brought to bear in any attempt to understand the full complexity of women's relation to culture: contradictions at an intrapsychic level; contradictions between conscious and unconscious fantasies and the discourses that conflict with or discredit these fantasies; and contradictions between competing ideologies and discourses as they are reflected both in popular texts and in the audience's relations to these texts" (44).
4. Irena Klepfisz, *A Few Words in the Mother Tongue*, 225.
5. Simone Lotven Sofian, "Popular Fiction and the Limits of Modern Midrash," 95–96.
6. Ibid., 97.
7. Ibid., 102.
8. Ibid., 103.
9. Naomi Graetz, "Response," 106.

10. Ibid., 107.
11. Ibid., 108.
12. Ibid., 109.
13. See Andrew Furman's excellent summing up of this debate in "The Exaggerated Demise of the Jewish-American Writer." For an example of the skeptical attitude toward American Jewish literature and culture, and of the view of Hebrew and Yiddish as the Jewish imaginative mainstream, see Michael P. Kramer's, Ruth Wisse's, and David Roskies's chapters in Emily Miller Budick's *Ideology and Jewish Identity in Israeli and American Literature*.
14. Morris Dickstein, in *Ideology and Jewish Identity in Israeli and American Literature*, 75.
15. Sara Paretsky, "Keeping Nancy Drew Alive," v.

Bibliography

Andrews, Donna. "Stuart Kaminsky: Mysteries in Motion." Interview with Stuart Kaminsky. *Crescent Blues E'Magazine* 2, no. 1 (February 1999). 7 May 2002: <www.crescentblues.com/2_1issue/kaminsky2.shtml>.
Anidjar, Gil. "On the (Under)Cutting Edge: Does Jewish Memory Need Sharpening?" In *Jews and Other Differences: The New Jewish Cultural Studies,* ed. Jonathan Boyarin and Daniel Boyarin. Minneapolis: University of Minnesota Press, 1997.
Anski, S.. *The Dybbuk.* Trans. Joseph C. Landis. In *Three Great Jewish Plays,* ed. Joseph C. Landis. New York: Applause Books, 1987.
Antler, Joyce. "From Molly Goldberg to Sophie Portnoy: Changing Images of Twentieth-Century Jewish Mothers." Paper presented at Three Centuries of American Jewish Mothers session, Association for Jewish Studies (AJS) Conference, Sheraton Boston Hotel, Boston, 18 December 2000.
———. Introduction to *Talking Back: Images of Jewish Women in American Popular Culture,* ed. Joyce Antler. Hanover, N.H.: Brandeis University Press, 1998.
Bader, Gershom. *The Encyclopedia of Talmudic Sages.* Trans. Solomon Katz. Northvale, N.J.: Jason Aronson, 1985.
Bakhtin, Mikhail. "Discourse in the Novel." In *The Dialogic Imagination: Four Essays by M. M. Bakhtin,* ed. Michael Holquist, trans. Caryl Emerson and Michael Holquist. Austin: University of Texas Press, 1981, 259–422.
Band, Arnold. "Popular Fiction and the Shaping of Jewish Identity." In *Jewish Identity in America,* ed. David M. Gordis and Yoav Ben-Horin. Los Angeles: Wilstein Institute, 1991.
Barker, Kenneth. "One Day the Rabbi Speculated." *Theology Today* 48, no. 4 (January 1992): 426–435.
Barthes, Roland. *A Lover's Discourse: Fragments.* Trans. Richard Howard. New York: Hill and Wang, 1984.
Bauerlein, Mark. *Literary Criticism: An Autopsy.* Philadelphia: University of Pennsylvania Press, 1997.
Baumgarten, Murray. *City Scriptures: Modern Jewish Writing.* Cambridge, Mass.: Harvard University Press, 1982.
Ben-Merre, Diana Arbin. "Murdering Traditional Assumptions: The Jewish-American Mystery." In *The Detective in American Fiction, Film, and Television,* ed. Jerome H. Delamater and Ruth Prigozy. Westport, Conn.: Greenwood Press, 1998.
Berger, Maurice. "The Mouse That Never Roars: Jewish Masculinity on American Television." In *Too*

Jewish?: Challenging Traditional Identities, ed. Norman L. Kleeblatt. New York: The Jewish Museum/New Brunswick, N.J.: Rutgers University Press, 1996.

Berman, Rabbi Israel V., ed. and trans. *The Talmud: The Steinsaltz Edition.* Vol. 5, Tractate Bava Metzia, part 5. New York: Random House, 1992.

Biale, David, Michael Galchinsky, and Susannah Heschel. "Introduction: The Dialectic of Jewish Enlightenment." In *Insider/Outsider: American Jews and Multiculturalism,* ed. David Biale, Michael Galchinsky, and Susannah Heschel. Berkeley and Los Angeles: University of California Press, 1998.

Bialik, Hayim Nahman, and Yehoshua Hana Ravnitzky, eds. *The Book of Legends: Sefer Ha-Aggadah.* Trans. William G. Braude. New York: Schocken Books, 1992.

———. "Revealment and Concealment in Language." In *Modern Hebrew Literature,* ed. Robert Alter. New York: Behrman House, 1975.

Binyon, T. J. "Race for Revenge." Rev. of *The Boys From Brazil,* by Ira Levin. *Times Literary Supplement,* 11 June 1976: 688.

Blood Money page. Amazon.com. 8 March 2000: <http://www.amazon.com>.

Boland, John. Rev. of *Monday the Rabbi Took Off,* by Harry Kemelman. *Books and Bookmen,* September 1972: 89.

Borges, Jorge Luis. "Death and the Compass." In *Crime Classics: The Mystery Story from Poe to the Present,* ed. Rex Burns and Mary Rose Sullivan. New York: Penguin Books, 1990.

Boyarin, Daniel. *Unheroic Conduct: The Rise of Heterosexuality and the Invention of the Jewish Man.* Berkeley and Los Angeles: University of California Press, 1997.

Boyarin, Jonathan, and Daniel Boyarin, eds. *Jews and Other Differences: The New Jewish Cultural Studies.* Minneapolis: University of Minnesota Press, 1997.

[Rev. of] *The Boys From Brazil,* by Ira Levin. *The New Yorker,* 1 May 1976: 130–131.

Brahm, Laura. "Clueless: Jewish Women's Mystery Novels." Rev. of: *The Ritual Bath,* Faye Kellerman; *Angel of Death,* Rochelle Krich; *Death Comes As Epiphany,* Sharan Newman; and *Survival Instincts,* Marissa Piesman. *Pakn Treger* (fall 1998/5759): 34–36.

Breines, Paul. *Tough Jews.* New York: Basic Books, 1990.

Brettschneider, Marla, ed. *The Narrow Bridge: Jewish Views on Multiculturalism.* New Brunswick, N.J.: Rutgers University Press, 1996.

Browne, Nick. "The Spectator-in-the-Text: The Rhetoric of *Stagecoach.*" In *Narrative, Apparatus, Ideology,* ed. Philip Rosen. New York: Columbia University Press, 1986.

Budick, Emily Miller, ed. *Ideology and Jewish Identity in Israeli and American Literature.* Albany: State University of New York Press, 2001.

Bunzl, Matti. "Jews, Queers, and Other Symptoms." *GLQ: A Journal of Lesbian and Gay Studies* 6, no. 2 (2000): 321–341.

Cahan, Abraham. *The Rise of David Levinsky.* New York: Penguin Books, 1993.

Canby, Vincent. Rev. of *The Boys from Brazil* dir. by Franklin J. Schaffner. *New York Times,* Section 2, 3 December 1978: 13

Castle, Terry. *The Female Thermometer: Eighteenth-Century Culture and the Invention of the Uncanny.* New York and Oxford: Oxford University Press, 1995.

Cawelti, John. *Adventure, Mystery, and Romance: Formula Stories as Art and Popular Culture.* Chicago: University of Chicago Press, 1976.

Chametzky, Jules, John Felstiner, Hilene Flanzbaum, and Kathryn Hellerstein, eds. *Jewish American Literature: A Norton Anthology.* New York: W. W. Norton and Co., 2001.

Chandler, Raymond. *The Long Goodbye.* New York: Ballantine Books, 1978.

———. "Twelve Notes on the Mystery Story." In *Raymond Chandler: Later Novels and Other Writings,* ed. Frank MacShane. New York: The Library of America, 1995

Cunningham, Valentine. "Pincers," rev. of *The Boys From Brazil,* by Ira Levin. *New Statesman* 91, 16 April 1976: 514.

de Lauretis, Teresa. "Through the Looking-Glass." In *Narrative, Apparatus, Ideology,* ed. Philip Rosen. New York: Columbia University Press, 1986.

DesPres, Terrence. *Praises and Dispraises: Poetry and Politics in the Twentieth Century.* New York: Penguin Books, 1989.

———. *The Survivor: An Anatomy of Life in the Death Camps.* New York and Oxford: Oxford University Press, 1976.

Desser, David, and Lester D. Friedman. *American-Jewish Filmmakers: Traditions and Trends.* Urbana: University of Illinois Press, 1993.

Dickstein, Morris. "The Complex Fate of the Jewish American Writer." In *Ideology and Jewish Identity in Israeli and American Literature,* ed. Emily Miller Budick. Albany: State University of New York Press, 2001.
Du Bois, W.E.B. *The Souls of Black Folk.* In *Three Negro Classics,* ed. John Hope Franklin. New York: Avon Books, 1965.
Durham, Philip. *Down These Mean Streets a Man Must Go: Raymond Chandler's Knight.* Chapel Hill: The University of North Carolina Press, 1963.
Ebert, Roger. Rev. of *A Stranger among Us,* dir. by Sidney Lumet. *Chicago Sun-Times,* 17 July 1992: <http://www.suntimes.com/ebert reviews/1992/07/767458.html>.
Eisen, Arnold. "In the Wilderness: Reflections on American Jewish Culture." *Jewish Social Studies* 5.1–2 (fall 1998/winter 1999): 25–39.
Etshalom, Rabbi Yitzchak. "Shiur P'tichah." *Rambam's Hilkhot T'fillah.* Rambam Archives: Project Genesis, March 1996: <http//www.torah.org>.
Ezrahi, Sidra DeKoven. *By Words Alone: The Holocaust in Literature.* Chicago and London: University of Chicago Press, 1980.
Feingold, Henry. "Shoah Business," rev. of *The Holocaust in American Life* by Peter Novick. *Congress Monthly* 66, no. 5 (September/October 1999): <http://www.ajcongress-ne.org/booklets/cong_monthly/cong_monthly_999.htm>.
Feuerman, Ruchama King. *The Secret of the Hotel DelaRosa: A Bina Gold Mystery.* Brooklyn: Aura Press, 1996.
Finkielkraut, Alain. *The Imaginary Jew.* Trans. Kevin O'Neill and David Suchoff. Lincoln: University of Nebraska Press, 1994.
Finkelstein, Norman. *The Ritual of New Creation: Jewish Tradition and Contemporary Literature.* Albany: State University of New York Press, 1992.
Finkelstein, Norman G. *The Holocaust Industry: Reflections on the Exploitation of Jewish Suffering.* London and New York: Verso, 2000.
Fish, Stanley. "Interpreting the *Variorum.*" *Critical Inquiry* 2, no 3 (spring 1976): 465–485. Rpt. in *Contemporary Literary Criticism: Modernism through Post-Structuralism,* ed. Robert Con Davis, New York and London: Longman, 1986.
Fishman, Sylvia Barack. *Jewish Life and American Culture.* Albany: State University of New York Press, 2000.
———. "Our Mothers and Our Sisters and Our Cousins and Our Aunts: Dialogues and Dynamics in Literature and Film." In *Talking Back: Images of Jewish Women in American Popular Culture,* ed. Joyce Antler. Hanover: Brandeis University Press, 1998.
Fiske, John. "Culture, Ideology, Interpellation." In *Literary Theory: An Anthology,* ed. Julie Rivkin and Michael Ryan. Oxford: Blackwell, 1998.
———. *Understanding Popular Culture.* Boston: Unwin Hyman, 1989.
Forché, Carolyn. *The Angel of History.* New York: HarperCollins Publishers, 1994.
Foucault, Michel. *Discipline and Punish: The Birth of the Prison.* Trans. Alan Sheridan. New York: Vintage Books, 1995.
Freedman, Jonathan. *The Temple of Culture: Assimilation and Anti-Semitism in Literary Anglo-America.* Oxford: Oxford University Press, 2000.
Furman, Andrew. *Contemporary Jewish American Writers and the Multicultural Dilemma: The Return of the Exiled.* Syracuse, N.Y.: Syracuse University Press, 2000
———. "The Exaggerated Demise of the Jewish-American Writer." *The Chronicle of Higher Education* 6 July 2001: B7.
———. *Israel through the Jewish American Imagination: A Survey of Jewish-American Literature on Israel, 1928–1995.* Albany: State University of New York Press, 1997.
———. "The Secret Jews of Sixteenth-Century Lisbon," rev. of *The Last Kabbalist of Lisbon,* by Richard Zimler. *Midstream,* September/October 1998: 39–40.
Galchinsky, Michael. "Scattered Seeds: A Dialogue of Diasporas." In *Insider/Outsider: American Jews and Multiculturalism,* ed. David Biale, Michael Galchinsky, and Susannah Heschel. Berkeley and Los Angeles: University of California Press, 1998.
Geertz, Clifford. "Blurred Genres: The Refiguration of Social Thought." *American Scholar* 49 (1980): 165–179.
———. *The Interpretation of Cultures.* New York: Basic Books, 1973.
"Genizah." *Encyclopedia Judaica.* CD-ROM Edition. Tel Aviv: Keter Publishing House, 1999.
Gilman, Sander. *The Jew's Body.* New York and London: Routledge, 1991.
Glazer, Miriyam. "'Crazy, of Course': Spiritual Romanticism and the Redeeming of Female Spirituality

in Contemporary Jewish-American Women's Fiction." In *People of the Book: Thirty Scholars Reflect on Their Jewish Identity*, ed. Jeffrey Rubin-Dorsky and Shelley Fisher Fishkin. Madison: University of Wisconsin Press, 1996.
Goldman, B., and A. B. Biegel. *Ner Ma'aravi*. Brooklyn: Tova Press, 1991.
Gosselin, Adrienne Johnson. "Multicultural Detective Fiction: Murder with a Message." In *Multicultural Detective Fiction: Murder from the "Other" Side*, ed. Adrienne Johnson Gosselin. New York: Garland Publishing, 1999.
———. "The Psychology of Uncertainty: (Re)Inscribing Indeterminacy in Rudolph Fisher's *The Conjure-Man Dies*." *Other Voices: The (e)Journal of Cultural Criticism* 1.3 (January 1999) 13 February 2000. <http://www.english.upenn.edu/~ov/1.3/agosselin/harlem.html>.
Graetz, Naomi. "Response." *Conservative Judaism* 54, no. 3 (spring 2002): 106–110.
Greenberg, Rabbi Irving. "Jewish Denominationalism Meets the Open Society." In *One Nation Under God?: Religion and American Culture*, ed. Marjorie Garber and Rebecca L. Walkowitz. New York and London: Routledge, 1999.
Grella, George. "The Hard-Boiled Detective Novel." In *Detective Fiction: A Collection of Critical Essays*, ed. Robin W. Winks. Englewood Cliffs, N.J.: Prentice-Hall, 1980.
Hall, Stuart. "The Whites of Their Eyes: Racist Ideologies and the Media." In *Silver Linings: Some Strategies for the Eighties*, ed. G. Bridges and R. Brunt. London: Lawrence and Wishart Ltd., 1981. Rpt. in *Gender, Race, and Class in Media*, ed. Gail Dines and Jean M. Humez, Thousand Oaks: Sage Publications, 1995: 18–22.
Harap, Louis. *In the Mainstream: The Jewish Presence in Twentieth-Century American Literature, 1950s–1980s*. Westport, Conn.: Greenwood Press, 1987.
Harris, James W. "Stuart Kaminsky: No Mystery—He's A Libertarian." *The Liberator OnLine* 3, no. 17, 21 August 1998. 7 May 2002 <http://www.self-gov.org/liberator/v003n017.shtml>.
Hartman, Geoffrey. "On the Jewish Imagination" *Prooftexts* 5 (1985): 201–220
———. "Tele-Suffering and Testimony in the Dot Com Era." In *Visual Culture and the Holocaust*, ed. Barbie Zelizer. New Brunswick, N.J.: Rutgers University Press, 2001.
Haut, Woody. *Pulp Culture: Hardboiled Fiction and the Cold War*. London: Serpent's Tail, 1995.
Hershinow, Sheldon. "Harry Kemelman." In *Dictionary of Literary Biography 28: Twentieth-Century American-Jewish Writers*, ed. Daniel Walden. Detroit: Gale, 1984: 127–133.
Hershinow, Sheldon ,and Margaret J. King. "Judaism for the Millions: Harry Kemelman's 'Rabbi Books.'" *MELUS* 5 (winter 1978): 83–93.
Hirsch, Marianne. *Family Frames: Photography, Narrative, and Postmemory*. Cambridge, Mass.: Harvard University Press, 1997.
Homicide. Dir. by David Mamet, perf. by Joe Mantegna, William H. Macy, Natalija Nogulich, and Ving Rhames. Columbia Tristar, 1991.
Holquist, Michael. "Whodunit and Other Questions: Metaphysical Detective Stories in Postwar Fiction." In *The Poetics of Murder: Detective Fiction and Literary Theory*, ed. Glenn W. Most and William W. Stowe. New York: Harcourt Brace Jovanovich, 1983.
Horowitz, Sara R. "Gender, Genocide, and Jewish Memory." *Prooftexts* 20, no. 1 (2000): 158–190.
Howe, Irving. *Celebrations and Attacks: Thirty Years of Literary and Cultural Commentary*. New York: Harcourt Brace Jovanovich, 1979.
Hubin, Allen J. Rev. of *Sunday the Rabbi Stayed Home*, by Harry Kemelman. *New York Times Book Review*, 2 March 1969.
Hubner, Carol Korb. *The Haunted Shul and other Devora Doresh Mysteries*. New York: Judaica Press, 1981.
———. *The Silent Shofar and other Devora Doresh Mysteries*. New York: Judaica Press, 1983.
———. *The Tattered Tallis and other Devora Doresh Mysteries*. New York: Judaica Press, 1979.
———. *The Twisted Menora and other Devora Doresh Mysteries*. New York: Judaica Press, 1981.
———. *The Whispering Mezuzah and other Devora Doresh Mysteries*. New York: Judaica Press, 1979.
Huyssen, Andreas. "Mass Culture as Woman: Modernism's Other." In *Studies in Entertainment: Critical Approaches to Mass Culture*. Bloomington and Indianapolis: Indiana University Press, 1986.
———. "Present Pasts: Media, Politics, Amnesia." *Public Culture* 12, no. 1 (2000): 21–38.
Hyman, Paula E. *Gender and Assimilation in Modern Jewish History*. Seattle and London: University of Washington Press, 1995.
Ingraham, Col. Prentiss. *The Jew Detective; or, The Beautiful Convict*. New York: Beadle's Dime Library, 1 July 1891.
Irons, Glenwood, ed. *Feminism in Women's Detective Fiction*. Toronto: University of Toronto Press, 1995.

Itzkovitz, Daniel. "Secret Temples." In *Jews and Other Differences: The New Jewish Cultural Studies*, ed. Jonathan Boyarin and Daniel Boyarin. Minneapolis: University of Minnesota Press, 1997.
Jewish Gothic Home Page. 29 May 2001: <http://www.jewishgothic.com>.
Jochnowitz, Eve. "'Send a Salami to Your Boy in the Army': Sites of Jewish Memory and Identity at Lower East Side Restaurants." In *Remembering the Lower East Side*, ed. Hasia Diner, Jeffrey Shandler, and Beth Wenger. Bloomington and Indianapolis: Indiana University Press, 2000.
Joselit, Jenna Weissman. *The Wonders of America: Reinventing Jewish Culture, 1880–1950*. New York: Hill and Wang, 1996.
Kael, Pauline. "Current Cinema." Rev. of *The Boys from Brazil*, dir. by Franklin J. Schaffner. *The New Yorker* 9 October 1978: 164–166.
Kamenetz, Rodger. *The Missing Jew: New and Selected Poems*. Saint Louis: Time Being Books, 1992.
Kaminsky, Stuart M. "Confession." In *Mystery Midrash: An Anthology of Jewish Mystery and Detective Fiction*, ed. Lawrence W. Raphael. Woodstock, N.Y: Jewish Lights, 1999.
———. *Lieberman's Choice*. New York: St. Martin's Press, 1993.
———. *Lieberman's Day*. New York: Henry Holt and Co., 1994.
———. *Lieberman's Folly*. New York: St. Martin's Press, 1991.
———. *Lieberman's Law*. New York: Henry Holt and Co., 1996.
———. *Lieberman's Thief*. New York: Henry Holt and Co., 1995.
———. "The Tenth Man." In *Criminal Kabbalah: An Intriguing Anthology of Jewish Mystery and Detective Fiction*, ed. Lawrence W. Raphael. Woodstock, N.Y.: Jewish Lights, 2001.
———. *When the Dark Man Calls*. New York: St. Martin's Press, 1983.
"Kaminsky, Stuart M." *St. James Guide to Crime and Mystery Writers*, 4th ed. Detroit, Mich.: St. James Press, 1996. Reproduced in *Biography Resource Center*, Farmington Hills, Mich.: The Gale Group, 2002. 3 April 2002 <http://galenet.galegroup.com/servlet/BioRC>.
Karlinsky, Rabbi Shaya. *Maharal Derech Chaim*. Maharal Archives: Project Genesis, March 1996. 21 March 1996 <http//www.torah.org>.
Kauffmann, Stanley. Rev. of *A Stranger among Us*, dir. by Sidney Lumet. *The New Republic*, 17 August 1992, 34.
Kaufman, Margo. "Happiness Is a Warm Subplot." Rev. of *Prayers for the Dead*, Faye Kellerman. *Los Angeles Times* 22 Sept. 1996: Book Review, 8.
Kellerman, Faye. *Day of Atonement*. New York: William Morrow and Co., 1991.
———. *False Prophet*. New York: Fawcett Gold Medal, 1992.
———. *Grievous Sin*. New York: Fawcett Gold Medal, 1993.
———. *Milk and Honey*. New York: Fawcett Gold Medal, 1990.
———. *Prayers for the Dead*. New York: William Morrow and Co., 1996.
———. *The Ritual Bath*. New York: Fawcett Crest, 1986.
———. *Sacred and Profane*. New York: Fawcett Crest, 1987.
———. *Sanctuary*. New York: Avon Books, 1994.
Kemelman, Harry. *Common Sense in Education*. New York: Crown Publishers, 1970.
———. *Conversations with Rabbi Small*. New York: Fawcett Crest, 1981.
———. *The Day the Rabbi Resigned*. New York: Fawcett Crest, 1992.
———. *Friday the Rabbi Slept Late*. New York: Fawcett Crest, 1964.
———. *Monday the Rabbi Took Off*. New York: Fawcett Crest, 1972.
———. *The Nine Mile Walk*. New York: G. P. Putnam's Sons, 1967.
———. *One Fine Day the Rabbi Bought a Cross*. New York: Fawcett Crest, 1987.
———. *Saturday the Rabbi Went Hungry*. New York: Fawcett Crest, 1966.
———. *Someday the Rabbi Will Leave*. New York: Fawcett Crest, 1985.
———. *Sunday the Rabbi Stayed Home*. New York: Fawcett Crest, 1969.
———. *That Day the Rabbi Left Town*. New York: Fawcett Crest, 1996.
———. *Thursday the Rabbi Walked Out*. New York: Fawcett Crest, 1978.
———. *Tuesday the Rabbi Saw Red*. New York: Fawcett Crest, 1973.
———. *Wednesday the Rabbi Got Wet*. New York: Fawcett Crest, 1976.
Klein, Kathleen G., ed. *Diversity and Detective Fiction*. Bowling Green, Ohio: Bowling Green Sate University Popular Press, 1999.
———. *The Woman Detective: Gender and Genre*. Urbana: University of Illinois Press, 1988.
Klein, Zachary. *No Saving Grace*. New York: Fawcett Columbine, 1993.
Klepfisz, Irena. *Dreams of an Insomniac: Jewish Feminist Essays, Speeches, and Diatribes*. Portland, Ore.: Eighth Mountain Press, 1990.

———. *A Few Words in the Mother Tongue: Poems Selected and New (1971–1990)*. Portland, Ore.: Eighth Mountain Press, 1990.
Klingenstein, Suzanne. *Jews in the American Academy, 1900–1940: The Dynamics of Intellectual Assimilation*. New Haven, Conn.: Yale University Press, 1991.
Knight, Stephen. *Form and Ideology in Crime Fiction*. Bloomington and Indianapolis: Indiana University Press, 1980.
Krich, Rochelle Majer. *Angel of Death*. New York: Mysterious Press, 1996.
———. *Blood Money*. New York: Avon Twilight, 1999.
———. "The Holocaust in Her Soul, Romantic Comedy in Her Heart: An Interview with Rochelle Majer Krich." Interview with Reed Andrus. August/September 2000. 19 July 2001 <http://www.rochellekrich.com/Rochelle%27sBio.htm.>
Kristeva, Julia. "Ellipsis on Dread and the Specular Seduction." In *Narrative, Apparatus, Ideology*, ed. Philip Rosen. New York: Columbia University Press, 1986.
Kroll, Jack. "Little Hitlers," rev. of *The Boys from Brazil*, dir. by Franklin J. Schaffner. *Newsweek*, 9 October 1978: 92
Kugelmass, Jack. "Jewish Icons: Envisioning the Self in Images of the Other." In *Jews and Other Differences: The New Jewish Cultural Studies*, ed. Jonathan Boyarin and Daniel Boyarin. Minneapolis: University of Minnesota Press, 1997.
Landrum, Larry. *American Mystery and Detective Novels: A Reference Guide*. Westport, Conn.: Greenwood Press, 1999.
Langer, Lawrence. *Admitting the Holocaust: Collected Essays*. New York and Oxford: Oxford University Press, 1995.
———. *Holocaust Testimonies: The Ruins of Memory*. New Haven and London: Yale University Press, 1991.
Lefkowitz, Lori Hope. "Inherited Memory and the Ethics of Ventriloquism." In *Shaping Losses: Cultural Memory and the Holocaust*, ed. Julia Epstein and Lori Hope Lefkowitz. Urbana and Chicago: University of Illinois Press, 2001.
Lester, Julius. "What Do American Jews Believe?" *Commentary*, August 1996), 63–65.
Levin, Ira. *The Boys from Brazil*. New York: Dell, 1976.
Levitsky, Ronald. "Jacob's Voice." In *Mystery Midrash: An Anthology of Jewish Mystery and Detective Fiction*, ed. Lawrence W. Raphael. Woodstock, N.Y.: Jewish Lights, 1999.
Liptzin, Sol. *The Jew in American Literature*. New York: Bloch Publishing Co., 1966. Locke, Helen. *A Case of Mis-Taken Identity: Detective Undercurrents in Recent African-American Fiction*. New York: Peter Lang Publishing, 1994.
Lyons, Gene. Rev. of *The Boys from Brazil*, by Ira Levin. *New York Times Book Review*, 14 March 1976: 4–5.
Lyotard, Jean François. *The Differend: Phrases in Dispute*. Minneapolis: University of Minnesota Press, 1988.
Maryles, Daisy. "Harry Kemelman: Creator of the World's Best Known Rabbi." *Jewish Digest* (December 1975), 45–47.
Meravi, S. T. "Undercover Plot." *Jerusalem Post*, 17 March 1989.
Merivale, Patricia, and Susan Elizabeth Sweeney, eds. *Detecting Texts: The Metaphysical Detective Story from Poe to Postmodernism*. Philadelphia: University of Pennsylvania Press, 1999.
Mintz, Alan. *Popular Culture and the Shaping of Holocaust Memory in America*. Seattle and London: University of Washington Press, 2001.
Modleski, Tania. *Feminism Without Women: Culture and Criticism in a "Postfeminist" Age*. New York and London: Routledge, 1991.
Moore, Deborah Dash. "Jewish Migration in Postwar America: The Case of Miami and Los Angeles." In *The American Jewish Experience*, ed. Jonathan D. Sarna. New York: Holmes and Meier, 1997.
Morrison, Toni. *Playing In the Dark: Whiteness and the Literary Imagination*. Cambridge, Mass.: Harvard University Press, 1992.
Most, Glen, and William Stowe, eds. *The Poetics of Murder: Detective Fiction and Literary Theory*. New York: Harcourt Brace Jovanovich, 1983.
Mulvey, Laura. "Visual Pleasure and Narrative Cinema." In *Narrative, Apparatus, Ideology*, ed. Philip Rosen. New York: Columbia University Press, 1986.
Munt, Sally R. *Murder by the Book?: Feminism and the Crime Novel*. New York and London: Routledge, 1994.
Newton, Adam Zachary. *Facing Black and Jew: Literature as Public Space in Twentieth-Century America*. Cambridge: Canbridge University Press, 1999.

Norden, Edward. "Holy Hollywood," rev. of *A Stranger among Us*, dir. by Sidney Lumet. *Commentary*, November 1992: 51–52.
Norton, Charles. *The Hebrew Detective*. Chicago, 1914.
Omer, Ranen. "The Metaphysics of Lost Jewish Identity in David Mamet's *Homicide*." *Yiddish* 11, no. 3–4 (1999): 37–50.
Paretsky, Sara. "Keeping Nancy Drew Alive." Introduction to *The Secret of the Old Clock*, by Carolyn Keene. Bedford, Mass.: Applewood Books, 1991.
Pavletich, JoAnn. "Anzia Yezierska, Immigrant Authority, and the Uses of Affect." *Tulsa Studies in Women's Literature* 19, no. 1 (spring 2000): 81–104.
Pellegrini, Ann. "Interarticulations: Gender, Race, and the Jewish Woman Question." In *Judaism Since Gender*, ed. Miriam Peskowitz and Laura Levitt. New York and London: Routledge, 1997.
Piesman, Marissa. *Alternate Sides*. New York: Dell Publishing, 1996.
———. *Close Quarters*. New York: Dell Publishing, 1994.
———. *Heading Uptown*. New York: Dell Publishing, 1993.
———. *Personal Effects*. New York: Pocket Books, 1991.
———. *Survival Instincts*. New York: Dell Publishing, 1997.
———. *Unorthodox Practices*. New York: Pocket Books, 1989.
Prell, Riv-Ellen. "Cinderellas Who (Almost) Never Become Princesses: Subversive Representations of Jewish Women in Postwar Popular Novels." In *Talking Back: Images of Jewish Women in American Popular Culture*, ed. Joyce Antler. Hanover, N.H.: Brandeis University Press, 1998.
———. *Fighting to Become Americans: Jews, Gender, and the Anxiety of Assimilation*. Boston: Beacon Press, 1999.
Prescott, Peter S. "Love Your Führer," rev. of *The Boys from Brazil*, by Ira Levin. *Newsweek* 23 February 1976, 83,86.
Priestman, Martin. *Detective Fiction and Literature: The Figure on the Carpet*. New York: St. Martin's Press, 1991.
Punter, David. *A Companion to the Gothic*. Oxford and Malden, Mass.: Blackwell Publishers, 2000.
———. *The Literature of Terror*, vol. 2. *The Modern Gothic*. London and New York: Longman, 1996.
Pyrhönen, Heta. *Mayhem and Murder: Narrative and Moral Problems in the Detective Story*. Toronto: University of Toronto Press, 1999.
Radford, Jean. *The Progress of Romance: The Politics of Popular Fiction*. New York and London: Routledge, 1986.
Radway, Janice A. *Reading the Romance: Women, Patriarchy, and Popular Literature*. 1984. Chapel Hill: University of North Carolina Press, 1991.
Raphael, Lawrence W. "Assimilated, Acculturated, or Affirming: The Jewish Detective in America," rev. of: *American Judaism in Transition*, by Gerhard Falk; *Justice*, by Faye Kellerman; and *The Day the Rabbi Left Town*, by Harry Kemelman. *Judaism: A Quarterly Journal of Jewish Life and Thought* (winter 1997): 122–126.
———, ed. *Criminal Kabbalah: An Intriguing Anthology of Jewish Mystery and Detective Fiction*. Woodstock, N.Y.: Jewish Lights, 2001.
———, ed. *Mystery Midrash: An Anthology of Jewish Mystery and Detective Fiction*. Woodstock, N.Y.: Jewish Lights, 1999.
Rapping, Elayne. "Gender Politics on the Big Screen," rev. of *A Stranger among Us*, dir. by Sidney Lumet. *The Progressive*, October 1992, 36.
Ray, Robert. *A Certain Tendency of the Hollywood Cinema, 1930–1980*. Princeton, N.J.: Princeton University Press, 1985.
———. *The Avant-Garde Finds Andy Hardy*. Cambridge, Mass.: Harvard University Press, 1995.
Reedy, Gerard C. "The Best Springtime Reading," rev. of *The Boys from Brazil*, by Ira Levin. *America*, 1 May 1976, 385.
"Reviving the Jewish Gothic." *Culture Currents* (October 1998). 29 May 2001 <http://www.jewishculture.org/publications_cult_curr_9810.html>.
Rich, Adrienne. *Your Native Land Your Life*. New York and London: W. W. Norton and Co., 1986.
Riddel, Joseph. *Purloined Letters: Originality and Repetition in American Literature*. Ed. Mark Bauerlein. Baton Rouge: Louisiana State University Press, 1995.
Rosenbaum, David. *Zaddik*. New York: Mysterious Press, 1993.
Roskies, David G. *The Jewish Search for a Usable Past*. Bloomington and Indianapolis: Indiana University Press, 1999.
Roth, Philip, *Goodbye Columbus, and Five Short Stories*. Boston: Houghton Mifflin, 1989.
———. *Operation Shylock: A Confession*. New York: Vintage, 1993.

Rudolph, Janet. "The Kemelman Capers: A Religio-Cultural Study of Harry Kemelman's Detective Fiction." Ph.D. diss., Graduate Theological Union, Berkeley, California, 1985.

Rukeyser, Muriel. *The Life of Poetry.* Ashfield, Mass.: Paris Press, 1996.

Rzepka, Charles J. "'I'm In the Business Too': Gothic Chivalry, Private Eyes, and Proxy Sex and Violence in Chandler's *The Big Sleep.*" *Modern Fiction Studies* 46, no. 3 (2000): 695–724.

Safrai, Shmuel. "Eleazar ben Simeon (tan.)." *Encyclopedia Judaica.* CD-ROM Edition. Tel Aviv: Keter Publishing House, 1999

Said, Edward. *Orientalism.* New York: Vintage, 1979.

Sarna, Jonathan. "The Cult of Synthesis in American Jewish Culture." *Jewish Social Studies* 5, no. 1–2 (fall 1998/winter 1999): 52–79.

Schickel, Richard. "Cloning Around," rev. of *The Boys from Brazil,* dir. by Franklin J. Schaffner. *Time,* 9 October 1978, 100–101.

Schonberg, Harold C. Rev. of *The Boys from Brazil,* dir. by Franklin J. Schaffner. *New York Times,* 6 November 1978, 54.

Sege, Irene. "Tuesday the Rabbi Made Headlines at 87." *Boston Globe,* 21May 1996, 77.

Seidman, Naomi. "Theorizing Jewish Patriarchy *in extremis.*" In *Judaism Since Gender,* ed. Miriam Peskowitz and Laura Levitt. New York and London: Routledge, 1997.

Selavan, Ida Cohen. "Friday the Rebbetzin . . . A Feminist Look at the Rabbi Small Series." *Lilith,* fall/winter 1977, 39–41.

———. "The Rabbi's Awakening Makes No Drowsy Tale," rev. of *Friday the Rabbi Slept Late,* by Harry Kemelman. *Jewish Chronicle* (Pittsburgh), 28 May 1965.

Shandler, Jeffrey. "Schindler's Discourse: America Discusses the Holocaust and Its Mediation, From NBC's Miniseries to Spielberg's Film." In *Spielberg's Holocaust: Critical Perspectives on Schindler's List,* ed. Yosefa Loshitzky. Bloomington and Indianapolis: Indiana University Press, 1997.

———. *While America Watches: Televising the Holocaust.* New York and Oxford: Oxford University Press, 1999.

Shaw, Marion, and Sabine Vanacker. *Reflecting on Miss Marple.* New York and London: Routledge, 1991.

Sheppard, R. Z. "Rosemary's Führer," rev. of *The Boys from Brazil,* by Ira Levin. *Time,* 23 February 1976, 64.

Sherwin, Richard E. "The Jewish Image in American Fiction." *Menorah Review* [Center for Judaic Studies of Virginia Commonwealth University] 40 (spring/summer 1997): 1–3.

Showalter, Elaine. "Rethinking the Seventies: Women Writers and Violence." *The Antioch Review* 39, no. 2 (spring 1981): 156–170.

Sicher, Efraim. "The Future of the Past: Countermemory and Postmemory in Contemporary American Post-Holocaust Narratives." *History and Memory* 12, no. 2 (2001): 56–91.

Silverman, Kaja. "Suture [Excerpts]." In *Narrative, Apparatus, Ideology,* ed. Philip Rosen. New York: Columbia University Press, 1986.

Smith, Gavin. "'That's The Way It Happens,'" interview with Sidney Lumet. *Film Comment* 28, no. 5 (September 1992): 50–61.

Sofian, Simone Lotven. "Popular Fiction and the Limits of Modern Midrash: *The Red Tent* by Anita Diamant." *Conservative Judaism* 54, no. 3 (spring 2002): 95–105

Soitos, Stephen. *The Blues Detective: A Study of African American Detective Fiction.* Amherst: University of Massachusetts Press, 1996.

Sokoloff, Naomi. "Jewish Mysteries: Detective Fiction by Faye Kellerman and Batya Gur." *Shofar* 15, no. 3 (1997): 66–85.

———. "Sleuths and Sages: Detective Fiction by American Jewish Women." *Midstream,* October 1997, 36–39.

Sollors, Werner. *Beyond Ethnicity: Consent and Descent in American Culture.* New York: Oxford University Press, 1986.

Speir, Jerry. *Raymond Chandler.* New York: Frederick Ungar, 1981.

Spencer, William David. *Mysterium and Mystery: The Clerical Crime Novel.* Ann Arbor: UMI Research Press, 1989.

Sragow, Michael. "Menagerie," rev. of *A Stranger among Us,* dir. by Sidney Lumet. *The New Yorker,* 27 July 1992, 55.

Steinberg, Janice. "Wailing Reed." In *Mystery Midrash: An Anthology of Jewish Mystery and Detective Fiction,* ed. Lawrence W. Raphael. Woodstock, N.Y.: Jewish Lights, 1999.

Stier, Oren Baruch. "Memory Matters: Reading Collective Memory in Contemporary Jewish Culture." *Prooftexts* 18, no. 1 (January 1998): 67–82.

A Stranger among Us. Dir. Sidney Lumet. Perf. Melanie Griffith, Eric Thal, John Pankow, Tracy Pollan, and Mia Sara. Hollywood Pictures, 1992.
Surette, Ray. "Prologue: Some Unpopular Thoughts about Popular Culture." In *Popular Culture, Crime, and Justice,* ed. Frankie Bailey and Donna Hale. Belmont, Calif.: West Wadsworth Publishing, 1998.
Swartz, Sarah Silberstein, and Margie Wolfe, eds. *From Memory to Transformation: Jewish Women's Voices.* Toronto: Second Story Press, 1998.
Thompson, Jon. *Fiction, Crime, and Empire: Clues to Modernity and Postmodernism.* Urbana: University of Illinois Press, 1993.
Walton, Priscilla L., and Manina Jones, eds. *Detective Agency: Women Rewriting the Hard-Boiled Tradition.* Berkeley and Los Angeles: University of California Press, 1999.
———. "Identity Politics: April Smith's North of Montana and Rochelle Majer Krich's Angel of Death." In *Diversity and Detective Fiction,* ed. Kathleen Gregory Klein. Bowling Green, Ohio: Bowling Green Sate University Popular Press, 1999.
Webber, Jonathan. "Lest We Forget." In *Modern Jewish Mythologies,* ed. Glenda Abramson. Cincinnati: Hebrew Union College Press, 2000.
———. "Modern Jewish Identities: The Ethnographic Complexities." *Journal of Jewish Studies* 33, no. 2 (1992): 246–267.
Weber, Donald. "Taking Jewish American Popular Culture Seriously: The Yinglish Worlds of Gertrude Berg, Milton Berle, and Mickey Katz." *Jewish Social Studies* 5, no. 1–2 (fall 1998/winter 1999): 124–153.
Whitfield, Stephen J. *American Space, Jewish Time.* Armonk: North Castle Books, 1996.
———. *In Search of American Jewish Culture.* Hanover, N.H.: Brandeis University Press, 1999.
Wieseltier, Leon. "Machoball Soup," rev. of *Homicide,* dir. by David Mamet. *The New Republic,* 24 April 1995, 46.
Williams, Linda. "Film Body: An Implantation of Perversions." In *Narrative, Apparatus, Ideology,* ed. Philip Rosen. New York: Columbia University Press, 1986.
Willson Jr., Robert F. "From Novel to Film: De-Sinistering *The Boys from Brazil,*" Literature/Film Quarterly 7 (1979): 322–324.
Wirth-Nesher, Hana. "Defining the Indefinable: What Is Jewish Literature?" In *What Is Jewish Literature,* ed. Hana Wirth-Nesher. Philadelphia and Jerusalem: The Jewish Publication Society, 1994.
Wisse, Ruth. "Reading About Jews." *Commentary,* March 1980, 41–48.
Yaffe, James. "Is This Any Job for a Nice Jewish Boy?" In *Synod of Sleuths: Essays on Judeo-Christian Detective Fiction,* ed. Jon L. Breen and Martin H. Greenberg. Metuchen, N.J.: Scarecrow Press, 1990.
———. *My Mother the Detective.* Norfolk, Va.: Crippen and Landru, 1997.
Yasgur, Batya Swift. *The Search for the Real Megan: A Bina Gold Mystery.* Brooklyn: Aura Press, 1996.
———. *The Secret of the Grandfather Clock: A Bina Gold Mystery.* Brooklyn: Aura Press, 1998.
Yerushalmi, Yosef Hayim. *Zakhor: Jewish History and Jewish Memory.* New York: Schocken Books, 1989.
Young, Robert J. C. *Colonial Desire: Hybridity in Theory, Culture, and Race.* London and New York: Routledge, 1998.
Zimler, Richard. *The Last Kabbalist of Lisbon.* Woodstock, N.Y.: Overlook Press, 1998.
Zipperstein, Steven J. *Imagining Russian Jewry: Memory, History, Identity.* Seattle: University of Washington Press, 1999.

Index

acculturation: "imaginary Jew" and, 173; imperfect, 79; Kemelman's strategy for, 23–24, 26, 30–32, 51–52; as literary theme, 24, 27–28, 257n16; of "modern ideas," 82–84; in popular arts, 3
Adam, crime and punishment of, 7
African Americans: detective fiction of, 6; double-consciousness of, 200; relations with Jews, 37–39, 152, 189, 191
"Africanist" characters, 152
Alter, Robert, 24
Alternate Sides (Piesman), 104, 105
amateur detectives: audience reception survey on, 232; women, 76–107
"Americanization of the Holocaust on Stage and Screen" (Langer), 141
American Jewish detective stories: analytical focus on, 227; audience reception survey on, 226–238, 249–252; beginnings of, 12, 19; in canon of Jewish literature, 11–12; children's, 1, 242–247; critical perspectives on, 6–7; critical reception of, 1–2; detective formula source materials for, 5–6; gender issues in, 235–236; Jewish source materials for, 7–10, 11; kosher hybridity concept and, 4–5; vs. literary fiction, 2–3; past in (*see* Holocaust; memory of past); pedagogical function of, 6, 10, 234–235; social function of, 2–3; viewer/reader positioning in, 13–14, 174–199; women in (*see* women; women detectives). *See also specific authors and works*
American Jewish writers: acculturation theme of, 24, 27–28, 257n16; displacement of, 258n20; memories of past, 25, 257n17; policing kosher hybridity, 238–242; popular culture and, 2–3; of popular fiction, 56, 238, 241–242
American Space, Jewish Time (Whitfield), 4
Angel of Death (Krich), 13, 141, 157–162
Ansky, S., 119, 259n2
Antler, Joyce, 78
Anzaldúa, Gloria, 6
audience reception survey, 226–238, 249–252

279

Avrech, Robert J., 177

Babi Yar (Kuznetsov), 140
Bakhtin, Mikhail, 4
Band, Arnold, 25, 56
Barker, Kenneth, 32
Baron, Salo, 25
Barthes, Roland, 76, 77–78, 254n17
Bauerlein, Mark, 3
Baumgarten, Murray, 92
Bellow, Saul, 25
Bialik, Hayim Nahman, 187–188, 190, 194
Big Fix, The (film), 26
Bina Gold mystery series, 1, 242, 243–247
Blood Money (Krich), 13, 141, 156, 162–168
borders and border crossings, 14, 175, 185, 197–198, 202
Borges, Jorge Luis, 194, 195, 196
Boyarin, Daniel, 9, 19, 28, 29, 31–32, 175–176
Boys from Brazil, The (Levin), 13, 141, 142–143, 144–151
Breines, Paul, 64, 256n1
Brice, Fanny, 25
brotherly collaboration, multicultural, 202, 203–210
Buber, Martin, 126, 128, 130

Cahan, Abraham: *The Rise of David Levinsky*, 53–55
Call It Sleep (Roth), 25
Castle, Terry, 131–132, 133
Chandler, Raymond, 53, 57
chavurah movement, 41
children's mystery series, 1, 242–247
Christianity, in Kemelman's Rabbi Small mysteries, 32
City Scriptures (Baumgarten), 92
classical detective formula: asocial attitude in, 35–36; defined, 14; in disciplinary society, 258n29; feminization of, 260n1; misogyny in, 44; woman detective in, 76
Close Quarters (Piesman), 104–105
Cohen, Arthur, 143

Cohen, Rich, 122
Coles, Tim, 151
collaborative community, 212–214
Common Sense in Education (Kemelman), 21, 22, 46
"Confession" (Kaminsky), 213–214
Conservative Judaism (periodical), 239
Conversations with Rabbi Small (Kemelman), 50
conversion, 49, 50, 70
Conversos, in Zimler's detective story, 133–134, 136
countermemory, 128–129, 132
Cranny-Francis, Anne, 79
Criminal Kabbalah: An Intriguing Anthology of Jewish Mystery and Detective Fiction (ed. Raphael), 1, 214
cultural studies, 3–4
Culture Currents (newsletter), 121

Daniel (film), 178
Davidowicz, Lucy, 145
Day of Atonement (Kellerman), 72
"Death's Head Revisited" (*Twilight Zone* episode), 144
Desser, David, 178
Detective Agency (Walton and Jones), 165
detective fiction: African American, 6; modernism and, 2; pulp culture, 56–58; source materials for, 5–6; women writers of, 260n1, 261n25. *See also* American Jewish detective stories
Devora Doresh mystery series, 1, 242–247
Diamant, Anita: *The Red Tent*, 238–240
Dickstein, Morris, 241
Din Torah (legal hearing), 28
Di rayze aheym (Klepfisz), 157
disciplinary society, 258n29
double-consciousness, 200
Du Bois, W.E.B., 200
Dupin, C. August (fictional detective), 20, 35–36, 44
dybbuk (evil spirit), 120, 121

Dybbuk, The (Ansky), 119, 259n2

Edelkayt (nobility), 29
Eichmann, Adolf, trial of, 143–144
Eisen, Arnold, 3, 255n36
Eleazar, Rabbi, 8–10, 11, 14, 174, 175–176, 231, 236
Ellery Queen Mystery Magazine, 21, 80
Ellin, Stanley, 6
Empire of Their Own: How the Jews Invented Hollywood (Gabler), 56
Engineer of Death: The Eichmann Story (television docudrama), 144
evil spirit (dybbuk), 120, 121
Ezrahi, Sidra DeKoven, 139, 140, 141, 143

Fair Game (Krich), 156
False Prophet (Kellerman), 72
Feldman, Irving, 143
Feuerman, Ruchama King, 245
Fiddler on the Roof (musical), 25
Finkelstein, Norman, 10–11, 255n39, 255n40
Finkelstein, Norman G., 151, 155
Finkielkraut, Alain, 14, 173, 177, 197
Fish, Stanley, 267n11
Fishman, Sylvia Barack, 5, 78
Fiske, John, 254n17
Forché, Carolyn, 111
Forsyth, Frederick, 144
Fortunoff Archive, 164, 264n41
Forward (newspaper), 226, 230
Foucault, Michel, 165, 258n29, 263n13
Freese, Peter, 6
Freud, Sigmund, on the uncanny, 131
Friday the Rabbi Slept Late (Kemelman), 21, 23, 24, 27–32, 45
Friedman, Bruce Jay, 25
Friedman, Lester D., 178
Funny Girl (musical), 25
Furman, Andrew, 39, 132

Gabler, Neal, 56
Geertz, Clifford, 253n9
gender. *See* women; women detectives

Gentiles. *See* Jewish-Gentile relations
ghost story, 118–121
Glazer, Miryam, 69, 260n16
God in Genesis, as detective, 7
"Gold Bug, The" (Hubner), 245
Goldman, William, 144
Goodbye, Columbus (Roth), 24, 27
Gosselin, Adrienne Johnson, 6
Gothic. *See* Jewish Gothic
goyim naches, 31–32, 34, 243
Graetz, Naomi, 239–241
Green, Gerald, 140, 141, 143, 145
Grievous Sin (Kellerman), 64, 72, 73–74
Gur, Batya, 232, 233

Haddad, Carolyn, 76
Hall, Stuart, 199
Harap, Louis, 24
hard-boiled detective formula: in audience reception survey, 232; defined, 14–15; ethical model in, 201; in Holocaust justice, 141–142, 157–169; individualist ethos of, 202, 266n3; influence of, 13; and Kaminsky's Lieberman, 205; and Kellerman's Decker, 57–58; and Nazi hunter, 148–150, 154–155; as outsider, 152–153; as proxy, 150
Harel, Isser, 144
Harland, Henry (Sidney Luska), 7–8
Hartley, Marilee, 93
Hartman, Geoffrey, 10, 11, 264n41
Hasidim: as Holocaust survivors, 152–153; as icons of Jewish authenticity, 180, 265n20; as Jewish Others, 176–186; recovered and reinvented memories of, 123–124, 125–130
"Haunted Shul, The" (Hubner), 244
Haute, Woody, 56–57
Heading Uptown (Piesman), 100–104, 105
Hellerstein, Kathryn, 157
Hemingway, Ernest, 20
Hersey, John, 140
Herzog (Bellow), 25
Hirsch, Marianne, 114

Hitchcock, Alfred, 197
Hitler's War (Irving), 145
Holocaust: in documentary fiction, 140; and Eichmann trial, 143–144; exploitation of memory of, 151, 155; historical memory of, 113; in Jewish Gothic, 127–128, 131, 132–133, 137; and obsession with past, 112; popular cultural constructs of, 140–141, 144; video testimony on, 164–165, 168, 264n41
Holocaust, American justice and, 139–142; changing image of victims, 13, 141, 153–154, 155, 160; child of survivors, detective as, 156–162; hard-boiled detective in, 162–169; Nazi hunters, 141, 142, 144–151, 154–155, 161–162, 237
"Holocaust" (television docudrama), 140, 141, 143, 145, 146, 147
Holocaust in American Life, The (Novick), 151
Holocaust Industry, The (Finkelstein), 151, 155
Holquist, Michael, 194
Homicide (film), 1, 14, 19, 174–175, 176–177, 186–196, 198
Horowitz, Renee B., 76
House on Garibaldi Street, The (Harel), 144
House of Mirth, The (Wharton), 20
Howe, Irving, 257–258n20
Hubner, Carol Korb, Devora Doresh series of, 1, 242–247
Huyssen, Andreas, 263n23
Hyman, Paula, 260n15

ibbur (good man's soul), 120, 121
"imaginary Jew," 173
"In Dreams Begin Responsibilities" (Schwartz), 3
Ingraham, Prentiss, 7–8
intermarriage, 13, 213, 231; Cahan's Levinsky on, 54–55; conversion and, 49, 50, 70; cultural, 55, 70–74
Irving, David, 145
Isaacs, Susan, 76
Israel, Jewish identity and, 39–40

Israeli-Palestinian conflict, 67–68, 218–221, 245–247
"Is This Any Job for a Nice Jewish Boy?" (Yaffe), 6–7
Itzkovitz, Daniel, 20

"Jacob's Voice" (Levitsky), 118–121, 132
Jewish American Princess (JAP), 101, 103
Jewish cultural studies, 3–4, 253n7
Jewish detective stories. *See* American Jewish detective stories; women detectives
Jewish-Gentile relations: with African Americans, 37–39, 152, 189, 191; with Arab Americans, 218–220; audience reception survey on, 233; brotherly collaboration, 202, 203–210, 213, 214, 219; in *A Stranger among Us,* 177–186; visibility of Jewish body and, 175–176. *See also* intermarriage
Jewish Gothic: defined, 121–122; mystical tradition and, 122–123; place of future in, 132–137, 138; returned memory in, 123–129; terror of memory in, 130–131, 138; uncanny as theme in, 123, 131–132
Jewish gothic.com, 122–123
Jewish Journal (newspaper), 226, 230
Jewish mother stereotype, 80–83, 86–87, 94, 261n11
Jewishness: authentic, 185, 197, 265n20; collaborative community and, 212–214; defining, 7–9; double-consciousness and, 200–201; and ethical behavior, 14, 202, 210–217, 218; food-related, 56, 213; idealization of, 173, 198; inauthentic, 173; Israel and, 39–40; libertarianism and, 10, 203, 266n4; memory and, 112, 132; midrash and, 10–11; multiculturalism and, 203–204; as Other, 173–174, 180; popular culture formulations of, 20, 51–52;

spiritual accountability and, 130; visibility of, 174, 175; *Yidishkayt,* 173, 229
Jewish Other, 3, 173–174, 176–186
Jewish women. *See* women
Jewish writers. *See* American Jewish detective stories; American Jewish writers
"Jew's closet," 20, 51, 256n2
Jones, Manina, 165
Judah, Alvin (fictional detective), 7–8, 12
Justice (Kellerman), 64

kabbalah, 134, 173
Kael, Pauline, 146
Kafka, Franz, 92
Kahn, Sharon, 76, 232
Kamenetz, Rodger, 200–201
Kaminsky, Stuart, Abe Lieberman mysteries of, 1, 14, 201–225, 231; Jewish ethical conduct in, 202, 210–217, 218; Jewish identity in, 202, 203, 217–225; libertarian viewpoint in, 202–203; multicultural brotherhood in, 202, 203–210, 213, 214
  WORKS: "Confession," 213–214; *Lieberman's Choice,* 208–210; *Lieberman's Day,* 207, 215–217, 218; *Lieberman's Folly,* 205–207, 210–212, 223; *Lieberman's Law,* 203, 217–223; *Lieberman's Thief,* 207, 213, 214–215; "The Tenth Man," 214; *When the Dark Man Calls,* 204
Kellerman, Faye, detective fiction of, 1, 12–13, 52, 55–75; audience reception of, 231, 233, 234, 236; cultural intermarriage in, 55, 70–74; gender divisions in, 55, 69–70; Jewish cultural identity in, 56, 61–65, 74; middle-ground modern Orthodoxy in, 65–68; pulp culture detective in, 56–61; spiritual hero in, 55, 68–69, 73
  WORKS: *Day of Atonement,* 72; *False Prophet,* 72; *Grievous Sin,* 64, 72, 73–74; *Justice,* 64; *Milk and Honey,* 67, 72; *Prayers for the Dead,* 69; *Ritual Bath,* 56, 57–66, 68, 69, 70, 72–73; *Sacred and Profane,* 71; *Sanctuary,* 65, 67
Kemelman, Harry, detective fiction of, 1, 12, 19–52, 232, 234; Americanness defined in, 42–43; critical reception of, 26, 43; educational mission of, 21–27, 47–48; feminized Jewish male in, 19–21, 29; misogyny in, 43–51; Nicky Welt mysteries, 21–22, 23, 49; resistance to social and cultural change in, 36–42; social and cultural setting for, 24–26; Talmudical analysis in, 20, 28–35
  WORKS: *Common Sense in Education,* 21, 22, 46; *Conversations with Rabbi Small,* 50; *Friday the Rabbi Slept Late,* 21, 23, 24, 27–32, 45; *Monday the Rabbi Took Off,* 39–41; *The Nine Mile Walk,* 21, 22, 46; *Sunday the Rabbi Stayed Home,* 36–39; *That Day the Rabbi Left Town,* 51; *Thursday the Rabbi Walked Out,* 35; *Tuesday the Rabbi Saw Red,* 45–50; *Wednesday the Rabbi Got Wet,* 41–43
"Kidnapped" (Hubner), 246–247
kitchen Judaism, 56
Klarsfeld, Serge and Beate, 147
Klein, Kathleen Gregory, 261n25
Klein, Zachary, 19; *No Saving Grace,* 13, 141, 151–155
Klepfisz, Irena, 157, 229
klezmer music, memory of past and, 115–118
Knight, Kathryn Lasky, 76
Korelitz, Jean, 76
kosher hybridity: audience reception and, 226–238; defined, 4–5; gender and, 12–13; memory and, 13; policing, 238–242; suture concept and, 197–199; viewer/reader positioning and, 13–14, 174–197

Krich, Rochelle, 1, 76, 141–142, 231; *Angel of Death,* 13, 141, 157–162; *Blood Money,* 13, 141, 156, 162–168; personal history of, 156–157
Kugelmass, Jack, 265n20
Kuznetsov, Anatoli, 140

Langer, Lawrence, 141, 264n41
Last Kabbalist of Lisbon, The (Zimler), 13, 132–137
Lefkowitz, Lori Hope, 157
Lester, Julius, 70
Levertov, Denise, 143
Levin, Ira, 1; *The Boys from Brazil,* 13, 141, 142–143, 144–151
Levitsky, Ronald, 1, 13, 139; "Jacob's Voice," 118–121, 132
Lieberman's Choice (Kaminsky), 208–210
Lieberman's Day (Kaminsky), 207, 215–217, 218
Lieberman's Folly (Kaminsky), 205–207, 210–212, 223
Lieberman's Law (Kaminsky), 203, 217–223
Lieberman's Thief (Kaminsky), 207, 213, 214–215
Lilith (periodical), 43
Loew, Judah, 259n9
logocentrism, 8, 9
Long Goodbye, The (Chandler), 57, 149–150
Looking for Mr. Goodbar (Rossner), 98, 99–100
Loshitzky, Yosefa, 141
love relationships vs. professionalism, 87–91, 97–107
Lumet, Sidney: *A Stranger among Us,* 14, 174–175, 177–186
Luska, Sydney (pseud.), 7–8
Lyons, Gene, 146

Maltese Falcon, The (Hammett), 149
Mamet, David: *Homicide,* 14, 19, 174–175, 176–177, 186–196, 198
Marathon Man (Goldman), 144, 147
Marjorie Morningstar (Wouk), 83
memory of past: in American Jewish fiction, 25, 257n17; delivery systems for, 112, 113, 143; Jewish Gothic and (*see* Jewish Gothic); klezmer music as touchstone for, 115–118; material dimension of, 114–115; obsession with, 112, 263n23; possession by, 118–121; postmemory and countermemory, 114, 128–129, 132; seduction of, 111, 113, 114, 116, 123, 129, 130, 135; terror of, 111, 113, 123, 128–129, 130, 130–131, 138; Torah memory, 134. *See also* Holocaust
"Message from Tangiers" (Hubner), 245
midrash, modern: defined, 10–11; feminist, 238–241; involuntary or insubordinate, 10, 11; Orthodox, 242, 244; pop cultural, 34
Milk and Honey (Kellerman), 67, 72
Miller, Avigdor, 222
Mintz, Alan, 141, 145, 168, 264n41
Mirror, The (Singer), 122
misogyny, 43–51
Modleski, Tania, 228
"Mom in the Spring" (Yaffe), 84–85
"Mom Knows Best" (Yaffe), 77, 80, 82–83
"Mom Makes a Bet" (Yaffe), 83
"Mom Makes a Wish" (Yaffe), 84, 85–86
"Mom Remembers" (Yaffe), 87–90, 105
"Mom Sheds a Tear" (Yaffe), 83–84
"Mom Sings an Aria" (Yaffe), 84
Monday the Rabbi Took Off (Kemelman), 39–40
Morrison, Toni, 152
multiculturalism: defined, 266–267n6; Jewish identity and, 203–204; in Kaminsky's collaborative brotherhood, 202, 204–210
Munt, Sally, 261n25
"Murders in the Rue Morgue" (Poe), 44, 45
My Mother the Detective (Yaffe), 80

Mystery Midrash: An Anthology of Jewish Mystery and Detective Fiction (ed. Raphael), 1, 7, 213–214
mysticism, 122–123, 125–128

Nancy Drew mysteries, 243–244
National Foundation for Jewish Culture, 121
Nazi hunters, 141, 142, 144–151, 154–155, 161–162, 237
Newton, Adam Zachary, 187, 188–189, 194
Night Gallery (television series), 144
Nine Mile Walk, The (Kemelman), 21, 22, 46
Norden, Edward, 184
North of Montana (Smith), 162
No Saving Grace (Klein), 13, 26, 141, 151–155
Novick, Peter, 151

Odessa File, The (Forsyth), 144
Omer, Ranen, 187–188, 194
Operation Eichmann (film), 144
Operation Shylock (Roth), 3, 168
outsider status, of amateur women detective, 77–78

Pakn Tregr (periodical), 1
Paretsky, Sara, 244
past. *See* memory of past
patriarchy: as psychological male violence, 102, 103; right conduct and, 217
Pavletich, JoAnn, 90–91
Pawnbroker, The (film), 178
Pellegrini, Ann, 259n36
Personal Effects (Piesman), 93, 98–100, 107
Pi (film), 122
Piesman, Marissa, detective fiction of, 1, 13, 76, 77, 78, 91–107, 232; as courtship drama, 92–93; "hybrid" characters in, 99–100, 104–105; Kafkaesque protagonist in, 92; love relationships vs. professionalism in, 97–99, 105; social roles in, 93–96, 100, 107; urban Jewish identity in, 101–104, 105–106
WORKS: *Alternate Sides,* 104, 105; *Close Quarters,* 104–105; *Heading Uptown,* 100–104, 105; *Personal Effects,* 93, 98–100; *Survival Instincts,* 105–106; *Unorthodox Practices,* 91–98
Poe, Edgar Allan, 20, 35–36, 44
police procedurals, 58, 177
Popular Culture and the Shaping of Holocaust Memory in America (Mintz), 141
"Popular Fiction and the Limits of Modern Midrash" (Sofian), 238–239
postmemory, 114, 128–129, 132
Prayers for the Dead (Kellerman), 69
Prell, Riv-Ellen, 107
Price Above Rubies (film), 122
Psycho (film), 197
pulp culture detective: defined, 56–57; and Kellerman's Decker, 57–61
Punter, David, 130–131
"Purim Mystery, A" (Hubner), 244–245
"Purloined Letter, The" (Poe), 44

queer theory, 256n4

Radway, Janice, 162, 228
Raphael, Lawrence, 1, 7, 213
Rawlings, Ellen, 76
Ray, Robert, 6
Reading the Romance (Radway), 228
Real Megan, The (Yasgur), 243
Red Tent, The (Diamant), 238–240
Rejoice O Youth (Miller), 222
Reznikoff, Charles, 143
Rich, Adrienne, 64
Riddel, Joseph, 42, 44
Rise of David Levinsky, The (Cahan), 53–55
Ritual Bath (Kellerman), 56, 57–66, 68, 69, 70, 72–73
Ritual of New Creation, The (Finkelstein), 255n39
Rosen, Norma, 143

Rosenbaum, David, 1, 19; *Zaddik*, 13, 123–130, 139
Rosenbaum, Eli, 147
Rosenberg, Robert, 232
Roskies, David, 258n20
Rossner, Judith, 98, 99–100
Roth, Henry, 25
Roth, Philip, 3, 24, 27, 168, 261n11
Rukeyser, Muriel, 2–3, 198, 257n17
"Russian Connection, The" (Hubner), 245
Rzepka, Charles J., 150

Sacred and Profane (Kellerman), 71
Said, Edward, 253n9
Sanctuary (Kellerman), 65, 67
Sarna, Jonathan, 4, 5
Saturday the Rabbi Went Hungry (Kemelman), 32–35
Schulberg, Budd, 122
Schwartz, Delmore, 3
Secret of the Grandfather Clock, The (Yasgur), 244
Secret of the Hotel DelaRosa, The (Feuerman), 245
Sedgwick, Eve Kosofsky, 20
seduction of memory, 111, 113, 114, 116, 123, 129, 130, 135
Selavan, Ida Cohen, 43–44, 52
Selling the Holocaust (Coles), 151
Serling, Rod, 144
Shadows on the Hudson (Singer), 122
Shandler, Jeffrey, 141, 143
Shapiro, Karl, 25
Shoah Foundation, 164
Showalter, Elaine, 98
Sicher, Efraim, 139
Siegel, Don, 204
Silverman, Kaja, 197
Simon, Roger, 19
Singer, Issac Bashevis, 25, 122
Smith, April, 162
Sofian, Simone Lotven, 238–239, 240–241
Soitos, Stephen, 6
Sokoloff, Naomi, 79
Spielberg, Steven, 164
Spielberg's Holocaust (Loshitzky), 141

spiritual renewal, women as agents for, 55, 68–70
spiritual romanticism, 69, 260n15
Steinberg, Janice, 1, 13, 76, 232; "Wailing Reed," 115–118, 132, 139
Stevens, Serita, 76
Stranger among Us, A (film), 1, 14, 174–175, 176, 177–186
Sun Also Rises, The (Hemingway), 20
Sunday the Rabbi Stayed Home (Kemelman), 36–39
Surette, Ray, 254n12
Survival Instincts (Piesman), 105–106
suture concept, 197–198

Tales of the Hasidim (Buber), 126
Talmudical analysis: in Kemelman's detective fiction, 20, 28–35; Yaffe on, 7
"Tattered Tallis, The" (Hubner), 245
Telushkin, Joseph, 232
"Tenth Man, The" (Kaminsky), 214
terror of memory, 111, 113, 123, 128–129, 130, 130–131, 138
That Day the Rabbi Left Town (Kemelman), 51
Thompson, Jon, 2, 35–36, 44, 258n29
Thursday the Rabbi Walked Out (Kemelman), 35
Torah memory, 134
tough Jews, 64, 205, 256n1
Tough Jews (Cohen), 122
Tuesday the Rabbi Saw Red (Kemelman), 45–50
"Twisted Menora, The" (Hubner), 244

uncanny, 123, 131–132
undercover detectives: Gentile, 177–186; Jewish, 186–196
Unheroic Conduct (Boyarin), 9, 19, 175–176
Union of American Hebrew Congregations (UAHC), 238, 239
Unorthodox Practices (Piesman), 91–98
Uris, Leon, 140

video testimony on Holocaust, 164–165, 168, 264n41

viewer/reader positioning, 13–14, 174–175, 225; in *Homicide,* 176–177, 186–196; social identity and, 197; in *A Stranger among Us,* 176, 177–186

"Wailing Reed" (Steinberg), 115–118, 132, 139
Waldman, Ayelet, 76, 232
Walton, Priscilla L., 161–162, 165
War against the Jews (Davidowicz), 145
Webber, Jonathan, 112
Wednesday the Rabbi Got Wet (Kemelman), 41–43
Wharton, Edith, 20
What Is Jewish Literature? (Wirth-Nesher), 11
What Makes Sammy Run? (Schulberg), 122
When the Dark Man Calls (Kaminsky), 204
While America Watches: Televising the Holocaust (Shandler), 141
"Whispering Mezuzah, The" (Hubner), 242–243
Whitfield, Stephen J., 4, 7, 257n16
Wieseltier, Leon, 194
Wiesenthal, Simon, 142, 147
Wirth-Nesher, Hana, 11
Wisse, Ruth, 34–35
Witness (film), 177
women: in the classic detective formula, 44; Jewish mother stereotype, 80–83, 86–87, 94, 261n11; and love relationships vs. professionalism, 87–91, 97–107; midrash and, 238–241, 242; misogynistic view of, 43–51; and negative Jewish femininity, 83–84; social roles of, 93–96, 100–101, 107; as spiritual heroes, 55, 68–70, 73, 236; spiritual romanticism and, 69, 260n16; subservience to patriarchy, 102, 103; and transmission of Jewish knowledge, 260n15; urban identity and, 101–104, 105–106
women detectives, 76; amateur, 76–77; audience reception survey on, 232–233, 234–235; generic limits of, 163; in girls' stories, 242–247; Holocaust justice and, 141–142, 157–169; outsider status of, 77–78; Piesman's Nina, 91–107; stereotypes of, 78–80; as undercover Gentile, 177–186; Yaffe's Mom, 80–91
Wouk, Herman, 83

Yaffe, James, detective fiction of, 1, 6–7, 12, 13, 19, 52, 77, 78, 79, 80–91; acculturation of "modern ideas," 82–84; gender masquerade in, 84–87; Jewish mother stereotype in, 80–83, 86–87; love relationships vs. male professionalism in, 87–91. WORKS: "Mom in the Spring," 84–85; "Mom Knows Best," 77, 80, 82–83; "Mom Makes a Bet," 83; "Mom Makes a Wish," 84, 85–86; "Mom Remembers," 87–90, 105; "Mom Sheds a Tear," 83–84; "Mom Sings an Aria," 84
Yasgur, Batya Swift, 243, 244
Yerushalmi, Yosef, 112
Yezierska, Anzia, 90
Yidishkayt, 173, 229
Yuppie Handbook, The (Piesman and Hartley), 93

Zachor (Yerushalmi), 112
Zaddik (Rosenbaum), 13, 123–130, 139
Zimler, Richard, 1; *The Last Kabbalist of Lisbon,* 13, 132–137

About the Author

LAURENCE ROTH is an assistant professor of English and Jewish studies and coordinator of the Jewish Studies Program at Susquehanna University. He is the editor of *Modern Language Studies*.